I0820834

TO

FROM

DATE

Visit Christian Art Gifts, Inc., at www.christianartgifts.com.

Man of God: 366 Devotions to Seek God Daily

Previously published by Wisdom Hunters, LLC under the title *Seeking Daily the Heart of God*.
Copyright © 2013. Revised and updated.

Published by Christian Art Gifts, Inc., Bloomingdale, IL, USA.

First edition 2025.

Designed by Christian Art Gifts, Inc.

Cover and interior images used under license from Shutterstock.com.

Most Christian Art titles may be purchased at bulk discounts by churches, nonprofits, and corporations. For more information, please email SpecialMarkets@cagifts.com.

ISBN 979-8-89678-193-6

Printed in China.

30 29 28 27 26 25
10 9 8 7 6 5 4 3 2 1

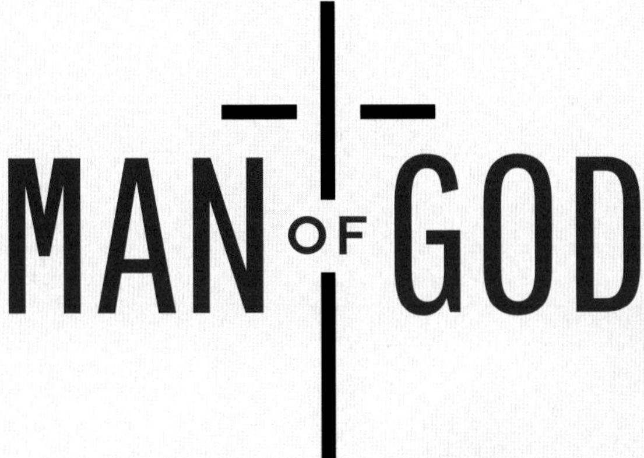

MAN OF GOD

366 DEVOTIONS TO SEEK GOD DAILY

BOYD BAILEY

DEDICATION

To my late grandmother,
Kastell Goss

&

Rita's late Gandi Mama,
Lucille Isbill

Thank you both for romancing God's Word
with passion, persistence and prayer.

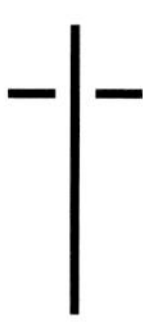

ACKNOWLEDGMENTS

Thanks to my wife **Rita** and the girls: **Rebekah, Rachel, Bethany** and **Anna,** and our two sons-in-law **Todd** and **Tripp** for letting me do life with you.

Thanks to **Brittany Thoms** for encouraging me, reminding me, and editing for me. Your boundless energy around this book kept me focused on finishing well.

Thanks to **Andy Thoms** for giving his pregnant wife permission to quarterback this project, and for his informal marketing and sales of the book.

Thanks to **Cliff Bartow** who asked me to stretch myself and compile 366 daily devotionals that could encourage people from all walks of life, especially business leaders.

Thanks to **Jim Reimann** for meeting with me monthly and coaching me to become a writer to the heart and head who is concise, clear, compelling and Christ centered.

Thanks to **Bob Lewis**, my business coach, whose wisdom and counsel gets me out of trouble and keeps me out of trouble.

Thanks to the **MinistryVentures** staff that stays focused on Christ and serving people like no team I know of. I am so proud to serve the Lord with you.

Thanks to **Lee McCutchan,** my original editor of the daily devotional, *Wisdom Hunters … Right Thinking*. Lee, your faithfulness fires me up everyday!

Thanks to **Don Kooima** and **Todd Headen** who were precise in every detail required to print and publish this project with excellence.

Thanks to **Paul Ryden** and **Sheila Maufer** for their meticulous attention to grammar, punctuation, spelling and clarity!

Thanks to the encouraging many who regularly write to tell me how the Lord has led you into a deeper walk with Him, as a result of regular time in His Word.

Thanks to my heavenly Father for loving me, extending His grace and blessing through the power of the Holy Spirit, and for giving me His inspired written word: the Bible.

TABLE OF MONTHS

INTRODUCTION

When I think of a man of God, what comes to mind is not a pious, holier-than-thou life, but rather a man who loves well—loved by God, loves and obeys God, and loves others well.

The Lord God Almighty called Moses "My servant." Imagine God's servant standing before Pharaoh's throne, staff shaking in weathered hands, yet his voice steady: "Let my people go." Here's a man who'd rather tend sheep than lead nations, yet God chose him anyway. Moses earned the title "man of God" not through self-promotion but through stubborn obedience. He climbed mountains to meet with the Almighty, came down with a glowing face, and somehow managed to lead two million complaining Israelites through a wilderness without losing his mind—well, mostly.

Then there's Samuel, the boy who heard God's voice in the night and spent his life listening for more. When Israel demanded a king like other nations, Samuel didn't throw a theological tantrum. He prayed, listened, and reluctantly anointed Saul, then David. Samuel shows us that being a man of God sometimes means blessing decisions you wish people wouldn't make.

Elijah bursts onto the scene like a desert storm—calling down fire, raising the dead, and outrunning chariots. Yet this same prophet who single-handedly confronted 450 prophets of Baal later cowered under a broom tree, begging God to let him die. Elijah teaches us that men of God aren't superhuman; they're simply humans who have learned to depend on a super God.

His successor, Elisha, focused more on miracles with a gentler approach—healing bitter water, multiplying oil for widows, and raising sons from the dead. Where Elijah was like thunder, Elisha was more like steady rain. Both were exactly what their generation needed.

David, the shepherd-king, never officially wore the "man of God" label, but he lived it through poetry and warfare, through triumph and spectacular failure. His psalms reveal a heart that wrestled with God, complained to God, and ultimately surrendered to God. David shows us that men of God aren't perfect—they're forgiven.

Fast-forward to the New Testament, where Paul explicitly calls young Timothy "man of God," charging him to "pursue righteousness, godliness, faith, love, endurance and gentleness." Do you notice that shopping list? It's not about platform or power—it's about character development in the crucible of daily life.

Paul himself embodied this calling, trading prestige for prison cells and choosing beatings over bowing to popular opinion. His letters are filled with passion for Christ and people, showing that men of God are characterized more by what they're willing to sacrifice than what they hope to gain.

And then there's Jesus—not just a man of God but God as man—who perfectly demonstrated what humanity looks like when it's fully surrendered to the Father's will.

What binds these men together across centuries? They spoke God's words when it was inconvenient, lived with integrity when compromise was easier, and led others toward truth even when following was costly. They prayed more than they preached, listened before they spoke, and chose humility over self-promotion. Faithfulness is the Lord's measurement for success.

These weren't men who had it all figured out—they were simply men who figured out that God was worth following, whatever the cost. In a world obsessed with building personal brands, they were content building God's kingdom, one faithful decision at a time.

The words in this book are daily doses of courage to grow more like Jesus and to become a man of God.

Will you step up as God's man in a world starving for authentic love lived out?

Love in Christ,
Boyd Bailey

JANUARY 1

WISDOM SEEKERS

The whole world sought audience with Solomon
to hear the wisdom God had put in his heart.
1 KINGS 10:24

Wisdom is a cherished commodity. It is insight from the Lord, so its value is enormous. Because wisdom must be sought and asked for, we pursue it by attending church, listening to good Bible teaching, and engaging with older mentors. Wisdom doesn't come naturally; it's a gift from God (Proverbs 2:6). For all of these reasons, wisdom is precious. People are drawn to wisdom because it is attractive and winsome. It is also a gift that protects us from decisions that could haunt us for a lifetime and a weapon God wields on behalf of His warriors. Wisdom cuts through confusion and replaces it with clarity.

The wise, however, are not immune to sin. A wise man or woman still needs accountability, maybe more so. Indeed, the wise are susceptible to pride (Jeremiah 9:23). A wise heart intermingled with pride thinks it can rise above the rules. It can be subtle at first, but inner convictions begin to rot like a termite-infested foundation. If pride is not kept in check, it will convert wisdom into cockiness. Sad is the state of a once-wise leader who allowed pride to water down his fear of God. Wisdom is God's gift to carry out His kingdom-initiatives. If spent on oneself, it becomes destructive.

So seek out truly wise people whose top priority is God. Search for wisdom in the Bible, books, people, circumstances, film, life experiences, and creation. Once you find it, don't take it for granted. Thank God for wise outcomes. Be wise for His glory and for His purposes. Allow wisdom to humble you, rather than give you a sense of superiority. We are all seekers of God's wisdom. We will seek it until we get to heaven.

Wisdom is active and alive, and always in need of a fresh infusion from God. Use prayer as a bridge to the wisdom of God. Ask Him often for His perspective and His heart on the matter in front of you (James 1:5). Allow wisdom to draw you closer to your heavenly Father in worship and dependence on Him.

Finally, be a generous dispenser of wisdom to others. Make time for people to get to know your heart and understand the life-lessons through which God has forged your faith (1 Kings 4:34). We all have wisdom we can offer to others. Carve out time just to listen to another's travails. Their "top of mind" issues need attention. Be available to listen patiently with understanding, and then, in humility, offer options for their consideration. Wisdom is gentle. It gives answers in a spirit of grace, as a fellow wisdom-seeker.

Seek wisdom and give wisdom always
motivated by humble submission to God.

RIGHT THINKING

"For my thoughts are not your thoughts, neither are your ways my ways," declares the Lord. "As the heavens are higher than the earth, so are my ways are higher than your ways and my thoughts than your thoughts."
ISAIAH 55:8-9

God's will does not always make sense. Usually this is because we approach it from our own understanding. If we were left to make sense of life by our limited knowledge and experience, we would be miserable. Thankfully, there is a greater pool of knowledge reserved for us in Christ. Do not underestimate its value and availability. Divine direction saves us from running down winding paths that waste our time and the time of others. God's way may not make sense now, but it will later.

God's thoughts and ways are accessible to us by faith. Faith is our constant connection to God-thinking, but we struggle with this because we have been programmed differently. Some of us wrongly think we don't deserve God's grace or that we don't need it. We try to muddle along on our own, but we cannot live the Christian life without the grace of God. God's way is the grace way. We give Him glory and He gives us grace. We give Him praise and He gives us peace. We give Him worship and He gives us confidence. This is the way of God. He created the original "road less traveled." Avoid the mindless masses and follow God. His ways may not be the most popular, but they are the most productive. His thoughts transcend our thoughts.

God-thinking takes grace and discipline. This temporal world does not necessarily reward eternal thinking. For example, it may criticize you for believing that people outside of Christ are lost in their sins and bound for hell. The world assumes you are narrow in your thinking. Though this way of thinking may not be popular, it is true. As a follower of Christ, you can think like God because you have the mind of Christ (1 Corinthians 2:16). Your conversion experience infused you with a new worldview. By faith you anticipate what God can do, and you focus on God-centric thinking. When you think like Jesus you do not have to be in control. You trust Him to handle people and circumstances in His timing. This is tapping into the mind of Christ that exists to renew your thinking on a moment-by-moment basis. God-thinking is only a faith-step away.

Think God-sized thoughts and expect God-sized results. Make His ways your ways and incorporate His thinking into your thinking. It may seem peculiar at first, and others may label you as strange, but you know better.

Thinking by faith and seeking the mind of Christ is right-thinking. You can't go wrong with right-thinking!

CALL FOR WISDOM

My son, do not let wisdom and understanding out of your sight, preserve sound judgment and discretion; they will be life for you, an ornament to grace your neck.
PROVERBS 3:21-22

Wisdom is required more often than we realize. Wisdom cuts through emotion and gets to the reality of the situation. "What is the wise thing to do?" is an effective question in decision-making. "What is best for the mission?" is a wise question to ask as it relates to business and ministry. Many times God speaks through money, or the lack thereof. So, if money is tight, then we need to be extremely careful with expenditures. Wisdom says cut back on expenses and do not add additional costs. At this point it is not about lack of faith, it is about being a wise steward with what you have.

Another characteristic of wisdom is that it is not impatient or desperate. Wisdom takes a step back and thoroughly evaluates a situation before charging ahead. Do you solicit wisdom on a consistent basis and in crisis? Knowledge and experience mixed with common sense and discernment combined with prayer and obedience is a great recipe for wisdom. Wisdom seeks to understand God's perspective on matters. This is why the wisdom found in God's Word is so relevant for living.

The Bible is a treasure-trove of wisdom waiting to be discovered by the wisdom hunter. Therefore, pray, read, and meditate on the Bible, but also seek out the wise (Matthew 12:42). Look for people with gray in their hair who exhibit wise behavior. The wise will help you validate the inklings of wisdom you are beginning to grasp from your study of Scripture. Read books and listen to messages of wise men and women. If you hang out long enough with wisdom, it will rub off on you. Take every opportunity to practice wisdom. Be wise in your relationships. Be wise with your money. Be wise with your time. Before you realize it, your wisdom will attract others who are hungry for the same.

Wisdom begins (and ends) with fearing the Lord. "The fear of the Lord is the beginning of knowledge, but fools despise wisdom and discipline" (Proverbs 1:7). The fear of God positions you to receive wisdom. Having no fear of God means you lack wisdom. No wonder our world is filled with fools. We have lost our fear of God, and wisdom has eluded us. Love God but fear Him. Worship God but fear Him. Learn of God but fear Him. Serve God but fear Him. Your fear of God qualifies you for wisdom.

Wisdom awaits your harvest call. Pluck it and enjoy, like plump, luscious fruit on a hot summer day. Taste and see that wisdom is good. No one has ever complained of attaining too much wisdom. Call on wisdom often.

Seek out the wise and ask them and God for wisdom. This is the wise thing to do!

WISDOM FROM HUMILITY

When pride comes, then comes disgrace,
but with humility comes wisdom.
PROVERBS 11:2

Wisdom is packaged with humility. If you want wisdom, you will cultivate a humble heart. The humble person understands his need for the wisdom of God. He does not pretend to be a guru who already knows everything. Humility is crystal clear that we need Christ's thoughts to intersect our own intelligence. Humility is smart enough to confess what it does not know.

Much of life is beyond the reach of human reason. There has to be more than man's comprehension. We are not objective enough to figure out the best choice with our own limited understanding. We need the wisdom of God to wash our thinking and leave His clarity. Humility positions us to receive wisdom from God and others. It is a growth process.

Pride pushes you out of position to receive wisdom. It is like a first baseman in baseball lining up in left field. He is out of position once the ball is hit. No one is on first base to receive the ball. Without humility you are out of position to receive wisdom. You may desire wisdom, but without humility you will be hollow in heavenly instruction. God rarely imparts His wisdom to a proud person because He knows he cannot be trusted. Why entrust wisdom to one who will squander it or spend it all on himself? God knows the humble man will be a good steward of wisdom. Indeed, humility sharpens a hunger for wisdom. It gives you an appetite for wisdom's morsels.

Once you adjust your spiritual diet to consume wisdom, you will never go back to the junk food of worldly wisdom (1 Corinthians 1:20-30). The world's wisdom is positioned in pride. It is a power struggle over who can be the shrewdest and the quickest to outsmart their opponent. Everything is competition to the proud. Pride foolishly jockeys for power. Humility, on the other hand, is patient to wait on God.

Better to be humble and follow the ways of wisdom.
Wisdom rests well. Wisdom gives grace.
Wisdom gets results with no regrets.
So, humbly invite the gracious wisdom of God!

WISDOM'S WEALTH

But where can wisdom be found? Where does understanding dwell? Man does not comprehend its worth. ... "The fear of the Lord—that is wisdom, and to shun evil is understanding."

JOB 28:12-13, 28

Wisdom is like money well-invested. Its value compounds over time. If you regularly add wisdom to your life, you become wealthy in the ways of God. This is why it is imperative that you get wisdom above most everything else in your life. Wisdom is your ally that will assist you in defeating the enemy. Satan is toothless in the presence of the wisdom of God. Do not attempt to defeat the devil with your own limited understanding. Rather, crush him with the weapon of wisdom. A life built on the foundation of wisdom can withstand the winds of change and the waves of adversity (Proverbs 28:26).

Wisdom keeps you engaged with God's perspective. It is a life preserver for the drowning, a compass for the lost explorer, and a light on a dark and perplexed situation. Wisdom begins and ends with the fear of God. The fear of God means you engage His teaching with your heart and mind (Proverbs 15:33). Wisdom precludes a passive relationship with God. Wisdom means you meditate on His ways and truths. You prayerfully and respectfully ask Him why, what, and how as it relates to His way of doing things. Through contemplating on His Word and understanding His truth, wisdom will begin to reign in our everyday life.

Wisdom originates from God and resides with Him. Anyone who attempts to take credit for its effectiveness may risk losing the rights of its use. Humility tempered with wisdom leads to wise decision-making. Take time to listen and learn from wise people. This could save you heartache from a relational train wreck or the loss of money from a bad financial decision. Be wise; listen to both God and His wise mentors.

You get wisdom to give wisdom, sharing wisdom's wealth with those who steward it well!

TEACH CHILDREN WISDOM

"Pains as of a woman in childbirth come to him,
but he is a child without wisdom; when the time arrives,
he does not come to the opening of the womb."
HOSEA 13:13

Children need to be taught wisdom. Yes, sometimes it's hard for them to grasp its meaning because of their age and stage in life, but it is still good to begin early. Wisdom comes through understanding and applying God's Word to life experience. Wisdom is one of the wonderful gifts you can give your child.

Make the pursuit of wisdom inviting and practical. Tell stories of individuals who made wise decisions and the positive effects that followed. Then contrast these uplifting illustrations with stories of those who chose an unwise path and have suffered harm as a result. Stories arrest the heart and illuminate the mind. Engage your children in conversations about real-life people.

Wisdom comes by allowing children to spread their wings and begin making decisions while they still live under your roof. Start by helping them make money decisions. Show them the pattern of "share, save and spend" from your own financial management. Then lead them to do the same. Watch them smile as they experience the joy of generosity. Be proud as their patience grows when they save for something they want and then purchase their prize with cash. Financial wisdom is a practical gift you can give to your child (Ephesians 6:4).

Encouraging good judgment in choosing friends is another facet of teaching your child the ways of wisdom. Make sure children understand the propensity to be like the people they hang out with (Proverbs 13:20). It's wise to choose a friend whose faith is growing and robust. Encourage them to choose friends who lift up instead of those who pull down. Wisdom does not settle for the shallow acceptance of just any friend. Wisdom has a high standard for friendship. Challenge your children to pray for friends who encourage their faith and who move them closer to their heavenly Father. Wise friends rub off on your children in wise ways.

Lastly, discuss with your child regularly the wisdom of God. He gives wisdom (Proverbs 2:6). Read with them from the Bible and discuss its meaning. Make the discussion of Scripture a part of your everyday life. Take your Bible to church. Underline the phrases that leap from the page into your heart and mind. Then discuss its application to your life over lunch. Ask your child to hold you accountable to the truth God is teaching you.

God's wisdom will follow your children the rest of their lives. It will be with them when you are absent. You can be at peace when you have a child who is wise in the ways of God.

You are wise when your goal is to grow up a wise child.
Wise children become wise adults!

WISE FEAR

The fear of the Lord is the beginning of knowledge,
but fools despise wisdom and instruction.
PROVERBS 1:7

There are good fears. The fear of God is one of them. It is foundational. It feeds all other good fears. Wise is the man who first fears God. Fear of God is fervent at the beginning of your faith walk. But, if the fear of God is neglected, you drift into disobedience (Psalm 36:1). Like any other belief or discipline, the fear of God needs to be fostered by faith and obedience. Fear of God keeps you honest with Him and with yourself. It is the beginning of accountability. The grace of God, without the fear of God, is an illusion. There can be no grace without fear, just as there is no fear without grace. Foolish is the one who does not fear God. The fruits of not fearing God are foolish choices and undisciplined living.

Sadly success can be an enemy to fearing the Lord. The more you experience success, the more you are prone to trust yourself and to stop fearing God. However, the opposite needs to be true. The more successes you enjoy, the more you need the fear of God and the fear of sin's consequences. Be brutally honest with yourself. You can't handle success without accountability. David couldn't, and he was a man after God's heart (Acts 13:22). No one is above accountability.

Wise is the leader who builds accountability into his faith, finances, family, work, and leisure. Those who don't think they need it, need it the most. Maybe you start by hiring a personal assistant of the same gender who is with you at work and on business trips. This is your opportunity to mentor a young, up-and-coming leader, and it is his opportunity to hold you accountable. We all do better when others are watching. Invite accountability from your spouse, board, boss, and accountability group. Be transparent with your professional and personal finances. Tell your spouse when you become emotionally attached to someone else. Be very intentional about your alone time. Idleness leads to indiscretion. You are wise to reserve solitude for your Savior, your spouse, and special friends.

Fear of God is your friend. Fear of the consequences of sin is smart. Fear of being unaccountable is wise. Fear of God is freeing. Therefore, fear God, hate sin, and trust Him!

WISE WEALTH

People who have wealth but lack understanding are like the beasts that perish.
PSALM 49:20

Wisdom sees the small value of riches without God's redemption. Wisdom is otherworldly in its view of wealth. The creation of wealth is for Christ's purposes, not the world's ways. This is why the wealthy, when they are wise, seek to understand God's game plan for their gold. They prayerfully come up with a plan, and then they commit their actions to the Almighty, trusting that God will bring the best results (Proverbs 16:3).

Prayerful planning is the process by which the Spirit leads and brings about success. Plans without prayer miss God's best. Actions committed to Christ carry-out God's game plan. Wealth requires responsible stewardship not to be taken lightly. Wisdom believes that the Lord's blessing is much larger than our own life and can be used for the Lord today.

Always remember that finances are finite. You have a window of generosity that will close one day. Don't wait until riches grow wings and fly away (Proverbs 23:5) to some faithful soul who understands the significance of "stuff" before the Lord.

Riches are like hailstones; they fall from heaven in different sizes, garnering our attention while rattling on the tin roof of our trust. But after a while, riches melt away into the silent ground, gone. So it is with "stuff." It can be "here today and gone tomorrow." It is wise to give aggressively what you have today instead of hoping to give what you may not have tomorrow.

Missionaries need malaria medicine now. Orphans need homes today. Growling stomachs need more than gruel immediately. Churches are waiting to be built once they receive their necessary start-up capital. Humanitarian work and the spreading of the Gospel will happen exponentially as the wealthy collaborate with Christ and obey. Run the risk of liberating your wealth for the Lord. It is His to give.

God has made us to be generous and not beastly in our view of wealth. Animals are driven by self-preservation and by instinct. But we are children of our heavenly Father. He is gracious and generous in bestowing His good gifts (Matthew 7:9-11). We should follow God's example by using wealth for His ways and not our own. Sanctify your "stuff" for your Savior. Look to the Lord for wisdom to know how to save, invest, spend, and give.

Wise wealth wraps itself around God's redemptive plan through faith. It understands and applies God's generous game plan!

WISE SAVER

Joseph stored up huge quantities of grain,
like the sand of the sea; it was so much that he stopped
keeping records because it was beyond measure.
GENESIS 41:49

There are wise savers, and there are greedy savers. People are attracted to wise savers. Wise savers are responsible and trust God to provide through their careful planning. God expects us to save, and He blesses our efforts. A "Joseph Fund" represents foresight to prepare for hard times. There is great wisdom in realizing good times may one day come to a screeching halt. Hardship may come in the form of healthcare needs, a collapsing career, or a depressed economy. Financial fatigue, even famine, may not be far off in our future. Therefore, it is imperative to store up for the lean times. This does not mean hoarding to the extent of not helping those in need. But it does mean spending less than you make, giving generously, and saving the rest.

We save so we can better serve. Faith and savings are not opposite ideas. They actually complement each other. Because we have faith in our heavenly Father, we prepare for the worst and hope for the best. Do not spiritualize away saving. Be cautious of blaming God for your lack of preparation. He gives us faith and good fortune to further His kingdom. Start today by diligently saving (Proverbs 21:5).

Use debt wisely or even avoid it completely. Ask yourself: what is the worst thing that can happen if you are left holding a balance sheet full of debt with little savings? You could lose everything, be bankrupt, and have to depend on family or friends. Debt can be devastating, so spend and save wisely.

Seek to be a saver and not an impulsive spender. Plan to save little-by-little (Proverbs 13:11). Faith and presumption are two opposite strategies. One trusts God with a plan, and the other lives life without a plan, blindly hoping things work out. Systematically save with both a short-term emergency fund and a long-term contingency fund. An emergency fund is there to keep you from going into debt when cars break down, appliances need to be replaced, or the house needs painting. A long-term contingency fund helps you finance college costs for your children, or it supplements your income when you are unable to work. Saving is sensible and spiritual.

Consistent savings may mean a lifestyle change. Pull the plug on presumptive living. Cut-up credit cards that prop-up an unrealistic lifestyle. Credit card living will eventually collapse like a house of cards. By God's grace save more and spend less.

You save so you can give. Savers are wise!

WISE WARNINGS

They serve at a sanctuary that is a copy and shadow of what is in heaven. This is why Moses was warned when he was about to build the tabernacle: "See to it that you make everything according to the pattern shown you on the mountain."
HEBREWS 8:5

Wise warnings come from wise people. They are wise because they speak from experience with pure motives and reliance on God and His Word. Do not dismiss lightly those whom the Lord brings into your life. They remind you of right and warn you of wrong.

You are wise to pursue this quality of friendship. Wise friends have not always lived their lives in "a bed of roses," but they have persevered through their problems by the grace of God. They overcame because they regularly obtained grace and mercy from their heavenly Father (Hebrews 4:16).

Listen to couples with imperfect, but growing marriages. Learn from them from their past mistakes. Take to heart their warnings of neglect and indifference in marriage. Good and maturing marriages take time and intentionality. Your marriage is destined for a train wreck if you do not heed the warning signals of apathy and anger. God has designed your lives to receive encouragement and instruction from wise mentors; listen intently and learn from them (Proverbs 12:15).

Apply wisdom to relationships at work as well. Before you engage a new employee, call his last employer; validate his credibility and competence. Honest past employers will give you a fair warning about a flaky ex-employee. People may interview well but fit in poorly after they are employed. Let the wisdom of your interviewing team protect you from professional relationships that are not a cultural fit.

Heed wise warnings from people who love the Lord and follow Him faithfully. If you ignore these warnings, you expose yourself unnecessarily to foolish decisions. Listen also to warnings in your own mind and heart regarding relationships or decisions. God's protection thrives in the heeding of wise warnings. If several people you respect tell you to slow down, then you need to slow down. If more than one person questions your attitude, then ask them to hold you accountable for an attitude adjustment. Use the rule of three. If you hear the same thing three times in godly counsel, God is speaking loud and clear.

Watch for wise warnings and process them.
This is God speaking. Wise people apply wise warnings!

JANUARY 11

WISE CHILDREN

Listen, my son, to your father's instruction and do not forsake your mother's teaching. They will be a garland to grace your head and a chain to adorn your neck.

PROVERBS 1:8-9

Wise children listen to their parents. They listen to their mom or dad, whether their parents love God or not. God has placed parents over their children for protection and teaching. Some parents may not provide either of these, but they can still be used by God to deliver His instruction. Therefore, listen to your parents. Listen when it hurts and listen when you don't completely understand. Let them know that you want to honor them by listening to their advice. It pleases the Lord when you obey your parents (Colossians 3:20). The older you get, the harder it becomes to listen to your parents. It becomes harder because you want to be your own person and because you begin to discover that your parents are fallible and sometimes even fragile in their faith. They can be overprotective, insensitive, and angry. Yet they still love you with their whole heart. They want God's very best for you, though they sometimes struggle with how to relate and care for you.

Be patient with your parents. Do not dismiss them as irrelevant. Learn how to lovingly listen to your dad and mom. Learn how to patiently process their instruction and teaching. They sometimes seem redundant, condescending, and patronizing. Remember, they love you. They stick their nose into your business because they care. Indeed, a disengaged and apathetic parent communicates a careless concern. But wise children still care for their careless parents, because they know it is the right thing to do. Unselfish service to selfish people will build a bridge to the Savior. Your life may be the only book about Jesus your unrepentant parents are willing to read.

Therefore, listen and learn from your parents, even if they are lazy in their faith. You honor them when you learn from them (Ephesians 6:1-3).

Your love for your parents may very well ignite their love for Him!

JANUARY 12

WISE LEADERSHIP

"Chose some wise, understanding and respected men from each of your tribes, and I will set them over you."
DEUTERONOMY 1:13

The selection process for wise leadership can make or break an organization. We are constantly faced with this in our families, church, work, schools, civic groups, and professional associations. So where do we look for wise leaders? A good place to begin is within the ranks of those who already exhibit wise leadership (Acts 15:22). You see it in the open and authentic environment they create in their work and home by their own honesty around personal weaknesses and strengths. Wise leaders are excellent listeners. They listen with the intent to understand. You observe their wisdom in one-on-one conversation as they know what questions to ask. They challenge you to think and offer counsel as is appropriate.

Wise leaders are not gurus or know-it-alls. Instead, they are smart enough to understand the vastness of what they don't know, and they seek the expertise of others. Moreover, a wise leader is respected (1 Timothy 3:8). Those who know them the best respect them the most. If those in the inner circle lack respect for a leader, so will those outside their circle of influence. Indeed, respect comes over time. It is the result of doing what you say. It is integrity in living out what you say you believe. Consistent Christ-like behavior invites raving reviews of respect. Wisdom and respect go hand-in-hand.

Last of all, wise leadership points to God. Wisdom can only thrive in a humble heart. It is within the incubator of humility that wisdom germinates and flourishes. Therefore, a wise leader shows humility in his heart for God.

Follow wise leaders and be a wise leader.
Patiently and prayerfully select and appoint wise leadership!

WISE LIVING

Who is wise? He will realize these things. Who is discerning?
Let them understand. The ways of the LORD are right;
the righteous walk in them, but the rebellious stumble in them.
HOSEA 14:9

Wise living keeps the realization and understanding of God at the front of your thinking. God-awareness is central. Asking, "What would Jesus do?" becomes a way of life. His desires, His motivations, His thoughts, and His character become paramount in your thinking. This leads to wise living because it is based on Christ-like living. God's ways are the path to wisdom.

However, it takes conscious effort on our part for the wisdom of God to penetrate our thinking. We must become men of the book. Joshua said it best, "Do not let this Book of the Law depart from your mouth; meditate on it day and night, so that you may be careful to do everything written in it. Then you will be prosperous and successful" (Joshua 1:8).

Wise living includes the ability to discern right from wrong and good from best. Use the Bible as your guide for wise recommendations. Your ability to discern truth and goodness will grow as you mature in faith. You may be a pretty good judge of character, but God wants to grow you in this area. Your discernment can become a gift to your wife for her protection against unwise decision-making (1 Corinthians 2:14). Present your thoughts with grace and humility. By faith, extract your overly aggressive emotion and replace it with a prayerful appeal. Hold your suggestions with an open hand and trust God to work in His timing.

Be patient. Plant seeds, pray, and watch the Holy Spirit turn the heart of your wife in the right direction. It is not about you convincing her; rather it is all about the Spirit of God convicting and leading.

Wise is the husband who listens to his wife.
Therefore, be humble and teachable. Understanding
and discernment will follow. This is wise living!

WISE LISTENER

"Listen now to me and I will give you some advice, and may God be with you." ... Moses listened to his father-in-law and did everything he said.

EXODUS 18:19, 24

Sometimes God sends people your way who offer great advice. Therefore, listen intently—you never know who may be speaking on behalf of God. These may be people you trust or people you barely know. Either way, do not allow pride to stand in your way of listening to what they say. Wisdom can come from the most unlikely sources. Therefore, listen with discernment. Do not be a non-thinking listener. Wise listening involves a functioning brain. The intent of wise listening is to separate the "wheat from the chaff."

Like Moses in the verse above, you may be laboring away unnecessarily in stress and anxiety. You need wise advice (like Jethro gave Moses) encouraging you to develop a better system for processing the needs of people. You may also be trapped in the never-ending cycle of busyness. Your life and organization are more complex than even six months ago. You need help identifying a better process for handling issues and complaints. People are starting to grumble. You are weary, and they are frustrated. This may be the optimal time for you to let go and trust others. Listen to what other proven leaders have to say, and obey.

So who in your life is currently offering you advice and counsel? Is it your wife? Is it your father or father-in-law? Is it your mother or mother-in-law? Is it your boss? Is it your employee? Is it your friend? And are you truly listening? Or are you just going through the motions and not really adjusting or modifying your behavior?

This time of uncertainty may be a good time to evaluate the basics of life and work. What is the purpose? What do you do best? What is your capacity? Do you value quality over quantity? Do relationships have priority over tasks? What is your motive? This honest self-evaluation, coupled with the counsel of others, will help take you to the next level of living. Proverbs 1:5 states it well, "let the wise listen and add to their learning, and let the discerning get guidance."

Above all else, listen for the Lord's voice among the various voices that vie for your attention. Obey the voice of God!

JANUARY 15

WISE PROCESS

Then the king said, "Bring me a sword." So they brought a sword for the king. He gave an order: "Cut the living child in two and give half to one and half to the other."

1 KINGS 3:24-25

Every decision requires some sort of process. While King Solomon's "process" in 1 Kings 3 seems severe, it worked to reveal truth from falsehood. A wise decision-making process protects. It protects life. It protects relationships. It protects resources. It protects commitments. The process on the surface may not seem smart, but time wins you over with its wisdom.

One example of the value of process is when you are responsible for hiring a new employee or appointing someone to be a leader at church. During the process of interviewing you may discover new issues related to what the job really requires. You may even rewrite the job description. Perhaps this process of employee or leader selection needs to include four or five other interviewers. Their perspective and wisdom are invaluable as you seek to discern the best qualified person for the position. These "people processes" need to not be rushed, so everyone is protected from unwise decision-making.

Jesus understood this. He spent a 30-year process of preparation before He embarked on a relatively short three years of ministry. In addition, He took His followers through a process of discipleship, teaching, and on-the-job training. His process with people was pregnant with questions, discovery, and hands-on experience. Ultimately, His process culminated with the cross and the resurrection. Some processes require death before there can be life. The death of a vision may be needed, before it can be realized.

We are all in a process. We are learning along the way, in preparation for God's next assignment. Process trains you for greatness. If you run ahead of the process, you may very well disqualify yourself from greatness. Therefore, it is wise to be patient in the process and enjoy its excursions.

Above all else, implement prayer as the first step of any decision-making process. Make Christ your process consultant. Default to "what does Jesus think" before you ask Him to bless your "seat-of-the-pants" process. Prayer is your best process. Employ it well and employ it often. Allow prayer to define the process, initiate the process, and conclude the process. Prayer that seeks the wisdom of God and the wisdom of godly counselors is almost guaranteed success. Therefore, weave prayer throughout the process, and watch God work. Allow the Holy Spirit to drive the process.

Hearts, minds, and spirits align around a prayerful process. You can't beat a process interwoven with intercession and punctuated by prayer!

JANUARY 16

GOD'S WISDOM

"I will give you what you asked,
I will give you a wise and discerning heart."
1 KINGS 3:12

The wisdom of God goes beyond your ability to understand right and wrong. It gets to the heart of the matter. Wisdom asks, *Why do you want to do what you want to do? What is your motive? Is your priority: God first, others second, and you third?*

Opportunities should become options to further God's kingdom, rather than a way to exploit your own power and status. This is the motive God looks for when He pours out His blessing of wisdom (Ecclesiastes 2:26). He is looking for people whose heart's desire is to obey God and follow His ways.

God's wisdom comes from God and is received through a heart of character. God does not entrust His thoughts to someone who will prostitute His wisdom for wrong purposes. He is looking for a heart of humility and honesty. Someone who, like a child, says, "I need you and I need your direction." And without the wisdom of God, "I am lost and unclear on God's ways."

Humility is the gateway to wisdom (Proverbs 11:2). It is what sustains it. Your humility means you are teachable by God. Your humility means you will use God's wisdom in an honorable way. Wisdom can be used to settle disputes between individuals or organizations. It can assist you in becoming an expert in a career that serves others. Wisdom extracts nuggets of knowledge and becomes a paintbrush in the hands of a skilled artist who can translate information into a beautiful portrait.

Wisdom is not microwavable; it marinates in your mind. It becomes digestible over time. Therefore, be patient; talk to God about your need for wisdom. He will answer your prayer. The other things that consume your thinking will take care of themselves. Wisdom eventually wins. It is a steady and sure road.

Ask God for wisdom. It is His reward (Proverbs 9:12).
Wisdom is a wise request!

JANUARY 17

BIG VISION

In the beginning God created the heavens and earth.
GENESIS 1:1

God has a big vision. His vision is enormous. He wrote the book on vision. He is the original visionary. His vision is so large, we are unable to wrap our minds around its implications. He expressed His vision in the creation of the earth, the sun, the moon, the stars, plants, animals, sky, water, and most importantly man. Man was the crown jewel of God's creation, because he was created in the likeness of God (Genesis 1:27). Our Lord is an extraordinary visionary. He takes nothing and makes something. He lifts up what seems to be insignificant dirt and breathes life into it so it becomes a beautiful human being.

God is the expert at taking colorless capability and crafting it into a technicolor transformation. His vision is macro: He illustrates His creativity and complexity through the creation of earth and all it contains. His vision is also micro, because He has created no two people the same. Each plant and animal is unique.

Above all else, His vision is personal. God has a vision for your life that is larger than you think. We tend to limit the Lord's vision with our unbelief and fears. Therefore, lift your heart and mind to the Lord, and ask Him what His vision is for your life. By faith, do not be afraid to stretch yourself into seeing things like He sees things. What we see as obstacles, He sees as steppingstones. What we see as limitations, He sees as His provision. What we see as fear, He replaces with faith.

Do not grow tired of doing well. Tackle life with the energy and excitement of someone consumed with a fresh vision from heaven. Ask the Lord to baptize your vision under the water of His wonder. Ask Him to take your old and stale vision and bring it to life with faith and hope. Raise the bar of your belief, so you are bold to ask things of God you have never asked, to believe things from the Lord you have never believed, and to do things by faith that you have never done. Go to the one who is Lord over all visions and ask Him to infuse yours with life and largeness. Do let your education, income, relationships, or past failures limit you in your pursuit of His vision for your life. Indeed, your failures are His opportunities to flourish with a fresh vision for you and your family. Pray for the Holy Spirit to birth a God-sized vision in your soul. It may mean moving. It may mean changing careers. It may mean more education. It may mean admitting failure and starting over. Whatever it means for you, focus on God and His vision for your life. By faith, ratchet up a more robust vision.

Look to the Lord of vision and craft your vision around His. He has a big vision!

DOUBT GOD

Now the serpent was more crafty than any of the wild animals the Lord God had made. He said to the woman, "Did God really say, 'You must not eat from any tree in the garden'?"
GENESIS 3:1

Satan's first goal is to get you to doubt God. After all, what good is faith that is watered down by doubt? We may go through seasons of doubt as disciples of Christ. But doubt is not the ongoing pattern of a serious and faithful follower of Jesus. Thomas was a doubter for a time, but when he came face-to-face with his resurrected Savior and Lord, his doubts fled like an exposed bandit. Do not underestimate the enemy's endeavors to get you to doubt God. If he is successful in planting and growing seeds of doubt, your faith will be choked to death by weeds of worry and by the crab grass of the cares in this world.

In some ways, it was easier to trust God when you first believed. Now that you have aged in years as a Christian, you may feel like the miraculous has been replaced by the mundane. Questions of doubt have replaced God's promises of assurance.

Did God really say my relationship with Him is based on my belief in Jesus Christ as His Son, the only way to heaven (John 14:6)? Did God really say that those who believe in Jesus go to heaven and those who reject him are separated from God eternally in hell (Revelation 20:15)? Did God really say that I am to pay my taxes that are due the government as an example of a good citizen (Mark 12:17)? Did God really say I am to honor my parents even if they are undeserving of honor (Ephesians 6:1-3)? Satan may be seducing you with these subtle messages of doubt. Did God really say to volunteer in the church, start tithing, stay in this marriage, forgive my friend, invest in my family, and help my neighbor? Did He really say to trust Him even when I don't feel Him? Am I to obey Him when I don't understand why or how? The answer—no doubt—is yes.

Just say yes to God's Word, in opposition to the enemy's subtle and sometimes not so subtle questions of doubt. Answer the devil's leading questions of doubt with a resounding vote of confidence in what God has told you to be true. Satan will try to convince you that God is somehow holding back on what's best for you. He may be holding back, but only for your good, not for your detriment or frustration. Be aware of Satan's schemes. He is determined for you to doubt God and thus doubt yourself and others. But you know better. Replace his temptations to doubt God with God's assurance of faith.

Doubt the devil, yes. Doubt God, no!

GOD BACKFILLS

"I will repay you for the years the locusts have eaten—the great locusts and the young locust, the other locusts and the locust swarm—my great army that I sent among you."
JOEL 2:25

God can make up for wasted time. He specializes in redeeming rough seasons in our life. What has become a torturous transition, He can use to love you into a closer relationship with Him. Where else can you go for eternal life than to the one who is eternal (John 6:68)? Allow God to backfill this blot on your past. He can rebuild what has been broken and even destroyed.

You may have been embarrassed and humiliated, but this is not beyond God's long arm of restoration. Injustice may have invaded your unsuspecting life. Unexpectedly you lost everything you had spent a lifetime building. Poof, in a twinkle of an eye, it was gone. Your career was gone. Your family teetered on division. Your reputation was tattered and all but obliterated. Your joy was gone. Your finances were depleted. Your energy was sapped. And your faith was shot full of holes. Your desire to move forward in life was severely stalled. Worst of all you wondered where the Lord was in all of this reversal of fortune. You were on the fast track to bitterness, because of your feelings of betrayal.

You may have hit rock bottom and now there is nowhere to look but up to Jesus. He is your hope, your rock, and your refuge. Look up to the Lord even though He may seem a million miles away. Now is the time to practice what you told others all those years. Trust God during this time of turmoil. God wants to backfill your loss. Your pit of pity He can fill with hope (Psalm 40:2). Your broken relationships that are buried in a cistern of hurt, He can retrieve with forgiveness. Your financial black hole, He can shine the light of His provision and opportunity.

In Christ, your best days lie ahead. Submit to His healing. Let go of your hurt and pride. Hang on to Him. He is the best thing you have going for you. Let these failures forge a stronger faith in God for you and your family. Face the fact that you are forgiven and move forward in the power of the Holy Spirit. Lean on the Lord. He can handle it. He is your stability in this storm of insanity.

God will bring you through this crisis of faith to allow you to coach others through the same. You are a living and breathing testimony of the grace and love of God. Proclaim His faithfulness to other fledgling followers of Jesus. Let the Lord backfill the hole in your heart and life with His love and faithfulness. His filling of right attitudes and actions will bar the door of your mind from bitterness. Invite the Holy Spirit to backfill your soul with His fruit of love, joy, peace, self-control, purity, forgiveness, and humility. What God fills proves faithful. What God fills He controls and comforts.

Use the lessons of the past as a reminder for the Holy Spirit's filling in the present. His backfilling results in faithfulness going forward!

LIVE IN HIS PRESENCE

After two days he will revive us; and on the third day he will restore us; that we may live in his presence.
HOSEA 6:2

Live in His presence, so you can better live in the present. God's presence provides a reality check. His presence is pure and is purifying. You cannot live in the presence of the Lord and not be changed. Christ expects Lordship over His followers. This is why we submit to Him each time we enter into His presence. His looming presence means He is Lord of our life. Since He is ever-present, we are perpetually in His presence. So whether we acknowledge His presence or ignore it, Christ is still there.

Always look for ways to humbly crown Christ as the Lord over your life. It is in His presence that our own sin comes to light. This is why you intentionally enter into His presence. You need the reminder more than He needs the recognition. At the same time, it is a form of honor to regularly recognize the one you love most. Come into Christ's presence out of sheer love and respect, with no agenda but worship.

When you live in Christ's presence, you can live in the present. His presence arrests your worries, and locks them away, so you can live in today. His presence purifies your heart and mind (1 Thessalonians 3:13). His presence comforts and encourages like none other. It is living in His presence that provides strength for your life-long journey. His presence is where love lingers and holiness hovers. It is in the presence of Jesus that your perspective is aligned with the Almighty's. God is great at giving a gut check. Take the time to tarry with the Lord. Christ can keep you from insignificant commitments. His presence points to your spot in His will.

The presence of God is experienced positionally and volitionally. You know in your head that He is always present. But your heart must volitionally engage with Him for you to experience Him practically. Learn to practice His presence. Think about Him often. Invite the Lord in through the front door of your heart's faith. He does "stand at the door and knock" (Revelation 3:20).

Practicing His presence produces lasting relationships and right results. It revives and restores!

DIVINE DIRECTION

LORD, that a man's life is not his own;
it is not for man to direct his steps.
JEREMIAH 10:23

We do not own our lives. We have been bought with a price (1 Corinthians 6:20). As followers of Jesus, His sacrificial blood purchased our freedom from the fire of hell, sin, and death. By faith, we are owned by Him. A great exchange took place when you believed in Jesus. What's yours became His, and what's His became yours. The life of Christ became your life. It is not your life to define, but His. He has wrapped a wonderful definition around who you are in Him. You are a child of God. You are secure, because your Savior keeps you. You are valuable, because the Lord values you. You are protected, because the Almighty owns you.

The Bible is God's glossary of how to define oneself. Scripture gives you a family tree of faith for you to trace your religious roots. It is also a mirror of how God sees you. He sees you as accepted in His Son, though you might suffer rejection from others. Cherish and enjoy the acceptance of Jesus. Your mistakes are His opportunity to affirm His acceptance. There are still consequences to your sin, but He is always available to receive you back, because you are His. He accepts and welcomes His own.

Furthermore, He directs His own (Isaiah 48:17). His desire is for you to understand and follow His plan for your life. Praise God, it is a step-by-step process, and He directs your steps! Some days you may feel like it is three steps forward and two steps back, but do not be discouraged or dismayed. God is still directing your steps. Though tedious and laborious at times, the Lord leads you in lockstep with His steps. In His steps is the wise way to walk. Do not run ahead thinking you have to set a record for speed or quickness. In fact, fast steps may cause you to backtrack and have to learn all over again what God was trying to teach you. Walk patiently with Him and watch Him at work.

The Holy Spirit is your step director. You are in His step class for instruction in His Word and exercise in faith. Learn how to let the Lord direct your steps. Prayerfully listen to the quiet prompting from His Spirit. Stop when you need to stop. Speed up when you need to speed up. Slow down when you need to slow down. God directs the steps of a submitted and surrendered man.

Stubbornness is hard to direct (Psalm 81:12). Pride resists direction. Independence attempts to self-direct. Listen to your wife or close friend. God may speak His next steps through them. Self-direction is like traveling alone to a new destination without a map, or an orientation to your surroundings. It is futile and frustrating. God-directed steps, on the contrary, lead to peace. You can rest in His far-reaching perspective and other-worldly wisdom. Step by step He leads you. You can trust that His way is the best way.

Trust in your walk with Him.
Allow His direction to define your steps!

FIERY HEARTS

But if I say, "I will not mention his word or speak anymore in his name,"
his word is in my heart like a fire, a fire shut up in my bones.
I am weary of holding it in; indeed, I cannot.
JEREMIAH 20:9

The word of God flows through the human heart like orange hot lava out of an erupting volcano. Nothing can hold back the effects of God's word. It penetrates the hardest of hearts and disturbs apathy. It ignites a tender and teachable heart with confidence and gratitude. The heart cannot contain the Word of God any more than a mother can hold back her joy after the birth of her baby. There is an explosion of endurance and excitement that happens when Scripture seeps into the soul. It cuts into your being (Hebrews 4:12). You cannot remain unchanged by the living word of God.

Any open-minded person who seeks to understand the Bible will benefit now and for eternity if he embraces its claims. You cannot silence a person who has been spoken to by the Lord, via His Word. The Bible is a conduit for knowing Christ. It facilitates faith like nothing else. As a follower of Jesus you engage with eternal purposes when you hide God's word in your heart. You hide it within, but it explodes without. Truth in is truth out.

Jesus was a man of the Word. The Scripture was fire in His bones. He spoke like no one else because His authority was not in His words, but in the words of His heavenly Father. You can stand confident in Christ when your decisions and rationale are based on the Bible. The Word of God perseveres. It is your teacher. The Bible defines your belief system.

Lastly, learning and obeying the Bible frees you from the excuse of not knowing what the right thing to do is. If you really want to comprehend and increase your own accountability, then teach the Scripture. Teachers adhere to a higher standard (James 3:1). A teacher who does not teach feels frustrated and worn out. The things you are learning have to come out, or you are hard to live with. Don't hold back any longer what the Lord is teaching you. A teacher must tell, or they will not feel well. The Bible begins to boil in a heart full of truth.

For a heart simmering with God's Word, sin surfaces to the top and the Lord skims it away by His grace and forgiveness. The fruit of the Spirit has the potential to flourish in a heart that is purified by the Word. Faith and hope hang out in a heart recalibrated by Christ's words.

The Bible is your reality check. Though Holy Scripture is up to 3,000 years old, it keeps you relevant today. Carry Scripture with you. Read and study it with others. It is a fire that melts fear and burns away bad attitudes. Scripture leads you to your Savior.

Stoke the fires of your faith with God's Word.
Watch it burn brightly. You will see Him!

JANUARY 23

BUILT TO LAST

"Woe to him who builds his palace by unrighteousness,
his upper rooms by injustice, making his own people
work for nothing, not paying them for their labor."
JEREMIAH 22:13

Anything worthwhile is worth doing well. If you are building a family, frame it well. Furnish it with faith, love, hope, and the fear of God. If you are building a business or ministry, grow it relationally and systematically. Pour its foundation with honesty, trust, and excellent work. If you are building a life, develop it with discipline, forgiveness, humility, grace, service, and obedience to God. Spend your time building people, processes, projects, and enterprises that are sustainable and eternal. Above all else, dedicate your building to God (Nehemiah 3:1).

If you are positioned as a leader, then lead well. In mid-life, men often have the privilege of mentoring, or even mentoring mentors. Steward this responsibility well. Build spiritual disciplines into faithful followers of Christ.

Do not neglect developing disciples. Disciples of Jesus need a firm foundation of faith. It is imperative to model for them mastery of the Master's words. Let the Word of God flow freely from your speech. Speak it and live it on behalf of your Savior. You build lives that last when you ground them in the Good Book.

The legacy you leave is predicated on the people in whom you invest. Therefore, keep your children "top of mind." Make them your number one building project. Begin telling them about Jesus when they are tiny. As they grow, instill the principles of Scripture into their hearts and minds. Tell them stories of God's faithfulness in your life all these years. Confess how your heavenly Father forgave you at your points of failure. This authentic home environment grows small children into giants of the faith. Build into your children now and they will leave a legacy of faith. Build for generations to come (Psalm 48:13).

Moreover, build your ministry or business into one that lasts. A business or a ministry that is built to last is carefully constructed with the bricks of vision, mission, and values. Strategy, objectives, goals, and metrics all rest upon this foundation. There is a compelling cause that everyone is motivated around: This is vision. There is clarity of purpose of what needs to get done: This is mission. And there is agreed-upon behavior that defines the culture: these are values. If your vision is too small, only small people will venture forth. If your vision is so massive that it becomes unrealistic, then no one will take you seriously. However, if your vision is prayerfully aligned with God's will, He will accomplish great things through you and others. Cast a God-sized vision that can last beyond your lifetime.

What God builds lasts as long as He wills!

INFLUENTIAL ADVOCATE

Furthermore, Ahikam son of Shaphan supported Jeremiah, and so he was not handed over to the people to be put to death.
JEREMIAH 26:24

We sometimes need influential advocates. We need people who can plead our case with authenticity and authority. We are all limited in our ability to influence our own outcomes. This is why God uses advocates to further His purposes on our behalf. It may be at work that you need another person to introduce you to someone significant within a particular department. Without his support you will be severely limited in your progress and productivity. Do not allow your pride to keep you from seeking a sponsor or advisor. Make sure you have an influencer go ahead of you who can create a safe environment of acceptability. If you run ahead with unbridled zeal, you may run into a brick wall and then wonder why you have stalled. Sometimes it's appropriate to "ride the coat tails" of someone else's character.

Later, after you have proven yourself, you will be able to navigate without waiting on an influential advocate. It is much better for another to praise you than for you to "toot your own horn" (Proverbs 27:2). If you are perceived as a self-promoter, then you will be placed in the penalty box of opinion by your peers. People shun self-promoters. But let another influencer pave the way for your project, and all will be pleased. Be patient and pray for this. Stay prepared, and pray for God to use another influential advocate to convince others of your creditability. You need the support of other influencers to succeed.

The flip side of this equation is your opportunity to be an influencer on behalf of others who are pregnant with potential. Prayerfully consider being an advocate but be very careful to whom you lend your endorsement. Your influence is extremely valuable and needs to be stewarded wisely. People will not seek out your recommendations if you continually send them crummy characters. Be responsible and do due diligence to those desiring your introduction. Normally you can feel good about "going to bat" for another if you, or someone you trust, have known them for a long period of time. You have witnessed their interactions with their family, their friends, and their faith. There is a consistency in their character. They are honest. They are teachable. They are humble. They submit to authority. They are grateful and content. They manage their home and their finances responsibly. They are competent. You can be an aggressive advocate of influence for this quality of person.

Above all else, appeal to your most influential advocate, Jesus Christ, for yourself and others (1 Timothy 2:5). His influence is persuasive, and it never wanes!

PRAYER REVEALS

"Call to me and I will answer you and tell you great and unsearchable things you do not know."
JEREMIAH 33:3

Prayer reveals the heart of God. His heart is full of lovingkindness. He has loved you with an everlasting love (Jeremiah 31:3) and has drawn you to Himself. This faithful love is what prayer reveals. Prayer is designed to align the Almighty's heart with yours. Relish the revealed heart of God. Indeed, it is in this quiet place of prayer that you see His face. The friendly face of your heavenly Father is waiting to welcome you into an understanding of Him and His will for your life. His face is inviting and confident. Rejection is not part of His repertoire. Intimacy is His intention.

Prayer places you up close and personal with your Lord and Savior, Jesus. Prayer offers the reassuring tone of His voice as we read and recall Scripture. We recognize and respond to Jesus' voice because we are His sheep (John 10:26). His tender call has the rhythm and rhyme of compassion and hope. Yes, there are times we detect firmness in His words. This is for our protection. He is not a killjoy, but rather a joy-giver.

There is no other voice like His. Listen to His voice, and you will learn to be content. Listen to His voice, and you will understand how He communicates with clarity and conciseness. Prayerful meditation on God's Word is the place His voice is best understood. Prayer unlocks the language of the Lord.

Prayer also extends the eternal hand of God. He reaches down to lead you through dreaded decisions. His hand is ever extended to guide you into eternal purpose, and not leave you caught up with inconsequential activities. The hand of your heavenly Father caresses your worried soul with comfort and calmness. His arms embrace you like the hug of a loving parent locked around a fearful child.

The arms of your Maker are never so short that they cannot meet your point of need (Numbers 11:23). We all need a hand from time to time, especially a hand from our heavenly Father. Bow in prayer and allow God to place His hand of blessing on your head. His commissioning is your confidence and hope. Prayer is the air of eternity. Inhale and exhale it often. Do not smother your soul with prayerlessness. An asphyxiated soul is dead to the ways of God. Keep it robust with prayer's revelations.

Call, and He will answer you!

PUT INTO PRACTICE

"Therefore everyone who hears these words of mine and puts them into practice is like a wise man who built his house on the rock."
MATTHEW 7:24

The purpose of learning truth is to use it. Unused truth expires and becomes stale. When you hear truth and put it into practice, you are wise. When you hear truth and ignore its application, you are foolish. Foolish is the man who acknowledges truth outwardly but never applies it inwardly. His foundation for faithfulness is fragile, so when the winds of adversity strike, his character collapses under its crushing blow.

Someone may show up for the Bible study or attend a soul-stirring retreat and hear truth but never change for the better. How can this be? This happens when people do not follow through with what they know to be right and true. There is a "disconnect" between their head and their heart. The discipline to stop bad habits and start new ones is rationalized away with convincing excuses. We deceive ourselves by saying, "I don't have enough time," "I am not spiritual enough," "I will get around to this one day," or "God will understand if I wait." John described self-deception's effect on truth, "we deceive ourselves and the truth is not in us" (1 John 1:8).

Truth cannot co-exist with deception, so jettison deception and apply truth now. If you wait, you will wander from its application. The present is the wisest occasion to receive His gift of grace and apply it to your life. You are responsible for the truth you have received. Therefore, steward it wisely. Use it before you lose it, by being a practitioner of truth.

Lastly, apply truth in doses that can be digested into your character. Do not be overwhelmed by multiple things in your life that need to change. Choose one thing, like loving your wife with full commitment and sensitivity. Paul said in Ephesians 5:25 for the husband to "give himself up" for his wife. Without saying a word, serve in secret so that your wife can experience your unselfish care and concern. Get into her world by loving her at her point of interest. It may relate to entertainment, cooking, or yard work; serve in ways that will show your wife you care.

At work, you have the opportunity to put into practice the radical teaching of Jesus, to treat others like you want to be treated, "Treat people the same way you want them to treat you, for this is the Law and the Prophets." (Matthew 7:12 NASB). Think of a colleague you need to forgive for letting down the team. If you were in his or her shoes, you would appreciate this gift of mercy. God has filled you with His grace, so you can live a gracious life. Focus on building the foundation of your life and character with one brick of truth at a time. This architecture designed by the Almighty will endure.

Put His principles into practice and persevere!

COME TO ME

"Come to me; all you who are weary and burdened, and I will give you rest. Take my yoke upon you and learn from me, for I am gentle and humble in heart, and you will find rest for your souls. For my yoke is easy and my burden is light."
MATTHEW 11:28-30

Sometimes, your soul needs to catch up with your body. There is a disconnect created by distractions and busyness. You are weary of life and work. This soul fatigue will follow you until it finds rest. The warning lights of weariness flash in the face of your faith. You are tired and troubled with nowhere to turn. This is when you can turn your eyes upon Jesus. He offers a constant invitation to come to Him. Burdens of responsibility bear down on your back like a ton of bricks, but Jesus is there to ease the pressure. Health issues assault your body like unceasing fire from the enemy, but Jesus is there to soothe the pain through prayer. Marriage confusion has overwhelmed you, and you are ready to give up, but Jesus has the answers as the supreme counselor. You can carry on with Christ. Submit to His restful invitation. Take Him at His word and yoke up with His humility and gentleness. His invitation to rest is received by faith. The yoke of Jesus gives hope and encouragement to the soul.

Start by aligning your calendar with Jesus' time. A partnership with Christ requires time and attention. You cannot maintain a relationship with Him without investing in it. Jesus went to the mountain to commune with His heavenly Father, and when He came down, large crowds followed Him. Why? People follow leaders they know they can trust. When you spend time with Jesus, you build trustworthiness. You go to the mountains alone to pray, and you come back surrounded by followers. They know you have been with Jesus (Acts 4:13). When others know you have been with Jesus, they are reassured that you are depending on Him for wisdom and direction. They can trust that your motives are pure and that this business or ministry is not your deal but His. You gain instruction from Him on how to execute His plan. Followers take great comfort when their leader pauses to pray and takes time to receive the Holy Spirit's discernment over issues of vision and strategy.

Slow down each day and listen to the voice of the One who created the world with a word. His words are powerful and freeing. They are comforting and convicting. The Word of God will save you from unwise decisions and free you to make wise ones (Psalm 119:1-3). Organize your priorities around the priorities of Christ. Get away, and get with Him. Give your soul a break when it is strained under the barrage of activity. Take a step back and reevaluate. This requires faith. A well-kept soul results in robust living. Go to Jesus, for He is asking you to come.

Come quickly to Christ. Your soul deserves to rest.

DIVIDED AGAINST ITSELF

Jesus knew their thoughts and said to them,
"Every kingdom divided against itself will be ruined,
and every city or household divided against itself will not stand."
MATTHEW 12:25

Humility unites; pride divides. Patience pauses; anger accelerates. Indeed the nature of division is to reduce someone or something into a lesser status or significance. This is what division does. It divides. It divides families, nations, and cities. It ruins communication and intimacy. It ruins teamwork and trust. It ruins peace and contentment. Indeed, the devil uses division as one of his primary weapons for worry and fear. If he can divide husbands and wives, he has conquered husbands and wives. The enemy has won when husbands and wives think the other has become the enemy. Division deceives both parties into thinking that they cannot work together, so they fight. It is irrational and irresponsible.

Division is the fruit of pride. Pride allows no room for compromise; much less death to self. It drives couples to unreasonable demands and proud pontifications. Division creates losers and lasting regrets. It is a road that leads into a downward spiral of ineffective living.

Therefore, unite around humility. Humility relates from a position of brokenness. There is an appeal to the common sense of Christ and the wisdom of God. Mutual submission to your Savior Jesus becomes the starting point of discussion. This is how division is defeated. There is a determination by everyone involved to depend on God and godly counselors for instruction and accountability. Emotional hostage-taking is prohibited, and manipulative moves are unacceptable. Instead, the fruit of the Spirit (Galatians 5:22) is the baseline for discussions. Unity is fostered around respectful and responsible discussions. This is the place where patient and cool heads prevail.

Identify your true enemies as pride, fear, selfishness, and the demons of hell. Make a frontal assault of faith against the adversary instead of backstabbing each other with betrayal. Unity flourishes in a foray of forgiveness. "Forgive first and discuss second" is a good rule of thumb. Unity requires thinking the best of each other. Past failures are not held over the other as a hammer of guilt, and current hurts are not glibly dismissed. As your heads hit the pillow each night, pray for one another before you slip into sleep. Unified, your marriage and ministry will stand; divided it will fall. Therefore, unify around God and His Word. In Christ you will stand (Romans 12:5).

Stand strong with your Savior.
He forgives. He saves. He unifies!

LACK OF FAITH

And he did not do many miracles there because of their lack of faith.
MATTHEW 13:58

Jesus blesses faith. There is no doubt about it; faith matters. God, of course, can do anything, and He is willing to do big things on your behalf, but He is looking for faith. He is searching for men and women who trust him for great things. We serve a mighty Lord who deserves a giant vision, fueled by great faith. Yet sometimes we mope around like God has lost control, and Christianity is hurling into irrelevance. Where faith is alive the church is on fire. Prayer is prevalent when the faith community believes God for big things (Acts 4:24).

Your faith expands as it remains focused on the Faithful One. Like the disciples, Jesus is your rabbi (John 1:38). It is the dust from His feet that flies back in your face as you follow Him. Spending time with Jesus marks you with His character and confidence. You are a Jesus-follower, by faith. Therefore, be bold in your belief. He is the one who has called you to this eternal endeavor, and He is the one who will pull it off.

Keep your motive pure by glorifying Him. Enlarge your vision of what He wants you to do by tenfold, maybe a hundredfold. Do not sell short your Savior. Why settle for a few who might find Christ, when you can trust God for hundreds, even thousands who will grace the gates of glory.

Trust God to take His vision wherever He likes. An unleashed vision has limitless possibilities. Give God your five loaves and two fish of ability (Mark 6:38-44). Watch Him pray over it and bless it bountifully and beautifully. Trust and be amazed at what the Almighty accomplishes through you. You lose only if you lack faith. Therefore, be one who believes big in Him. Miracles matter to your Master, because He manufactures them by faith.

God's industry is all about doing the impossible.
Faith facilitates the miraculous!

GRATITUDE FOLLOWS GENEROSITY

You will be enriched in every way so that you can be generous on every occasion, and through us your generosity will result in thanksgiving to God.
2 CORINTHIANS 9:11

Gratitude to God follows generosity for God. Thank God for the generous people He has placed in your life. People with the gift of giving have an uncanny ability to match resources with compelling needs. Paul described these dear people, "We have different gifts, according to the grace given us … if it is giving, then give generously." (Romans 12:6, 8). It brings generous people great joy when they are able to significantly leverage their stuff for kingdom outcomes. It is not a matter of if they are going to give, but *where* they are going to give. Generous givers prayerfully scan their surroundings to discern where God is working and where they can invest around their passions. Evangelism, discipleship, and church planting grip the hearts of many visionary givers. A compelling vision for these things causes them to give themselves to greater participation.

Furthermore, it is in the middle of generosity that God can be found. God is a giver (Deuteronomy 26:1). He gave His only son (John 3:16). He gives daily bread (Proverbs 30:8). He gives eternal life (John 10:28). Indeed, generous givers grow in their faith because God is in close proximity. There is a very good possibility that a generous giver is growing closer to God rather than away from God. Thank God that generous givers give others the opportunity to know the Lord, and follow Him in discipleship and maturity.

Lastly, finances without faith in Christ provide a temporary solution at best. Therefore, godly generous givers understand the strategy of giving to causes that lead to their Savior. Where He is preeminent, He sustains the work. If you are a gifted giver, then exercise your gift to the glory of God. Pray for the right giving plan and then give generously to heavenly causes. Keep Christ in the center of your giving. He is the exit strategy into eternal life in heaven. You cannot out give God, but you can partner with Him on opportunities that both of you are passionate about.

Above all else, be extremely grateful to God for the generous givers in your life. Emulate them and thank them!

RUMBLINGS OF GRUMBLINGS

"When they received it, they began to grumble against the landowner. 'These men who were hired last worked only one hour,' and you have made them equal to us who have borne the burden of the work and the heat of the day."
MATTHEW 20:11-12

Grumbling is not fun to be around. It grates on both the giver and the receiver. Grumbling loves to draw a crowd that is sympathetic to its mistreatment. Often, grumbling does not disclose all the facts; there is a skewed understanding of the situation. Instead of taking the high road of humility and acceptance, grumbling attacks authority and acts like the grumbler is the center of the universe. Grumbling lacks integrity around commitments and makes excuses based upon perceived injustice. But Jesus was clear; He said to "stop grumbling" (John 6:43).

Grumbling is not good. It gets everyone lathered up in distracting and detrimental behavior. It is easy to constantly compare yourself to others and grumble under your breath that you are better and somehow deserve more. You complain because others receive more pay and forget that when you started the job, you were the highest paid. Greed can fuel grumbling as much as anything.

Grumbling is relational suicide because it feeds on gossip and ingratitude. The tongues of perfectly good people become tainted under the influence of grumbling. It is a sad sight to watch. Grumbling converts good people into grumpy whiners. However, grumblers can get a life. Grumbling can easily be escorted out the back door of your life through maturity, trust, acceptance, and responsibility. Grumbling is for small people, and contentment is for big people. Grumbling ceases in the face of fulfillment from your heavenly Father. Israel experienced this in the wilderness (Exodus 16:12).

Lastly, God-grumbling is the worst kind of grumbling. Anytime you murmur against your Master, you are setting yourself up for disappointment. Yes, you can complain to Christ, but do not obsessively worry over matters out of your control. Express your disappointments and fears to your heavenly Father and then trust Him with the outcome. There is no need to go on an extended tirade against God and others. He knows and understands you and your situation. He is more concerned about changing you than about changing your circumstances. He is interested in you becoming more like the character of His Son Jesus. It is the character of Christ that matters most in the middle of unfair or unjust situations. A heavenly focus puts into perspective earthly expectations. Free yourself from grumbling by giving it over to God. Trust Him that His plan and process are perfect for you and are what is best for others. Replace grumbling with gratitude and applaud those ahead of you.

**Grumbling gets you nowhere,
but gratefulness gets you all you need.
Reject the rumblings of grumbling!**

FEBRUARY 1

SURVIVAL MODE

All her people groan as they search for bread; they barter their treasures for food to keep themselves alive. "Look, LORD, and consider, for I am despised."
LAMENTATIONS 1:11

A person can be in "survival mode" for a lot of different reasons. For some, it means searching for the next meal. For others, it means struggling with a teenager. For still others, it is desperately seeking a way to make ends meet. For some, it is the slow healing of a broken and wounded heart. For others, it is withstanding conflict at home and work. For some, it is the bearing the unending and confining responsibility of being a caregiver. And for some it is struggling inwardly to trust God. In all of these circumstances, a person experiences a sense of desperation. This is not all bad. It is when we reach the end of ourselves that we most need the Almighty.

Sometimes, our circumstances strip us naked before our Creator. We feel exposed, vulnerable, embarrassed, and exhausted. It is an uncomfortable position. Life seems to be swirling out of control. We feel as if we are two steps away from total despair and depression. Survival mode means we are on the verge of giving up. We are not sure the marriage is worth it anymore. We are not convinced that Christ is all that He is cracked up to be. Life stinks and we are just trying to get through another day. Our goal is to eke out a living and get by the best we can. Indeed, survival mode can become a way of life without divine intervention.

Do not become satisfied with survival mode; instead let the Lord love you through your despair. Scripture teaches, "No, in all these things we are more than conquerors through him who loved us" (Romans 8:37). The abundant life (John 10:10) in Christ is much more than survival mode. So, use survival mode to lead you to revival mode. Ask God to use this time of desperation to revive your relationship with Him (Psalm 85:6). Pray for the Holy Spirit to ignite your soul and revive intimacy with your Savior, Jesus. Repent from watering down the Word of God and revive its application to your everyday life. Survival may be for the fittest, but revival is for the faithful. It is not those who "gut it out" alone who experience God, but those who invite the Lord and others into their inner circle of influence. Break the cycle of cynicism by turning your hurts over to Christ, your caregiver. Allow the gentle Spirit of God to lead you through survival to revival. Do not continually strive to survive. Instead, rest in Him to revive. A revived soul does more than survive. It flourishes by faith in God.

Live through survival mode into revival mode.
But do it all by the grace of God.

JOY IS GONE

Joy has gone from our hearts; our dancing has turned to mourning.
LAMENTATIONS 5:15

What happens when the joy is gone? It's not fun anymore. What we are experiencing is not what we signed up for. Indeed, a joyless state is not a good place to. Maybe you just lost a loved one suddenly and without warning. You grieve because of your tremendous loss, but their great gain is that they knew Jesus. It is not unusual for joy to rise from the ashes of our grief. Joy comes at dawn after the dark night of the soul (Psalm 30:5). Your heart laments and longs for one more conversation and warm embrace from the dear one departed to heaven. But joy comes when you know they are with Jesus.

Jesus understands that joy comes from obedience and faithfulness to God's call even through suffering. It was for the joy that was set before Him, that He endured the cross and despised its shame (Hebrews 12:2). Consider Christ's model of endurance and obedience when you are in the middle of opposition and persecution. Do not grow weary and lose heart. The Lord provides a lesson in joyfulness. Jesus never forgot the bigger picture of hope for a better tomorrow. Hope ultimately leads to heaven. Joy is set before us in the person of Jesus Christ, reigning on His throne of grace. It is imperative that we stay fixed on Him. Our faith flees when it loses perspective. Joy is found in Jesus.

Joy lies dormant within every disciple of Jesus Christ. Therefore, awaken it from its slumber if you have slid into a joyless state. Look to the Lord for an infusion of His eternal joyfulness. Joyfulness is found in hopefulness. Do not allow joy killers to rob you of hope and peace. For the follower of Jesus Christ, a definition of reality without hope is wrong. Therefore, reject joyless jabs from revisionists touting a hopeless reality. Instead, seek out companions in Christ committed to seeing Him as the joy giver.

Jesus is a dispenser of joy. You know His love; this is joy. You know His forgiveness; this is joy. You know His faithfulness; this is joy. You know His mercy; this is joy. Joy is not based on changing circumstances, but on knowing an unchanging Christ. Seek Him in your sad state, and you will not have to search far for joy. When you find Jesus, you have found joy.

Therefore, receive Jesus and give Jesus, because He is joy.

SHATTERED PLANS

My days have passed, my plans are shattered.
JOB 17:11

Sometimes, our plans do not go as we had hoped. In fact, they are shattered. They're obliterated in front of our very eyes. Certainly, plans are made to be adjusted, but this one blew up in your face. You were devastated. Even now, your emotions vacillate between bewilderment and anger toward God, and your future feels gnarled and disjointed.

Now you are positioned to start over. It is hard to muster the energy to withstand another assault on your vision, but it is not time to give up and give in to defeat because God is still in control. He controls your plans and their successful launch. He can still be trusted going forward. Just because things have not worked out according to your timetable is no reason to quit trusting Him. Trust the Lord with a reengineered plan that will be better than the old one. His ways are much better than your ways (Isaiah 55:8-9). There is no human comprehension to what God has in store if you remain faithful to Him.

His ways (Isaiah 2:3) can be hard to understand. The cycle of digesting His will into your mind and soul is like "chewing cud," a repetitive process that requires time and patience. The desires of your heart need validation. This is part of His plan, and this is where prayer plays a vital role. Take the broken pieces of your plan and place them at the feet of Jesus. He will take your shattered plan and piece it back together with His enhancements. A crushed plan in the hand of Christ has much more potential than your perfect plan buried in your grasp.

Lastly, like the expressed genius of an artist, the new plan formed by God has the depth and breadth of a masterpiece. Therefore, do not settle for anything less than your Master's plan. Your desires may be dead, but now is the time to submit to God in a fresh and humble way. Watch in delight as He resurrects your desires to align and connect with His. He has slowed you down so your plans partner with His. See your shattered plan as a blessing, not a curse. God loves to take what is broken, lift it up, and make it whole again. Place your plans and your heart in His hands. He is the author and the finisher of your faith (Hebrews 12:2).

God is the plan provider, and He makes shattered plans better.

TIMES OF TROUBLE

But I will sing of your strength, in the morning
I will sing of your love; for you are my fortress,
my refuge in times of trouble.
PSALM 59:16

Times of trouble are ever looming in our life. They are approaching us, surrounding us, or engulfing us. Times of trouble are never too far off, so we should not be surprised when they arrive. It may be relational trouble in your marriage. Maybe you're in trouble at work. Perhaps financial cuts and layoffs are the new reality. The business has gone from times of abundance to times of trouble. The naïve man acts as if things will always be all right, while the prudent man plans ahead (Proverbs 22:3).

Times of trouble can take us down if we are not rooted in the Word of God. God's Word is our anchor in adversity. It reminds us to place our hope in heaven, and not on earth. The principles of Scripture teach us how to act and what we need to do while we wait on God. We gain our strength from our Savior, Jesus. We trust Him when we know Him, and we come to know Him through His Word. Times of trouble tempt us to lose our trust in God. However, trust looks trouble in the eye and is not terrified. Trust trumps trouble. This was Daniel's demeanor in the lion's den (Daniel 6:22).

Furthermore, there is an urge to overreact during times of trouble. Instead of giving God control, we try to seize it and won't let go. A closed hand cannot trust, while an open hand releases control to Christ. Let go and let the Lord lead you through this time of trouble. We think we are in control, but in reality, we never have been and never will be. God is in control. The Almighty is all-powerful. The Lord is large and in charge. Therefore, you can praise Him for His all-encompassing power (2 Chronicles 20:22). Your song of satisfaction is for God alone because you have experienced His lovingkindness in the midst of your times of trouble. Above all else, praise God for His provision of peace during times of trouble.

Trouble is your ticket for trust.

FAITH VERSUS FEAR

When I am afraid, I put my trust in you.
In God, whose word I praise—in God I trust
and am not afraid. What can mere mortals do to me?
PSALM 56:3-4

Fear is a formidable foe of faith. It lurks about, looking for ways to lead us into distrust of our Lord. Fear is subtle with its sneak attacks on our attitudes and bold in its frontal barrage on our beliefs. Fear always fights back, even when we extinguish it for a time with our total trust in God. And it doesn't let up until we get to heaven. Fear is like fire ants. You can eliminate their unholy mound, but they regroup and rebuild nearby.

Trust in the Lord is the terminator of fear, but fear seems to recreate itself with whatever appendage of doubt is left. It grows within the next uncertain circumstance that comes our way. Fear thinks it has us in check on the chessboard of our life, but the truth is that Jesus checkmated fear on the cross. Now it is up to us to appropriate His triumph by trusting in God.

There are many times when we are in transition from fear to faith. It's in the transition of trust in God that our cares co-mingle with Christ's care. There is a holy tension in our transition into trust. It is in this dawn of trust that light gradually overcomes darkness. Faith dissolves doubts as the sun drives away the mist.

Your mind may be a little murky, but you renew your thinking (Romans 12:2) with the truth that God is ever present. Your confidence may be crumbling, but you keep your eyes on your Savior. Your prayers may be clumsy, but you still cling to Christ. Hope trusts in this transition from fear to faith.

Followers of Jesus have the eternal seal of their Savior as their newfound identity (Ephesians 4:30). Do not allow the patterns of your old life to feed any fading fears in your new one (Romans 6:6). The fears of your proud past have been replaced with faith, love, and hope in your humble here and now. Faith has banished fear. Therefore, you can continually celebrate. So praise Him, trust Him, and fear no one. No one can take from you what you have already given to Him.

Faith is a fear-killer; it overcomes.

FEBRUARY 6

HOW LONG?

My soul is in anguish. How long, Lord, how long?
PSALM 6:3

"How long?" is a fair question to ask of the Lord. He does not expect us to suffer in silence. In fact, it's okay and desirable to pour out our petitions to Him. We need heaven's healing. When we verbalize our confusion to our loving heavenly Father, we feel relief. Just to know that the Lord listens to our heartfelt cries, no matter how petty or profound, is reassuring. Sometimes we can't sleep well at night. We wake up in anguish, our mind racing. A troubled heart has a hard time with sweet dreams because there is a dread or disappointment that destroys its quality of rest. However, deep sleep accompanies those who are able to rest in Him. We can rest in the Lord's presence (Exodus 33:14).

The pain will linger until you see Jesus face-to-face, but the Lord will get you through this difficulty. Therefore, do not let this momentary affliction keep you from experiencing God. Adversity is meant to engage us with eternity (2 Corinthians 4:17). If everything were easy, we would be prone to forget our heavenly Father. So while on earth, it is okay to ask, "How long?" Questions keep us from being clueless with Christ by driving us to our knees in dependency on Him. How long before you can be married? How long before your parents will be more understanding? How long before your teenager will mature? How long before the doctors can diagnose your ailment? How long before you can change careers or get a promotion? How long before finances are not such big issues?

All of these are fair questions and need to be asked. It is wise, healing, and hopeful to lift our concerns to Christ. But once we go to God with our questions, it is imperative that we listen to His answers. It is not enough just to question. We must be willing to listen to the Lord. His answer is simple yet profound. "As long as it takes," is His compassionate reply. As long as it takes to accomplish His will; as long as it takes to mold us into the image of His son Jesus; as long as it takes for us to learn the lessons of faith, patience, love, and forgiveness; as long as it takes to break our stubborn pride and replace it with gracious humility; as long as it takes to die to ourselves; as long as it takes for God to glorify Himself through our lives.

Questions keep you coming back to Christ for His love and direction. His unfailing love wipes the tears from your eyes and holds you close, where you are secure in Him. So above all else, in your state of questioning and confusion, receive God's unfailing love. How long before the Lord can love you? Right now.

His love will see you through, so invite Him to love on you as only the Lord can.

WAIT IN EXPECTATION

In the morning, LORD you hear my voice; In the morning
I lay my requests before you and wait in expectation.
PSALM 5:3

After we pray, we wait in expectation. That means we don't fret or wait fearfully. We wait, expecting God to engage. Faith fills our soul with expectation. However, be careful with flippant prayers that are shot off randomly with no recognition of royalty in the room. Do not dishonor Christ's kingship by praying aimlessly or distractedly. Do not grow weary of waking up each day in prayer. You shouldn't ignore the care of your soul any more than the rest of you when preparing in the morning. It is when you are the freshest that you engage best in prayer. One hour of prayer in the morning is worth two hours at night because your mind has yet to be tired from the complexities of the day. Morning prayers sow seeds of selflessness that bear fruit during the day in patience, peace, and productivity.

Indeed, you wait prayerfully, expecting God to answer in His timing and in His way. But your waiting is not without doing. As you pray and wait for the Lord to send out workers into His ripe harvest (Matthew 9:37-38), you venture into the world yourself and learn to love people. As you pray and wait to be healed from a dreaded disease or aggravating ailment, you go to a well-trained doctor to administer the latest medicines and treatments to help remedy your illness. As you pray and wait for a job, you go out and enlist in projects or labor that expose you to new opportunities and provide for your family in the interim. As you pray and wait for a relationship to be repaired, you reach out and seek to love the person with encouraging words and acts of kindness. You do your part as you wait expectantly on God to do His part. Waiting listens to the Almighty and then acts.

Expectations of God are good. Just be sure to align your expectations with His in prayer. No expectations may mean no disappointments, but this is where prayer and faith fill in the gaps. You can expect good things from God: "Now to him who is able to do immeasurably more than all we ask or imagine, according to his power that is at work within us." (Ephesians 3:20). God is trustworthy 100% of the time. He can be trusted regardless, so expect this of Him. He loves to see His children wait expectantly on Him. This trusting posture invites Him to answer prayers you never dreamed possible. You trust Him exclusively as you wait expectantly.

And oh, He knows how to exceed your expectations. Wait and see.

LOVE IS PATIENT

Love is patient …
1 CORINTHIANS 13:4

Love is patient. It is patient because it is more concerned with the welfare of another than its own needs. It is patient because it is more motivated to make the relationship right than to be right. Patience is the job description of everyone who loves because patience is the fruit of people filled with the Holy Spirit. Patience comes out of your heart when love dominates it (Ephesians 4:2).

Furthermore, patience stunts anger's growth by not feeding its appetite. It lovingly replaces anger with grace and forgiveness. Patience understands that most anger is destructive and self-centered, so it deflects anger by being other-centered. It looks out for the welfare of other human beings for their sake and for the purpose of being an image bearer of Christ. When people see patience, they see an example of Jesus' attitude and behavior. However, He was more patient with sinners who didn't know any better than He was with religious leaders who should have known better (John 8:7).

Patience is a priority for people who seek to love as their Savior loves. So, learn to love in a patient manner. The reason you are patient with your wife is because you love her. The reason you are patient with people who make you uncomfortable is that you love them. There is a difference between being reluctantly tolerant and lovingly patient. The second greatest command is to love others as you love yourself (Matthew 22:37-39). Jesus patiently loves you just as you are. Therefore, you can strive to love others and exercise patience in the same unconditional way Christ loves you. Patient people actively and meaningfully plan to love. Pray for patience, and you will increase your capacity to love.

Be like Jesus and be a patient lover of people.

LOVE IS KIND

... Love is kind.
1 CORINTHIANS 13:4

Love is a "killer application" for Christians because we "kill with kindness." Kindness means you are pleasant to be around because your countenance is inviting and shows interest. It is as much an attitude as anything. Kindness means you go out of your way to love someone. People who are unlovable become prime candidates for your kindness. A family member who is far from God has a deep desire for unconditional love and kindness. Kindness is the ability to be accepting when everything within you wants to be rejecting.

Love keeps you kind, especially toward those who are closest to you. They do not deserve you dredging up hurtful, bitter, and unforgiving words from the past. Love is kind in its conversations. Harsh and abrasive speech is absent from kind conversation. Love produces words that are "kind and tenderhearted" (Ephesians 4:32). Love is able to extend kind words that cheer up heavy hearts (Proverbs 16:24). Pray to God for kindness to reign in your relationships with kids and teenagers. We all have blown up and lost our temper over disrespectful attitudes and actions from our offspring. The temptation is to disrespect when we have been disrespected, and the natural response is to become angry when someone else spews out his or her frustrations on us. But God has not called us to natural responses but supernatural ones. Kindness in the face of frustration is a fruit of the Spirit, and only through submission to your Savior will kindness become front and center. The fullness of the Holy Spirit in your life is what causes kindness to come forth.

Lastly, loving others with kindness does not preclude difficult decisions. Kindness is authentic care and concern, and it is able to deliver hard truth that softens hard hearts. You can dismiss an employee with kindness. Likewise, you can disagree in a heated debate with kindness. Harshness has no hold on those who are controlled by Christ. Therefore, kindly love people through difficult situations. Kindness is king for followers of King Jesus, so love with kindness and watch people come around and embrace Christ. Allow Jesus' loving-kindness to flow through you, for kindness toward the needy honors God (Proverbs 14:31).

Kindness resides where love is applied, because love is kind.

LOVE IS NOT ENVIOUS

It does not envy …
1 CORINTHIANS 13:4

Love is not envious. It celebrates the good fortune of others and smiles when someone succeeds because love is an envy eraser. It can't wait for someone else to reach their goals and get the attention and accolades, for it is emotionally secure and mature. Love is content knowing that God "rains on the just and on the unjust" (Matthew 5:45). God's grace and blessing cannot be figured out or bottled in a formula, for He withholds or gives His blessing at His discretion. Love understands this and is not envious of those who are lavishly blessed by the Lord.

Christ, of course, has established principles that, if obeyed, lead to blessing (Psalm 119:1-2). If you obey your parents, you will be blessed by their wisdom, experience, and love. If you follow the laws of the land, you will be free from serving a prison term or paying fines. Both believers and unbelievers can apply and benefit from God's truth. His ways work; so don't get worked up when the wicked succeed. Success in life is an option for anyone who implements the principles embedded in God's Word. Therefore, choose to ignore envy and its dead-end road that results in comparison and disappointment. Envy attracts the immature, the insecure, the greedy, and the faithless. Comparing oneself to other people is an incubator for envy. Instead, reserve your comparisons for the character of Christ and be humble. Your personality, your looks, and your gifts are from God, so be whom God created.

Love is well-versed in congratulating. Love takes time to revel in the moment of accomplishment and looks for reasons to recognize the good in others. For example, completed projects, anniversaries, and birthdays are celebrated as a team. A sure remedy for envy is giving. Love gives sincere compliments, money, credit, time, and it gives the benefit of the doubt. Love's generosity deflates envy's influence. Love your enemies (Luke 6:35) and pray for them. Envy leads to a life of discontentment and sorrow, but love is Christ-centered, content, and joyful.

Envy has no place for a person who lavishly loves God and people.

LOVE DOES NOT BRAG

... it does not boast ...
1 CORINTHIANS 13:4

Love does not need to brag because it is secure. Those who boast seek security in the praise of others, and they do not rest in the eternal love of God. This is a struggle for all of us because we want our peers to admire our abilities and our accomplishments, and we want them to see us as intelligent and capable. We want to be perceived as spiritually mature and to have a reputation as a man who loves and respects his spouse and family. Our flesh lobbies for recognition.

Even the most committed disciples of Jesus struggled to tame their egos. James and John wanted to know on which side of the throne they would sit when Christ entered into His kingdom (Mark 10:37-40). Love learns to leave these matters in the Lord's hands. It is the ability to tell a story without having to be the lead actor in the plot. Love lifts up others and lowers itself. Love is not all about you, but all about others.

Love seeks ways to give God credit for accomplishments. It is not a flippant, "Praise the Lord!" Rather, it is heartfelt humility and thankfulness. There is communication—with body language and words—that acknowledges without God we would have failed. He answered prayer. He opened and closed doors, and He transformed hearts. He grew our character and forgave our sin. He blessed us with family and friends who love Him. Love looks long and hard at the goodness of the Lord. Boasting is limited to Him and to heaven's benefits.

James said, "As it is, you boast in your arrogant schemes. All such boasting is evil." (James 4:16). Boasting *takes* what is not deserved—praise—while love *gives* what is not deserved—grace. Love serves in silence since its goal is not selfish ambition (Philippians 2:3-4). Love is so caught up with reaching out to others that it forgets to stick a feather in its own cap. Love trusts God to reward His servants in His timing. Boasting repels people, but love draws them in. Therefore, invite people in with your love and lead them to the Lord. He gets the glory and you get the incredible satisfaction of following Him. Above all else, let your love brag on Jesus.

Give God glory and give people credit for your success. This is love, to brag on others and to lift up Christ.

LOVE IS NOT PROUD

. . . it is not proud.
1 CORINTHIANS 13:4

Love is not proud. Indeed, there is no room for pride in a heart of love. Pride struggles against love because love requires taking the focus off oneself and turning toward others. Pride is deceptive, and it always negotiates for its own benefit.

Pride's feeling of superiority slices into the soul like a poisoned arrow. It inserts its influence deep and wide. You can be controlled and wired by pride and not even know it. Love seeks to defuse pride's time bomb. Love drives pride from your controlling heart and frees you to become trusting and humble. Love teaches you to seek the blessing of others.

Love listens; pride talks. Love forgives; pride resents. Love gives; pride takes. Love apologizes; pride blames. Love understands; pride assumes. Love accepts; pride rejects. Love trusts; pride doubts. Love asks; pride tells. Love leads; pride drives. Love frees up; pride binds up. Love builds up; pride tears down. Love encourages; pride discourages. Love confronts; pride is passive-aggressive. Love is peaceful; pride is fearful. Love clarifies with truth; pride confuses with lies.

Love and pride are mutually exclusive. Pride withers love, but humility nurtures it. Humility invites love to take up permanent residence in the human heart. Love covers a multitude of sins (1 Peter 4:8). Love forgives even the worst of sinners, while pride struggles in a life of bitterness and resentment, thinking somehow it is paying back the offender. This state of unresolved anger only eats up the one unable to love and forgive.

Furthermore, humility positions you to love and be loved. Humility knows it needs help in the arena of receiving love. Your humble heart yearns for love from your Lord Jesus Christ. Once you receive the love of your heavenly Father, you become capable of giving love. Therefore, let the Lord love on you and allow others to love you, so you can, in turn, love.

Proud hearts melt under the influence of intense and unconditional love.

LOVE IS NOT RUDE

[Love] does not behave rudely …
1 CORINTHIANS 13:5 (NKJV)

Love rejects rudeness. Rudeness is impolite and disrespectful. Indeed, a rude reply stands ready on the lips of an unlovely life. Rude people use coarse words that rub their listeners the wrong way. They pride themselves in being without airs, but they are insensitive to the timing and the tone of their conversations. They hurt feelings at the drop of a hat and seem to alienate people on purpose. However, love is the light that leads rudeness out of darkness.

A rude person is impossible to work alongside because you never know when they are going to offend you or someone else. You lose confidence in rude people because of their volatile nature. Rude people become loners by default. Over time, no one can tolerate a barrage of irreverence and sarcasm. Even the most accepting and forgiving saints grow weary of rudeness which has no place in a caring culture.

Love expunges rudeness like a healthy body does a virus. Love requires you to be very direct and matter-of-fact in your communication with a rude person. Direct conversation is the only way they begin to "get it." Love takes the time to be very candid and clear with rude people who run roughshod over others. However, be careful not to be rude in dealing with the rude. Do not lower your standards to theirs. Be prayed up and filled up with the Spirit before you encounter the rude with truth (Romans 9:1).

Love is able to find at least one thing they admire in someone else. Even if a person is full of himself, there lies dormant, within him or her, some redeeming quality. Love is able to pull out the potential for good that lies deep within a selfish soul—the way Barnabas saw possibilities in Saul (Acts 9:27). Love looks beyond the hard, crusty exterior of someone's character and understands that fear may have locked his or her love into solitary confinement. Love is able to get past this barrier.

The Almighty's rude awakening transforms an impolite heart into one full of kindness and grace. When love has its way, rudeness runs away. Stay committed to your rude roommate, relative, parent, child, or colleague. Love them to Jesus, and your unconditional love will melt away their iceberg-like insecurities. Pray they will see themselves as Christ sees them. Love loves the rude and is not rude.

Therefore, be persistent by staying engaged in unconditional love. Watch the rude walls come down as you bombard them with consistent acts of love.

LOVE IS NOT SELF-SEEKING

… it is not self-seeking …
1 CORINTHIANS 13:5

Love is not self-seeking. It seeks instead the kingdom of God and His righteousness (Matthew 6:33). Like a heat-seeking missile, love is locked onto the warm heart of God. Self is lowered to the bottom shelf and God is elevated to the top shelf. Love seeks its Savior, Jesus, moment by moment, for wisdom and direction.

While selfishness seeks its own way; love seeks God's way. Self seeks praise; love seeks to praise. Self is fearful of being found out; love is an open book. Self is self-absorbed; love is saturated in the Spirit. Self is preoccupied with pleasing people; love is compelled to follow the commands of Christ. Love dies daily to self and comes alive for Christ.

There are competing forces that vie for your attention. Therefore, default to prayer. Prayer may be your most potent, precluding power against a self-seeking mindset. The very nature of prayer assumes you are seeking God and not seeking self. Prayer aligns with the Almighty's agenda and is a confession that you are submitting to God's will. Prayer is your expression of love for the Lord. It is very difficult, if not impossible, to remain self-seeking when seeking the Lord in prayer, confession, and repentance (Hosea 10:12).

This attribute of love also applies to our horizontal relationships with people. Love seeks to meet the needs of others first. Love understands and is not afraid to deny self for the sake of a spouse or friend. Families provide a daily opportunity for selfless living where you must choose between demanding your own way or lovingly serving others. Churches and communities also provide opportunities to put others first. It is far more fulfilling to seek the welfare of widows and orphans than your own leisure. Use your position and influence for the good of other people by giving sacrificially. This is counter-intuitive and countercultural. Someone may take advantage of your good will, but any cross you bear is a reflection of the cross Christ bore.

Jesus' goal was to do the will of His heavenly Father (John 17:4). Jesus loved by doing God's will over His own will. He subjugated His selfish desires to eternal interests. Since Jesus trusted His heavenly Father, so can you. Your choice to love others may mean death to your own desires, but it will provide life in your relationships. As Jesus said, "But many who are first will be last, and many who are last will be first" (Matthew 19:30). Love may finish last in man's eyes, but will win the gold in God's eyes.

Love seeks its Savior first, and it serves others.
Love is a Savior-seeker, not a self-seeker.

LOVE IS SLOW TO ANGER

... it is not easily angered ...
1 CORINTHIANS 13:5

Love is not easily angered. It is not in a hurry to get angry because it knows God is at work. Love knows God can handle the irritating person and the stressful situation. Most of the time, the best thing love can do is refrain from anger. A calm response diffuses an angry outburst (Proverbs 15:1). Anger toward injustice and bullying is appropriate, and sometimes we need to respond proportionately, but love overlooks the silly things that really don't matter much.

A friend or family member who is rarely on time is no reason to get angry. Instead, adjust your expectations and build a time buffer into your schedule. Why get angry when a little bit of adjustment remedies the situation? Love adjusts rather than stews in anger. Love calms the nerves, while anger wreaks havoc with your blood pressure. Love-filled living is by far healthier physically and emotionally.

Love is able to keep the big picture in mind. It understands that tomorrow is another day and there is no need to stress over this temporary setback. God will work things out in His timing, for He can be trusted. It is much wiser to trust God with your spouse, instead of attempting to change her with your anger. God's discipline is much more thorough and precise. He puts His finger on an attitude or action and won't let up until He is satisfied with the resulting change. Love knows how to trust God. Therefore, pray to God before you get angry. Ask the Lord to increase your love quotient. Love understands there are better ways and a better day ahead.

However, sometimes love sees the need for anger. You must lovingly confront the abuses of drugs and alcohol. These are enemies that wreck relationships and take lives. Love doesn't stick its head in the sand of isolation and detachment but engages by encouraging wise choices and compassionate counseling.

Love confronts sin. Love is angered by sin's control of a loved one's soul. It drives us to our knees in our own confession of sin and to our feet to be a part of the solution. Love reserves anger for the right occasions. Even Jesus administered anger at the appropriate time (Mark 3:5; John 2:15). Love will be angry at times, but only after much prayer and patience. Love more and be angry less.

Above all else, be rich in love and slow to anger (Psalm 145:8). This high road to heaven illustrates the long-suffering love of the Lord.

LOVE FORGETS

... it keeps no record of wrongs.
1 CORINTHIANS 13:5

Love forgives continually and it forgives comprehensively. Forgiveness wipes clean the slate of offense. Forgiveness was close to the heart of Jesus. Some of His dying words were to ask God's forgiveness for the ignorant acts of His offenders (Luke 23:34). Christ's greatest act of love was the forgiveness He extended by His voluntary death on the cross (Colossians 2:13-15). Jesus described His own act of love when He said, "Greater love has no one than this: to lay down one's life for one's friends." (John 15:13). Jesus was the epitome of love and forgiveness. He owns the trademark.

Forgiveness is the fuel for living a life free from the clutter of cutting words or unjust acts. A life without forgiveness is a lonely life locked up in the solitary confinement of sin. Forgiveness flows when you have been authentically and thoroughly forgiven. Unless the forgiveness of God has graced your heart and soul, your capacity for forgiveness will be foreign and futile. It is the grace of God and faith in Him that fuels forgiveness in followers of Christ. The job description of Christians is to love with forgiveness because we have been forgiven (Colossians 3:13). Think about the depth and breadth of God's forgiveness when we turn to Him in genuine repentance. Ignorant acts are forgiven. Drunkenness is forgiven. Lust is forgiven. Immorality is forgiven. Hate is forgiven. Ignoring God is forgiven. Unbelief is forgiven. Love forgives because it has been forgiven.

Remember where you were BC (before Christ) and reflect on where you would be today without His love and forgiveness. Recall what it was like to be lost and bound up in your sin and celebrate how far God has brought you. Love is extremely grateful for God's goodness and redeeming power. Forgiveness is second nature for those who are consumed by Christ's love. When you have been forgiven much, you love much (Luke 7:47).

Your capacity to love is directly tied to your willingness to receive Christ's forgiveness. Accept the Almighty's forgiveness and extend forgiveness. Love by forgiving your family members who may not even know they hurt your heart. Love by forgiving your friend who violated your confidence. Forgiveness forgets the past, engages in the present, and hopes in the future.

Reject the temptation for indignation and humbly receive God's grace instead. Love liberally by regularly relying on forgiveness. Love forgives.

LOVE AVOIDS EVIL

Love does not delight in evil …
1 CORINTHIANS 13:6

Love avoids evil by not entertaining its alluring temptations. Evil seeks to destroy love. It is relentless in its pursuit to replace love with lust. Sin takes well-meaning workers and grinds them into workaholics. It takes people under extreme pressure and turns them into alcoholics. It portrays drugs as fun and romantic. But love sees beyond the momentary escape, the temporary release, and the artificial high. Love longs for the authentic and the real.

Sin is the enemy, and love does not sleep with the enemy. Love does not flirt with sinful people or experiment with sin; it is not worth it. Sin breaks the heart of God. Sin may lure you in with good looks and false promises, but its outcomes are outrageously bad. Satan will continue to unleash his evil strategies until our Savior returns. He will cast the devil and his evil endeavors into the lake of fire forever (Revelation 20:10). For now, the role of love is to reject any demonic evil advances.

Jesus Christ is the focus and attraction for those motivated by love. Faith is not lukewarm for those who love God (Revelation 3:16). Without deep and committed love, you are disqualified to engage in kingdom initiatives. Furthermore, love does not perceive church attendance as a perfunctory exercise done out of obligation or guilt. Love sees the church as the "bride of Christ," and it is not cold or dispassionate toward Christ or His church.

The passion of Jesus-followers is to love and obey God. When your focus is on Him, there is no room for evil. The agenda of love is to delight in the Lord; it is preoccupied with pleasing God. Love can't wait to commune with Christ because its desire is intimacy with Almighty God. Love flushes out evil desires and sinful thoughts as it loves and obeys God. Love has no time for sin because it is caught up with Christ. Therefore, stay away from sin, run from evil, and run toward God. Disengage from people who lean toward evil. Be true to the One who loves you most.

The cross of Christ—His love—overcame evil.
So above all else, express your love by delighting in Jesus.

LOVE ENJOYS TRUTH

... [Love] rejoices with the truth.
1 CORINTHIANS 13:6

Since love enjoys truth, it seeks it out and rejoices in applying it. Love knows truth comes from the Father. Truth is a tremendous asset to love because it illuminates the way. Truth teaches love where to apply itself. Truth delivered in love brings joy and healing and restoration. Love is pleased to give and receive the truth. However, love without truth is shallow and sentimental because it has no lasting effect. Truth without love is harsh and abrasive and is rarely received well. Love and truth need each other. Together they make a dynamite duo.

Jesus modeled this when He lovingly spoke to both the woman caught in adultery and to her accusers. He confronted the sin of both parties with the offer of redemption and love (John 8:3-11). Indeed, love is eager to understand and apply truth, because it knows truth's positive outcomes. A life shaped by truth—patterned after the character of God and the life of Christ—is beautiful and blessed. For example, truth reveals disrespectful attitudes and replaces them with respect. Truth exposes a lack of love and invites confession and repentance.

Love takes the time to speak the truth (Ephesians 4:15). Many times, you can most effectively deliver truth with questions. Help people discover truth without telling them what to do. Ask questions like: "What do you think you need to do?"; "Why do you want to do this?"; "Have you prayed through this?"; "What does the Bible say about this issue?"; "What do your spouse and friends think?" Loving questions help sincere seekers get to the essence of truth through their own self-discovery.

God used a question from the very beginning when He asked Adam where he was in the garden (Genesis 3:9). God knew the answer, but He wanted Adam to think through his curious condition. God loved and respected Adam so much that He gave him the opportunity to reason and reflect on truth. Socrates may have branded the questioning method, but God invented it.

Love leads others into truth because it is a patient lover of truth. Love longs for truth to be exposed and embraced. This is what it means to love God with your mind (Matthew 22:37-39). The wisdom of this world lacks authentic love, but the wisdom of the Lord is pregnant with real life love. Be glad that your parents, friends, and teachers lovingly lead you into the discovery of the truth. As a Christ-follower, celebrate truth and urge others to pursue it.

Above all else, express your love by embracing truth and rejoicing in its outcomes.

LOVE ALWAYS PROTECTS

It always protects …
1 CORINTHIANS 13:7

Love always protects. It protects because it loves, and it loves because it protects. A husband and father's love protects physically. If you love your wife or children, you do not want them to suffer bodily harm. You provide a safe home for them. You shield them from harmful substances that might damage their bodies. You keep them safe by obeying the speed limit and not driving recklessly. You protect them by not endangering their lives with unnecessary risks. If you love those entrusted to your care, you protect them.

Wives love to be protected; it makes them feel valued and cherished. They yearn for physical, financial, and emotional protection. Husbands, when you keep your wife safe you speak her love language. Your provision of a dependable automobile and a secure home screams love. Because you love your family, you protect them from unwise financial exposure. For example, you don't "bet the farm" and place your house at risk. Your temperament might be able to handle high risk and even thrive on it, but because you love your family, you do not personally expose them to on-the-edge endeavors. You do not want them to fear being unprotected.

Love also protects emotionally because it understands the feelings and concerns of others. Emotional protection allows young children to grow up well-adjusted and loved. Adolescents are vulnerable and tender; they need the loving protection of their parents. Love prays for the ones it loves. Pray for their hearts to be protected from the evil one and from unwise influences. Pray for the Holy Spirit to protect loved ones from straying away from God's best in relationships. Furthermore, pray for your own tendency toward selfishness and self-deception. If not careful, you can justify almost anything. Sometimes, you can become your own worst enemy, so pray for protection from yourself, and be accountable.

Lastly, think of ways to protect your friends and work associates. Your wisdom and counsel provide loving protection (Proverbs 4:6). A small, encouraging word may protect peers from overcommitment. Your colleagues may need your permission to say no. Do not underestimate your actions. Your model of appropriate behavior with female friends and coworkers protects you and provides an example of discretion for those you influence (Proverbs 2:11). You love others by creating an environment of protection.

Therefore, pray for God's protection and provide protection. Love always protects.

LOVE ALWAYS TRUSTS

… [Love] always trusts …
1 CORINTHIANS 13:7

Love always trusts, for trust is a staple of love. If you are always suspicious and uncertain, then love is lacking. Love thrives in an environment of trust but shrivels up with distrust. Trust is necessary for a relationship to flourish and take root. Therefore, look for the best in someone else and be ready to trust them, even though they may not have been trustworthy in the past. Love is all about second chances. Don't blindly believe everything everyone tells you, but be ready to extend grace and trust. Have a policy of "trust and verify." Love does not write someone off when they fail to meet expectations or when they blatantly fail. Love picks them up and says, "I will trust you again. I have not given up on you. You are a child of God, therefore you deserve another opportunity to succeed."

Love is all about making people successful. When you love someone, you trust them to carry out the plan. Love sees potential where others see disqualification. Love sees success where others see failure. Love sees a hurting human being where others see someone who is just angry. Love thinks the best, but distrust thinks the worst. Love and trust feed off each other; they propel one another to greater heights.

Love always trusts. This is especially true with Almighty God. Love trusts God, for He is trustworthy. His track record of trustworthiness is without blemish. He can be trusted. If you love Him, you will trust Him. Your affection and love should originate in heaven not on earth. Love leans on and listens to the Lord because it trusts Him.

So the goal is to fall more deeply in love with God. Go deeper with God and you will become more and more delighted with Him and His ways. John explains it well: "And so we know and rely on the love God has for us. God is love. Whoever lives in love lives in God, and God in them" (1 John 4:16). Indeed, a loving relationship with God is based on trust. You can trust God to love you authentically and unconditionally. He has no limitations in His love toward you.

You love better when you regularly receive the love of God. Because you love, you trust. Sad is the soul that has not learned the secret of loving by trusting. The conditional lover is always looking over their shoulder in distrust. Cynicism creates a cold heart. However, your heavenly Father wants to flood your heart with love. Trust Him with this.

People come back to where they know they are loved. Love always trusts.

LOVE ALWAYS HOPES

... [Love] always hopes ...
1 CORINTHIANS 13:7

Love always hopes. It hopes for the best while it is prepared for anything. Love is hopeful because its hope is in the Lord. As the old hymn proclaims, "My hope is built on nothing less than Jesus' blood and righteousness." When we love God, we also hope in Him because we are sure of His promises that provide assurance—promises such as, "Never will I leave you; never will I forsake you" (Hebrews 13:5). Moreover, faith helps us be sure of what we hope for. As it says in Hebrews 11:1, "Now faith is confidence in what we hope for and assurance about what we do not see." Faith, hope, and love are all first cousins; they complement each other and support one another.

Love hopes because it knows the end of the story, and heaven is its destiny. It bridles its emotions to not fear because love casts out fear (1 John 4:18). Hope conquers death and fear because Jesus has gone before us and done the same (Acts 2:23-24). You can be hopeful because you get to be in heaven with your Lord and Savior, Jesus. However, there is something just as big that you can hope for even now. You can hope that others you love might place their faith in Jesus Christ. You know God is willing to save them from their sin (2 Peter 3:9). Your part is not to save them, but to love them toward the Lord. Some plant and some water, but it is God who makes faith grow (1 Corinthians 3:6). It is the Lord who convicts and draws people to Himself. But be hopeful. If God can save us, He can save anybody. Do not give up on praying for and loving on your family and friends because love always hopes.

Love always hopes, especially when you are drowning in adversity. You may feel like you can only come up for air one more time. The undertow of your circumstances may be sucking you out into the sea of despair. Your emotional energy may be overspent and close to bankruptcy. Your marriage may seem hopeless, but you are still called to love. Your health may be ravaged, but you are still called to love. A relationship may be hopeless, but you are still called to love. Your finances are struggling, but you are still called to love. You can only love in trying circumstances when you hope in God. It is okay to not like what you are going through but trust God's goodness and hope in His plans for you, then continue to love. Hope fuels love, and love fuels hope. Hope follows love as ducklings follow their mother.

Love especially when you don't feel like loving.
Be hopeful, for love always hopes.

LOVE ALWAYS PERSEVERES

... [Love] always perseveres ...
1 CORINTHIANS 13:7

Love always perseveres. It does not give up. This is why the love commitment of husbands and wives is "till death do us part." This is the assurance that supports love, for it insists upon loyalty in the face of hard times. "I don't love you anymore" is not an option for couples committed to Christ. Love always perseveres. It perseveres through problems; it perseveres through misunderstandings; it perseveres through uncertainty; it perseveres through messy arguments; it perseveres through suffering and hardship. Love becomes better instead of bitter when experiencing challenges because it perseveres.

God's grace and steadfast love enable our love for others. The unconditional love of Jesus becomes a template for our own love. This is why parents persevere in their love for their children. They can only give up on loving a son or daughter when their heavenly Father gives up on loving them. Parents persevere with their children because they know what it is like to be loved by a Father who never gives up. Even through the hurt, rejection, selfishness, financial irresponsibility, and anger, love for a child still stands. Love will not stand down to the devil's strongholds in a young person's mind and heart.

Moreover, love perseveres in reminding them of the truth and their identity is in Christ. Your believing child is forgiven by you and by God; remind them of this. God has uniquely gifted your child; remind them of this. Love perseveres in reminding and revealing truth to those it loves. Pray that the eyes of your child's heart will see and understand the truth of who they are from God's perspective. They are longing for love, so be the lead lover in their life.

Lastly, persevere in your love for your parents. Parents can be distant and disinterested but still love them. To some degree, they may still be licking the wounds of past hurts and disappointments. They need love as much as or more than anyone else. Love your mom and dad while they are still alive. One day they will not be around to love, so express all your love for your parents in this life. You plan for no regrets when you aggressively love them now. Persevere in your love, and one day you will be grateful you did.

Love is an invaluable investment because it leaves no regrets. It always perseveres.

LOVE NEVER FAILS

Love never fails.
1 CORINTHIANS 13:8

Failure is not an option for love. You can labor in love with someone for a long period of time, yet they still seem unfazed by your unconditional "agape." Even in these situations, you are still successful. You get an A for your consistent effort to love. Some may describe your scenario as unsuccessful, but you know better. You know that if you have been obedient to love, the results are in God's hands (Deuteronomy 30:16). He can soften a hardened heart, and He is the one who can change a person's mind. Love never fails because Almighty God is its author.

Your part is to love, and His part is to draw people to Himself (Jeremiah 31:3). Love in your leadership, and you are successful. Love in your marriage, and you are successful. Love in your friendships, and you are successful. Love in your speech and behavior, and you are a roaring success. Make it one of your goals to be as successful in your loving as you are in your business or career. Long to out-love your peers and you will experience extraordinary outcomes.

The Bible paints a beautiful picture of love as a matter of obedience: "Now that you have purified yourselves by obeying the truth so that you have sincere love for each other, love one another deeply, from the heart" (1 Peter 1:22). This is why moms are celebrities of love; they love long, and they love hard. Moms are unselfish lovers because they love when no one is looking. In the middle of the night, they minister to their little ones. Moms are the unsung heroes of unselfish love.

You may feel like a failure with your children because parenting is hard. It is hard to teach, train, and lead your children to obey God. Sometimes it is even hard to love them through tantrums and whining and all manner of things that come from sinful hearts. Furthermore, in parenting, it is hard to measure your effectiveness. It may be that your child is well into adulthood before you really know their commitment to God. But even in your parental frustrations, you still love your child. You never stop loving them. And because you never stop loving them, you do not fail. Indeed, there are lots of ways you can fail. You can fail in your job; you can fail in your finances; you can fail in school; you can fail to follow up. But you can never fail when you love. By faith, place yourself in a better position to love more robustly.

Heaven gives you high marks for your unconditional love, so stay enrolled in the school of love, and graduate when you get to glory. Lovers succeed, for love never fails.

LOVE IS THE GREATEST

And now these three remain: faith, hope and love.
But the greatest of these is love.
1 CORINTHIANS 13:13

Why is love the greatest out of three worthy contenders? It is the greatest because God is love (1 John 4:8). The apex of God's attributes is love. God is the lover of your soul, and the love of God far exceeds earthly, limited love. This is the reason you look to Jesus as the supreme example of how to love. Love is God's gold standard; it rises above other compelling character traits such as faith and hope because it is the foundation for everything else.

Love is the theme that covers your character, seasons your service for Christ, and flavors your faith. Love brings brilliant technicolor to our otherwise bland black-and-white loveless living. You can serve, provide for your family, mow the lawn, feed the poor, attend church, and even worship, but if these lack love, you lose. You lose the blessing of God, and you lose heaven's reward because your motivation was not for your Master, Jesus Christ. Love is the greatest because it aligns your heart with Almighty God.

You are the greatest when you love because it draws attention to Jesus. So meditate on love as you rise in the morning, work during the day, and eat dinner at night with your family. Your wife longs to be loved; this is her greatest need from you. So love her lavishly in ways she wants to be loved. Think often on love, and your actions will begin to follow your thoughts. What drives you? Is it love? Make love your motivation, and your happiness will spill over on to others. Love jumpstarts joy and prolongs peace; it decreases pride and increases humility. Therefore, love long and hard, love unbiased and unencumbered, love early and love late. Love the rich, the poor, and everyone in between. Love during the good times and the bad. Love the deserving and undeserving. Love faithfully and you will have a lasting influence for the Lord.

Lastly, great love takes on different forms. Your situation may require tough love, full of accountability and action. Or your friend may be crying out for tender love, rich in encouragement. Pray for God's wisdom and discernment on how to love, then trust Him with its application. Your greatest contribution to mankind is love on behalf of the Lord Jesus Christ. Your greatest gift to God and others is love. Because He loved you first, you can love (1 John 4:19). God is great and He makes you great with love. You are your greatest when you get and give love.

Therefore, by the grace of God, seek to be a great lover. Love is the greatest in God's eyes.

HONOR MARRIAGE

Marriage should be honored by all, and the marriage bed kept pure, for God will judge the adulterer and all the sexual immoral.
HEBREWS 13:4

Marriage is a sacred institution of God and it is not to be taken lightly or treated with disrespect. It is easier in most cases to get a marriage license than a driver's license, but this does not give you a license to have a reckless marriage. To honor marriage means there is an understanding of commitment and preparation for its success. Marriage requires much more than love. It is not just a convenient way to guarantee sex. You don't just walk away from marriage when you get tired of one another or stop loving one another. To honor marriage is to make a lifetime dedication to one person. Just as Jesus is committed and faithful to His bride, the church, for eternity (Revelation 19:7), so are you committed to your wife.

Keep your marriage bed pure. You honor marriage when you keep the Lord's definition—a man and a woman exclusively devoted to loving each other—under the submission of Almighty God. Do not chase after a fantasy of sexual perfection with someone other than your spouse. Sex outside of marriage is wrong and it breaks the heart of God and crushes your wife's spirit. It is not a causal infraction, for its effects last a lifetime. Most important, prevent unfaithfulness by keeping your marriage bed pure and honorable and by falling deeper and deeper in love with the wife God has given you.

Lastly, create boundaries together, such as committing to one another that divorce is not an option. Agree to never be alone with someone of the opposite sex. This is a way to honor each other and to not find yourselves in compromising situations. At the very least, you will avoid the appearance of evil. A marriage discipline of fidelity takes effort, definition, and accountability. Yes, you trust your wife, but do not be naïve to think that temptation, Satan, and other lonely souls are not out to snare your spouse (Proverbs 7:10-23).

Be on the offensive by planning purity. One way to plan purity is to honor your spouse with your words. Words of disappointment and dissatisfaction about your wife—shared indiscreetly with another woman—fuel the fires of unfaithfulness. Unfaithfulness starts with words, is furthered by a disrespectful attitude, and is executed by actions facilitated over a meal or a walk with a "friend." Therefore, remain true to your marriage vows and your wife by exercising kindness and respect.

Above all else, honor your marriage by first honoring God.

SUCCESSFUL MARRIAGES

"For this reason a man will leave his father and mother and be united to his wife, and the two will become one flesh."
EPHESIANS 5:31

Even successful marriages are fraught with mistakes. Marriage lessons are learned by "trial and error" or "trial and terror," as some couples have experienced. Indeed, successful marriages don't just happen by chance. They are not created like a clock, to be wound up and never given attention. You become one flesh, but in reality it takes a lifetime of hard work, forgiveness, love, and respect to enjoy oneness. One flesh implies unity of purpose. It is alignment around beliefs and behavior, and if this is void in marriage, you become vulnerable to misplaced expectations and perpetual misery.

Marriage requires at least as much work as your work. Hard work is necessary for successful marriages. This seems obvious, but we tend to drift toward being selfish. However, hard work is the fuel that keeps a marriage moving forward. We see the fruit of hard work in our career as it produces satisfaction and significance. But these results come from many hours of planning, communicating, training, and teaching. Indeed, your marriage is a direct result of the amount of effort you have expended. Don't expect a harvest of marriage success if the seeds of forgiveness, love, and respect have not been planted in the soil of humility and trust. Furthermore, the weeds of busyness have to be intentionally pulled out, before they choke out your love and friendship with your spouse. Busyness is the enemy of the best marriages, so labor toward a marriage with much margin. Robust marriages take time and trust.

Forgiveness in marriage means you take the time to say, "I was wrong" and "I am sorry." It means you take responsibility to confess your anger and selfishness. Moreover, it means you do not hold a grudge. God-like forgiveness forgives regardless of the offense that has been committed (Colossians 3:13). It accepts apologies and does not bring up past hurts as a club of resentment. Forgiveness is the footers in the foundation of a successful marriage.

Above all else, successful marriages are made up of unconditional love and radical respect. No wife has ever complained of too much love, or a husband of an over-abundance of respect. Love is emotional, physical, and volitional. Husbands, you are to love sensitively, intimately, and willfully (Ephesians 5:25). Furthermore, marriage is your laboratory for growing as a follower of Christ because you learn to live for the Lord by learning to live for each other. You die to yourselves and come alive to each other.

Successful marriages reflect your oneness with your Savior. Be a marriage success as God defines success.

PRAYING HUSBAND

Isaac prayed to the Lord on behalf of his wife, because she was childless. The Lord answered his prayer, and his wife Rebekah became pregnant.
GENESIS 25:21

A praying husband appeals to the Lord for the sake of his wife. He bombards heaven on behalf of his bride, and he is consistent in praying for his wife every day for important matters such as peace and security. Prayer is one of God's select weapons that a husband can wield in defense of his wife. God has called you to be the spiritual warrior of your home, and prayer is your first line of defense. If prayer is compromised, then you have no air support from your heavenly Father. Without prayer covering your home and your wife, you and your family are open to blistering assaults from the devil and his demons. So pray for God's hedge of protection (Job 1:10).

The strategy of the enemy is to keep you busy and distracted with only fragments of prayer on your breath. An overly active man is probably a prayerless man; a man consumed with his own deal is probably a prayerless man; a man absorbed by pride is probably a prayerless man; a man who serves a small God is probably a prayerless man; a man angry at his wife is probably a prayerless man. A husband whose prayers are hindered is a man who knows he needs to pray for his wife but doesn't. He is a man powerless as a spiritual leader (1 Peter 3:7).

Prayer for your wife leads you to forgive your wife and to love your wife. You cannot pray for your wife and stay mad at her. You cannot pray for your wife and not want to hang out with her, for prayer facilitates intimacy. Prayer changes your heart and hers. Therefore, agree together for a time apart just to pray (1 Corinthians 7:5). Prayer unleashes the resources and the blessings of God. Satan shudders at the thought of a praying husband. A husband will win the battle for his family if he fights the enemy on his knees. It is a posture of desperation for God that brings victory and reconciliation. Husbands, prayer is your most potent marriage resource.

Therefore, get on your knees and do not get up until you have persevered in prayer for your helpmate. Courageously cry out to God on her behalf. Pray for her inner beauty to be reflected in her countenance. Pray for her to feel God's love and security. Pray for her to feel your love, support, and respect. Pray for her to be at peace with God, herself, and you. Pray for her to have wisdom and discernment as a wife and a mom. Pray for her to love God and hate sin. Thank God for your wife and thank Him for her love for you. Thank Him for her unselfish service. Thank Him that she puts up with your idiosyncrasies.

**Prayer for your wife is profitable;
it solicits heaven on her behalf.**

RISK AND REWARD

And Caleb said, "I will give my daughter Acsah in marriage to the man who attacks and captures Kiriath Sepher." Othniel son of Kenaz, Caleb's younger brother, took it; so Caleb gave his daughter Acsah to him in marriage.

JUDGES 1:12-13

Risk often precedes reward. War is risky because you endanger life and limb. The stakes are high. However, the rewards of war are life, liberty, and the pursuit of happiness. The victor enjoys the spoils of war, while those humiliated in defeat suffer loss. Marriage is risky because it entails the co-mingling of money, time, trust, and loyalty. What's yours becomes hers, and what's hers becomes yours. But the rewards of marriage are love, joy, peace, companionship, sex, children, and spiritual/emotional maturity, to name but a few. The many risks of marriage are overshadowed by the mammoth rewards it hands out to the husband and to the wife.

Business and ministry can also be risky undertakings. Like David, your model of risk-taking may inspire others to greater vision (1 Chronicles 11:19). You have the reward of positioning yourself to invest in and influence kingdom endeavors. Keep this your goal, regardless of whether you fail or succeed. Success will always be accompanied by mini-failures. So stay focused on God and stay obedient to His calling. Risk and reward are kept in the right perspective through prayer. God will lead you by His Holy Spirit because these initiatives come from a divine directive. Therefore, there is no need to take unnecessary risks. Be patient, and God will lead you to just the right opportunities at just the right time.

Over a lifetime, there are limited God-ordained opportunities that require risk. Therefore, allow the Almighty to guide you through the risky terrain of life. Avoid shortcuts and, instead, wait on Him. Pay the price of patience and seize the moment only when your faith, His Word, and godly counsel validate your direction. Persevere in the process because God may ask you to do things that seem larger than life. He has prepared your way with people and resources, so follow hard after Him. And what may seem risky to others will be peaceful to you.

For some, the rewards remain dormant until death. Your risk may be living an obscure and obedient life to Christ, with the joy of remaining faithful as your only earthly reward. But the reward of knowing and obeying Him is eternal, and it is enough.

What a privilege to honor, serve, love, and worship Jesus. And then your greatest reward is when you see Him face to face and hear, "Well done" (Matthew 25:23).

PARENTAL GIFT

Marry and have sons and daughters; find wives for your sons and give your daughters in marriage, so that they too may have sons and daughters. Increase in number there; do not decrease.

JEREMIAH 29:6

For a parent, it is hard to give away a child in marriage. When an adult child marries, you do gain a son or daughter, but you still feel like you are losing something. For some parents, it is much easier to give away time and money than to give away a child in marriage. Even when you know in your heart it is absolutely God's will, it is still difficult. However, this is another opportunity to turn to God, for His timing is impeccable.

It may be hard to accept that marriage for your child is imminent. You may reflect, "This soon-to-be married adult child can't already be ready for marriage." It seems like yesterday when they were still in diapers, bumping into things as they learned to walk. Walking led to talking; talking led to reading; reading led to writing; and writing led to graduation. They graduated from kindergarten, middle school, high school, and college. You were there for their first step, their first day of school, their first sleepover, their first sickness, their first school play, their first athletic event, their first date, and hopefully, by God's grace, their first and only marriage.

It is hard to entrust your baby to someone you have known for only a short time. Even if this new in-law loves God, it is still difficult. You know in your heart this person is the one, and you know they are meant for each other. You know their character and maturity is robust and real. This is the right relationship, in the right way, at the right time. It is right. Now as the parent, you have to loosen your grip and let go. This is similar to the process you have gone through in each of your children's transitions through life. During the good or bad stages, you held them with an open hand and trusted God with their lives. This is a transition of trust for you as you let them leave so they can cleave. (Mark 10:7).

God can be trusted with your adult child, as you have trusted Him in all other areas of your life. Your children are not exempt from this total trust. He will do a much better job of watching over them than you ever could with your limited time and wisdom. This is the role of our heavenly Father. He takes care of your children because they are His children.

When your child marries, you have gained a son or daughter, and your heavenly Father is smiling and well pleased (Matthew 3:17).

CHANGE MANAGEMENT

"Therefore, this is what the LORD says: 'I will return to Jerusalem with mercy, and there my house will be rebuilt. And the measuring line will be stretched out over Jerusalem,' declares the LORD Almighty."
ZECHARIAH 1:16

Change is inevitable. It may come from external forces out of your control or internal initiatives. Your home is a hotbed of change, so be aware and prepare. Prepare your family for the change from home to school and train them in how to transition from a single adult into a married adult. The same can be said about change at your workplace. People are afraid of what they might lose: jobs, status, pay, or influence, to name a few concerns. Leaders need to take responsibility during change to negotiate its transitional turns. Like hugging a steep and curvy road without the benefit of guardrails, the leader needs to handle change carefully and prayerfully.

Embrace change and enjoy its benefits, for it comes sooner or later. Those who accept change use it wisely and esteem its value. Those who reject change die a slow death of denial. So be careful not to fight change, for it will bloody your stubborn nose of resistance. As on a river, enjoy following the current and do not exhaust yourself by fighting to paddle upstream. Moreover, people need a wise leader who can frame change positively. Many times, something has to die. An old way of doing things may need to be put to rest. At the beginning of change, there is an invitation to bury out-of-date expectations and methods. Laugh a lot at yourself and with others, because humor is like WD-40 for the hinges of change.

Above all else, never lose the spirit and wisdom of Christ during the shifting courses of change. His values, principles, and purposes never change, so embrace the never-changing Christ throughout the process of change (Colossians 2:8). On the other hand, Christ is the ultimate change agent, and you can trust that He manages change for His purposes (Proverbs 21:1). So don't lose sight of the Lord's leading. Lean heavily on the Lord during these uncertain seasons. Change is inevitable, and Christ creates change. Therefore, walk with Christ through transitions, and you will be changed for the better.

Change will manage you or you will manage change.
So enjoy today in anticipation of tomorrow.

MARCH 2

SEDUCTIVE SHORTCUTS

When Pharaoh let the people go, God did not lead them on the road through the Philistine country, though that was shorter. For God said, "If they face war, they might change their minds and return to Egypt." So God led the people around by the desert road toward the Red Sea. The Israelites went up out of Egypt armed for battle.

EXODUS 13:17-18

Shortcuts are seductive because they are appealing and inviting. They caress our pride, stroke our ego, and garner immediate gratification. We sometimes seek shortcuts while driving, preparing for school exams, career advancement, marriage maturity, parenting skills, financial success, and spiritual development. Shortcuts are attractive to your clever side because you think that with enough ingenuity and smarts you can bypass much of the work that is usually required. However, the downside of shortcuts is that their promise of a faster way may be short-circuiting God's best. Just because it is easier does not qualify it as the will of God. In fact, ease of execution may be evidence against God's will. Instead, a season of suffering may be His plan (1 Peter 4:19).

Do not depend on circumstances alone as the compass of where God is leading you. You may feel pressure from people, pride, politics, or finances to take the most expedient route. But be careful because expedience can be an excuse for the impatient and the distrusting. Do not underestimate His wisdom if you find you're going through a laborious and sometimes painful process. If you rush, you may miss God's best.

God's glory should be our main objective (1 Corinthians 10:31). This means using God's glory as your litmus test, and then watching your other initiatives take care of themselves. Have faith that God is facilitating His will even if some of your questions remain unanswered. He's got your back even though the enemy may be breathing down your neck and whispering words of doubt. God is in control. It is much better to take the longer route with God than the shorter one without Him.

Many times, God's approach is unconventional. This is the nature of God, for He will not be hemmed in or backed into a corner. Cut God some slack by giving Him the latitude to lead you however and wherever He desires. Just because a friend of yours went down a road does not mean you should follow. God's will for you may be just the opposite. One thing is for sure: He will get the glory when you are patient to follow Him in trust and obedience.

**Travel instead on the proven path of providence.
Faith in Christ rejects seductive shortcuts.**

TIES THAT BIND

I drew them with gentle cords, With bands of love,
And I was to them as those who take the yoke
from their neck. I stooped and fed them.
HOSEA 11:4 (NKJV)

You were not created to bear your burdens alone. God is there to come alongside you and lift your burdens with His love and kindness. Burdens borne alone will break your spirit and crush your confidence. It is the compassion of Christ that lifts you to new levels of love and assurance. Do not hide your burdens, for if you stuff the hurt into the back of your mind, it will slowly seep back out in unhealthy behaviors. Praise your Savior for He daily bears your burdens (Psalm 68:19).

Someone may have let you down in a big way. Because you loved them much, they have disappointed you greatly. You love profoundly, but they rarely reciprocate with the same degree of love and kindness. This subtle and sometimes not so subtle rejection has grown into a big-time burden. You've tried to ignore its effect on your heart. But over time, your heart has become calloused. This burden of hurt feels as though it might crush you.

Go to you heavenly Father and lay your burdens at His feet. Allow Him to tie up and bind your broken heart with His kindness, love, and forgiveness. He alone can bear this burden, so trust Him to bear this on your behalf. His Word is restorative like a hot meal. His answered prayers are cool, refreshing, living water that results in mature faith and garners hope for your heart. He will nurse your hurt heart back to health (Matthew 13:15). A healthy heart made whole by its Maker is in a position of strength to do the same for friends. He bears your burden so you can be a burden-bearer for another (Galatians 6:2).

Make it a point to ask others about their tears and trials. Your kindness and love can be the tie that binds someone's sick condition of despair into one of hope and encouragement. Look for a way to bear a brother's or sister's burden in prayer, for it positions you to leverage kindness and love on behalf of the Lord. Prayer is extremely efficient and effective, so be a channel of Christ's love and kindness by saying a simple prayer. So share your burdens with your heavenly Father and those you can trust.

Bear the burdens of other people in the faith.
These are the ties that bind and lift you to live.

BE GLAD

*Be glad, people of Zion, rejoice in the Lord your God,
for he has given you the autumn rains because
he is faithful. He sends you abundant showers,
both autumn and spring rains, as before.*
JOEL 2:23

The follower of Jesus cannot remain sad. Yes, there are seasons of sadness, but you are not meant to stay there. Yes, pain is ever-present. Emotional pain may emerge often, your physical pain may be perpetual, and financial pain could be flirting with your peace of mind. Relational pain may be assaulting you with rejection. Pain will try to steal your gladness and replace it with sadness. It will show up on your face as a scowl or a jutting jaw. Instead, be glad and allow the calm of Christ to caress your countenance.

Gratefulness to God can begin with the little things such as rain, the warmth of the sun, and the cool of the night. God Almighty is the author of all of these, and He is forever creating good things for His children: relationships, laughter, a full stomach, a good night's rest, healthy children, a free nation, and the opportunity to share all of our gifts from God. His blessings elicit smiles on the face of His children. Giving gladness is a vital role of your heavenly Father; even in the middle of severe sadness, He dispenses gladness. The gladness of God is uncanny in its ability to keep you poised with a peaceful perspective.

Therefore, go to God often for the gift of gladness. Receive His roaring laughter (Job 8:21) as a reminder not to take ourselves, others, or situations too seriously. Fight sadness with gladness so that when you are tempted to torture your mind with sad thoughts, you will choose instead to fill it with glad memories of good things. Slow down and let your trust in the Lord massage your mind. Trusting in Christ brings you glad tidings.

This is why we worship God rather than the things of this world. Anything outside of the Lord has the potential to let you down. Money will fall short and even contribute to sadness. Children can break your heart, and your spouse will make you sad. Friends will fail you, and circumstances can crush your motivation to care. But Christ-followers have a heavenly Father who gives gladness in the middle of sadness.

Peace and contentment are first cousins and fruits of a glad attitude. Anybody can live a chronically sad life, but those who look to their Savior, Jesus, cannot help but be glad. He is the giver of all good things that satisfy (Psalm 103:5). Therefore, be glad for the grace of God that gushes from heaven like a generous geyser. Such gladness results from your resting in the presence of God and engaging with a community of Christ-followers.

**Allow grace to govern your thinking,
because gladness grows in a heart overflowing
with gratitude for God's grace and all His good gifts.**

BAD TO WORSE

It will be as though a man fled from a lion only to meet a bear, as though he entered his house and rested his hand on the wall only to have a snake bite him.
AMOS 5:19

Sometimes, things have to get worse before they get better. Your finances, relationships, job, and health may all have to get worse before they get better. This is not fun, but it is reality. Adversity can be agonizing, but it does not have to be forever. Indeed, it is hard to follow hard after God when times are hard. Use this time in the downward spiral to look up to your Savior, Jesus. Let go and allow Him to love on you. It is during this time of crumbling circumstances that dependence on Christ needs to be front and center.

Yes, fear may be pursuing you like an uncaged beast. In your mind, there is a lion behind you and a bear in front of you. Get down on your knees in prayer and then get up and lead on in the power of the Holy Spirit. Confess and repent of your sin and then rise with a radical faith that will see you through. Now is the time to increase your dependence on God and decrease your need for clever tactics. Do not miss the fact that faith in Him is your greatest asset. Reject fear, and replace it with raw reliance on the Lord. Paul experienced survival with his Savior: "I have worked much harder, been in prison more frequently, been flogged more severely, and been exposed to death again and again. Five times I received from the Jews the forty lashes minus one. Three times I was beaten with rods, once I was pelted with stones, three times I was shipwrecked, I spent a night and a day in the open sea, I have been constantly on the move." (2 Corinthians 11:23-26).

Faithful is He who has called you, for He will do it (1 Thessalonians 5:24). Face your fears in faith, for you are kept and protected by the grace of God. The Lord is good, and while things may get worse, His will always prevails. You can look forward to the better, knowing you did not compromise your convictions. You stayed true to your calling because you knew Christ was in control. He will see you through this, so follow Jesus by faith. Through the thick and thin, be true to Him. His work will not be stopped, and what He initiates, He completes.

Allow your character to become better during this bad time. Christ is your Master, not circumstances. Therefore, walk with the Lord from bad to worse to better.

COMPLACENT SECURITY

Woe to you who are complacent in Zion, and to you who feel secure on Mount Samaria, you notable men of the foremost nation, to whom the people of Israel come!
AMOS 6:1

Complacent security believes an illusion, for it acts as if everything is okay when it isn't. It is just a matter of time before the walls of deception come tumbling down. Passivity is subtle and subversive. It is a house of cards waiting to fall as the winds of adversity begin to blow. Pride and hyperactivity can lull you into thinking things are all right when they have, in reality, gone wrong. You think you are safe, but you are in real danger (Deuteronomy 29:19). It is unwise to make assumptions about God or others by remaining in a state of complacent security. You cannot act as if it is business as usual if the financial foundations of your business or home are crumbling.

You can deal with the passive decision-making or it will deal with you. Yes, it is humbling and sometimes humiliating to admit our mistakes of inaction but thank God for second chances. You can change before it's too late. Your pride may have delayed the inevitable by isolating you from people who know better, so invite them back into your life. Ask them for their advice and then follow their wise counsel. Seek out their perspective and how they define the problem. If you ignore the obvious and plow ahead instead, it will be to your downfall. Sincerely apologize and remain accountable, for your confession is healing for everyone (James 5:16).

You can break out of your complacent security with the help of your Savior, for Christ is not complacent. His security is based on the Word of God, not on the ways of the world. Stay engaged with the agenda of eternity, and it will puncture the protective bubble that shields you from life's inevitabilities. The opposite of complacent security is concerned security; it depends on Christ and His definition of reality. Concerned security initiates and gives full disclosure of the facts to preclude any misunderstandings. Information is freely given, not fearfully withheld. Concerned security collaborates with others in carrying out the plan.

Therefore, ask God and others often for a reality check. Be secure in Christ and concerned about connecting His character and will to your behavior and actions. Pack up and leave your little insecure world and experience God's abundant life. Live large for the Lord and stay connected and secure in Him.

**It is a mature faith that stands the test of time.
Your concerned security replaces complacency.**

MARCH 7

THE VISION

The vision of Obadiah. This is what the Sovereign LORD says about Edom—We have heard a message from the LORD: an envoy was sent to the nations to say, "Rise up and let us go against her for battle."

OBADIAH 1:1

If you feel that God has placed a vision in your heart, it can be hard to ignore. Indeed, your vision can be daunting, for it likely will require extraordinary faith. This is God's way of growing. Some days you might tremble with feelings of anxiety, unsure of how the next few phases of the vision can become a reality. Money and time may both be short, but your provision flows from the Lord (1 Timothy 6:17).

Yes, God's provision is at its best when you feel overwhelmed with responsibilities and worry. A vision starts with an acorn of an idea but then grows into an oak tree of influence. This takes time and resources that you cannot control. The more patient you are, the more opportunities you'll have to see God work. Your ambitions for Christ will need time to mature. Like an infant in the womb, the vision needs time to grow, so it can be birthed in good health.

Lastly, the vision God has lodged in your life requires all of you to be fully focused. There are two focuses: the focus of the vision and your focus on the vision. Start by crystallizing the idea Christ has placed on your heart. If you cannot clearly articulate the vision in a sentence, it is not focused. Clear communication of the vision is concise and compelling. If others see it, they can conceive it. Secondly, focus on the vision in prayer and do not be distracted by other good opportunities. Furthermore, the vision is top of mind for you, but it takes time to register in the hearts and minds of others. Your part is to cast the vision; their part is to catch the vision. So present the vision in a relevant way to your audience and seek to align with those of like-minded passions. Communication of vision takes repetition. What is familiar to you may be foreign to your followers. However, in the process, the vision becomes better focused, you are more focused, and it comes into focus for others.

Your vision of God determines the quality and quantity of your vision. So stay fixated by faith on your heavenly Father, for the vision flows from Him.

MARCH 8

GOD INTERRUPTION

The word of the Lord came to Jonah son of Amittai: "Go to the great city of Nineveh and preach against it, because its wickedness has come up before me."
JONAH 1:1-2

God may be interrupting your plans. He does this from time to time according to His will. You were going in one direction, and He stopped you in your tracks and led you in an about-face. It can be disconcerting and more than a little scary. But do not be surprised if this happens to you. Your current path may be the opposite of what He intended. Maybe you got in a hurry and ran ahead without Him or maybe you have been reluctant to move forward and missed Him.

Interruptions from the Lord are not to be ignored. Some people will be relieved when God leads them in a different direction, but others will resist. When God interrupted Jonah's plans, he disobeyed and stayed put, failing to preach repentance to those who needed to hear it. Clearly, the consequences of disobedience are not isolated. They ripple throughout our relationships, and the people God gives us responsibility for. Don't wait for people to be hurt before you say yes to heaven's directive.

God interrupts for a reason and for a season. The reason may be to protect you from bad decision-making. You don't know what's around the corner in your life, but He does. He is watching out for you, so this severe turn in His will may be to protect. Promptings from the Holy Spirit make pride uncomfortable because it means giving up control and submitting in humility. If you continue to drive forward in pride, you are destined for unnecessary pain. God is moving you out of your comfort zone and into His arena of obedience. Take this interruption as a sign from God to slow down, reevaluate, and recalibrate.

He has something better if you are willing to be bold in your obedience. God, many times, interrupts your plans through a decrease in time, money, or resources. His interruptions are intended to get you into environments where you can be blessed. He will prepare you and provide for you as you move in this new direction. He is ever faithful to furnish us with every provision needed to follow his path for us. So, see His interruptions as a step up, not a step down.

Thank Him that He cared enough to stop you in your tracks and redirect you down a better path.

Invite divine diversions. You are wise when you follow the Lord's interruptions.

TAKE RESPONSIBILITY

"Pick me up and throw me into the sea," he replied, "and it will become calm. I know that it is my fault that this great storm has come upon you."
JONAH 1:12

Leaders take responsibility for actions—both their own actions and for the actions of their team. There is no "he said, she said." A leader knows when he could have done a better job of planning, collaborating, and communicating. So when the expected results do not materialize, the responsible leader takes a step back and asks why. This pause for retrospection is key. If blame is shifted or ignored, then an opportunity is lost for everyone to grow. Mature leaders take the blame and, without making excuses, take responsibility.

It is interesting why some leaders do not want to take responsibility for negative outcomes. Many times, there is the fear of losing something. There may be a fear of the loss of respect, reputation, control, leadership, effectiveness, momentum, or even in extreme cases, the loss of a job. Ironically, a leader who comes clean with his failures and takes responsibility gains instead of loses. He gains perspective, respect, and another opportunity to succeed. He gains resources and more committed followers.

You want a leader with a sense of urgency around realistic concerns, but not one who panics because he is engulfed by fear. Fear is a lousy long-term motivator. It can jump-start apathy but, over time, it erodes a leader's confidence and leadership. Fear assumes the worst, jumps to the wrong conclusions, and, like Jacob, makes unnecessary, drastic changes (Genesis 32:7).

It is in the climate of change that a leader has a greater responsibility to lead. Without intentional and prayerful leadership, everyone will default to doing what is right in his own eyes (Judges 21:25).

Responsible leaders understand God's goal of transformation for themselves and for the team. So, be a responsible leader who takes the blame for failure and who shares the credit for success. Christians can be the world's best at smiling on the outside while disagreeing on the inside. It is the sin of silence that comes home to roost in relational confusion and hurt. The responsible leader helps their followers communicate and understand each other. The responsible leader loves and leads the team. The goal is to improve processes and grow people, to the glory of God.

Trust the Lord and lead others to do the same. In Christ there is calm. Therefore, take responsibility and trust Him.

ASK FOR RELIEF

My son, if you have put up security for your neighbor, …
[if] you have been trapped by what you said, … do this, my son,
to free yourself, since you have fallen into your neighbor's hands:
Go—to the point of exhaustion—and give your neighbor no rest!
PROVERBS 6:1-3

Sometimes you need relief. You need relief from pain, from work, from an obligation, a relationship, a financial commitment, or from overcommitment. The discomfort has become distracting, as you have become ensnared by an unwise decision. You need some radical relief. However, relief is not a pass to be irresponsible. It is an opportunity for you to humble yourself and to ask for a change in something that is out of your control. You may or may not receive the needed relief, but at least you have positioned yourself for the possibility. Relief many times is the result of a humble request.

Anytime you feel trapped, it is natural to request some level of relief. Maybe you need relief in the area of time, for your margin account is overdrawn and you are suffering from daily relational fees of frustration. Asking for relief might look like canceling or rescheduling an appointment. More than likely people will be more understanding than you think. Other times, seeking out relief will involve sitting down with a boss or supervisor. Heart to heart, eye-to-eye—go in person, share your burden, respectfully ask for relief, and hope for the best. God will bless your honest and humble efforts.

Without fail, relief comes through the channels of humility and action. Always pray for an attitude of humility and respect before you request relief. Don't wait so long that the pressure you are feeling crushes your spirit and produces panic. Humility is willing, early on, to get everything out in the open for discussion and discernment. When you stifle your fears, you set yourself up for a resentful attitude. People under severe pressure suffer resentment under the burden of unprocessed feelings. So, in humility, go and share your heart. Take a chance and process your fears and worries with the authorities God has placed in your life. Humility goes a long way toward disarming the one you are appealing to for relief. Agree with their concerns and, at the same time, offer them creative solutions. Humility is not irresponsible, so it doesn't walk away and leave the other party in the lurch. But humility does come in the form of a prayerful and action-oriented appeal.

Above all else, seek the Lord first for relief,
for He is your most dependable reliever.
Ask for relief and watch God work.

MARCH 11

INTEGRITY LOST

Her leaders judge for a bribe, her priests teach for a price, and her prophets tell fortunes for money.

MICAH 3:11

Integrity is not for sale to those who love their Savior, Jesus. There is no amount of money or status that can lure integrity away from someone who values its influence, accountability, and positive outcomes. Integrity is your calling card for leadership, and it is evidence of your faith in Christ. Integrity may be your greatest value that is not itemized on your balance sheet, and it is not for sale with serious followers of the Lord. Like Esau selling his birthright (Genesis 25:25-34), you might be tempted to exchange your integrity for instant gratification. But it's a lopsided loss to let go of a lifetime of faithfulness for a moment of problematic pleasure.

The love of money makes you vulnerable to losing your integrity (1 Timothy 6:10). Money can maneuver your motives into a less than desirable position, so be sure not to masquerade your good works around a drive for wealth. You cannot reason your way around wrong methods of obtaining money, even for the sake of worthy outcomes. You do not have to compromise your God-given convictions to grow your net worth.

How much is your credibility worth? Certainly, it is more valuable than anything money can buy (Proverbs 22:1). Effective leaders in the long run are given respect, trust, and goodwill because of their position, authority, and track record of integrity. Indeed, integrity is being true to yourself and to God's calling on your life, so be who you are in Him. Integrity does not have to prove itself. Rather, it rests in being itself.

If you have lost your integrity, it can be found in Christ. So, go to Him in honesty and humility. Be forthright with your heavenly Father about your failures and blown opportunities. Let Him love you through this time of transition and rebuilding of trust. Align your doing around your being, for this integration is the essence of integrity.

If you have hurt others by your lack of integrity, it will take time to heal and reconcile. But the longer you prove to yourself and others that you are the real deal, the more your integrity will blossom. A track record of faithfulness fertilizes the roots of integrity and produces lasting fruit. Cultivate integrity through prayer and service, then watch it grow.

"Whoever walks in integrity walks securely, but whoever takes crooked paths will be found out" (Proverbs 10:9). Therefore, gain it, retain it, and do not sell it out at any price.

MARCH 12

HOPEFUL WAITING

But as for me, I watch in hope for the Lord,
I wait for my Savior; my God will hear me.
MICAH 7:7

Hope allows you to wait patiently on the Lord. Because of the things that are out of your control, it is wise to practice hopeful waiting; otherwise, you will live in frustration and fear over matters you can't control. This is where hopeful waiting pays great dividends. You choose to hope in Christ rather than place your trust in ever-changing circumstances. This is a wise bet.

If, however, your hope is in an organization or institution, all bets are off. Both can and will fail to meet your expectations, but hopeful waiting trumps the company's broken promises. It gets you to place your trust and hope in God's provision rather than in the corporation's ever-changing commitments.

The same can be said of what we should expect from people. They can be fickle and undependable. Indeed, some people hurry away when things get tough. They make excuses or excuse themselves from responsibilities. Difficult times lift up heroes and bring down imposters. Therefore, faithful people learn hopeful waiting in their dealings with others. They wait on people, not in a naïve and irresponsible way, but in a way that honors them and Christ. Even when people fail, we will not be shaken if our trust is ultimately in the Lord.

Wait on Him and hope in Him. God is not going anywhere without you (Deuteronomy 31:6). Circumstances change and people leave, but He is still there for you to trust and obey. His wisdom is there for the asking. His stability becomes a firm footing for you when you faithfully wait on Him in hope. Allow the Holy Spirit to lead you, even while people swirl out of control.

God is listening, so speak to Him often in prayer. So go to Him quickly. This is what hope does. It depends on Christ. He will come through, as He has in the past. You can wait hopefully in Him because He fulfills His promises with pleasure. Be patient and hopeful as you wait on Him. He will do what He set out to accomplish. Trust Him with this and do not be overwhelmed by inactivity. His hope is certain and true. Therefore, remain faithful to the One who is most trustworthy.

Wait on Him and hope in Him, for this prayerful sequence with your Savior is security indeed. Watch, wait, and hope, for He hears your heart and feels your pain.

GOD ENABLES

The Sovereign Lord is my strength; he makes my feet like the feet of a deer, he enables me to tread on the heights.
HABAKKUK 3:19

God is your enabler, for there is nothing you cannot do that He has destined you to accomplish. The next phase of your character growth may be painful. The development of your business or ministry to the next level could be daunting. The demands you face as a parent are scary, and it seems impossible to balance work, home, and hobbies. But God is bigger than your frailties, fears, and family. He will enable you if you let Him, so do not carry this burden alone. In your own strength you will remain frustrated, frazzled, and stuck. There is no amount of self-discipline that by itself can accomplish God's results.

It is through the empowering of the Holy Spirit that you are able to endure and to execute the will of the Lord (Isaiah 63:11). As a child of God, you can offload your fatigue to your heavenly Father and rest in Him. You can outsource your anxieties to the One who can enable you to execute eternity's agenda. His grace qualifies you to carry out this life's assignment. You have been crucified with Christ (Galatians 2:20) and sealed by His Spirit (Ephesians 4:30).

This season of life may be hard for now. It is difficult because you are not sure how to navigate everything that needs to be done, and some things need to be left undone. Allow the Sovereign Lord to enable your actions or inactions. Seek out His power before you traverse up this next path of trust. Pray for His eternal enablement, for He is your strength as you embark on the next steps.

Part of accepting God's enablement is admitting areas of weakness. No amount of prayer can transform you into something God never intended you to be. This is important to accept. If you are good with numbers, then allow Him to grow you in this area of data analysis. If not, then free yourself by allowing another to enjoy the responsibility of drawing financial conclusions and estimates. Stop striving to be someone you are not. Know your limitations and humble yourself by confessing them to others.

Change and transition expose weaknesses and strengths. Use this time of vulnerability and let God grow you and develop new skills in you. Like a photo developer in a darkroom, this dark time is illuminating the Lord's best for you. God's enablement may mean letting go of the good and focusing on what you do best. Cooperate with the Holy Spirit; He strengthens what He enables. God's enablement gives you the resources and the wisdom to carry out His plan.

Look to the Lord often for His eternal enablement. His enablement strengthens and lasts forever.

MARCH 14

QUIET LOVE

"The Lord your God is with you, the Mighty Warrior who saves. He will take great delight in you; in his love he will no longer rebuke you, but will rejoice over you with singing."
ZEPHANIAH 3:17

The love of God quiets the soul. There is nothing more soothing to the soul than the love of a Savior. The world's remedies can be loud and obnoxious, but not the Lord's love. His love penetrates the proudest of hearts with gentle promptings of care and concern. Pride likes to figure things out without assistance from the love of the Lord, for it sees the receiving of love as a sign of weakness. To be loved means you are dependent on something other than yourself for significance. But the love of God provides purpose for every recipient. Quietly and effectively, God's love calms your nerves and reminds you of whose you are. You are important because you are His. You are the object of God's quiet and lavish love, for He loves whom He values. Love covers a multitude of sin and sorrow (1 Peter 4:8).

If you are stressed, let Him quiet you with His love; if you are fearful, let Him quiet you with His love; if you are angry, let Him quiet you with His love; if you are rejected, let Him quiet you with His love; if you are confused, let Him quiet you with His love; if you are desperate, let Him quiet you with His love.

His love is active and effective. It is not a lost love waiting to be found. His love initiates and it is seeking to find you and love you at your point of need. The love of the Lord is calling out for you, like a mom who stands at her front door calling her children to come in from play. Don't get so busy playing or working that you miss God. He is with you, and He is mighty to save. He delights in you and desires His very best on your behalf. He loves you simply because you are His. He cannot not love you, so be still and be loved by the Lord.

Your Savior's love is safe despite unsafe surroundings. When all hell breaks loose, you can be comforted by heaven's love. You are your Father's child, and you are very, very precious to the One who has saved you from loveless living. Act like you are loved, as a loved one of Jesus. Let Him love you often and allow Him to love you completely. His love pursues you with a calm and quiet persistence. His love rejoices when you rejoice and cries when you cry. His love understands, and the Lord's love never lets up. He is relentless in His concern, care, and compassion.

Above all else, allow Almighty God to embrace you with His radical love.

SORROW REMOVED

"I will remove from you all who mourn over the loss of your appointed festivals, which is a burden and reproach for you."
ZEPHANIAH 3:18

Sorrow can be like a stab in the back—painful and alarming. Sorrow is not easy to swallow when it is sudden, like an unexpected car accident. Or it can tarry like a terminal disease. Sorrow saps hope from your heart and courage from your countenance. It is a drain on the disposition in the mightiest of men. You cannot hide sorrow, for it shows in your face and flows through your words. Like an uninvited guest, sorrow may stay longer than you intended and become a nuisance that never seems to go away. Sorrow makes a heart sad, it weighs on the mind, and it steals away most of your motivation.

Sorrow comes with death. When you lose someone you love dearly, sorrow is a natural and healing outcome. In most cases, you must first tread through the sand of sorrow before you can arrive at the sea of gladness.

Whatever the source of your weeping, give it over to the Lord. Your sorrow may be the natural outcome of grief or regret. But it will eventually be time for Christ to bring closure and heal your heart. Sorrow need not keep you sad indefinitely, for it is a pass-through to His peace. Your sorrow may be the result of unconfessed sin, in which case you might require repentance before you find healing. Furthermore, do not bear your burden alone. Allow your community of Christians to love you through this time of trial. Joy is with you in Jesus and His followers.

Your Savior was a man of sorrow who was acquainted with grief (Isaiah 53:3). Sorrow, for your Lord, is not a foreign language. He is fluent and has survived its purging process. When sorrow arrives at the doorstep of your life, your Savior's presence becomes more precious than ever before.

His grace is like a miracle-working detergent that removes sorrow's deepest stains. He can erase sorrows that have etched themselves into your emotions. He can lift sorrows that have burdened your heart and have weighed down your actions to the point of inertia. Therefore, allow His love to squeeze the sorrow from your weeping heart as if from a water-soaked towel. He can wring the sorrow out that has disabled your discipleship. It is okay to be sorrowful, but it is not okay to remain sorrowful. Jesus can remove your sorrow by His comfort or His cleansing.

Sorrow is for a season, but joy and peace are for an eternity. Tomorrow's hope deletes today's sorrow.

MARCH 16

CONFRONT TO CONNECT

Faithful are the wounds of a friend,
but the kisses of an enemy are deceitful.
PROVERBS 27:6 (NKJV)

Confrontation means there has been a disconnection. Something has severed trust. It may be relational, emotional, or financial. Maybe you feel you have lost someone's love and respect. Whatever the reason for the disconnection, confrontation needs to seek out a reconnection. This is what a caring, faithful friend does. They seek to reconnect where there has been a disconnect. Caring confrontation creates a culture of trust.

This is true in marriage. A wife may confront her husband when she feels she needs more help. This is a natural response when her spouse is distant or not involved enough. Depending on the context of the confrontation, the husband may respond positively (if he is smart!) or he may push back defensively. Questions like, "Sweetheart, can we sit down sometime today to discuss the children's schedule for the upcoming week?" can be helpful. In this situation, healthy confrontation gives a couple the organizational connections they need to be more effective in managing their family responsibilities. Your spouse will always be most receptive when they have time to prepare and process, and they know they have your respect.

Your salvation in Jesus brought you into relational wholeness with heaven so you could model the same on earth. Scripture teaches, "All this is from God, who reconciled us to Himself through Christ and gave us the ministry of reconciliation" (2 Corinthians 5:18). However, if ignored, delayed confrontation deteriorates into disconnection. It dilutes understanding, trust, and intimacy. This is why it is wise to keep short accounts.

If someone experiences feelings of frustration, they will naturally distance themselves from friends or colleagues. But if they confront early on, in a spirit of respect and understanding, they stay engaged—at church, work, or with individuals—and therefore avoid creating a culture of control and distrust.

So, most importantly, start by connecting with Christ. Vertical relational reconnection facilitates horizontal relational reconnection. Sin subtly or not so subtly severs relationships, but confession leads to connection. David, a most effective leader, said it well: "Then I acknowledged my sin to you and did not cover up my iniquity. I said, 'I will confess my transgressions to the LORD.' And you forgave the guilt of my sin" (Psalm 32:5).

Therefore, make your motives and methods of confrontation for the purpose of reconnection. Friends who care confront to connect.

RIGHT MOTIVES

"Ask all the people of the land and the priests, 'When you fasted and mourned in the fifth and seventh months for the past seventy years, was it really for me that you fasted? And when you were eating and drinking, were you not just feasting for yourselves?'"

ZECHARIAH 7:5-6

Right motives can be illusive. One minute you can be as pure as the driven snow in why you do what you do; in the next you can subtly slip into suspect behavior. Therefore, you need to be relentless and honest in reviewing your motives. Sure, you can never shake self-preservation and some level of pride, but you can ask the Lord to cleanse your motives and mark them with His purposes.

Wrong motives have a ripple effect on relationships and organizational dynamics. Unhealthy motivation that seeks attention and credit will compromise principles and values. Misguided motives are driven by whatever means it takes to justify worthy results, but lasting fruit results from the seeds of pure motives.

You can use Jesus as a model for right motives. "Why would Jesus do this?" is a wise question that helps you get to the heart of the matter. The "why" question reveals intent and encourages honesty. Regularly asking "why?" addresses your motives. You may want to give to someone, but why? I may want to serve someone, but why? You may want to sacrifice an opportunity, but why? Where does your devotion reside? What drives you to do good things? If your reasons are self-serving, then you have missed managing your motives for eternal purposes.

If you serve because it makes you feel better or to feed your ego, your motives are dysfunctional. God does not like to be used for anything other than His glory. If you are trying to make up for your shady past or you are driven by guilt, then you have truly misunderstood the point of Christianity. Faith keeps you focused on your heavenly Father, and He replaces your pride with peace and contentment. Jesus can be trusted with our deepest regrets, because He bore our sins and shame on the cross.

Therefore, do an audit of your authenticity, and stop doing acts of righteousness that draw people to yourself instead of to your Savior. Serve when no one else is watching and you are guaranteed to not get the credit. Ask about others instead of talking about yourself. Help make other people successful, instead of using them for your success. Focus on the Almighty's accomplishments and not your own. Fast and pray with discretion and give anonymously (Matthew 6:5-6). Instead, do all for the glory of God. Let your love of the Lord and people lift your motives to a more noble level. Continually allow the Holy Spirit to scrub your motivations.

**Ask often, "Why would Jesus do this?"
Then mirror your Master's motives,
for right motives reap God's rewards.**

GENTLE AND HUMBLE

Rejoice greatly, Daughter Zion! Shout, Daughter Jerusalem!
See, your king comes to you, righteous and victorious,
lowly and riding on a donkey, on a colt, the foal of a donkey.
ZECHARIAH 9:9

Jesus is gentle and humble, and He is powerful and brave. Gentleness does not eliminate power, nor does humility cross out courage. Jesus is King of creation and ruler over the world, but He rules and leads with gentleness and humility. He describes Himself this way: "Take my yoke upon you and learn from me, for I am gentle and humble in heart, and you will find rest for your souls" (Matthew 11:29). A gentle and humble leader uses his position of influence to serve others and help them to be their best. He brings to bear resources and relationships that facilitate the unity of the team. His gentle and humble approach to people leaves no room for creating fear or leveraging intimidation.

Fear is a leadership technique of the insecure and incompetent leader. Obtaining results is no excuse to use intimidation as a tool. Certainly there are seasons of intensity that call for elevated effort and focused attention above the norm. But these windows of change are opportunities for the leader to provide stability and calm. It is a demeanor dependent on the Lord. Gentleness is power under the control of the Holy Spirit, and humility is courage that is first committed to Christ.

Yes, gentleness and humility risk rejection and risk being trampled upon, but you cannot go wrong emulating the character of Christ. Your position of influence as a parent, pastor, executive, volunteer, sole proprietor, or teacher is not a place for pleading or passivity. Instead, use your influence to gently lead by example and to humbly confront those who are stuck on their agenda.

Gentleness and humility are children of great faith. A gentle follower of Christ has been broken before God. Like a wild and robust stallion, your will must be broken and aligned with the Almighty's purposes. Use this time of resistance to graft the gentleness of Jesus into your soul and to embed the humility of your heavenly Father into your heart. Stay true to your personality and temperament; be loud and bold if this is your wiring. But whoever you are, do everything in a spirit of gentleness and with a humble heart. Deflect attention from yourself and trust Him for the proper recognition in His timing.

Turn away from arrogance and pride.
Embrace gentleness and humility, for they are
twins birthed from transformation in Jesus.

LEADERSHIP VOID

The idols speak deceitfully, diviners see visions that lie; they tell dreams that are false, they give comfort in vain. Therefore the people wander like sheep oppressed for lack of a shepherd.
ZECHARIAH 10:2

People wander aimlessly due to lack of leadership, but they want to be led. They want to be led by loving leaders who listen to the Lord and who listen to them. Look for leaders like Solomon, who petitioned the Lord on how to lead: "Give me wisdom and knowledge, that I may lead this people, for who is able to govern this great people of yours?" (2 Chronicles 1:10). This is God's design, for He has wired people to resist wandering and to want leadership.

People often wander around, disconnected and disinterested, because they are unsure of where to turn. But eventually, someone will fill the leadership void by default. Some ambitious soul will fill the empty shoes of leadership even if he is unable to lead effectively. An uncalled character, backing into leadership by default, is worse than no leadership at all. This happened to the people who begged Samuel for a king, then later regretted their request (1 Samuel 8:4-21). Therefore, be prayerful and patient; God will send His called leader in His timing. It is better to have an open position of leadership than to fill it with the wrong person. It may be a pastor, CEO, headmaster, administrative assistant, or COO that you need; so continue to trust God for His choice. Don't just fill a slot for the sake of expedience. Make vitally sure their chemistry, character, and competence align with your culture. It is expensive and emotional to extract an inadequate leader. Wait and work toward God's best.

If you are already in a position of leadership, lead. A good motto is to "lead, follow, or get out of the way." People expect you to lead, and they are confused if you don't. What are you waiting for? You will not lead perfectly, but press on. Indeed, leaders who love God and people will never lack a following. Let go of your fear of leading, release control, and have faith that God has placed you in this position of leadership. He equips those He calls to carry out His assignment. You may just lead here for a season, so lead with abandon on behalf of the Almighty. Seek the Lord as the leader of your life, work, family, and ministry. Follow hard after God so you can effectively lead people. Ask Him for wisdom and stay focused on the mission. Get your marching orders from on high and then execute them down low.

Therefore, on behalf of your Lord, and by His grace, lead. Follow Him and lead them.

MARCH 20

EXPECTS RESPECT

"A son honors his father, and a slave his master. If I am a father, where is the honor due me? If I am a master, where is the respect due me?" says the LORD Almighty.
MALACHI 1:6

Almighty God deserves your respect, for He is your heavenly Father, your Lord and Master. The quantity of respect due Him makes respect to the monarchs of this world look minuscule. This is one reason followers of Jesus attend church; it honors Him. Worship, teaching the Bible, and fellowship with other followers of Christ show respect for the Lord. It may be subtle, but people slip into a role reversal when they expect respect from people on earth while they extend little or no respect toward heaven. It is because of your honor and admiration of Him that you can't help but exclaim His goodness and glory.

Respectful people are quick to extend respect. They do not sit back and wait for respect but take the time to offer it. So, love God as your heavenly father and submit to Him as your Master. It is disrespectful to disregard the things of God and drive ahead in your own strength. However, respect slows down, listens to the Lord, and connects with Christ's wisdom. You show respect by relishing your role as follower and God's role as leader. Be respectful by way of regular prayers and following His voice. Respect for the Lord leads to respect for others. This is a natural place to grow in your respect for people. People are all made in the image of their Maker, and they long for respect. God honors His children, and He honors you as the apex of His creation. He does not disrespect His own; you are a work of His grace and a reflection of His glory. Once you receive God's honor, give it to others, even when they are disrespectful. Your loving-kindness leads to respect. Wisdom says, "A kindhearted woman gains respect." (Proverbs 11:16).

Respect does not mean you mutter in disagreement on the inside and smile on the outside. It means you voice your concerns and conflicting ideas clearly, concisely, and with a spirit of humility and calmness. Respect resists attacking people and instead challenges assumptions and processes, so it goes a long way in relational growth. There is a good chance a wife will experience deeper love at a more consistent level when she respects her husband. The Bible teaches the husband is to love his wife and, "The wife must respect her husband" (Ephesians 5:33). Respect sets the table for love, as it is an invitation to be loved. Respect is foundational for relational intimacy, so use it well and extend it often.

No one has ever complained about too much respect. Therefore, exhibit respect often to God and man.

"D" WORD

"Therefore what God has joined together, let no one separate."
MARK 10:9

For followers of Christ, divorce is not an option. In circumstances of abuse or abandonment, Scripture makes some exception, but the ideal is faithful, loving commitment for a lifetime. Yes, human frailty wants an out. It doesn't want to be uncomfortable or inconvenienced, but marital challenges are God's process of purifying us. Marriage mandates fidelity and faith in God, for it is not a relationship of convenience, rather one of conviction.

Moreover, marriage is a reflection of your Master. Whatever God does is not to be taken lightly, for the Lord is in the marriage-making business. He joins a man and a woman together in marriage as a mirror of the church's relationship with Him—it is final and forever. Marriage is a not man's free pass for sex or a woman's gateway for security. Marriage is a divine appointment for a lifetime.

When the bubble of marital bliss bursts, be kind, patient, and forgiving. Don't run and hide when you let your spouse down but be open and honest. Allow Christ to cleanse your heart because, left on its own, the heart becomes selfish, proud, immature, and demanding (Matthew 15:19-20). Jesus came into your life, enabling you to be a servant to all, especially your spouse. He gives you peace so you can be a peacemaker in your home. Christ-centered marriages create peace and quiet, so submit to the Lord together and experience Him, who produces a peace that passes all understanding (Philippians 4:7-9).

Lastly, God's marriage design overcomes divorce's destruction by creating environments of encouragement and by the building up of one another. Children feel the safest in a family where divorce is not an option. One way to decrease divorce is to exalt marriage. Make marriage mean something by seeing marriage as a mandate from your Master. Accept marriage as a privilege and a responsibility. God uses marriage for His glory and as a reflection of His unconditional love and forgiveness. See your marriage as sealed by the Holy Spirit, never to be separated by man. Your marriage is not a mistake, so be hopeful by persevering.

You were joined together in marriage by Jesus and for Jesus. And your marriage is not to be destroyed by man's decree of divorce.

MONEY MOTIVATED

Jesus entered the temple courts and began driving out those who were buying and selling there. He overturned the tables of the money changers and the benches of those selling doves, and would not allow anyone to carry merchandise through the temple courts.

MARK 11:15-16

Money motivation is not the best motivation; in fact it can make you downright miserable. It frustrates you and those around you because money-motivated people are never content. They have an insatiable desire for the next deal or the next opportunity to make more. An all-consuming desire for money leads you to compromise common sense and character. Ironically, your family suffers the most even when your desire is for them to enjoy the benefits money may produce.

Moreover, money-motivated individuals stoop as low as using the Lord to line their pockets. Religion and church become means for cash creation. This angers God, for He is moved to righteous indignation when His bride is prostituted for worldly purposes. The church is a conduit for Christ, not a clearinghouse for economic gain. It is a house of prayer (Isaiah 56:7).

Dollar-driven institutions are often problematic. Businesses that are driven by bottom-line performance alone quickly develop unhealthy cultures. People are willing to work somewhere for less if they know the culture has a much bigger vision than just making money. There is so much more to life and work than money (Matthew 6:25).

Money motivation is the antithesis of mission motivation. A church bound up in debt can quickly become ineffective. If the bride of Christ is preoccupied with paying the bills, then the mission will be watered down and even ignored. The focus ought to be on excellent work accompanied by eternal expectations. The mission is what drives you to do more, because a transcendent spark ignites within your soul. Money becomes a result, not a reason, when the mission creates a culture of care and collaboration.

The mission gives you permission to say no. Enterprises and individuals are defined more by what they say no to than by what they say yes to. A well-focused team makes it a habit to defend the mission. There is a discipline in decision-making that characterizes mission-driven people and organizations. Paul said, "But one thing I do: Forgetting what is behind and straining toward what is ahead, I press on toward the goal." (Philippians 3:13-14). Mission is the master of money, so focus on the mission of your Master, Jesus, and you will be much more productive in the long run.

Mission motivation keeps you trustworthy, effective, and blessed by God.

MARCH 23

WHY ME?

"But why am I so favored, that the mother of my Lord should come to me?"
LUKE 1:43

Sometimes you wonder why God has blessed you so much. You often question why you are the recipient of God's magnificent grace. The magnitude of His blessing seems to be greater than normal because you are the object of Almighty God's sovereign selection of unmerited favor. It is good that you have not gotten over your gratitude to God. Your faith would be suspect if you routinely expected God to go over the top on your behalf. This type of presumption regarding God's favor is influenced by pride because it not only expects but demands the blessing of God. However, joyful obedience is God's expectation of you; He expects your surrender and submission.

You pinch yourself because of the overwhelming blessing of God. It may be gratitude for life itself or for a new baby. It may be the blessing of God a good friend is experiencing. Your joy may be because your children married godly spouses or because your career has taken off to a level of success you never imagined, and your financial abundance exceeds your expectations many times over. His blessings take all forms.

Doing His will is the least you can do, for He has chosen you for this opportunity to exalt Him. Furthermore, embrace those who have been graced with God's blessing. Wish only His very best for them. Do not be jealous because you did not receive what they received. The Bible says that the Lord made us all unique. "Since we have gifts that differ according to the grace given to us, each of us is to use them properly" (Romans 12:6 NASB). Be grateful that you can hang out with those on whom God's hand rests. He will choose to bless others differently than you, but blessing differentiators are meant to promote celebration, not division. This is how God expresses His sovereign control. He even blesses those outside the faith to promote His kingdom.

God has you where you are for a season. Seize this time to learn from those who know how to lean on the Lord. Be thrilled that He has trusted you with this relational stewardship. God's blessing is bountiful, so be aggressively appreciative that you and others are so blessed. Gratefully accept His blessing on your life and the lives of others.

When you ask, "Why me?" remember it is because He wants you to be blessed on His behalf. Therefore ask, "Why not me?"

FEELING EXCLUDED

"Blessed are you when people hate you,
when they exclude you and insult you and reject
your name as evil, because of the Son of Man."
LUKE 6:22

No one likes to feel excluded; it's disrespectful and distasteful. Exclusion may come in the form of blatant rejection or simply being ignored by others. In either case, the one excluded feels left out of the loop. Maybe you already know this from personal experience. You may have been excluded intentionally or by accident. If your exclusion was an oversight, this helps sooth your sensitivity. But if you were left out on purpose, then you have to wonder if you are really needed. Either way, the result is ugly. Exclusion communicates: "I don't care what you think," or "I don't need you."

Exclusion is counterproductive to building a culture of care. Wise and teachable leaders will extract exclusion from the enterprise by identifying its source and addressing the issue. Exclusion is also an enemy of high morale and quiet confidence. When excluded, people tend to believe the worst. Mistrust and miscommunication then gain ground and undermine the personal development of people. Healthy organizations, on the other hand, exclude exclusion. There is a conscious attempt to include the team in strategic decision-making. This takes time, especially in an environment of rapid change. There needs to be enough lead time to process information. Be sure to build buffer time into your corporate calendar to allow for clear communication. This will save you time in the long run. Therefore, eagerly exclude exclusion by building a culture of collaboration.

At home, work, or church don't forget the ones who have been around the longest. And don't forget the silent ones. Inclusion means you collaborate on defining the meeting agenda. You trust others to craft their own procedures, objectives, and goals, but you verify with an efficient process. You learn to manage the process and lead people. Inclusion requires servant leadership and prayerful attention to detail. If you run too fast, you will rush right past the opportunity to include others in a better decision. The wisdom of the whole far exceeds the insight of one, so slow down, include others, pray, and plan.

Fortunately, our Lord and Savior, Jesus Christ, is all-inclusive. He accepts repentant sinners and saints alike. He includes rich and poor, educated and uneducated, nationals and foreigners, new and old. The cross of Christ invites all who believe to belong to His family. "The Spirit and the bride say, 'Come!' And let the one who hears say, 'Come!' Let the one who is thirsty come; and let the one who wishes take the free gift of the water of life." (Revelation 22:17 KJV).

Most important, you are integrated into God's will and you are a significant part of providence's plan. Even when men exclude you, He includes you.

OVERCOME BY FEAR

Then all the people of the region of the Gerasenes asked Jesus to leave them, because they were overcome with fear. So he got into the boat and left.
LUKE 8:37

Faith and fear are always at odds with one another. This is especially true when your chronic fear relates to money. Money, more than anything, can make you myopic to faith in God. You get so consumed by the crises of current affairs that you forget your anchor in Almighty God. Money, or the lack of it, may be what's killing you. However, money is a symptom of something else beneath the surface of your fears. Money is not the answer; Jesus is the dependable security you desire.

Do not dismiss prayer and patience just because you feel out of control. This is where you are tempted to behave like an atheist. You say you believe in God, He is in control, and you trust Him, but then your behavior betrays your beliefs. You act like an unbeliever when your actions marginalize your Master. Indeed, it is when the bottom falls out that faith in the Lord needs to be your mainstay. "Be still, and know that I am God" (Psalm 46:10).

Satan loves to see you alone. He wants you to battle him in your own strength. He wins when fear drives you away from Jesus and into irrational actions. Fear keeps you looking over your shoulder in doubt. And all the while, your Savior is right beside you, waiting to be your calming force. Take the time to tarry in trust with the One who is totally trustworthy. Rise up from under the load of your languishing condition and come to Christ. Look to Christ for perspective and patience. Don't panic. Exorcise your overwhelming fear by faith.

Now is your opportunity to stand firmly and courageously in Christ. Talk is easy, but your walk with Him is what matters most. He desires an authentic and teachable heart. He can do this for you by faith. Go deeper with Jesus during desperate days. When fear attacks, be comforted by Christ's confidence and warm embrace. Say with David, "The Lord is my light and my salvation—whom shall I fear?" (Psalm 27:1). Furthermore, be real with those around you. Some of them have gone before you; learn from them. Trust them as a resource, for fear is flattened by the faith of friends. Trust them and Him.

Fear flees in the face of faithfulness, so escort the fear of failure out the door. Above all else, be strengthened by faith's reassurance, and not weakened by the fear of financial loss.

SELF-JUSTIFICATION

"You have answered correctly," Jesus replied.
"Do this and you will live." But he wanted to justify himself,
so he asked Jesus, "And who is my neighbor?"
LUKE 10:28-29

Christians know that justification comes through faith alone, in Christ alone. There is no need to hide anything. Self-justification, however, always has an excuse. There is no taking responsibility but instead, looking for a loophole in obedience. Contrary to one committed to Christ, those who seek self-justification are moving away from the Lord; they avoid accountability for their actions. There is always a reason why something didn't get done or can't be done. They may have even delegated a responsibility but not maintained accountability. Accountability is not a friend of those seeking to justify themselves.

Self-justification remains silent when it needs to speak up for clarification. It has an aversion to trust and an allergy to reality. It may smile in agreement but still not change. Self-justification is for those who want to make the rules, and decide which ones apply to them. This lifestyle choice is a house of cards that over time tumbles down under the facade of obedience. Eventually, these types of people implode. Their relationships unravel and their status becomes suspect. Their influence remains inward, and they become victims of the small world of self-justification.

However, those justified by faith have an entirely different take on life. They understand the need to listen to, understand, and follow the ways of Jesus. They are compelled to mature their faith in Christ. There are no excuses on their lips, only questions from their heart on how to be transformed by the Holy Spirit. They eagerly submit to authority and are looking for ways to better communicate and be held accountable. They are set free from their little world and are thoroughly engaged with eternity and the team around them. Their goal is to integrate their faith into every aspect of their lives. Christ is the focus when you are justified by faith. The Bible says, "So the law was our guardian until Christ came that we might be justified by faith" (Galatians 3:24).

As you trust Jesus to deliver you from your sins, you learn how to flee from those same sins. You are attracted to His and others' questioning of your actions. You invite accountability and strive to grow in personal holiness, becoming more like Christ in your motives. Justification by faith means God has made you righteous. Trust God and others with your strengths and struggles. Be a good neighbor by getting beyond yourself. Faith-filled living focuses on the needs of others and takes responsibility.

It trusts Christ; it doesn't test Christ. By faith,
Jesus has already justified you now and forevermore.

MARCH 27

CONNECTION AND TRUST

"So he got up and went to his father. But while he was still a long way off, his father saw him and was filled with compassion for him; he ran to his son, threw his arms around him and kissed him."

LUKE 15:20

Connection is a common craving for those created in the image of God. You were made to connect with Christ, your spouse, your parents and children, friends and those with whom you have daily contact. You want connection with the Body of Christ and with your community. Connection is critical to relational health. Without it, you feel alone and fearful. There is a much higher probability of mistrust and misunderstanding when there's no connection.

Indeed, you can be disconnected from someone and not realize what's happened. You may feel like everything is just fine, because on the surface things are running smoothly. But when you take the time to do a relational audit, you may discover that some degree of unintentional disconnection has transpired. Take the time to build back this trust. Do not blame others or ignore its reality. Instead, with a posture of humility and a position of brokenness, extend an apology and accept the love and forgiveness of the offended party. This is the spirit of mature men and women. Relational restoration is the goal of all who are seeking to follow Jesus Christ. You have a ministry of reconciliation (2 Corinthians 5:18).

Moreover, connection with Christ is the noblest need. As Christians, we are called to connect to Jesus by trusting in Him. However, when you experience a divine disconnect, you become prey to Satan's fearful lies. The enemy exploits relational disconnection with fear, anger, and suspicion. He does this in your marriage and in your working relationships. However, sincere and humble faith in God Almighty links you with the Lord. He lifts up those bowed in submission to Him and loves them. When you humbly receive the love of Christ, you connect. When you humbly receive the love of people, you connect. Love leads to connection, because love covers a multitude of sins (1 Peter 4:8).

Pray about how to best connect with your spouse, child, or friend. Commit to this over the long haul and assure them that disconnection is not an option. Give and receive love and respect, then watch connection progress aggressively. Go often for hugs from your heavenly Father and linger long in the love of the Lord. Connection with Christ sets the table for connection with people. The fruits of connection are peace, assurance, and trust.

Stay connected for Christ's sake. Stay joined to Jehovah, and feast on the fruit of faith.

EXHAUSTED FROM SORROW

When he arose from prayer and went back to the disciples,
he found them asleep, exhausted from sorrow.
LUKE 22:45

Sorrow is exhausting. It saps your energy deep down into the depths of your soul. It is fatiguing to experience and to watch, as sadness slits open a hurting heart. It is the fruit of anticipated or actual loss and it seems to linger longer than is needed. Patience runs thin when sorrow relentlessly rocks your world and reminds you of your limitations. Wise decisions become difficult during a rainstorm of sorrow. You become flooded with fear and are pelted with unbearable drops of dread.

This is a natural outcome of a broken heart, a diseased body, or a depressed mind. There is no getting around sorrow in this lifetime, since it is a consequence of original sin (Genesis 3:16-17). Many times, sorrow seems unfair and unnecessary, for it causes you to pause when you are ready to move on.

It is during seasons of sorrow that Satan's deceptions are alive and well. He will try to convince you that you are not loved or appreciated. He will try to lead you to look for love in all the wrong places. Temptation is untamed during times of sorrow. Furthermore, the devil is delighted for you to stay mad at God and His people. He knows that anger exhausts you. However, it is through prayer and meditation on the Word that your Maker will comfort and heal your hurting heart (Psalm 119:28).

During times of sorrow you can connect with God and people in authenticity. It is through prayer that you are reminded of the awesome God you love, serve, and worship. He reigns over heaven and earth, and He is Lord over life and death. Prayer protects you during sorrow's times of vulnerability. It is meant to draw us close to Christ. Sorrow is a path to prayer, and prayer brings vitality and focus.

Prayer pries open the prison doors of pride and fear; it gets the attention off you and onto others. It is in prayer that sorrow is laid at the feet of the Man of Sorrows, Jesus (Isaiah 53:3). He knows you hurt. He knows you are afraid. He knows you need Him, and He wants you to awaken to His assurance. Use your sorrows as an excuse to hang out with your Savior. Take some advice from a gospel song, "Have a little talk with Jesus. Tell Him all about our troubles. He will hear our faintest cry. He will answer by and by."

Pray for a resurrection of joy to follow the death of sorrow.
Ask Jesus to strengthen your exhausted soul.

BEST FOR LAST

"Everyone brings out the choice wine first and then the cheaper wine after the guests have had too much to drink; but you have saved the best till now."
JOHN 2:10

Jesus sometimes saves the best for last. He delights in delivering the unexpected to the unsuspecting. He waits until there is opportunity to show up where the needs are rampant, but the solutions are few. Then He meets the need unconventionally and boldly. Many times, this is His method because Christ is counterintuitive. He wants others to ask "Why?" Why did Jesus save the best for last? One reason the Lord saves the best for last is to honor the recipients. Those who persevere deserve the best. For example, in relationships, the fruit of long-term commitment produces the best experiences. Trust, contentment, and fulfillment all earn their right in relationships that resolve to remain true. God blesses those who wait: "Hope in the Lord and keep his way. He will exalt you to inherit the land." (Psalm 37:34).

Waiting on the best brings out the best, for trust in God fosters hope that there must be something better to look forward to in the future. You experience the best God has to offer when you save yourself for marriage. Sex within the bonds of marriage exceeds exponentially the settlement of premarital capitulation to hormonal-driven sex. Waiting protects you from impatient impulses that can instantly implode.

Your productivity and potential are severely limited if you attempt to do everything yourself. You will be restrained by your time, energy, and intellect. Your capacity is a drop in the bucket, compared to the resources of an aligned team; you need each other's gifts and skills (Romans 12:4-5). Waiting for the best is difficult at times because it often requires depending on others to accomplish the goal. It is your best that brings out the best in others, and vice versa. Therefore, be the best at what you do, and expect others to do their very best. Best breeds best.

Lastly, trust Jesus to take people and circumstances under your influence and bring out His best. Let go and let the Lord run with the opportunity. He may surprise you with joy. Your humble request of God will result in much more than you ever expected. Do whatever He says, and watch Him carry out His very best because obedience leads to His best. Believe the best is yet to come, and don't settle for less. Believe the best in others. Trust Him for the very best. Expect the best and be your best.

Pray and ask God for His best. Be patient, wait on Him, and remind yourself often: He saves the best for last.

MARCH 30

REAP THE BENEFITS

"I sent you to reap what you have not worked for. Others have done the hard work, and you have reaped the benefits of their labor."
JOHN 4:38

It is okay to reap the benefits from the work of others, for this is the Lord's law of the harvest. You cannot do everything yourself, but you can build on the efforts of others. Work and ministry are not done in a vacuum. They are the result of the prayers and perseverance of other people's faithfulness. Moreover, there is a harvest of character. You reap today what was previously placed in your heart.

If the Scriptures were sown into your mind and heart by your parents or teachers, then you will experience a harvest of character by the power of the Holy Spirit. You are a product of faithfulness: God's, yours, and others'. You reap the good and the bad, depending on what was sown into your life all these years. Indeed, be grateful for the positive examples God has placed in your life. Parents, teachers, mentors, leaders, and friends may have all sown good seeds into your life all these years. Many faithful men and women have unashamedly labored for the Lord, so you imitate them and Him (1 Thessalonians 1:6).

Therefore, do not miss this unprecedented time of harvest. The fields are white, so do not be yellow with fear, unwilling to trust God. Resist conveniences that may dilute your courage in Christ. Forgo the fear of moving out of your comfort zone and into a different time zone. Now is the time to enter into the harvest of souls for your Savior with abandon and anticipation. Two thousand years of sowing has produced a ripe harvest never before seen in human history. This is His story that needs to be told. Malaria-stricken missionaries have not labored in vain. It is no accident that technological advancements have flattened our world for the exposing and expanding of our faith. Economic and evangelistic opportunities are begging for attention. The time is now. The fields of faith are ripe and waiting for obedient individuals to go where God is already working.

Yes, there are plenty of people at home who need Him, but why should someone hear the good news twice when many in the world have not heard it even once? Harvest requires work, but its labor is full of joy and fulfillment, so venture out and experience the bountiful benefits of experiencing heaven in the harvest. Be grateful for those who have gone before and steward the fruit of their faithfulness. Be radically obedient. Weep over the need for reapers.

Pray to the Lord of the harvest to send forth laborers. Say yes to your prayer for laborers until He says no.

SMALL GROUP

Then Jesus went up on a mountainside and sat down with his disciples.
JOHN 6:3

A small group is necessary for sincere disciples of Christ. It is in the confidentiality of a small group that you really grow in understanding yourself, others, and God. Without the reality check of the group, your perspective drifts into detrimental living. Jesus structured a small group prayerfully, by inviting those who were teachable and available. He knew small groups were wise wards of the soul. It is within the care and concern of a small group that special things take place. Prayers are answered; tears are shed; joy erupts; frustrations are vented; teaching occurs; truth is unleashed; dumb decisions are averted; wise actions are initiated; work is found; families are freed up; accountability is invited; love is applied; character is cultivated; fun flows.

It is in the confines of a Christ-centered small group that the Holy Spirit so often works in our hearts. He freely roams and draws souls to Himself. No wonder the work of the enemy seeks to lure you away from the safety of a small group. Outside the security of the group, you are fair game for his demons of destruction. Wavering disciples become sitting ducks when they struggle alone, dying in desperate silence. You give up the good and give in to the bad without the guardrails of the group. The early church modeled this idea of a home care community (Acts 2:46).

So, engage with those you would like to get to know better. Seek out spiritually mature followers of Jesus. You are secure in Christ, and your small group feeds these feelings of security. A healthy small group is not co-dependent, rather interdependent and Christ-dependent. The group rises to the occasion when a crisis occurs. They minister hope to each other. It is a microcosm of the Body of Christ. Large groups leverage wonderful corporate worship and praise. Gifted teachers thrive in throngs. However, accountability and care get lost in largeness. It is in the small group that the teaching is synthesized down for personal and practical application. Questions and answers flow unguarded under the influence of the small group. Furthermore, prayer proceeds specifically and supportively within a community of trust. Your prayer life goes to a whole new level because the Lord becomes more intimate through specific supplications.

So, be a small group that submits to the authority of the Lord and His church. A small group led by the Spirit encounters Christ.

APRIL 1

COMPELLING CROSS

When you were dead in your sins and in the uncircumcision of your flesh, God made you alive with Christ. He forgave us all our sins, having canceled the charge of our legal indebtedness, which stood against us and condemned us; he has taken it away, nailing it to the cross. And having disarmed the powers and authorities, he made a public spectacle of them, triumphing over them by the cross.

COLOSSIANS 2:13-15

The cross is compelling because Christ is compelling. His love is compelling by the extent of its capacity; His holiness is compelling by the respect it demands; His forgiveness is compelling by the thoroughness of its cleansing; His power is compelling by its ability to disarm the enemy and deem him powerless. Therefore, the cross compels Christ's followers to be like Him.

There is nothing neutral about the cross. Either it compels you or it repels you. The cross either frees you to forgive or it drives you away, stuck in a cycle of cynicism. The cross either leads you into a life of hope or it discourages you to remain in a state of fear and uncertainty. You cannot embrace the cross and self at the same time. It is not possible. A house divided will not stand (Luke 11:17). A heart divided will collapse under the weight of diluted loyalties.

Go back to the foot of the cross. This is where the love and the blood of Christ flowed down together for you. This is a rare combination that for generations has compelled millions to extend the love of God to the lost and the least. "For the message of the cross is foolishness to those who are perishing, but to us who are being saved it is the power of God" (1 Corinthians 1:18). When you and I kneel at the cross, our lives have an exponential upside in the hand of God. Your outrageous obedience has a ripple effect that transcends cultural barriers and is felt around the world. The cross launches you to live for the Lord.

The cross you bear is compelling (Luke 14:27). It is compelling because it reflects the sacrifice and salvation of the cross of Christ. Moreover, the cross you hold high in word and deed draws all men to Jesus (John 12:32). Christ compels all cultures, denominations, races, and socioeconomic classes. His cross invites and even demands a response. To remain neutral is not an option. The cross either compels you to repent, or it repels you to remain in your sin. You can choose a divine destiny or one of your own making. The cross means death to self and sin, but life in Christ. "Whoever wants to be my disciple must deny themselves and take up their cross and follow me" (Mark 8:34).

Be captivated by the cross and you will become fully alive in Him and for Him.

APRIL 2

FOLLOW HIM

And whoever does not carry their cross
and follow me cannot be my disciple.
LUKE 14:27

The Lord's leadership is perfect, potent, and practical. Where He leads you, follow. Where He sends you, go. Therefore, pursue Him as a faithful follower. You follow Jesus because of His invitation and His worthiness; You follow Jesus because His way is the best way and because you are His disciples; You follow Jesus because there is none other who offers an abundant life on earth and eternal life in heaven; You follow the Lord because He leads you toward His will. He is worth following because He can be trusted; He will never lead you astray. His path will be painful at times, but it is in your pain that He purifies. Do not hold back one ounce of obedience and loyalty to your leader, Jesus Christ. Follow Him and you will be forever grateful, for He does not disappoint.

Follow Him through your difficult days. Do not give in to the temptation to quit. The Lord is still leading you through this valley of despair. Do not give up on Him, for He has not given up on you. He still lovingly leads even though your soul feels resistance. He will pull you through this present predicament. Use this time of challenge to strengthen your faith in Him. Stay behind Jesus and depend on His wisdom and care. If He can handle the forces of hell, He can handle whatever circumstance is crushing your confidence. Follow Him through the fog of fear. He is just ahead and can be trusted without reservation. Where else is there to go? This is the insightful question Peter posed (John 6:68).

Follow Him in your success. These good days may be for a season, so praise God for your accomplishments. Progress is a cause for celebration and praise to the Lord. Make sure everyone knows that you answer to a higher authority in Almighty God. Follow Him through this season of success so you will not be tempted to depend on self. Self-followers self-destruct. Jesus-followers, on the other hand, handle success with humility. Give God the glory during these good times. Use the Lord's blessing for His kingdom. Follow Him.

Jesus is in the soul-saving business. So, as you follow the Lord you become very interested in His business. You take stock in saving souls because this is the industry of His kingdom. His investments provide the greatest long-term return. You fish for men and women because your heavenly Father longs for their love and loyalty. You follow Him so others may follow Him. Follow Him so your family, friends, and foes may follow Him.

Faithfully follow God and you will inspire others to do the same.
Disciples follow their wise and loving leader, Jesus.

AVOID EXTREMES

Whoever fears God will avoid all extremes.
ECCLESIASTES 7:18

Extremes tend to get you into trouble. They put relationships on edge and require an exorbitant amount of energy to maintain. Anything taken to the extreme causes damage somewhere. It may be emotional neglect of your family, or the lack of time to maintain your home. You say, "But I need extra time at work to get my business (or ministry) off the ground." This may be true, but if you launched your business two years ago and are still working overtime, something needs adjustment. What was meant to be extreme for a season can become a habit for a lifetime. Left unchecked, extreme behavior is destructive.

Ironically, you start out with a goal of productivity, but the result can become counterproductive. Maybe for a season you need to reverse these adverse trends with extreme actions in the opposite direction.

Your physical, spiritual, and emotional well-being may depend on a sabbatical from years of overcommitment or abuse. You may need to totally abstain from alcohol because it has begun to control you. Extremes, oftentimes, need to be battled by their opposite extremes. But be careful, because extremes can start a vicious cycle that never ends.

The fear of God is your lasting remedy for extinguishing extremes. Embrace the eternal, and you will counter extremes with balance and brevity. Because you fear God, you will trust Him to help you live a balanced life. Fear of God keeps your passion to love and obey Him as your top priority. Christ becomes your mode of operation. Look to Jesus and admire how His heart and schedule followed the will of His heavenly Father. He prayed, "Not my will, but yours be done" (Luke 22:42). This is the pattern for people who want to exhibit abundant living. He said yes to what most would say no to. He was countercultural and counterintuitive with His choices. His focus on the eternal made His time spent with a Samaritan woman seem extreme to His disciples, but it was normal to Jesus (John 4:4-26).

Jesus redefined extreme. His life is the normal Christian life. God desires men who fear Him and who consistently walk in His ways (Psalm 128:1). He is looking for steady obedience over the long haul. People who have extreme fluctuations from "everything is great" to "everything is terrible" are undependable. Their availability is based on wavering circumstances, instead of their unwavering Lord. Your rock and refuge is Jesus. He gives you the foundation for stable living, so fear God and you will be free from harmful extremes. It may take longer than you like, but be consumed by Him, and you will marginalize extremes. This can be extremely difficult, but with the Lord all things are possible.

Trust Him and reject earthly extremes. Your family and friends will be extremely grateful you did.

FAINT-HEARTED FAITH

From the ends of the earth I call to you, I call as my heart grows faint; lead me to the rock that is higher than I. For you have been my refuge, a strong tower against the foe.

PSALM 61:2-3

Sometimes it seems like you are a million miles away from Jesus. It's as if He's doing big business on the other side of the world. Your small concerns seem trivial in the big scheme of our Savior's strategy. As in the Parable of the Talents (Matthew 25:14-30), your Master has left you to faithfully manage His stuff while He has gone away. However, you grow impatient, bored, and even faint-hearted from fear or fatigue. You wonder if faithfulness to your heavenly Father is really worth the effort, and you question the cause and your calling. It was exciting when you first started on this journey of faith, but now it is unfocused and uncertain. You may become melancholy or depressed. Your heart may grow faint without the fire of fresh faith. Left unchecked, a crevice of concern can become a canyon of crisis between you and Christ.

Life may have brought you onto a fearful ledge and you are paralyzed for fear of falling. However, now is the time to grab hold of the Lord's arm for stability. Even when you are on the verge of despair, God is there. No spot is too dreary, and no condition is too deplorable. Even in life-or-death situations, prayer is available. Prayer helps you plow through heaven's portal in the midst of your trials. You may be experiencing provocation from insensitive souls. An undiagnosed illness that saps your energy may be gnawing on your nerves. Your faithfulness goes unnoticed and unrewarded, and that perplexes you. You may be overwhelmed because of your total lack of control over the cruel circumstances that you wake up to every morning.

One or all of these trials may be smothering your heart. Because your heart is faint, it is unable to pump the blood of belief to the extremities of your faith. Your eyes are moist with tears. It's okay to cry. Cry out to Christ, for it is heaven's substitute for spiritual speech. God is the center of life, hope, love, and joy. Christ is the spiritual cardiologist for your suffering heart. Look to the Lord to lead you into His next steps as He guides you to higher ground.

Move away from the ledge of illegitimate longings and move toward your trustworthy Lord. You lean into Him for grace upon grace. You ask Him to embolden your beliefs. Climb up with Christ while your heart pumps the blood of bold belief.

Above all else, you are faith-hearted and not faint-hearted when you journey with Jesus. Your trust in Him is a strong tower against your foes.

FAINTING FAITH

As the deer pants for streams of water, so my soul pants for you, O God. My soul thirsts for God, for the living God. When can I go and meet with God?
PSALM 42:1-2

A fainting faith is forever in search of its heavenly Father. There is a building intensity for closeness with the Almighty. Sometimes your faith faints from sheer exhaustion. It passes out for lack of prayer or even during prayer. This is not sustainable. Rest instead in the continual call of Christ. Service to God, without communion with Christ, leads to spiritual fatigue. Your soul's life is sucked out because fainting faith leaves you in a state of spiritual fatigue. The scary thing is that your faith can be on the brink of fainting, and you are unaware. So keep your life's pace governed by grace, or you will outrun your soul.

Time with your Master requires margin. In fact, any significant relational investments take place in the margin of your life. Carve out space on your calendar to be with your Savior. You can do this by faith, trusting that the Lord will make up for any lost time. Christ can get things done without you. "With man this is impossible, but with God all things are possible" (Matthew 19:26).

A deer, by instinct, has no other thought than to slow down and drink as often as needed. Your soul cannot stand sustained times without hydration either, but we sometimes fail to take the time. Jeremiah reprimanded the people for ignoring their need for the Lord, "They have forsaken the Lord, the spring of living water" (Jeremiah 17:13). Just as water is necessary for your body to function, so drinking from divine resources is required for your soul to sustain itself. Otherwise, your faith faints for lack of the Lord. Your soul's thirst is a perpetual appetite that can only be quenched by Christ.

You can meet with the Lord immediately. He is always accessible. Get on your knees and pour out your soul in prayer. Drink in the love of the Lord. Guzzle down the grace of God. Sip on the joy of Jesus. Go to church and lift up your soul in worship to your great and mighty God. Drink in the praise and adoration of God's glory with other sincere believers in Jesus. Your soul is satisfied in environments that engage you with eternity. Worship, Bible study, prayer, and community with Christ-followers quench our thirsty souls. The world parches your soul, but heaven hydrates your heart. Your faith will flourish and not faint as you take the time to quench your thirsty soul.

Drink often with Jesus. "For the Lamb at the center of the throne will be their shepherd; he will lead them to springs of living water" (Revelation 7:17). He refreshes.

FRIENDS COMMUNICATE

Tychicus will tell you all the news about me. He is a dear brother, a faithful minister and a fellow servant in the Lord. I am sending him to you for the express purpose that you may know about our circumstances and that he may encourage your hearts.

COLOSSIANS 4:7-8

Friends communicate, for this is at the heart of friendship. Like a plant without water, friendship without communication dries up. Friendship requires an intentional effort to understand how each other are doing. You pick up the phone, write a letter or e-mail, or make a personal visit. You may send a message through a friend, though this is not quite the same as showing up in person. Yes, friends can go for years without seeing each other and still connect. However, a vibrant and growing friendship needs communication.

New friends are a blessing, but what about the friends who have been with you throughout the years? They have been faithful and have not discarded or ignored you like an old pair of shoes. It's easy to fall into the trap of only being with friends who can do something for you, but friendship is a two-way street. Sometimes, friendship requires that you be the initiator. Your friend may find himself in a high-maintenance stage of life. Do not let his or her one-way communication discourage you. You are a friend indeed when you communicate regularly with someone preoccupied with life issues.

Most important, make Jesus your best friend and communicate with Him often. He is an ever-present friend. Your Christian maturity naturally leads to friendship with Jesus (John 15:14-15). What a friend you have in Jesus, so communicate with Him regularly. He is a friend who is always available and who always cares. He listens attentively and cares compassionately. He cares about you and invites your communication. If you have faith in Christ, you are a friend of Christ. Like Abraham, you are God's friend (James 2:23). You are friends, so you can talk with Him directly and openly about your feelings and fears. However, you cannot be a friend of the world and of God's at the same time. "Anyone who chooses to be a friend of the world becomes an enemy of God" (James 4:4).

So, talk to the Lord in prayer, and ask others to talk with Him on your behalf. Allow them the joy of praying to their best friend for another friend. This builds friendships in both directions because friendship with God and people can feed off each other. If you want to feel close to God, talk with Him like a friend. "The LORD would speak to Moses face to face, as one speaks to a friend" (Exodus 33:11). He is still Lord and holy, but He is also a friend.

Communication is a great tool of friendship, so reach out with the goal of encouraging them, and watch your friendships flourish.

HONOR FAITHFULNESS

... but honors those who fear the Lord,
who keeps an oath even when it hurts.
PSALM 15:4

Faithfulness naturally flows from your fear of the Lord. This fear is honorable because its focus is reverence and respect. Because of the fear of God, you stand in awe of the Almighty; you obey Him because you fear Him; you worship Him; you remain faithful even when it is costly. The fear of the Lord facilitates faithfulness.

Beyond honoring God Himself, you also ought to honor those who fear Him. You may have a parent or grandparent who has remained faithful in their love for Jesus all these years. Their life is a résumé of repentance and obedience to God. Honor them, for they have prayed with you and for you. Make a big deal out of their faithfulness to do the right thing even when it requires sacrifice. Honor elderly saints in front of your children so these young ones can appreciate a life that has been invested wisely in what matters to God. Hopefully, they will emulate the admirable traits of those you honor. Honor too the faithful Christian workers in your life. They may be a pastor, missionary, evangelist, or teacher. Honor them for the sake of the next generation.

How do you honor those who fear the Lord and are faithful to do the right things? By listening to their wisdom and applying it to your life. You honor the faithful when you receive truth from them and integrate it into your behavior. God designed your heart to be a sanctuary and refuge for truth. Wisdom is God's daughter who is not shy about going public (Proverbs 1:20). When you learn and apply the principles of the faithful, you become a man of principle. Your obedience to God honors those who obey God. Honor takes on the characteristics of Christ and His followers. Your obedience under fire will not go unnoticed in heaven or on earth. Your heavenly Father honors your faithfulness. Those who love you the most honor your faithfulness. Therefore, remain honorable and honor faithfulness in others, for this honors God.

Jesus said, "All may honor the Son just as they honor the Father. Whoever does not honor the Son does not honor the Father, who sent him" (John 5:23).

LEADERSHIP AND FRIENDSHIP

Wounds from a friend can be trusted,
but an enemy multiplies kisses.
PROVERBS 27:6

If God ever puts you in a position of leading in a context with friends, it is important to lead first and be a friend second. As the old saying goes, "Lead, follow, or get out of the way." Wise and intentional leadership is necessary for the health of businesses, churches, and any sort of team. Leadership is watered down when friendships distract from the strategic direction. Friendships should forge the team, but not unduly dilute excellent outcomes based on courageous leadership decisions. If a leader is preoccupied with what a friend may think or do, then he risks diminishing his decision for the sake of sparing someone's feelings. The values and principles of the organization are the standards by which leadership decisions are made.

Be sure your leadership is grounded in principle so your friendships will not get in the way of doing what's right. Let a friend know up front how much you value him, but not to the detriment of what's best for the business or ministry. Friendship can become a fruit of wise leadership, but it is not meant to drive wise leadership. Indeed, loyalty to friends is an important and valued attribute of an effective leader. But do not allow loyalty to cloud your rationale of what's best for the team.

Friends can be the hardest or the easiest to lead. It all depends on your and their expectations. Does your friend perceive you as a partner or a boss? Do you value a team member because of their merit or a personal fondness? Lead first in humility, courage, and clarity. Let your friends know up front what you value as a leader and how they fit into the big picture. Constantly ask, "What's best for the team?" instead of "What does my friend want?" Sometimes, the best thing you can do for the team and your friend is to either fire him or reassign him; you lead first by defining the role of friendship on the team, and you keep leadership a priority by not playing favorites.

Lastly, wise leaders will need to make hard decisions, even when they adversely affect his friends. Paul felt this tension when he decided that his friend, John Mark was not mature enough for the responsibility of a mission trip: "Barnabas wanted to take John, also called Mark, with them, but Paul did not think it wise to take him, because he had deserted them in Pamphylia and had not continued with them in the work" (Acts 15:37-38).

Balancing leadership and friendship isn't always easy.

SHARE CREDIT, TAKE BLAME

For by the grace given me I say to every one of you: Do not think of yourself more highly than you ought, but rather think of yourself with sober judgment, in accordance with the faith God has distributed to each of you. For just as each of us has one body with many members, and these members do not all have the same function.

ROMANS 12:3-4

Credit is not created for one person because, if any one person holds onto it, credit corrupts. It corrupts one's judgment by causing him to think more highly of himself. Confiscated credit gives you false confidence. It is a confidence based on the illusion of invincibility, instead of the reality of culpability. Credit is a "pearl of great price" that needs to be shared, so share it often and share it liberally.

Wise leaders quickly give away credit, whether it be to individuals or a whole team that they are working with. Credit given is recognition of the contribution, skill, and smarts of others. A leader who dispenses credit because he knows his own limitations. He will give credit where credit is due because a team represents the eyes and ears of your leadership. Secure leaders can't wait to give away the credit. It burns a hole in the pocket of their ego. Strong leaders understand how to value others and their unique contributions to the culture of the organization. Therefore, you ought to share credit by praising people publicly and privately for their character and values. This affirms them before their peers and puts the emphasis on what's really important. Recognize specific achievements. This encourages your team's growth and development.

A leader also takes the blame, when necessary, because this models responsibility for actions. A leader keeps the buck of blame instead of passing it on. He is as quick to take the blame as he is to share the credit. When there is a breakdown in process or a dropped ball of responsibility, the only name he mentions is his own. He is the culprit in a crisis. Like a surge protector, he buffers the blame from the team by standing in the gap with mature leadership. He has no claim to fame, but he does take the blame when things go south. A leader's example of blame-taking is infectious to followers. Followers unconsciously find themselves emulating the same blame ownership in their spheres of influence. "I am responsible" and "I missed the deadline" are common statements of blame-takers. When you learn how to effectively take blame and give credit, you are on your way to mature leadership.

Mature leadership trusts the Lord, who blesses trusting leaders. He empowers people through leaders who share the credit and take the blame.

APRIL 10

GREAT FAITH

When Jesus heard this, he was amazed at him,
and turning to the crowd following him, he said,
"I tell you, I have not found such great faith even in Israel."
LUKE 7:9

Great faith comes from believing in your great God. Awe accompanies the Almighty, for He is engaged in eternal matters. What matters to your Master matters to you. Great faith in our heavenly Father is produced in a heart of humility, contentment, gratitude, and dependence. You see yourself as an ordinary person blessed by an extraordinary Savior. You have been rescued from the snares of sin and placed into position as God's child. Your old life of self-focus contrasts with your new life of focus on others. You are free from fraternizing in trivial pursuits and are compelled to follow Christ's commands. Great faith helps you to grow more like Jesus.

Just as Jesus was under the authority of His heavenly Father (John 10:17), so you are under Christ's authority. God's kingdom requires surrender and submission to His authority, not you asking God to bless your efforts after the fact. Prayerfully and humbly submit your plans to the cleansing power of the Holy Spirit. Once the Spirit has scrubbed your intentions clean, then you are free to move forward. When you remain under His authority you are able to hear His commands clearly. Great faith acts on what it hears from the Lord, for instant obedience is evidence of great faith.

Great faith is not afraid to obey Jesus. Obedience may seem overwhelming at the time, but when God says so, it is done. So you are wise to instantly obey what He says. Do not hesitate when you hear from heaven. He has His reasons for wanting obedience from you now. For one thing, He knows you might forget if you fail to obey now. He knows your fragile memory can forget Him. When you instantly obey, you don't run the risk of forgetting your heavenly Father's instructions. Instant obedience feeds great faith in God.

Moreover, our great faith grows others. Your children see your great faith and are challenged to do the same. It serves them well when you are not around. Your friends and acquaintances see your great faith and they have hope. Your unbelieving relatives see your great faith and come to believe there must be a God behind such bold belief. Above all else, your heavenly Father sees your great faith and sees someone He can trust. He can trust you with His blessing, His healing, His wisdom, and His resources. Great faith is trustworthy because it is grounded in God. It is not blind and irresponsible, rather it believes the unseen and stewards it well. Great faith is found among the ordinary. It is engagement in everyday life that invites great faith.

Your role as a regular Christian makes
you a compelling candidate for great faith.
Most important, great faith promotes God's greatness.

GENUINE FAITH

These [trials] have come so that the proven genuineness of your faith—of greater worth than gold, which perishes even though refined by fire—may result in praise, glory and honor when Jesus Christ is revealed.
1 PETER 1:7

Genuine faith comes by the grace of God, and trials prove its authenticity. Fire exposes fraudulent faith. Perhaps your current challenge is a test in faithfulness? It may be hard to hold your head up in faith because of the difficulties you are experiencing. Your Savior seems to be on sabbatical, but you still seek Him. You fill in the blanks by faith, and you love Him even though you cannot feel Him. Furthermore, your faith under fire inherits inexpressible joy through prayer. That seems strange to the uninformed. People may become curious about the persistent peace and assurance that travels within the depths of your soul.

You know you are saved by the grace of God, for this is your baseline. Salvation by faith in Jesus Christ is your foundation and this was your launching pad for a life consecrated to Christ. Because you have entrusted Him with eternity, you can trust Him with your temporary trials. Because you trust Him with your soul, you can trust Him with the sorriest of situations.

Do not fret that your faith is under fire, for this affliction is meant to stoke the fires of your affections for Christ. Turn the tables on trouble by diving deeper into your devotion to Jesus. It takes troubles to tear off encumbrances to your eternal perspective. Lukewarm living tends to create cataracts in your spiritual eyes. When you start out as a new Christian, you quickly discover that your faith (like all relationships) grows from times of difficulty. Sometimes life pushes back with pressure and prickly circumstances, and when Christ comes into your conflict, your faith increases.

Your faith is the most valuable thing you possess. Jesus purchased your salvation on the cross. Therefore, the currency that Christ accepts is faith. Yes, give generously to good works, but do not depend on your benevolent acts as a surrogate for belief. Your faith either diminishes or compounds in worth. Allow your current crisis of belief to increase your faith. As it grows in your mind and heart, its value increases.

If your only faith experience is your salvation, then your faith is stunted. God wants to grow your faith. Therefore, see these tough times as a transition from your faith's adolescence to its adulthood. Genuine and growing faith emerge from fiery trials. Genuine faith is God's ultimate goal.

Genuineness is like gold. It's valuable, compelling, inviting, and everlasting. Above all else, it glorifies God.

LOVE HIM

Love the Lord, all his faithful people! The Lord preserves those who are true to him, but the proud he pays back in full.

PSALM 31:23

God commands His saints to love Him. He loves you so you can love Him. The question is not if you love the Lord, but how you love the Lord. Yes, your love for Christ pales in comparison to His love for you. But you love because the Lord is worthy of your love. He longs for your love, and He invites and desires it. Indeed, God is honored and worshiped when His saints love Him.

Unredeemed sinners cannot love the Lord because they are incapable of loving Him. This is an experience that only disciples of Christ can enjoy. Unless you have been converted by the free grace of God, you cannot love Him. Love for the Lord is not unlocked until you turn the key of faith. It affords you the opportunity to love the Lord. You will remain unfulfilled, lost, and confused until you are able to love Him.

Loving the Lord moves you out of the basement of loneliness to the balcony of basking in His presence. Love lifts you to the Lord, and He is drawn to your love. He loves to be loved by His children. Love of the Lord starts you out in faith and sustains your faith. Loving the Lord fuels your faith, energizes your soul, and galvanizes your beliefs. It inflames hope and feeds forgiveness. Loving the Lord is a catalyst for becoming more like Him. You take on the traits of whom and what you love. You reflect the objects of your affections. Therefore, love Him because you want to be like Him. Love is a magnet that draws you toward your model for living. Transformation into the character of Christ is the goal for those who love Him.

Indeed, your love for Him transforms your behavior. So, love the Lord with your whole being. Love Him with your body, soul, and spirit. Love Him physically by taking care of the body He created; keep it pure and healthy. Love Him emotionally by processing and expressing your feelings. Allow Him to convert your anger into holy passion. Allow your love for Him to explode in the emotions of thanksgiving, praise, and celebration. Love Him with your spirit. Connect with Christ in prayer and meditation on His Word. Jesus reveals His will to those who seek Him; so love Him in the morning, in the noontime, and love Him when the sun goes down.

Since loving Him is right, you don't want to be wrong.

APRIL 13

LOVE THE LORD

Love the Lord *your God and keep his requirements,*
his decrees, his laws and his commands always.
DEUTERONOMY 11:1

Some people are hard to love, but God is not one of them. He is easy to love because He is love (1 John 4:16). However, you can be so busy meeting your own needs that you forget to love the lover of your soul. You can love Him because He first loved you (1 John 4:19). It is a reciprocal love relationship in which you are privileged to participate. If you receive His love without loving Him back, you miss the full effect of love's design. A one-way love is not God's best. His best is to be loved by Him, and then to regularly and relentlessly love Him as your heavenly Father. He desires and can't wait to be loved by one of His children. Any lover loves to be loved, and God is no exception. His love is an invitation for you to love Him back. Do not be shy about loving God, for you can love Him even if you don't know exactly how. After all, how do you love someone who has everything?

One way is to love Him with your time. You spell love T-I-M-E, so it is impossible to love without investing time. Time may be the most valuable asset you have to give. Your investment of time is an expression of your love. If you say you love Him but fail to spend time with Him, then your love is shallow, sentimental, and expedient. A confessed love without commitment is a caricature of love. His unconditional love is your baseline for loving Him, for it is radical and redeeming. The love of God has no beginning or end, and it is boundless in its intensity and without borders in its expression. Your capacity to love is directly proportional to how much you allow Him to love you. If you are closed and conservative in your acceptance of His love, you will lack liberality in your love for Him.

Another way you love Him is by loving others. John's teaching is clear: "Dear friends, since God so loved us, we also ought to love one another. No one has ever seen God; but if we love one another, God lives in us, and his love is made complete in us" (1 John 4:11-12). You love Him when you feed, clothe, and care for others on behalf of Christ. You love Him when you season your actions with words of grace and hope. You love Him when you forgive a parent or a child who has disrespected and hurt you profoundly. You love Him when you remain faithful in your marriage even when your spouse, even on the days when it's hard. You love Him when you love the unlovely.

Humility finds reasons to love, while pride procrastinates.
Love Him with all your heart, and watch Him heal your heart.

APRIL 14

APPALLED BY UNFAITHFULNESS

"The leaders and the officials have led the way in this unfaithfulness." When I heard this, I tore my tunic and cloak, and pulled hair from my head and beard and sat down appalled.

EZRA 9:2-3

Be careful not to get comfortable with sin, especially the sin of leaders. That sin has a way of gaining respectability and acceptance. What was appalling a generation ago has become standard, everyday fare. There is a movement afoot to legitimize sin, and the victims will be you, your children, the church, and society. Even more appalling is the unfaithfulness of those in leadership. So be careful, for you become like those who lead you.

So, how will you respond to the desecration of divine direction? If you ignore it in hopes that it will go away, you will wake up one day under the total, dominating influence of unfaithfulness to God. If you accept it incrementally, it will slowly eat away at the moral fabric of culture until you are left barren and broken, with the next generation exposed. The unfaithfulness of a leader's behavior must become the line in the sand of tolerance. It is at this point of unfaithfulness that changes in leadership are required.

Tolerance of unfaithful leaders is irresponsible and unchristian. There is a time to become appalled by the unfaithfulness of leaders. It is responsible and right to be outraged by people who take advantage of public trust for their private pleasure. There are consequences for leaders who dismiss the Bible as irrelevant or who pick and choose which commands are expedient for their malign motives. The Bible is not a menu for unfaithful leaders to manipulate for their purposes. This is where God-fearing people take responsibility.

It begins by confessing and repenting from the acceptance of sin. The sin of silent acceptance needs to be awakened and banished from your behavior. Jesus was the hardest on the hypocritical and unfaithful religious leaders (Matthew 23:13-51). Therefore, judgment does start in the house of God (1 Peter 4:17), for His people are the ones who need to be so appalled by sin that they fall broken before the Lord. You cannot address unfaithfulness in your leaders until it is addressed in your own hearts. But once you have come clean with God, you have the moral authority and responsibility to confront unfaithful leaders. Unfaithfulness to God is a major offense in heaven; it should be so on earth. It is time for God's people to awake from their apathetic slumber over sin and sound an appalling alarm.

You can start with your own confession and repentance, and trust God with the sweeping effect of His Spirit across the land. Be appalled. He is.

APRIL 15

HIGH PLACES

The people, however, were still sacrificing at the high places, because a temple had not yet been built for the Name of the Lord. Solomon showed his love for the Lord by walking according to the instructions given him by his father David, except that he offered sacrifices and burned incense on the high places.

1 KINGS 3:2-3

"High places"—where you worship idols—haunt, hurt, and hinder your relationship with God because they are direct competitors with Jesus. They are altars of worship from your past that you never destroyed. You are deceived when you think they can coexist with Christ and not bring you harm. The wisest man in the world, next to Jesus, learned this the hard way. Solomon thought he was smarter than God (not so wise) and went to the high place of degrading marriage. But it blew up in his face by debilitating his family. His high place of pride kept him from finishing well.

Your high place may be the propensity to drink too much; indeed, alcohol has become your altar of escape. Or you may be secretly serving the god of sex. The Internet with its streaming video or publications with their glossy photos have captured your affections in direct opposition to your devotion to Christ. Your high place may be the residue of salty language, eating too much, or exercise—either the lack of it or the obsession with it.

High places are indiscriminate; they bring down celebrity Christians and everyday followers of Jesus. God's remedy is to rid them from your life and destroy them before they destroy you. Paul described your need for and the ability to discard your old habits and put on new spiritual disciplines in Christ: "You were taught, with regard to your former way of life, to put off your old self, which is being corrupted by its deceitful desires; to be made new in the attitude of your minds; and to put on the new self, created to be like God in true righteousness and holiness." (Ephesians 4:22-24).

Hunker down in your faith and ask God to help you obliterate the high places in your heart. Ask your spouse or a trusted friend to help you identify and define them. Then invite them to hold you accountable to a process of removing high places from your home and work. Your high place may be as obvious as anger or as discreet as undisciplined thinking, but the influence on your life requires a drastic step. Above all else, go to the low place of increasing your dependence on God and decreasing your dependence on yourself. He must increase and you must decrease (John 3:30).

Your worship is much higher than high places; it is Jesus and Jesus alone.

APRIL 16

POWER'S PRIDE

His fame spread far and wide, for he was greatly helped
until he became powerful. But after Uzziah became powerful,
his pride led to his downfall. He was unfaithful to the Lord his God.
2 CHRONICLES 26:15-16

Pride is a natural result of power, and left unchecked, pride will cause you to do regretful things. It is what keeps couples from communicating and it's what strains relationships, leaving them in a rut. It confines Christ to Sunday routines. Pride feeds a feeling of superiority. Therefore, be aware of surroundings that bestow invite pride.

Success invites praise of your skills, gifts, and abilities. You are trusted because of your character and track record. As a consequence, you will gain more and more autonomy while solidifying a powerful position. This is the time to install boundaries in your life, which help avoid the slippery slide to your downfall.

Indeed, one wise behavior is to share your power. Trust others with their area of expertise because you do not have the time or the know-how to do their job. Power's pride makes you feel as if you have to be in control. This false sense of superiority has its roots in insecurity. You will drive people away and drive them crazy with your desire for control. So give it up before people give up on you. The Lord sees through prideful tactics. The Bible says, "God will bring down their pride despite the cleverness of their hands" (Isaiah 25:11). Instead, replace your sense of power with service. Seek out another's felt need and serve them. Try to understand where others are coming from, and then release resources around their goals. Become a facilitator of another's agenda, and, before you know it, power will lose its grip on your psyche.

Above all else, fight power's pride with prayer. Your posture of humility will foster a spirit of security and trust in God. Prayer pries open a clinched fist of control. Prayer and humility will free you to trust others. Stay on your knees in gratitude to God for your position of influence. Daniel prayed, "I thank and praise you, God of my ancestors: You have given me wisdom and power" (Daniel 2:23). Seek Him for wisdom on how to serve, love, and lead your family and team. Power is not an opportunity to be served, but rather to serve. Servant leadership deflates power's pride.

Serve God and people with humility and patience.
Then watch pride fade into the background.
Instead of a downfall from power's pride,
you will witness a windfall from prayer's humility.

GOD'S PASSOVER

"The blood will be a sign for you on the houses where you are; and when I see the blood, I will pass over you. No destructive plague will touch you when I strike Egypt."
EXODUS 12:13

God's Passover for the Christian is the blood of Jesus Christ. The cross of Christ is the reason God's judgment of hell is withdrawn from believers. God prepared the blood sacrifice for those who desire to follow Him. The shedding of His only Son's blood was the final sacrifice for the sin of mankind. Yes, it was a gory event tied to a grace-filled consequence. Jesus went through the muck and the mire of man's sin to lead you to salvation. It was not a pretty process, but it was a radically redeeming one.

Christ's unconditional love on the cross has empowered you to love freely. His torturous death on the cross has equipped you to die daily to your worldly whims. Christ's focus on the will of His heavenly Father as He faced the cross compels you to pray, "Your will be done" (Matthew 26:42). It is the cross of Jesus that gives individual believers God's Passover. God gives you a pass from His judgment, and it is a pass stamped with the blood of His Son, Jesus. Once you believe in Jesus as the Lamb of God who was slain for your sins, your past, current and future sins are covered. God's Passover is thorough and complete. Therefore, celebrate religiously the radical love and grace of God's Passover. Do not take for granted this emancipation from sin, sorrow, and death. It is cause for solemn yet joyful celebration.

His Passover is meant to be celebrated corporately and individually. This is one reason to stay engaged with Christ's bride, the church. The church of Jesus Christ is designed to raise the roof in worship and celebration for God's Passover through His Son, Jesus. This weekly celebration is not meant to settle into a take-for-granted posture that is expedient for the moment. Rather, this first day of the week is set aside to celebrate God's Passover. Believers remember so they don't forget. It breaks the heart of God when a church with a steeple outside forgets the cross inside. Therefore, celebrate corporately and in community with energy and thanksgiving because of God's Passover through the cross of Christ. But celebrate God's Passover individually as well. Consider making a big deal out of the anniversary of your spiritual birthday. Perhaps as part of your physical birthday celebration you could tell the story of your spiritual birth. God's Passover in Christ is to be remembered and celebrated, both in community and individually.

God's Passover in Christ is preeminent.
Enjoy and be grateful for the great things He has done.

APRIL 18

DEATH'S FRUIT

Jesus replied, "The hour has come for the Son of Man to be glorified. Very truly I tell you, unless a kernel of wheat falls to the ground and dies, it remains only a single seed. But if it dies, it produces many seeds."

JOHN 12:23-24

There must be a death before there can be fruit. A seed is buried in the ground before it returns to life and bears fruit. This is why Jesus Christ is still fruitful after nearly 2,000 years. His death was meant to bear fruit, and it has. The fruit of His life-change is represented in the billions of lives that have been altered for eternity. The death of Jesus Christ advanced God's plan.

No one close to Jesus wanted Him to leave. How could anything come from losing the One who had given life, healed the sick, and taught with riveting truth? It didn't make sense that He had to die. He was just getting started. Why put the brakes on the momentum that was occurring in that part of the world? Yet, death was God's plan to give life.

Jesus died as the payment for all past, present, and future sins of mankind. This is where the fruit of faith begins. When you believe that the death of Jesus was predestined by God as a good thing, then you have a foundation for fruit-bearing. Yes, all things do work together for good (Romans 8:28). The cross of Christ is one of God's good things, so make sure you thank Him for the sacrifice of His only Son. He gave life so we could receive life. When you believe in His death for your sins, you receive His life. Christ in you has put to death your old life, so now that you have been crucified with Him, you are positioned to bear much fruit.

This is why you die daily. You die to yourself so you and others can live for God. Fruit results when you deny self and remain in Him. Jesus said, "Remain in me, as I also remain in you. No branch can bear fruit by itself; it must remain in the vine. Neither can you bear fruit unless you remain in me." (John 15:4). What is something you haven't died to that is holding back your fruitful living?

To not die to self and sin is to separate yourself from your friends and the fruit of faith. But you do not have to remain alone. On the contrary, daily death by faith frees you to experience fruitful living. The fruit of your other-centered living becomes abundant and ubiquitous. You pollinate other lives that, in turn, bear fruit. For example, your children's love for God will resonate for eternity. Your generosity will silence even the most outspoken critics. Your teaching will transform lives in the here and now.

Therefore, stay dead to yourself, and watch Him live through fruit-bearing. Death's fruit is rooted in the cross.

REMAIN FAITHFUL

This calls for patient endurance on the part of the people of God who keep his commands and remain faithful to Jesus.

REVELATION 14:12

It should be easier to remain faithful when the object of your faithfulness is as pure as the driven snow; yet faithfulness tends to be practiced by the few. For all committed followers of Christ, however, the clarion call is to remain faithful.

There is nothing about Jesus that doesn't elicit faithfulness. His fairness invites faithfulness; His grace and generosity generate faithfulness; His love longs for faithfulness; His holiness inspires faithfulness; His compassion creates faithfulness; His forgiveness foretells faithfulness; His judgment motivates faithfulness; His life models faithfulness. Jesus remained faithful to the very end and, in Him, so can you.

Who else can you go to for eternal life (John 6:68)? Faithfulness to Jesus is par for the Christian life. He is the standard by which you live. Even under the onslaught of illness, you remain faithful. As circumstances around you crumble, you remain faithful. When people mistreat you and misunderstand you, you remain faithful. When a close friend lets you down and rejects you, you still remain faithful to Jesus. Faithfulness to Jesus is the chorus of Christian living. Moreover, His faithfulness to you is the measure of your capacity to remain faithful. The indwelling of the Holy Spirit's power in your life provides you with the capability to remain faithful.

Remaining faithful to people is a natural byproduct of remaining faithful to Jesus; your faithfulness may be the very thing that draws others to Jesus. Certainly, your remaining faithful will give them pause to reflect on your radical love and forgiveness. Faithfulness reminds people of truth. Paul said, "I am sending to you Timothy, my son whom I love, who is faithful in the Lord. He will remind you of my way of life in Christ Jesus." (1 Corinthians 4:17). Therefore, make it a goal to remain faithful to even someone you feel is undeserving. This becomes a magnet attracting them to God, and not a detour to the devil. You may need to dissolve a working partnership, but you can still salvage the relationship. You can remain faithful even when the other party doesn't. Let your faithfulness, not your feelings, be the gauge for your giving, your service, your forgiveness, and your love.

Above all else, remain faithful to Jesus, for He is the Faithful One.

APRIL 20

PURE JOY

Consider it pure joy, my brothers and sisters,
whenever you face trials of many kinds, because you
know that the testing of your faith develops perseverance.
JAMES 1:2-3

Jesus-generated joy is discovered and developed in the face of trials. Until your faith has been refined through various trials, it will remain immature. You can understand others' perspectives and respect them more when you have been broken over your own inadequacies and sins. Trials slow you down enough to allow you to look into the mirror and ask what needs to change.

The presence of Christ gives you reassurance and peace. He is the joy-giver, while Satan is the joy-killer. Therefore, you can smile because your smile while enduring a trial is the result of pure joy. It's pure joy because God can be trusted. It's pure joy because your faith is real and robust and Christ is faithful. It's pure joy because you will persevere by faith. Indeed, untested faith is a naïve faith. Pure joy is the position and privilege of the person who follows Jesus Christ. How can you lead and serve your family and friends during this time of unprecedented turmoil and tentativeness? Pure joy comes as a result of your faith changing and growing.

God is your change agent. The work of God in and through your life produces pure joy. Change can be painful, but God administers pure joy at the point of your pain. It is the result of the Holy Spirit's fullness: "And the disciples were filled with joy and with the Holy Spirit" (Acts 13:52). Therefore, learn how to accept the pure joy of the Lord. It is available for you to receive. Sometimes, it takes trials and tests to slow you down enough to look into the joyful face of Jesus. He is the personification of pure joy.

Jesus understood pure joy because He was focused on following the will of His Father (John 17:4). His heart was full of joy because He knew He was about His Father's business. Yes, His heart broke at times, but He suffered out of joyful obedience (Hebrews 12:2). In the middle of His most adverse circumstances, Jesus still cried out to His heavenly Father. His intimacy with the Father was strengthened during difficulty. No person, circumstance, or the devil kept Him from pure joy. Invite the pure joy of God to reign over your anxious heart as well. You can smile and place your refined faith in Him. He is building your faith capacity for the long run. The Bible says, "May the God of hope fill you with all joy and peace as you trust in him, so that you may overflow with hope by the power of the Holy Spirit" (Romans 15:13). Pure joy does not depend on good circumstances; it thrives during trials and tribulations.

Unleash the pure joy that already lives within,
for He is faithful. Above all, promote
pure joy and persevere in its promise.

PARENTAL FAITH

I am reminded of your sincere faith, which first lived in your grandmother Lois and in your mother Eunice and, I am persuaded now lives in you also.
2 TIMOTHY 1:5

If your parents are faithful followers of Jesus, their faith is a gift that must not be taken for granted. They helped instill the fear and love of God in you early on. Your parents' faith has been a flame of passion lighting the path for your own walk with Christ. You watched them pray and learned to pray. You watched them trust God and learned to trust God. You watched them love people and learned to love people. You watched them forgive and learned to forgive. Your parents are models of faithfulness in the ways of God. What a gift! What a reason for joy, thanksgiving, and celebration.

Have you thanked your parents lately for their gift of sincere faith? Take the time to tell them how grateful you are for your upbringing in the faith. Thank them and God for your training and teaching in the great truths of the Bible all those years. Their faithful teaching and modeling of truth made it easy for you to embrace truth. Now you have the opportunity to do the same for your children. The Bible says, "For you know that we dealt with each of you as a father deals with his own children, encouraging, comforting, and urging you to live lives worthy of God, who calls you into His kingdom and glory" (1 Thessalonians 2:11-12). Model for your children what has been modeled for you: service, selflessness, confession and repentance of sin, faithfulness, and forgiveness.

Perhaps your parents were not followers of Christ, or they failed in modeling a life of faith. You still have an opportunity to be this kind of example for your own children. Do not lament your lot in life if your parents lacked faith. Instead, consider the faith of surrogate spiritual parents. Pause and thank God for "fathers" or "mothers" in the church who have encouraged and nurtured your faith. Look to them as models. You are positioned on a faith walk for your kids, so walk wisely. Keep giving the gift of faith to your family.

Sincere faith can be passed on from one generation to another. So, by God's grace, be relentless, passionate, and disciplined to keep the faith alive.

FAITH LIVING

"... but the righteous person will live by his faith."
HABAKKUK 2:4

Faith living is focused on God living. It is the road less traveled, but it really is the only way to live. Why settle for anything less? He is calling you beyond the honeymoon stage of faith to mature faith. The Bible teaches, "Anyone who lives on milk, being still an infant, is not acquainted with the teaching about righteousness. But solid food is for the mature, who by constant use have trained themselves to distinguish good from evil" (Hebrews 5:13-14). His desire is for you to come alive with a faith that is active and growing. A faith that only thinks of the past is anemic and stunted. A living faith is passionate about God's vision for the future, and it is focused on the possibilities of today.

God's ability to create relational opportunities is staggering. He is the network weaver par excellence. By faith, He can be trusted to lead you to just the right people. People you can serve, and people who can join you in accomplishing God's will. This is faith living. It is looking beyond the new relationship of today and sensing where God wants to take it tomorrow. Determine ways to bring value to another person. It is not about what you can get from them, but it is all about how you can serve them. This is faith living. It is placing the needs of others before your own and trusting God to meet your needs. The Bible says, "This service that you perform is not only supplying the needs of God's people but is also overflowing in many expressions of thanks to God" (2 Corinthians 9:12). He releases you to serve others with His freedom in Christ. This is normal Christian faith living.

However, faith living is not irresponsible living. Prayer and godly advice guide it. Faith is not lived in a vacuum but in concert with those around you. Abraham went by faith to a new country (Genesis 12:4-5), but he exercised this transition while taking care of the needs of his family. Faith living trusts God's timing and does not rush into battle unarmed and without a plan. You trust God to prepare you and provide the needed resources to carry out His will. You are no match for Satan without the weapons of spiritual warfare. Faith living recognizes our battle is not with "flesh and blood," but that our battle is waged in the spiritual arena (Ephesians 6:12). Therefore, do not see people as obstacles, but as part of God's plan to teach you His ways and to grow you in your faith. Allow God and others to utilize your strengths and shore up your weaknesses. Be who God created you to be.

Live by faith and not by sight. When you live by faith in God alone you are truly alive.

LOVE, COMPASSION, FAITHFULNESS

Because of the LORD's great love we are not consumed,
for his compassions never fail. They are new every morning;
great is your faithfulness. I say to myself,
"The LORD is my portion; therefore I will wait for him."
LAMENTATIONS 3:22-24

The love of God keeps you from being consumed by the fiery flames of grief. Your sorrows can overwhelm you, but He is there as your loving heavenly Father to see you through your sadness.

The love of God is a peacemaker when you become consumed with conflict. Conflict melts under the loving influence of God. Worry is all-consuming until it comes under the direct influence of God's love, for His love exudes peace. Thus, the peace of God and the worry of the world cannot coexist. Fear can be all-consuming. However, the love of God flushes out fear and replaces it with trust. Fleeting fear must be replaced by faith, or it will return to occupy your heart and mind. The love of God floods your soul with faith. Fear vanishes under the influence of faith. Moreover, His compassions never fail, for God has a deep awareness and concern for your heartache; His compassions never fail, for they give hope you can hang on to for future resolution; His compassions never fail, for they provide companionship with your friend, Jesus; His compassions never fail, for they extend forgiveness to a contrite and hurting heart. His compassions establish soul success.

Great is His faithfulness. His faithfulness is greater than the depths of the sea (six miles at its deepest point), and it is greater than the highest mountain (over 5 miles at its highest point). The entire universe cannot contain the faithfulness of God, for it is far-reaching and deep. People will fail you, but God is still faithful; work will fail you, but God is still faithful; your health, your finances, and your circumstances will fail you, but God is still faithful; you will fail, but God is still faithful. Great is His faithfulness!

God does what He says He will do, so you don't ever have to doubt the Lord. He is there for you, your family, your friends, and even your enemies. He is faithful. He will not be unfaithful. For God to be unfaithful would be like the sun failing to rise or the moon forgetting to shine. Therefore, wait on Him, for He is worth the wait. Use that time of waiting to trust and obey Him. The Bible teaches, "I wait for your salvation, LORD, and I follow your commands" (Psalm 119:166). He will be faithful to lead you to the right spouse, the right career, and the right friends. He can be trusted; so let go of your inhibitions and trust Him.

It's comforting to know that in a world of uncertainty,
you serve a great God full of love, compassion, and faithfulness.

APRIL 24

FAITHFULNESS REWARD

To the faithful you show yourself faithful,
to the blameless you show yourself blameless.
PSALM 18:25

Faithfulness in a relationship is a two-way street. You have expectations for others to be faithful to their commitments, and you want to model the same. The essence of faithfulness is doing what you said you would do. It is the integrity of following through with a commitment even when it is costly. Commitments are not to be taken lightly. So a verbal commitment, for instance, should be considered as binding as a written contract. When you keep your word, you are true to yourself and others.

If you make a verbal commitment, it behooves you to make sure there is an understanding among all parties. If there is not clear communication, then expectations may not be clear. That could result in a perception of unfaithfulness. The burden of responsibility is on the communicator, and margin-less living contributes to poor communication. If you are moving too fast and are overcommitted, your communication skills and follow through drop off. You may assume others understand you and know what is going on, but this is flawed thinking. Other people live busy lives as well, so they need you to slow down and show up with clear speech. Slow down, communicate more, and show up on time for appointments. Take a relational audit and create a "stop doing" list so you are free for follow through. Follow the Lord's example as a promise keeper: "Let us hold unswervingly to the hope we profess, for he who promised is faithful" (Hebrews 10:23).

Fortunately, as a follower of Christ, you have the Faithful One in your life to model the way. He has been faithful even in your unfaithfulness. He is faithful to forgive your sin and remember it no more (Jeremiah 31:34). He is faithful to flood your soul with peace, joy, and contentment. He is faithful to give you friends and family who love you despite yourself. He was faithful to follow through with the cross of Christ, even through the cries of His only Son and the ultimate sacrifice of His life. God understands what it means to keep a commitment even when it costs a great deal. He says in His Word to let our "Yes" be "Yes" and our "No" be "No" (Matthew 5:37). You do this because you want to be faithful to Him. Your faithfulness is rooted in God, and that faithfulness does not go unnoticed or unrewarded. One of the greatest rewards is the gift of trust. Faithfulness births and grows trust so that over time, you earn the reputation as a trustworthy person.

Be faithful because He is faithful. Those who can be trusted with a little can be trusted with much (Matthew 25:21), and that "much" is the reward of faithfulness.

SPIRITUALLY MIXED MARRIAGE

"They have taken some of their daughters as wives for themselves and their sons, and have mingled the holy race with the peoples around them. And the leaders and officials have led the way in this unfaithfulness."
EZRA 9:2

Marriage is between a man and a woman, and Christian marriage is between two Christians. This is God's plan, and attempts to circumvent His plan can lead to watered down faith and a lifestyle lived contrary to Christian principles. Marriage already has plenty of challenges without the added confusion brought on by mixed belief systems and values. Two contrasting faiths are like blending oil and water. It doesn't work, and it creates a mess. Opposites may attract, but a common faith is a must for a healthy marriage. People with differing faiths may be able to coexist, but they miss the intimacy of a mutual commitment to the same heavenly Father. It takes more than love for one another to have a happy, holy, and fulfilling marriage. A bountiful marriage is one in which both husband and wife are madly in love with Christ. He is the originator and sustainer of marriage. He models marriage, with the church as His bride (Revelation 21:9).

One good question to ask a prospective life mate is, "Do you love God more than you love me?" If the answer is yes, you will be in better hands as a husband. Without this level of faith in God, you lose the leverage of a loving Savior. Jesus Christ is the plumb line in marriage. He is the baseline and the standard. His life, His death, His teachings, and His example set the stage for Christian marriage. There are boundaries and expectations that He defines for a successful marriage. Therefore, the wise husband and wife look to God and ask Him for direction, forgiveness, and ways to love each other. Your gratitude to God for His great love and forgiveness becomes the model of how you love and forgive your spouse.

The goal of Christian marriage is to reflect our relationship with God. By faith, He will galvanize your hearts together; by faith, He will allow you to weather the storms together; by faith, He will give you joy together; by faith, He will allow you to experience life together to its fullest; by faith, He will give you wisdom to raise children together; by faith, He will give you grace to live the Christian life together. Most of all, by faith, He will allow you to enjoy Him and each other together. Let your marriage start with a common belief in the same God, the Father of your Lord Jesus Christ. Love Him and each other passionately and with abandon. This will pull your marriage together and drive you toward the same destination of hope and heaven.

A common faith commitment is a non-negotiable for the Christian marriage. Mold your marriage around your Master.

APRIL 26

SUFFERING SAVIOR

"I offered my back to those who beat me,
my cheeks to those who pulled out my beard;
I did not hide my face from mocking and spitting."
ISAIAH 50:6

The sufferings of Jesus cannot be totally comprehended. One thing is clear: Jesus experienced voluntary suffering. He offered himself as a sacrifice on behalf of the human race. His heartache and mistreatment were the will of His heavenly Father (Mark 8:31-33). This is hard to process for those who seek problem-free living. The way of the cross is not always a smooth road, for it is marked with its own bumps along the way.

Jesus offered Himself to His tormentors as His adversaries plotted and schemed to bring Him down. They wanted to put Jesus on display as a mad man. If He were truly God, they reasoned, He would not allow this injustice to occur. However, the Creator allowed His creation to beat and bludgeon His only Son. Christ's back was bruised and beaten for your sake. But Jesus submitted to this suffering only because He first submitted to God. Ironically, those committing these hideous crimes were the very ones who could benefit from the results. They could embrace His atonement for sin and receive His resurrected life.

Jesus carried this burden on your behalf and that of all mankind. It was not an exercise in how much pain could be endured by one person. It was love, as Jesus loved you all the way to the cross. "Greater love has no one than this: to lay down one's life for one's friends." (John 15:13). Jesus conquered death, sin, and Satan so you could do the same. His pain was your gain. The way of the cross is the path to redemption. He bought you from the servitude of sin. No longer are you bound up in yourself and others, for He has set you free. You are exonerated by faith because He endured the cross, despised its shame, and is now interceding on your behalf at the right hand of His heavenly Father (Hebrews 12:2). This is cause for celebration. God really does use all things for His good on behalf of those who love Him (Romans 8:28). Therefore, allow gratitude to well up and burst forth from your heart. You can because of the great love of God exhibited in the sufferings of Christ Jesus. He suffered for you. Can you do any less?

You serve a suffering Savior. You worship a suffering Savior who rose from the dead so He could save you to the uttermost.

APRIL 27

DIVISIONS DOWNFALL

Jesus knew their thoughts and said to them,
"Every kingdom divided against itself will be ruined,
and every city or household divided against itself will not stand."
MATTHEW 12:25

Division weakens, cripples, and eventually causes a downfall; it's an internal erosion that cannot stand up to conflicting turmoil from within. The greatest threat to a nation, an organization, a home, or an individual comes from the inside out.

A culture without a true north is like a ship without a captain. Whoever is the most persuasive, most persistent, and loudest gets his way. This is a prescription for disaster. A nation, an organization, or an individual that fights itself will lose. Think of two siblings who tussle against one another but then unite their efforts to defeat the bully. Avoid a civil war from within, and fight the devil and his minions that are from without.

A business that sells its soul to the almighty dollar will do whatever it takes to bolster the bottom line. Yes, there will be disagreements, but when all is said and done, there has to be unity of purpose. Conflicting values begin to divide. What started out as a business built on integrity devolves into one of worldly avarice. Short-term compromise may prop up earnings, but long-term effectiveness is impossible, and the business will be like a sheep led to the slaughter.

Even a church can become its own worst enemy. The color of the church carpet, the number of pipes in the organ, and church politics are not what we should live and die for. It is the battle for the souls of men and women that unites believers. It is the proclamation of the Word of God in teaching and living that compels us to follow the example of Jesus and the great saints of the ages. The rallying cry for serious followers of Christ is, "Seek first his kingdom and his righteousness" (Matthew 6:33).

Principles and values based on God's truth will stand, and whoever embraces them and lives for them will stand together. Your goal as a follower of Jesus Christ is to unite around faith in Him. He is your reason for living and dying. Jesus is the way, the truth, and the life (John 14:6). Therefore, unite forces around Him and His Word. Do not be distracted or divided by peripheral preferences.

Truth unifies believers. It flushes out the counterfeit and affirms the authentic. Jesus is the truth. Therefore, lift up the Lord. He says, "And I, when I am lifted up from the earth, will draw all people to myself." (John 12:32).

An exalted Jesus draws a diversity of people to Himself.
You can unite around the holiness and truthfulness of Jesus.

APRIL 28

DEATH AND LIFE

For if, when we were God's enemies, we were reconciled to him through the death of his Son, how much more, having been reconciled, shall we be saved through his life!
ROMANS 5:10

The death of Jesus leads to the life of Jesus. This is God's pattern for the follower of Jesus. Death leads to life. The cross of Christ reconciled us to God by faith. The resurrection of Christ empowered us for God by faith. The cross leads to the resurrection and the resurrection points back to the cross. You can't have one without the other. If the cross were the finality of Christ's work, then you would have no power to live the Christian life.

However, you do not have to live defeated, because Christ did rise from His grave. He arose to validate the significance of the cross and prove His claims of deity. But He did not stop with reconciliation to God. He also arose from the dead to give you His life. His resurrected life provides you with the power needed to follow, obey, and enjoy Him. His life in you emboldens you to witness for Him. His life in you sanctifies you during suffering. His life in you allows you to persevere, builds your character, and gives you hope. It is the life of Christ that energizes you to live for Christ. You can declare, as Paul did, "I have been crucified with Christ and I no longer live, but Christ lives in me. The life I live in the body, I live by faith in the Son of God, who loved me and gave himself for me" (Galatians 2:20).

This is the reality of living the resurrected life. It is Christ in you, the hope of glory (Colossians 1:27). You cannot live properly and purely without your resurrected Lord, Jesus, reigning over you and living through you. Without the life of Christ your faith is anemic, but with the life of Christ it comes alive. His life saves you from yourself to Himself. He spares you from selfish whims to unselfish service. He counsels you from irresponsible decisions to wise choices. He saves you from a life of drifting to one of determination to follow God. You are reconciled to God for the purpose of unleashing His life through you by faith. Die daily so that you can allow His life to live through you. Do not capitulate to casual Christianity, for the tomb is empty of Jesus so that your heart can be full of Jesus. His grave is lifeless so that you can have life. The cross is about dying. The resurrection is about living. His life in you is the life you longed for; so let Him live there by faith.

Death leads to life, and life points back to death.
He lives in you to live through you.

SOUND DOCTRINE

He must hold firmly to the trustworthy message as it has been taught, so that he can encourage others by sound doctrine and refute those who oppose it.
TITUS 1:9

Doctrine is a belief system that is accepted as authoritative. For followers of Jesus Christ, the Bible contains Christian doctrine that is believed, understood, and lived. Doctrine is critical because what you believe can be the difference between heaven and hell, and it is critical because it determines your behavior. Doctrine is valuable because it provides structure around faith, and thus bolsters and encourages you toward a lifetime of growing and learning. Yes, doctrine can be abused and used as a club to knock others into line. But doctrine is not designed to discourage, but to encourage. Doctrine is not meant to be an intimidator. Rather, it is designed to lovingly lead disciples toward the ways of God.

Your motive for understanding and learning doctrine is so that you can know God more deeply and intimately. Doctrine is not an end in itself. If your desire is to simply gain more knowledge, then doctrine will work against your Christian maturity. Sound teaching helps you discern false teachers. The Bible says, "Then we will no longer be infants, tossed back and forth by the waves, and blown here and there by every wind of teaching and by the cunning and craftiness of people in their deceitful scheming" (Ephesians 4:14).

Some of the doctrines of the Christian faith are the deity of Christ, His death and resurrection for man's redemption, and the indwelling of the Holy Spirit in the life of believers. God is your loving heavenly Father who judges fairly. Traditional tenets of the faith are the inerrancy of the Bible, the second coming of Christ, salvation by grace through faith in Christ, and the reality of heaven and hell. Other compelling truths are eternal rewards, God's ownership of everything, and the power of prayer. Allow these doctrines and others to marinate in your mind and heart. Let them become the foundation of your beliefs and behavior. Read about them, learn about them, and let them give you confidence that God has laid out a logical and inviting explanation for living and dying. Be sure that doctrine has been distilled into a life change for you. This is evidence of authentic disciples. Jesus said, "If you hold to my teaching, you are really my disciples" (John 8:31). The major teachings of the Christian faith are clear; so camp out there and do not be confused over other distracting issues. Make sure your doctrine leads you to evangelism and discipleship, because it exists for your encouragement and defense of the faith.

Above all, keep doctrine from feeding your pride and boring others. Use it wisely and do not abuse it.

ABUNDANT FORGIVENESS

Then Peter came to Jesus and asked, "Lord, how many times shall I forgive my brother or sister who sins against me? Up to seven times?" Jesus answered, "I tell you, not seven times, but seventy-seven times."
MATTHEW 18:21-22

Sin's offense hurts. There's no doubt about it. It wounds indiscriminately, and it is no respecter of persons. Sin builds walls, as it separates and ravages relationships. It is deceptive, carnal, Christless, unfair, sad, and sometimes sadistic. Sin follows a process of desire, conception, birth, maturity, and death. James describes its diabolical development. "Then, after desire has conceived, it gives birth to sin; and sin, when it is full-grown, gives birth to death" (James 1:15). So sin is not to be taken lightly and cannot be ignored for long.

Sin invites a response from the one it offends. One option is to fight sin with sin. This is messy and can be long and drawn out. No one (except Satan) really wins when sin battles sin. Sin is rampant, and no one is immune from its consequences. It divides, belittles, and brings on relational suicide. Nonetheless, when you are sinned against, you are to forgive. When someone's sin berates your work, you are to forgive him. When someone's sin violates your trust or steals your joy or crushes your dreams, you are to forgive him. This forgiveness is countercultural, but it is the way of Christ. Forgiveness is God's game plan.

You will lose if you don't forgive, for unforgiveness is torturous to the soul. It is unhealthy to the body and the emotions. Unforgiveness leaves hollow lives in its wake. However, forgiveness is able to let go and let God be the judge. Forgiveness cuts through the varying degrees of guilt and erases the entire debt. True forgiveness comes from the heart (Matthew 18:35). Forgiveness is letting go. It is letting go of the hurt, anger, and shame. When you forgive, you are free. You are free from the shackles of sin. When you forgive, you trust. You trust God to judge others in His time. His judgment is fair and just. God can be trusted with the consequences of sin's offense.

Continue to forgive others because your heavenly Father continues to forgive you. The Scripture teaches, "Be kind and compassionate to one another, forgiving each other, just as in Christ God forgave you" (Ephesians 4:32). Without Christ's forgiveness, you are lost and undone. Jesus does not deal in forgiveness quotas. The forgiveness of the cross was swift, full, final, and forever. Unlock your relational restraints with the key of forgiveness. Write a letter with tear-soaked ink that documents your forgiveness. Call or e-mail someone today and let them know that because you are forgiven, you forgive them. Set others free with forgiveness, and you will be free. There is freedom in Christ.

Forgive fast and forgive often.
The forgiveness of Christ is forever.

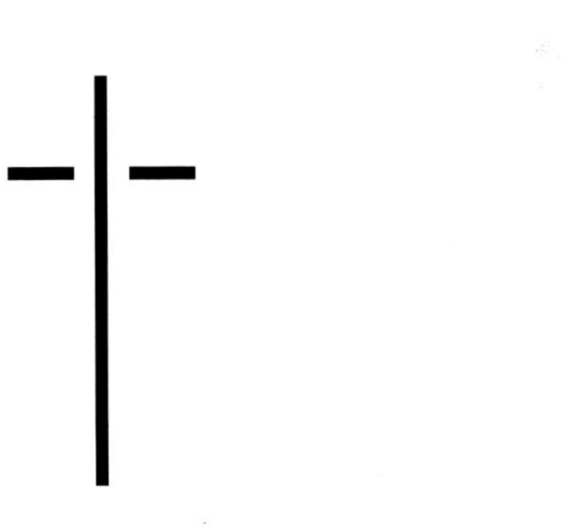

CARE BY CARRYING

"There you saw how the Lord your God carried you, as a father carries his son, all the way you went until you reached this place."
DEUTERONOMY 1:31

There is a parental passion around God's heart for you. It is a persistent and patient passion that is relentless in its care. So, not only does He walk with you through life (which is enough in itself), He goes a step further. When you are at your lowest of lows and fear has frozen your faith, or when your passion for God is paralyzed and has jumped the track, He is there to carry you. He lifts you out of your state of confusion and carries you in His loving and secure arms. You do not have to wander around in self-pity and despair. Turn to the One who truly cares. When others let you down, He is still by your side. He cares for you.

Therefore, let go of your anger, embrace Christ, and let Him carry you; let go of your fears, embrace Christ, and let Him carry you; let go of your hurt, embrace Christ, and let Him carry you; let go of your depression, embrace Christ, and let Him carry you. It's the wise thing to do. It may mean some of your goals need to be altered until you can regroup with Jesus. Plans may need to be put on hold and your vision realigned. That's okay; it is better to be in the arms of your heavenly Father than to be wandering around, bewildered without Him.

Just as the wind lifts the wings of an eagle, the Holy Spirit lifts you to soar with your Savior. To be carried by God is to need God; to be carried by God is to experience God; to be carried by God is to be loved by God. This is your time to go to a level of relational depth with your heavenly Father that you have not known until now. This is a season in your faith walk that will facilitate the maturing of your faith. Like a sensitive shepherd with a trapped sheep, He is bent over to untangle you from the snares of life and to carry you on His shoulders. Jesus said of a shepherd finding a stray sheep, "when he finds it, he joyfully puts it on his shoulders and goes home. Then he calls his friends and neighbors together and says, 'Rejoice with me; I have found my lost sheep.'" (Luke 15:5-6). You see close and up front the caring face of Christ when you are carried, so peer deeply into His compassionate eyes and enjoy Him.

You can carry on because He carries you, and He will carry you to His divine destination. This is total surrender to your Savior, Jesus.

WISE LEADERSHIP

"Choose some wise, understanding and respected men from each of your tribes, and I will set them over you."
DEUTERONOMY 1:13

The selection process of wise leadership can make or break an organization. We are constantly faced with this in our churches, jobs, schools, civic groups, and professional associations. Yet, wise leadership is not discovered through a popularity contest or a sterile assessment. Indeed, if someone is clamoring to fill a position of leadership, this is normally a red flag. A wise leader would rather be drafted by others than promote himself into a position.

So where do you look for wise leaders? A good place to begin is within the ranks of those who already exhibit wise leadership. Wise leaders are excellent listeners. They listen with the intent to understand. Wisdom desires understanding of what others are thinking and feeling. You observe their wisdom in one-on-one conversation; they know what questions to ask. They challenge you to think and they offer counsel when appropriate. Wise leaders are not gurus or know-it-alls. On the contrary, they are smart enough to understand the vastness of what they don't know.

Moreover, those who know them best especially respect wise leaders. If a leader fails to command the respect of someone in his inner circle, he will also lose the respect of those outside his immediate circle of influence. Respect comes over time by showing respect. It is the result of doing what you say and modeling integrity in living out what you say you believe. Consistent Christlike behavior invites raving reviews of respect. Wisdom and respect go hand in hand.

Wise leadership points others to God. Any infatuation with a leader as an individual is redirected to their heavenly Father. Wisdom will only remain in a humble heart. It is within the incubator of humility that wisdom germinates and flourishes. The Bible says, "He guides the humble in what is right and teaches them his way" (Psalm 25:9). So a wise leader exhibits humility with his heart for God. God can entrust wisdom to the humble of heart, but He is stingy in giving wisdom to the proud, for they cannot be trusted. The application of wisdom matures relationships, facilitates faith, and grows business and ministry. Hear from the wise before charging forward with a new opportunity. Wise leaders do not always tell you what you want to hear. Listen anyway. Their words are sometimes hard and can seem at the time to be intolerant and insensitive, for wisdom makes foolishness uncomfortable. But wise leadership leads you beyond selfish satisfaction. Wise leaders lead you to grow in your relationship with Christ.

So, follow wise leaders and be a wise leader. As the opportunity arises, prayerfully select and appoint wise leaders. Wise leadership promotes God's agenda, and His agenda is wisdom.

EARNEST EXPLANATION

"Far be it from us to rebel against the LORD and turn away from him today by building an altar for burnt offerings, grain offerings and sacrifices, other than the altar of the LORD our God that stands before His tabernacle."
JOSHUA 22:29

Always be willing to give an explanation for your actions, because good people may have interpreted your right behavior in a wrong light. If there has been a misunderstanding of motive, you need to take the initiative to clear up the confusion. This is the time to overcommunicate. So where you may have been wrong, make it right; and where you have been right, make it clear. Maybe your accusers are inaccurately associating your situation with an experience in their past. Help your critics understand the context; provide honest explanations, don't obstruct.

At times you may find yourself serving without the applause of people to bolster your efforts. This will reveal your true motives. Are you serving for the pleasure of the Lord or are you serving to please people? God is there to encourage you when you feel estranged from everyone. The Bible says, "The LORD upholds all who fall and lifts up all who are bowed down" (Psalm 145:14).

God is in control, and He will right any wrongs in His time. Trust that He will heal any harm inflicted on your reputation. Foolish is the man who flails back at his accusers with the harsh venom of vindication. Instead, be patient and allow Jesus to be your advocate. He will drive home your point with divine determination. The truth will prevail. It is your calm reaction that contributes to a positive perception. It is through humility of heart and a cool head that calamity ceases. The psalmist declared, "You save the humble but bring low those whose eyes are haughty" (Psalm 18:27).

You are in a position to reach out with an olive branch, so do everything you can to shore up the relational breach. Seek to understand why your friend's feelings are warping his words and clouding his thinking. Do not focus on winning the debate; stress instead the sovereignty of God and His goodness. He is in control, and He wants to give good things to His children. He can be trusted with this, so do the best you can, and then watch Him work. Allow prevailing prayer to puncture any building pressure, for Christ can defuse an explosive environment. Walk with Him in constant surrender, be earnest in your explanation to others, and then patiently trust God.

Christ is your life, and He is your defense.
"This is what your Sovereign LORD says, your God, who defends His people" (Isaiah 51:22).
Earnestly explain and then trust your Divine Defender.

LESS IS MORE

But the LORD said to Gideon, "There are still too many men.
Take them down to the water, and I will thin them out for you there.
If I say, 'This one shall go with you,' he shall go; but if I say,
'This one shall not go with you,' he shall not go.'"
JUDGES 7:4

Less of some things can mean an opportunity to trust in God with more things. This is why the sifting by your Savior need not be discouraging. His goal is not to harm you, but to strip you from any dependence on yourself or others and to rely solely on Him.

Your financial limitations are an occasion to watch Him provide in ways that give Him the glory for your life. Less money means you have the opportunity to trust Him with His creative provision. When some of your friends fall away, that stings; but your best friend, Jesus, still remains. If your life is driven by one new relationship after another, you will drown in shallow living. Having fewer earthly relationships means you have more time for your Heavenly One. Less is more.

Take the time to shed the weight of worry and watch God work. Now is the time to quit mourning your losses and move on. You have a new lease on life with the Lord, so follow His lead. Watch Him take your "five loaves of bread and two fish" (Matthew 14:17-19) and multiply them way beyond your efforts and enthusiasm. What God breaks, He rebuilds to be dependent on Him and more influential. This rebuilding process has simplified your life; so don't revert to complicated living. Less is truly more.

If "more is more" is your motto, you can easily become mean-spirited and hard to live with. A "more is more" mantra eventually becomes meaningless. You achieve and receive more, but to what end? There is no fulfillment outside of kingdom-minded motives. If it is all about you, you will become miserable. If, on the other hand, it is less of you and more of Him, everyone is happy. This is how God works. "He has brought down rulers from their thrones but has lifted up the humble" (Luke 1:52).

Therefore, wait in quietness. It may be time to talk less and listen more. Less worldly thinking and more heavenly thinking leads to discerning the will of God. Don't just stand in awe of His robust accomplishments through your meager efforts. Now is the time to use this momentum generated by your Master. God is on a roll, and you have the privilege of joining Him. By faith, stop doing two things before you add one. Slow down so God can speed up. Focus on quality and watch Him multiply the quantity. God wants to do more with less, so He gets the glory.

Decrease, so He can increase (John 3:30).
Less is more—less of you and more of Him.

POURED OUT

"Not so, my lord," Hannah replied, "I am a woman who is deeply troubled. I have not been drinking wine or beer; I was pouring out my soul to the Lord."

1 SAMUEL 1:15

Sometimes, your soul pours out in passionate prayer. The hurt is so deep, the loss so great, and the burden so heavy that your soul exceeds earnest prayer. Your emotions increase in intensity to the point that your prayers become speechless. Somewhere between the bottom of your soul and the tip of your lips the words evaporate. Sometimes your extra heavy heart feels constricted and emits groans that only the Holy Spirit can discern. "In the same way, the Spirit helps us in our weakness. We do not know what we ought to pray for, but the Spirit himself intercedes for us through wordless groans." (Romans 8:26). It's not only okay to go there, it's necessary. This level of soul-searching prayer is what brings peace to one painted with pain.

Latch onto your Lord and don't let go, for He is there for you. He is listening even when you don't speak or when your communication is nothing but moans. Continue to seek the face of your heavenly Father, for He is there as a present hope. It may seem silly to pour out your soul to One you cannot see, yet faith serves as the eyes that gaze upon your heavenly Father. Soul care is His passion, for what you pour out in grief and resentment, He replaces with comfort and forgiveness.

Once you pour out your soul to your Lord, you can leave it with Him and move forward in the power and peace of the Holy Spirit. Fill your now emptied soul with your Savior, and let Christ cover you with confidence, serenity, and security. If you leave your soul empty of the eternal, Satan will fill you with lingering lies such as guilt and worry (Jesus explains this principle in Luke 11:24-26). The Lord's love will lift you higher and higher to heights of affection that make angels envious. What is poured out, He fills; what is broken, He mends; what is hungry, He feeds; what is thirsty, He quenches; Allow Jesus to be the keeper of your soul. His nurture and care are unparalleled. Some people may think you are strange or weak to pour out your soul to God. However, you know better. When you pour out your soul to the Lord, He fills you up with Himself.

A life full of Jesus is the best place to live. You can trust Him with this level of transparency. Don't doubt; just pour out.

DIVINE DETOURS

Saul said ... "Come, let's go back, or my father will stop thinking about the donkeys and start worrying about us." But the servant replied, "Look, in this town there is a man of God; he is highly respected, and everything he says comes true. Let's go there now. Perhaps he will tell us what way to take."

1 SAMUEL 9:5-6

God's will for your life contains detours that build your trust in Him and build maturity in you. Your detour may seem dumb and a waste of time, but in reality, it is part of God's great adventure. Detours are very valuable and pregnant with life lessons that cannot be learned on a well-beaten and familiar path. Take this time to really understand your motives. "Remember how the Lord your God led you all the way in the wilderness these forty years, to humble and test you in order to know what was in your heart, whether or not you would keep his commands." (Deuteronomy 8:2). Divine detours are meant to grow your dependence on Him.

The more accurate your self-awareness, the more comfortable you become with yourself. Become better rather than bitter. Use this time and learn how to laugh at yourself, for it is freeing to laugh with others about your idiosyncrasies. It is at your points of weakness that God most wants to reveal Himself.

This detour is designed for you to go deeper with Him and in the significant relationships of your life. Be careful not to rush through this time and miss the blessings of becoming much better as a leader, friend, follower, husband, father, and child of your heavenly Father. Divine detours are designed to make you better.

During God's detours, you begin to see life from a different perspective. You value and respect people more authentically. Therefore, your relationships become more robust. You meet new friends and experience new things. The newness is a little daunting because you have never been here before. But the familiarity of your heavenly Father is still there. He is your one constant, and He is with you along this detour toward His best. Listen to the wise new friends He is sending your way. Honor them by prayerfully considering their advice and then follow it when appropriate. Without this detour, you would have missed the rich wisdom from these fellow pilgrims of the faith. New perspectives challenge old ones. Like a well-chiseled marble statue, the roughness of your life takes shape by the caring hand of your Creator. It is a gift of preparation, organization, and understanding, so listen to God through His Word and trusted advisors.

Detours traveled alone will consume you with fear of danger and failure, but with companions they mature, excite, and humble you. Therefore, look for your Savior's signposts of wisdom, for they lead you toward His best.

LOYAL FOLLOWER

"Do all that you have in mind," his armor-bearer said.
"Go ahead; I am with you heart and soul."
1 SAMUEL 14:7

Loyal followers are hard to find, but once they are discovered, wise is the leader who values them. They look for ways to make leaders successful in their God-given missions. They unselfishly serve behind the scenes, tirelessly and tediously. The loyal follower is an encourager and an implementer. They get things done by converting the leader's vision into reality. Without the skill and support of these dream enhancers, visionary leaders would only drown in their dreams.

Leaders without loyal followers are not effective over the long term. You can beg, bribe, and berate followers into results for a season, but eventually this type of leadership will drive loyal followers away and leave only the weak ones. The leader may start something, but it is the loyal followers who sustain the new initiative. They may be comfortable not getting credit, though the wise leader gives it gladly and gratefully. A wise leader learns to love loyal followers lavishly and unconditionally.

For followers, loyalty is not an end, but a means to something greater than themselves. They feel called to carry out the God-given mission of the ministry or business. Their loyalty is the fruit of their calling and the result of their respect. They respect because they are respected. Indeed, the respect of the leader toward followers elicits their respect in spades. When you honor and value your team or family you invite loyalty. You value them when you sincerely consider their ideas and opinions. You respect them when you start and end meetings and conversations on time. You honor them when you do what you say, and you respect them when you apologize for letting them down. You show respect when you listen and exhibit honor as you serve. You make them feel important because they are important. This type of environment of love and respect will cause loyalty to run rampant. You will be unable to control or contain its energizing effect. Loyalty that is given lasts, while loyalty that is demanded dies.

Jesus was loyal to the point of death on the cross, so be loyal to your Lord first, and loyalty to others will flow naturally. Loyalty to the Lord means you worship Him in His holiness, and you obey Him humbly and quickly. You love Him with passion and purity, and you follow Him by faith.

Stay loyal to your loyal Lord and to your loyal followers, for loyalty extends in all directions.

TRAINED AND SKILLED

Along with their relatives—all of them
trained and skilled in music for the Lord ...
1 CHRONICLES 25:7

Skill needs training, and training needs skill. You can be very gifted, but without the proper development of your gift, you are just scratching the surface of your potential. Therefore, it is imperative that you take the time to shore up your skills. Taking on training means you are teachable, and you care about developing your God-given abilities. You want to do the job well and with excellence but be very honest with yourself and others. Make sure God has given you the aptitude before taking on new responsibilities. Do not neglect your training, for you will regret it in the future. The narrower your role, the more specific skills are required. So, seek out well-defined training that is suited especially for you. Above all else, "Train yourself to be godly" (1 Timothy 4:7).

If you are pursuing a new role for status alone, you will struggle. However, if you relish the responsibility and would do it regardless of the pay, then you are on a productive path. God uses roles for service, not status. Your training and skill development is for the Lord. He is the one who got you here, and He is the one who will sustain you. Do not forget God. Your career development is not an end in itself; it is a means to an end: furthering His kingdom. Therefore, continue to dedicate your skills to Christ and allow Him to align your heart daily through prayer. He is the originator of your abilities. It is for the Lord's pleasure that you have been trained.

Make sure people know you are His and that your gifts come from Him. If not, others will heap praise on you that can puff you up. Honor that is not redirected to God and others can go to your head. Your excellent skills, honed by rigorous training, will invite accolades. So be prepared to say thank you, and then lay those kind affirmations at the feet of Jesus. He deserves all praise, honor, and glory. Your skill may give you an audience with kings (Proverbs 22:29). If so, do not be shy about your Savior. Focus on developing your talents with proper training and trust God to open doors.

Be a good steward of the skills God has given you,
and He will give back to you. Skills without training are dull,
but sharpened skills produce excellent results for His glory.

GOD'S PRESENCE

David also said to Solomon his son, "Be strong and courageous, and do the work. Do not be afraid or discouraged, for the Lord God, my God, is with you. He will not fail you or forsake you until all the work for the service of the temple of the Lord is finished."
1 CHRONICLES 28:20

God is with you, and He has called you to a specific endeavor. You can be strong, courageous, and confident in Christ. When you linger before the Lord in reflection and repentance, His confidence begins to well up within you in quietness and strength. Fear melts away in the presence of Jesus, for He is reassuring and restful. There is no need to lose sleep over the wall of work that is looming. The Lord is the author of your labor. Therefore, stay true to His original blueprint.

Do not be afraid to hand over the reins to one younger and less experienced. You may have brought the vision to this point, and now you have the privilege to hand off the responsibility of its completion to another. The goal is for God's will to be done and for Him to be glorified in the process. So who completes the project is not as important as getting the project completed in a God-honoring way. This is all about God and no one else. He is with you, and because He is with you, be careful to not take on more than He intends. You are a warrior representing another world. But the battle is His, not yours, so fight in His strength (1 Samuel 17:47). Comrades around you may have fallen, so take time to care for them and learn from their mistakes. People and processes are in your life to make you better and more effective for God. Therefore, stay true to your humble dependence on God and others. He will neither fail nor forsake you.

Do not interpret His temporary silence as a sign that He is unsupportive. This is a faith-builder and a faith-tester. Improper motives are manifested under pressure. He will use this time of pressure for purification. Your character will overcome tragedy, so do not falter into fear and discouragement, but stay true to the truth. This is His calling on your life; there is nowhere else to go. Be encouraged. His comfort may come in the form of the faithful's fervent prayers. Make much of His faithfulness and less of your fears. Fear drains, but faith fills. One day you will celebrate Christ's accomplishments through you. In the meantime, stay true to the task.

God is with you. He is here, and there is nothing to fear.

MAY 10

MADE RICH

You will be enriched in every way so that you can be generous on every occasion, and through us your generosity will result in thanksgiving to God.
2 CORINTHIANS 9:11

God's grace makes you rich in His ways. You are rich in mercy, love, patience, compassion, and wisdom. When Jesus Christ became the Lord and Savior of your life you received access to an eternal portfolio of resources. In Christ, you have just what you need, when you need it, and there are no shortfalls with the Lord.

No one can make a run on heaven's bank. You are rich with the resources of God. Like someone with oil reserves under the surface of property they manage, you have an abundance of energy of which you can take advantage. As the character of Christ continues to consume you, you can't help but receive the richness of His grace. People will begin to clamor for your time because they want to learn how to leverage love or apply patience. It is a remarkable truth that you have been made rich in the ways of God. Your eternal balance sheet is robust and real, so review what you already have in Christ, then daily count your many blessings. Account for the acts of God that overflow from your life.

Because you have been given so much, you are uniquely positioned to give. Grace can permeate your giving because grace permeates your life. You receive Christ so you can give Christ; you receive God's mercy so you can give mercy; you receive God's love so you can give love; you receive God's patience so you can give patience; you receive God's compassion so you can give compassion; you receive God's wisdom so you can give wisdom; you are rich in the ways of God so you can give the resources of God.

Happy are the generous, for thanksgiving and appreciation explode from the heart of a generous giver. God gives money and the capacity for serving others so they can be given away. A blessing that is not passed on can become a curse. Therefore, look on every occasion as an opportunity to give. Give spontaneously and give with structure, but with both, give prayerfully. Give money; give time; give expertise; give hospitality; give opportunity; give grace; give forgiveness; give resources. As Jesus says, "Give, and it will be given to you" (Luke 6:38). The best way to give is out of love, gratitude, and obedience to God. And when you give, you will receive. You will receive the peace and contentment of Jesus, knowing you modeled His motives and His generosity.

God has made you rich in His ways, for His sake, and the sake of others. Therefore, allow generosity to govern your giving for the glory of God.

CHOOSE YOUR BATTLES

"You will not have to fight this battle. Take up your positions; stand firm and see the deliverance the LORD will give you, O Judah and Jerusalem. Do not be afraid; do not be discouraged. Go out to face them tomorrow, and the LORD be with you."

2 CHRONICLES 20:17

Choose your battles wisely. Some are just the enemy's distraction. You'll find a never-ending supply of potential spats in parenting, marriage, or work. There always seems to be an issue to fight over. Let others fight these battles so these skirmishes don't keep you from following through with priorities that only you can accomplish. Wise is the leader who says "no" to fighting battles more than he says "yes." Some battles are not meant for you to fight. Yes, if you fight you may win, but why exert your time and energy toward this minor issue?

The Lord is your first line of defense, for the enemy is no match against the Lord's battle forces. God mows down pride with humility. He obliterates pretension with authenticity. He crushes prejudice with acceptance. You have the honor and privilege of receiving your marching orders from your commander, Christ Jesus. He has a way of winning battles without firing a single shot of cynicism. Sometimes, others simply implode as a result of their unwise choices. Jesus has warned them in His Word and with the wise words of others. But now is the time to wait and not force the issue. There is no need to plow ahead and make your point. Let the truth settle in and do its work at the right time. You will accomplish more by fighting from your knees, so kneel before Almighty God and ask Him to fight this battle. Prayer is your secret weapon of success. It is His aerial attack strategy. Prayer crosses over enemy lines and accomplishes the will of God. Your confused children may be exposed in warfare with the world. If so, stay diligent in the habit of covering them with prayer. Pray that God will fight for them even though they are unaware. Prayer matters—especially the fervent and faithful prayer of a parent, friend, or family member. Nevertheless, choose your battles wisely. Choose to fight fewer battles and trust God to fight more.

Most battles are distractions, so stay focused on Christ. He is your eternal Commander in Chief, ever engaged in battle on your behalf.

DANCING FOR DECADES

She is your companion and your wife by covenant. Did he not make them one, with a portion of the Spirit in their union?
MALACHI 2:15

My wife, Rita and I wed at 19—wow, really? How can that be? We didn't have a clue, just a whole lot of love and physical/emotional energy! But God, in His grace, gave us other couples a few steps ahead who could help us head off decisions detrimental to our relational health. Even with wise mentors, we still had our share of shame and suffering from immature acts and a lack of communication skills. Yet, we kept leaning into the Lord and each other. We had to learn to stop trying to change one another into our likeness and instead invite Christ to transform our individual selves into His likeness. And, in the process, draw closer to Him and to each other. We celebrate not a perfect marriage, but a marriage that our perfect Savior and Lord Jesus Christ is perfecting.

When I look at our long-term marriage mentors, Charlie and Patty, I don't see the airbrushed romance of movies. I see two people who've worn grooves into each other's lives—like favorite chairs that bear the imprint of thousands of evenings. Their faithfulness isn't the rigid loyalty of perfection; it's the stubborn choice to keep turning toward each other when the world offers easier options. Their forgiveness isn't immediate or photogenic. It sometimes arrives after doors have slammed and silent treatments have stretched too long. But it always comes. "You can't sustain a grudge and a marriage simultaneously," Charlie told me once. "Eventually, one has to go." And the fun? That's their secret weapon. The spontaneous living room dances to songs from their youth. The inside jokes so ancient that only they remember the punchlines.

Their love isn't perfect—it's better than that. It's weathered and worn and wonderful, like a map crossed with countless journeys. It's two people who don't just finish each other's sentences, but who've helped write each other's stories. That's what a marriage dancing for decades looks like: not one grand romance, but thousands of small choices to love again today.

But their most foundational element is built on God's faithfulness. When you understand you're loved by a God who never abandons, never grows bored, never withholds forgiveness—you gain courage to love each other the same way. The miracle isn't finding someone perfect—it's allowing an imperfect love to be continuously transformed by the One who invented love itself.

Remain faithful in heart, word, and deed to the one you vowed to love. Strengthen your bond with grace, patience, and joy rooted in God's covenant love.

MAY 13

NOT ABOUT YOU

For to me to live is Christ, and to die is gain.
PHILIPPIANS 1:21

Fourteen years ago, my reaction to hearing I had cancer was not pretty. I was *mad*, "Lord, I don't have time for this major life interruption, after all, I'm busy doing your work!" I was *sad*, "What if I miss experiencing our grandchildren growing up?" I was *afraid*, "I don't want to die, I have so much more life to experience!" Then the loving still small voice of the Spirit nudged my heart and opened my mind, "This is *not about you*, this is about Me, and My glory. My son, this is an opportunity to bless others so that you can live out, *in My strength*, what you believe. I want you to point people to Jesus ... the doctors, the nurses, and those you love ... point them to Me with your words, actions, and attitude." A game changer indeed ... It was not about me, but Him!

Paul writes Philippians 1:21 from prison. Picture a damp Roman cell where Paul, once a religious star and now a prisoner for Christ, writes the most joy-filled letter in Scripture. "For to me, to live is Christ, and to die is gain." These aren't words of desperate self-comfort; they're the revelation of someone who's discovered a viewpoint beyond circumstances. Writing from imprisonment, Paul faced two possibilities: execution or release. While most of us would obsess over our fate, he pondered which outcome would glorify Christ more. Paul viewed his chains as an opportunity—palace guards hearing about Jesus and believers growing bolder. What seemed to be a ministry-ending disaster had become a divine strategy.

This challenges our modern mindset. In a world fixated on personal happiness, Paul offers an alternative: a life where our highest aim isn't our wellbeing but glorifying the One who gave everything for us. The most exhausting journey is the one where you're the destination. We were never meant to be the point of our own stories.

When life becomes about redirecting attention from ourselves to Jesus, something shifts. Suddenly, both sunshine and storms serve the same purpose—showing others where true hope lives. That promotion? An opportunity to demonstrate grace rather than pride. That illness? A canvas for displaying supernatural peace. That ordinary Wednesday? A chance to love extraordinarily. The question transforms from "Why is this happening to me?" to "How might Jesus be seen through this?" There's energizing freedom in this holy redirection—we're no longer burdened with being the hero of our story. Instead, we become signposts pointing to the One who can actually bear the weight of glory our hearts were never designed to carry.

Today, surrender your pride and plans to the Lord. Remind yourself it's not about you. Let your life reflect the Lord's love, serve others humbly, and bring glory to His name.

MAY 14

THE ART OF GRANDFATHERING

The purposes of a person's heart are deep waters,
but one who has insight draws them out.
PROVERBS 20:5

I sometimes wonder what the best approach is to loving our grandchildren well. I watch my wife, Rita, effortlessly love the grandchildren in a manner that inspires and intimidates me. I am learning from Rita and other grandfathers that to love grandchildren well is to know and understand them. As Rita says, "Listen to what they say." In a recent car ride with two older granddaughters, I listened, and this is what I heard: Family, friends, music, sports, and school are important to them. I am learning that our twelve grands are real people with real fears, dreams, and desires. That moment when you realize your grandchildren are actual people—with opinions, passions, and inner worlds all their own—that's when the real adventure begins. The best grandparents aren't performing grandparenthood; they're genuinely curious about these young humans entrusted to them.

Try this: Create a "fascination file" for each grandchild. When they mention loving a particular artist or basketball player, jot it down. Later, read an article about that interest. Not to become an expert—just enough to ask one good question next time. "I heard Taylor Swift's new album broke records. What's your favorite song on it?" Watch their eyes light up when they realize you remembered. For the sports enthusiasts, attend their games without your phone in hand. Nothing says "you matter" like your undivided attention. For the music lovers, perhaps surprise them with concert tickets—with you tagging along not as a chaperone, but as a fellow adventurer.

Family dinners offer perfect opportunities to draw them out with questions like, "What's the best thing that happened this week?" or "What's something you're looking forward to?" The beautiful truth is that grandchildren don't need another coach or teacher. They need you—with your stories, your time, and your unique perspective. Remember: perfection isn't the goal—presence is. These young people don't need you to be cool; they need you to be consistent. Not trendy, but trustworthy. Not impressive, but interested. I am learning to let their agenda define my agenda.

Most of all, model the ways of Jesus to your grandchildren. I remember my grandmother's generosity and prayers and how, to this day, her love marks me. Your grandchildren are watching you—not just what you say, but how you live. When you pray over meals with genuine gratitude, when you extend forgiveness, when you serve others without fanfare, you're leaving fingerprints of faith on their hearts. My grandmother never preached sermons, but her life was one. Children may ignore advice, but they rarely miss an example. Your quiet consistency speaks volumes across decades.

Listen with love and patience as a grandparent.
Open your heart to truly hear, understand,
and connect with your grandchildren,
reflecting God's grace in every conversation.

MASTER MEMORIES

These days should be remembered and observed in every generation by every family, and in every province and in every city. And these days of Purim should never fail to be celebrated by the Jews— nor should the memory of these days die out among their descendants.

ESTHER 9:28

God-devised memories are one of His methods of encouragement and faith-building. Otherwise, we would run through life at breakneck speed and tend to forget God. One way we forget Him is by letting the stories of His faithfulness die out. Instead of being consumed with an attitude of "What has the Lord done for me lately?" we can celebrate the great things He has done in the past. The psalmist understood this: "I will remember the deeds of the LORD; yes, I will remember your miracles of long ago" (Psalm 77:11). These sorts of things are worth remembering and celebrating.

Most significant, He altered the course of your life and eternity with your soul's salvation, through faith in His Son, Jesus. This is a memory to be relived and retold. Let others know of this transition in your life, which has led to a lifetime of transformation. Sin had barricaded you in the back room of your soul. You were trapped, unable to break out of its bondage. But, by the grace of God and faith in Christ, you were set free. Your eternal emancipation is worth remembering and celebrating. It is a big deal to be "born again!" Tell your salvation story often, in fresh and meaningful ways.

Another good memory to relive is answered prayers. God answers prayers more often than you may recall. Therefore, consider recording and chronicling Christ's compassionate answers to your pelting of heaven with passionate prayers. As a result of answered prayer, He has saved souls, strengthened marriages, reconciled relationships, dispensed wisdom, revived those at the point of death, ceased wars, built churches, mended broken hearts, made whole the unhealthy, provided jobs, protected children, and orchestrated opportunities. He has created peace in the midst of turmoil, hope in the midst of despair, strength in the midst of weakness, victory in the midst of defeat, and forgiveness in the midst of rejection. His answered prayers have prevailed for posterity. These are worth recording and remembering for Christ's sake. Before you become discouraged, or consider giving up, recall His faithfulness to your daily supplications. Answered prayers compounded over a lifetime are staggering.

Memories with your Master were made to be memorialized. Therefore, relive them often, and watch them grow and multiply your faith.

FATHERING DAUGHTERS

*These commandments ... are to be on your hearts.
Impress them on your children. Talk about them when
you sit at home and when you walk along the road.*
DEUTERONOMY 6:6–7

My friend Woody has three daughters, and I have four. For three decades, we have prayed together, learned together, and grown together as dads. On days when I felt dazed and confused, Woody remained clear-minded, and on days he felt sad and unsure, I encouraged him. We were born "blue," but living in a world immersed in "pink" was not our native language. Having another dad to walk this journey is essential. We learned to be intentional with our girls.

Regular date nights with our girls grew beautiful bonds, helping our precious ones experience how a man should care for their hearts and respect them as God's beloved daughters. Something almost magical happens when a father looks his daughter in the eyes over a milkshake and asks about her day—really asks, then listens like her answers hold the secrets of the universe. Because in many ways, they do. We started "date nights" when our daughters could barely see over the restaurant table. Now, with adult girls, we understand what transpired on all those ice cream outings, shopping, and bookstore adventures. We weren't just keeping them entertained—we were writing their expectations for how men should treat them.

Every time you open her car door, you show her she deserves respect. When you put your phone away and give her full attention, you teach her that her thoughts matter. Each time you keep a promise, no matter how small, you demonstrate that her trust is worth protecting. These seemingly simple rituals create a sacred space where daughters learn to recognize genuine love—because they've experienced it firsthand from the first man in their lives.

The 24-hour rule helped our home when we disagreed and emotions were on edge. When one or more of us became upset on the verge of saying something we would regret, we hit the pause button on our conversation. By having a good night's sleep, we were able to let the sun go down to slow us down and, the next day, be in a much better frame of mind and heart to lovingly communicate. Your daughter doesn't need a perfect dad. She needs a present one who treats her mother well, apologizes when he's wrong, and consistently communicates her immeasurable worth through faithful presence. Dance with and date your daughter. She deserves you!

Love and care for your daughter with wisdom, patience, and tenderness. Choose words and actions to reflect the Lord's heart, shaping her with grace and truth.

WEDDING CELEBRATION

On the third day a wedding took place at Cana in Galilee. Jesus' mother was there, and Jesus and his disciples had also been invited to the wedding.
JOHN 2:1-2

A wedding is a celebration of two people committed to Christ and committed to each other. This is cause for raucous laughter and tearful gratitude. The solemn vows of the bride and groom are accented by their smiles and kisses. The parents celebrate God's goodness. It's a special blessing to see your child embrace a spouse who will cherish and respect your "baby." It's good to see your child happy and content. And it's good to see your child make wise choices and dance with joy. It is good to see your child obedient to his or her heavenly Father. Weddings where Jesus is invited are the best!

A wedding is a preamble to the constitution of marriage. It is a declaration of independence from self-interests. It is interdependence on each other and dependence on God. A wedding is costly, but not nearly as expensive as the marriage. A wedding mirrors a marriage's need for mentors, prayer support, and planning. A wedding done well is a template for marriage. You keep the fires of romance burning brightly. You plan together and communicate constantly. You spend budgeted money. You involve your family in ways that are appropriate and honoring. You keep God as the centerpiece of your life. A wedding is not a fleeting moment, but rather a memory to be relived over and over again.

Invite Jesus to your wedding. He is the ultimate wedding planner. Indeed, your public display of faith begins with your private devotion. Once you have developed a personal love relationship with Jesus, you can humbly exalt Him before friends, family, and the world. Private dedication precedes public declaration. An engaged couple who lack their individual engagements of faith is not ready for a wedding.

A wedding without Jesus is like an orchestra without a conductor. There is a ton of potential represented by a lot of well-meaning individuals, but there is no defined direction. There is no overall harmony of the musical instruments of husband, wife, family, friends, and faith. Jesus integrates the lives of all these well-meaning players into a beautiful concert called marriage. The wedding is but a prelude of the marriage concert, but what a beautiful beginning it births. Jesus is a gracious guest always looking for ways to intercede on your behalf—as the new couple—and on the behalf of your guests.

Keep inviting Jesus, the initiator of your wedding and the sustainer of your marriage.

FAMILY BUSINESS

King Asa also deposed his grandmother Maakah from her position as queen mother, because she had made a repulsive image for the worship of Asherah. Asa cut it down, broke it up and burned it in the Kidron Valley.
2 CHRONICLES 15:16

A family business can be a blessing or a burden. Working with people you love and trust can be a blessing. But family can also be challenging and burdensome.

You may be a son who works for your father, who wants you to take over the business one day, but your dad's faith is compartmentalized more to Sunday, while your faith is integrated throughout your everyday life. You have a strong desire to share your faith in the workplace, while your father perceives that approach to be unprofessional. So what are you to do? There is the tension of honoring two fathers, your heavenly Father and your earthly father. Be respectful, no matter what. There may need to be a clean break. This was the plan of Abraham and Lot: "So Abram said to Lot, 'Let's not have any quarreling between you and me, or between your herders and mine, for we are close relatives. Is not the whole land before you? Let's part company. If you go to the left, I'll go to the right; if you go to the right, I'll go to the left'" (Genesis 13:8-9).

Most family business conflicts can be resolved before they occur. You can preclude these squabbles with very clearly defined principles, values, and expectations. One business principle may be honesty. You may also value generosity, so include it as something that is non-negotiable. If everyone on the team agrees that the company should give back to the community, you may decide to give back 10% of your gross revenues. This becomes a company-wide discipline, and everyone enjoys giving to his or her favorite charity.

The point is to communicate and engage others. Give them ownership. Trust them to make the right decisions based on the agreed upon expectations. You may need a retreat or a family conference to hammer out your mission, vision, and values. But once defined, these values and principles become everyone's accountability. Family members must model the values of the family business, or it will fail. Do what you expect others to do and say what you expect others to say.

God's will is what is best for everyone.

ASK WITH ASSURANCE

Ezra came up from Babylon. He was a teacher well versed in the Law of Moses, which the Lord, the God of Israel had given. The king had granted him everything he asked, for the hand of the Lord his God was on him.

EZRA 7:6

When the Lord is with you, you can ask for anything with assurance. You can ask for prayer when the Lord is with you; you can ask for money when the Lord is with you; you can ask for protection, a friend, wisdom, or understanding when the Lord is with you; you can ask for forgiveness when the Lord is with you; you can ask others to consider Christ when the Lord is with you; you can ask for boldness, wisdom, humility, strength, kindness, and opportunity when the Lord is with you. Therefore, do not limit your "ask" to your influence; unleash your "ask" based on His influence.

Fear has plenty of reasons why you cannot ask. Pride will strangle the life out of your asking every time. The chance of rejection can lead you to postpone your asking for a more convenient time. However, the longer you wait, the harder it can become to simply ask.

Ask respectfully and responsibly. You are not a bull in a china shop, but a sheep in God's flock. So ask prayerfully and in a timely manner. Make sure your "ask" has been preceded by proper planning and prayer. You have a finite amount of relational and emotional capital to spend, so budget accordingly. Do not wear out your welcome. Make sure to punctuate your asking with thanksgiving. The number one reason people do not give is because they have not been asked. Blessings are left on the table when an "ask" is absent.

Above all else, stay immersed in Scripture. A proper perspective provides for a potent petition. When we lose perspective, our asking becomes anemic and even nonexistent. God's Word will flush out your fears and replace it with His calm confidence. Seek the Lord, and He will show you how and when to ask. His Word is clear that you "have not because you ask not" (James 4:2). Ask for His wisdom. It will facilitate your freedom to ask. Ask for humility, and God will use this to tie down the trepidation that holds you back. It is easier to ask God than to ask people. So, ask God so you can ask people. Asking is God's methodology for accomplishing His mission, and it is an expression of trust. Therefore, by faith, ask and you may be amazed at what you discover about yourself and God.

Don't ask, and you may never know what you missed. Do ask, and see what mighty things God has in store for those on whom His hand rests.

MAY 20

THOROUGHLY PREPARED

So I went to the governors of Trans-Euphrates and gave them the king's letters. The king had also sent army officers and cavalry with me.
NEHEMIAH 2:9

It is very hard to over-prepare. Indeed, most people do not struggle with over-preparation. Your temptation may be to neglect the real need for thorough preparation. Rushing ahead of God, exposes you to the nagging details about which you could have intentionally prayed and thought through. Pride tends to shun preparation, as it assumes too much and prays too little. When you take the time to prod those areas about which you are unsure, you discover insights that are invaluable to success. If, on the other hand, you go off half-cocked with a Pollyannaish naïveté, you are an excellent candidate for disappointment or, worse, failure. Irresponsible assumptions are foreign to faith because faith thoroughly prepares on one hand and humbly prays on the other.

You cannot pray too much about your methods and motives. Pray for God to be glorified and for His will to be done. Pray for His provision and resources. Pray for relationships you have yet to enter into that will become critical alliances in your God-sized project. It is through prayer that you persevere in preparation.

Change occurs primarily in the person praying. Their faith expands and so does their patience. Their love elevates and their vision grows. In a phrase, their character receives an extreme makeover. Prayer is the crowning jewel of thorough preparation. Prayer gives you courage to speak boldly and the wisdom to know what to say and how to say it. Prayer holds you back when you need to wait in silence. Prayer is preparation, as it aligns you with the Almighty's agenda.

Preparation also includes the involvement of others because you will not accomplish big things for God by yourself. He has placed people in your life whose hearts have been moved to join in life. Let them in and do not be intimidated because they possess skills and experiences that you don't. Instead of lamenting the different backgrounds, personalities, and skills that surround you, celebrate them. Help others prepare by removing obstacles. "Build up, build up, prepare the road! Remove the obstacles out of the way of my people" (Isaiah 57:14).

Thorough preparation is your friend. God does not waste preparation; He blesses it. Therefore, be thoroughly prepared then follow through with the plan with abandon and gusto.

Weave prayer throughout your preparation as if it were an intricately woven quilt and then watch God work. Thorough preparation positions you to be used by God.

MAY 21

CONSIDERED TRUSTWORTHY

I put Shelemiah the priest, Zadok the scribe, and a Levite named Pedaiah in charge of the storerooms and made Hanan son of Zaccur, the son of Mattaniah, their assistant, because these men were considered trustworthy. They were made responsible for distributing the supplies to their fellow Levites.

NEHEMIAH 13:13

God's primary prerequisite for service is trustworthiness. He is not looking for the most gifted, the most talented, the wealthiest, the most attractive, or the most popular. God is interested in bestowing His blessing on those who can be trusted. Trustworthiness is an attribute that invites God to participate. It is an invitation for His encouragement, His wisdom, and His responsibilities. Being in a position where God can trust you is a humbling place. His trust is both energizing and daunting. He trusts you with His reputation, His truth, His children, His wisdom, His church, His spirit, His work, and His kingdom.

You serve and love a trusting heavenly Father who enjoys extending Himself to those who can be trusted. Therefore, do not shrink back from God's trust. He has given you this opportunity because He trusts you. Continue to bathe each day in prayer and thanksgiving. Seek wisdom and counsel from those smarter and more experienced than you, for a trustworthy individual is teachable. You are a lifetime learner who understands the need to grow. Education and experience are meant to be tools for developing and extending your trustworthiness. Daniel trusted God in the middle of his test. "The king was overjoyed and gave orders to lift Daniel out of the den. And when Daniel was lifted from the den, no wound was found on him, because he had trusted in his God" (Daniel 6:23).

Your good name is your most valuable asset. Guard it with a God-fearing vigilance. If people love and respect you, this is an honor much greater than fame or fortune. People follow those they trust. Their investment of time and money is in direct proportion to your level of trustworthiness. "This is a trustworthy saying. And I want you to stress these things, so that those who have trusted in God may be careful to devote themselves to doing what is good. These things are excellent and profitable for everyone" (Titus 3:8). So let your life and actions—not your words—prove you are trustworthy.

Do more than what's expected. Keep your word and follow through. Attention to the little things builds big blessings. But, above all else, focus on "being" rather than "doing." Be who you are in Christ, and the proper "doing" will follow. In Christ, you are loved, accepted, forgiven, and trusted. Abide in Him, and others will clamor for your attention and time.

Are you considered trustworthy? If so, your life is an invitation for God and people to join you. Trust Him and others, and you will be trusted by both.

MAY 22

SHOW UP

When [the king] saw Queen Esther standing in the court, he was pleased with her and held out to her the gold scepter that was in his hand. So Esther approached and touched the tip of the scepter.

ESTHER 5:2

Successful living is about showing up, which means you arrive at the appointed time, ideally a little early. Your mode of operation is to say less and do more, as your actions speak for themselves. You show up for work as a diligent employee even when you don't feel like it; you show up to exercise when your body begs you to stay in bed; you show up for a funeral when you don't know what to say; you show up for church even when you feel guilty and insecure. Make it a priority to show up, and you may be surprised at the result.

You especially need to show up for God. Be relentless about not missing your God time. Show up for God when you are sleepy, lazy, or lonely. Your desire may be waning, but after you show up, your "want to" will grow. Show up for God and watch Him show up. It takes time to show up for God, but it is time well worth the effort and expense. You can't afford to not show up for your Savior. He is waiting patiently for you to show up and be loved on by Him. Slow down and show up. Then pour out your heart to Jesus.

It is time to level with the Lord, for His wisdom is waiting. You cannot maintain a breakneck pace with relational wreckage piling up around you. People feel manipulated and misunderstood, so pull up before you go over the cliff. You may need to burn busyness at the stake. Take the time now to show up for private prayer and petition to the great high priest, Christ. Show up in the presence of King Jesus, and He will invite you into His inner court of care and concern. Like the five virgins who showed up prepared. "At that time the kingdom of heaven will be like ten virgins who took their lamps and went out to meet the bridegroom. Five of them were foolish and five were wise. The foolish ones took their lamps but did not take any oil with them. The wise, however, took oil in jars along with their lamps" (Mathew 25:1-4). It is prudent to prepare to meet the grace, love, and holiness of God.

Show up in humility and see Him. Just show up for Jesus' sake, and you will be radically served by an encounter with your living Lord.

DISMAYED AND DISCOURAGED

But now trouble comes to you, and you are discouraged;
it strikes you, and you are dismayed.
JOB 4:5

Life can squeeze you like a cold and insensitive mechanical vise. Before you realize it, you're gripped by dismay and discouragement. Sometimes, you find yourself drowning in a cesspool of cynicism, unable to get out. The harder you try, the more difficult it gets. Problems loom larger than life, and there seems to be no hope. People let you down; they do dumb things and seem as if they couldn't care less. Dismay and discouragement have backed you into a corner. You have become alone and afraid.

It all seems unfair because you have done your best to please God. You have served with a sincere and diligent heart. You have done all the right things, but you can't get a break. You really don't know which way to turn. It seems like you have exhausted all your options.

However, you still have Christ and He has you. Together you can triumph over trouble, for it is temporary. Christ is eternal. He is your hope when life seems hopeless. He is your security when chaotic circumstances seem to be in control. He is your peace when fear locks its fangs into your faith. He is the truth when lies assault your thinking. Jesus understands your discouragement.

The Christian life is mostly lived between the valley and the mountaintop. Now you may be going through your valley experience, but there is a mountaintop that lies ahead. The path is not always easy or pretty, but you can count on Christ as your companion. No hurt is too deep that the depths of His forgiveness cannot heal. No rejection is so severe that His acceptance cannot comfort. No trouble is so crippling that the soothing waters of His trust cannot rehabilitate. Fear may have ambushed you, but His hope is there to rescue and release you from its prison of pride.

In times of despair, you can draw deep from the well of His grace. His grace is sufficient, generous, and good. So stay refreshed by His grace. Picture your life as an automotive engine powered by God's grace. Trouble will drain your tank dry, but trust refills it. Don't try to run without a full tank of grace or you'll sputter along and eventually break down and burn out. God's grace generates hope and trust. Cling to Christ and dismiss discouragement. Keep Job as your model, "In all this, Job did not sin by charging God with wrongdoing" (Job 1:22). Be not dismayed, but hopeful, and overcome trouble with trust in God.

This trouble is temporary, so look to the eternal.
Jesus is your friend that sticks closer than a brother.

FEW DAYS

Mortals, born of woman, are of few days and full of trouble.
JOB 14:1

Life is short. Relatively speaking, there are only a few days to do God's will. So how can one be a better steward of this brief time allotment? One idea is to budget your time as you would your finances. Time is a precious commodity that cannot be used twice. It is fleeting and needs to be used for God's purposes. Be careful not to wish away your today for a brighter tomorrow. Be present in the present, or discontentment will eat away at the quality of your life.

As a parent, you have only a few days to be dad to the children who live under your roof. Take advantage of this time; you have a captive audience. You can use this season of life to train and teach them in the ways of God. Do not allow your own life's distractions to keep you from your family. It may mean changing jobs so that you are not consumed by corporate responsibility. It may require lowering your standard of living and paying off your debt.

Give Him the first fruits of your few days and watch Him multiply the results in a significant way. When all is said and done, your hope is in Jesus Christ, in His blood and righteousness. He understands what it means to live wisely for a few days and then go home to His Father. His brief three years of ministry still resonate today. The quantity of your work/life ministry is not as important as the quality. Who are you developing in these few days who can carry on the mission of God's kingdom?

The management and wise use of time is a stewardship issue. Your agenda is meant to be a prayer list that validates your activity. Intentionality of your investment in others will pay dividends into eternity. You can use these few days that are left to be proactive in your prayer life. Spend these few days doing less and listening to God more. He will use the quality of your life to accomplish His quantity of results. It is not the extent of your activity that impresses the Almighty; rather, it is the focus of your heart on Him. A flurry of activity may actually cause your faith to falter. Take inventory of your time. Stop doing the trivial and the unnecessary and replace them with the eternal and the necessary. Focus on the inner circle of relationships that really matter: the Lord, your wife, your children, and your parents.

There are only a few days left, so choose to use them wisely in light of what really matters most. Make these last few days your best days.

MENIAL TASKS

After that, he poured water into a basin and began to wash his disciples' feet, drying them with the towel that was wrapped around him.
JOHN 13:5

Jesus was the master of menial tasks. He was not afraid to get His hands dirty—literally. There was nothing or no one that was beneath Him, for He valued everyone. Jesus put Himself into the shoes of others so that He could relate to their world and serve them well. Success did not shield Him from the ordinary. His heart was all about service, and He knew that service around menial tasks unlocks opportunities to influence. Jesus expects you, as a follower of His, to follow His example. "I have set you an example that you should do as I have done for you" (John 13:15).

No level of authority exempts you from serving others. Pride or dignity may cause you to resist things such as working in a soup kitchen, tutoring an underprivileged illiterate, vacuuming the house, unloading the dishwasher, taking out the garbage, washing clothes, running errands, maintaining the house, or returning phone calls. Yet, when you execute these menial tasks faithfully, you reflect Christ.

Menial tasks can become mundane over time. They can become boring and predictable, so stay fresh and challenged. Do not be satisfied with the status quo. Challenge the system and execute in a more excellent way. If you take for granted your position or technical skills, you may become sloppy in your service and lazy in your work. Always become better at what you do. Anybody can do anything for a short period of time. But it takes stamina and character to continue mastering the menial over the long run. Take continuing education classes. Improve your speaking and writing skills by engaging a speech or writing coach. Use technology to enhance and accelerate the menial. Nothing, however, will ever replace your need to give personal attention to important details.

The devil is in the details, so give attention to them. This keeps him from taking you hostage. Yes, delegate, but do not make the mistake and abdicate. People appreciate your thinking of the details that affect them. Your accountability to carry out the menial makes others want to do the same, so plan ahead. Serve others where they least expect you to get involved. Then it becomes infectious. So be a contagious carrier who reflects Christ.

There is no task too menial for your Master.
Join Him where He serves.

MAY 26

REMAIN TRUE

When he arrived and saw what the grace of God had done, he was glad and encouraged them all to remain true to the Lord with all their hearts.
ACTS 11:23

It is easy to sign up as a Jesus follower, but follow through requires faithfulness, so remain true to your commitment to Christ. It does matter that you follow through for Him. It matters to Him, to you, to your family, and to your credibility. It matters to those you have encouraged, those you are encouraging, and those you will encourage. It matters that you remain true.

Remain true to the Lord, for He has remained true to you. Remain true because the grace of God compels you to; remain true, for He knows what is best for you; remain true because you know it is the right thing to do; remain true while others encourage you; remain true because your obedience encourages others; remain true with all your heart so that the kingdom of God advances aggressively for His glory.

Satan will try to suppress your commitment by his limited power of disease, discouragement, and discontentment. He wants you to forget God's faithfulness and fall into his trap of temptation. He will feed your pride until you starve humility into nonexistence. Jesus said, "I know where you live—where Satan has his throne. Yet you remain true to my name. You did not renounce your faith in me" (Revelation 2:13). Begin by exposing any unauthentic living and seek to reconnect with Christ. The hand of the Lord is on those who remain true with all their hearts.

You can encourage others to remain true because God's grace has been extended to you. Grace encourages faithfulness. Encouragement extends hope rooted in a relationship with Jesus Christ. Your eternity-based encouragement is not sentimental or shallow. It is a heavenly hope evidenced by answered prayer. You encourage others exponentially when you petition Christ on their behalf. Cry out to your heavenly Father and ask that He keep your teenagers true to Him. Pray for your friend's body to be healed by the hand of God; pray for married couples to learn how to love and respect each other through the influence of the Holy Spirit; pray for your pastor to remain true to his calling and to the One who extended his call; pray for opportunities to pray with those you are encouraging. Prayer is without exhaustion in its encouragement. Above all else, receive encouragement from the Lord and others to remain true. Then simultaneously and spontaneously extend encouragement to others to remain true with all their hearts.

Remain true because there is no limit to what the Lord can do. Giving up is not for you.

CALL TO MISSIONS

While they were worshiping the Lord and fasting, the Holy Spirit said, "Set apart for me Barnabas and Saul for the work to which I have called them." So after they had fasted and prayed, they placed their hands on them and sent them off.

ACTS 13:2-3

A call to missions is spiritually motivated because it is initiated by the Holy Spirit and validated by mature leaders within the church. It is through worship, prayer, and fasting that God speaks clearly around calling. This is not to be taken lightly or half-heartedly, for a missionary's calling is a work of God. God longs for the crown jewel of His worldwide creation to come to Him, their Creator. The nations are never very far from the loving arm of Almighty God. He was born in the East and, after His death, His message spread like wildfire to the West. He is Lord over all the continents and countries on planet Earth. The first missionaries were compelled by Christ to tell His good news of the cross and resurrection. Their commitment to spread the Word of God was not deterred by stoning or shipwrecks. If anything, their imprisonment and hardships galvanized their calling to carry forth the transforming truth of faith in Christ.

It was so clear to these cross-cultural Christians that the birth, life, and death of Christ fulfilled many Old Testament prophecies. His miraculous signs and the miracles of the early church were further evidence that their heavenly Father had His hand on Jesus and His church. Peter proclaimed, "Jesus of Nazareth was a man accredited by God to you by miracles, wonders and signs, which God did among you through him, as you yourselves know. This man was handed over to you by God's deliberate plan and foreknowledge; and you, with the help of wicked men, put him to death by nailing him to the cross. But God raised him from the dead, freeing him from the agony of death" (Acts 2:22-24). He was the Messiah they had longed to see and hear. But the most riveting part of their missionary message was the resurrection. Jesus was the resurrected Lord and Savior of the Jews and the Gentiles. God has invited people of all languages on the planet to believe in Jesus. This is the message of the missionary called by God, set apart by the Holy Spirit, and sent out by the church.

This calling is not confined to the super-spiritual, but to all who love God and people. So prayerfully consider Christ's call to missions.

CITIZEN STEWARDSHIP

But Paul said to the officers: "They beat us publicly without a trial, even though we are Roman citizens, and threw us into prison. And now they want to get rid of us quietly? No! Let them come themselves and let us out."

ACTS 16:37

Citizenship in a free country is a gift from God. It is a stewardship with privileges and responsibilities. Citizenship gives you freedom for good or evil, so remind the culture of wise thinking and value-based living.

So your vote matters because your citizenship matters. This is the purpose of the regular election of government officials, for your vote is their performance review. Voting is a responsibility of citizens to provide feedback to the God-ordained institution of government. This authority is used by God to carry out His purposes. The Bible says, "Let everyone be subject to the governing authorities, for there is no authority except that which God has established. The authorities that exist have been established by God. Consequently, whoever rebels against the authority is rebelling against what God has instituted, and those who do so will bring judgment on themselves" (Romans 13:1-2). Therefore, elect men and women of principle who value life, especially in those who are unable to defend themselves.

The unborn and the elderly are on the top of their list of who to protect. They value marriage, one man and one woman engaged in holy matrimony. They reject a redefinition of marriage from those driven by money and immorality. Most importantly, they value God and His Word. There is a humble submission and respect to the authority of Almighty God.

Public service is a public trust. Pray for trustworthy men and women who are motivated by principle. Daniel was a government official of integrity. "At this, the administrators and the satraps tried to find grounds for charges against Daniel in his conduct of government affairs, but they were unable to do so. They could find no corruption in him, because he was trustworthy and neither corrupt nor negligent." (Daniel 6:4). Hold accountable those cowards who hide behind compromise or enrich themselves with personal profit. God is in control, but He expects participation from people of the state. Look for leaders who will return prayer and the fear of God back into the public arena. Expect the language of the Lord to pepper their speeches.

We are citizens of a greater kingdom who have a temporary assignment to engage in our earthly kingdom. Therefore, steward well your citizenship while you can. God expects engaged citizens.

UNMARRIED DAUGHTERS

Philip the evangelist, one of the Seven …
had four unmarried daughters who prophesied.
ACTS 21:8-9

Unmarried daughters need their dads. They need their moms, but they really need their dads. There is a transition that takes place during a daughter's teenage years that requires the wisdom, love, and affection from Dad. If his tender loving care is lacking, she will look for it in all the wrong places. Her emotions can become hostage to another male who does not have an objective agenda. They are fragile young ladies at the entrance of womanhood. The nurture, love, and encouragement of their earthly fathers go a long way in enhancing their relationship with their heavenly Father.

An unmarried daughter needs and wants her dad's attention. She wants you to look her in the eye and say everything is going to be okay. She desperately needs you to affirm your belief in her. So, value her by complimenting her beauty and brains. Praise her for her initiative and intuition. Hug her hard and often. Above all else, your unmarried daughter needs your unconditional love and acceptance.

It is probably easier to solve a work issue than to sit across from your teenage daughter over dinner. Engaging a teenager may be uncomfortable, but parenting is not for your comfort. Rather, it is for her confidence. She needs to know that you pray for her and care for her. Be there to ask her suitor for his plan to stay pure with your daughter, for a prayerfully co-created plan increases the probability for purity. Then hold them accountable to the plan.

One day your unmarried daughter will be married. Because you modeled for her the right kind of man, she will prayerfully pursue a like-minded husband. Do not downplay your valuable role as a dad. Let other things like travel and meetings wait so you can stay involved with her. Your relational investment earns you influence. Praise her often for her wise choices and aptly remind her of authentic accountability.

Pray for and be with your unmarried daughter. When she is married, she will want more of the same. Your baby will be married one day, so be a model of the man she needs.

SHAMEFUL LUST

Because of this, God gave them over to shameful lusts. Even their women exchanged natural relationships for unnatural ones. In the same way the men also abandoned natural relations with women and were inflamed with lust for one another. Men committed shameful acts with other men, and received in themselves the due penalty for their perversion.

ROMANS 1:26-27

Lust breaks the heart of God. It is a hybrid of covetousness and sexual immorality. But there is something darker than lust, and that is shameful lust. It is crafty in its pursuit of corporate benefits that validate its behavior. Shameful lust is well funded, well scripted, intelligent, and engaging. It is a Christless conspiracy set on redefining the natural with the unnatural.

Shameless lust claims to be true when it is a lie. Lust, to the Lord, is adultery in the heart. Jesus said, "I tell you that anyone who looks at a woman lustfully has already committed adultery with her in his heart" (Matthew 5:28). It is virtual sex and not to be taken lightly. It is a sin against God and others.

This type of lust is shameless in its pursuit of acceptance. The collapse of culture comes from within, so moral disregard and the redefining of marriage will bring a nation to its knees. The greatest enemy is the failure to stay true to God's truth. Moral decay rots society's security and is a slippery slope to irrational behavior and apathy toward God.

So what is the role of authentic followers of Jesus? Pray for Christians to repent from acceptance of shameful lust as normal. Pray for a revival of holiness. Pray for a return to the commands, principles, and values of Holy Scripture. Pray for the elevation of marriage as a picture of a believer's relationship with Christ. It is a covenant between a man and a woman for life. It is a relationship of fidelity, commitment, forgiveness, love, and respect. Exalt marriage and dethrone the debauchery of shameful lust.

God has not and will not bless shameful lust. Nor does God bless a man that condones truth-suppressing behavior. Silence is acceptance; ignorance is irresponsible. Pray for those seduced into shameful lust to be authentically loved by their Savior, Jesus. Pray that those who know the truth will speak it in love.

The love of God replaces shameful lust with legitimate love. Be like Jesus and love them to the Lord.

I AM SORRY

Godly sorrow brings repentance that leads to salvation and leaves no regret, but worldly sorrow brings death.
2 CORINTHIANS 7:10

Sincere sorrow means taking responsibility. "I am sorry" are three freeing words. "I was wrong," "You were right," "I apologize," "Please forgive me." All of these phrases communicate culpability. A more sincere apology occurs when you admit your error, transgression, or sin before you are found out. You take the first step to ask forgiveness because you know it is the right thing to do.

You initiate peace because your desire is to repair the relationship. Disharmony and disconnection are not acceptable options. Have faith that God expects behavior that brings reconciliation. You put the relationship at risk if you resist humbling yourself and apologizing. Someone has to start by saying, "I am sorry." Extend your apology as soon as possible. When others sense you have really changed, they extend trust. However, they may withhold that trust until you prove yourself worthy of it. Sorrow that does not lead to change results in relational death. Sincere sorrow makes you sick to think you let down the One who loves you the most.

Godly sorrow means wanting to change for Christ's sake. You have sinned against your Savior and those you love. The pain inflicted is not worth continuing with the same bad habits. No one ever regretted repenting of sin. Godly sorrow leads to repentance, which results in transformation. Change occurs around a humble and honest heart.

On the flip side, be patient with those who ask your forgiveness. Forgive them and give them a chance to change, while releasing your anger and their broken promises to Jesus. Give them over to the Lord and pray for their repentance. God can do more with a person's heart in a minute, than a lifetime of your nagging could ever accomplish. Do not hold them in contempt. Rather, entrust them to Christ. Give time for repentance to root out bad habits and destructive behaviors. Lies can be extracted by the everlasting love of God and replaced with His transforming truth. Accept apologies at face value and hope for the best. Pray for the work of the Holy Spirit to have His way in a humble heart. Be quick to forgive and just as quick to ask forgiveness. Replace fear with faith. Your sorrowful confession connects with Christ and with others. Therefore, take the first step and apologize.

Ask for forgiveness and surrender to your Savior. Become broken, for brokenness leads to freedom. Say, "I am sorry," and see how your Savior blesses your apology.

DARK DECEPTION

"The eye of the adulterer watches for dusk; he thinks, 'No eye will see me,' and he keeps his face concealed. In the dark, thieves break into houses, but by day they shut themselves in; they want nothing to do with the light."

JOB 24:15-16

Everyone has a dark side that tries to lead him astray. It is always attempting to seduce you into your old way of thinking and doing. It wants to pull a dark cloud over your soul and rain down discontentment and confusion. It knows that one decision can devastate you for a lifetime.

You are led to believe that enough lies can cover up your dark deeds. The dark side offers the illusion that adultery is harmless and recreational. It reasons with you that in the cloak of darkness, no one will ever find out. That, of course, is fiction. "You may be sure that your sin will find you out" (Numbers 32:23). The light will eventually pierce the darkness, and, like a scattering roach, you will be exposed. God is light; so in darkness, the light of His love exposes you. Why crouch in a dark corner of carnality, when you can be free in the light of Christ? Darkness promises freedom but delivers bondage. The promise of God is grace, which results in faith's freedom.

Your dark side will hound you until you get to heaven. So, in the meantime, it is imperative to live in the light. Live in the light of God's love, for that's where you are accepted and kept secure; live in the light of accountability, for that's where you have boundaries from the edge of darkness; live in the light of Christian community, for that's where others can pray for you and with you; live in the light of God's Word, for that's where you gain His wisdom and perspective. Simply live in the light of Christ, and He will repel the relentless rampage of your dark side. "But if we walk in the light, as he is in the light, we have fellowship with one another, and the blood of Jesus, his Son, purifies us from all sin" (1 John 1:7). Therefore, do not tamper with the temptations of your dark side alone, or you may suffer the scars of sin's consequences.

Walk away from the dangers of the dark side. Tell someone today your deepest, darkest secrets. Exposure is the enemy of your dark side. Freedom in Christ comes from accountability with other Christ-followers. Walk in the light together, as overcomers with God and people.

Alone, you backslide into your dark side. Therefore, surround yourself with lovers of the light. In the light you get it right.

CONTENTMENT'S CONCERN

My heart is not proud, Lord, my eyes are not haughty; I do not concern myself with great matters or things too wonderful for me. But I have calmed and quieted myself. I am like a weaned child with its mother, like a weaned child I am content. Israel, put your hope in the Lord both now and forevermore.

PSALM 131:1-3

Contentment is not concerned with matters out of its control. Anytime you try to manage circumstances out of your purview, you grow discontented. The world of discontentment is a dangerous place to live because it may lead you to make a hasty or unwise decision. On the other hand, contentment is patient and prayerful in decision-making. Most things do not have to be decided right away.

Contentment does not try to change people. That's God's job. Contentment accepts the fact that some people are best left to themselves. God will deal with them in His way and in His timing.

You don't have to be in the know about everything around you. Too much information can get you into trouble, for you are responsible for what you know. Be content and trust God with the issues that exceed your capacity to understand. Do the best in your current position and let opportunities come your way. The world of contentment is a great place to live in peace and quiet.

Contentment is found by placing your hope in God. Hope in the Lord can never be taken from you. All hell can break loose, but He is there. If you can trust Him with your soul for eternity, you can trust Him during this incredibly brief time on earth. Hope feeds contentment the way an appetizing meal feeds a hungry body. If you place your hope in anything other than God, you set yourself up for major disappointment. Everything else in life will let you down, but not your heavenly Father. He is there for you, and His desire is contentment. He desires contentment because He knows that pure joy and happiness are nurtured and able to grow there. Sad are the discontented; glad are the content. Driven are the discontented; called are the content. Restless are the discontented; peaceful are the content. Addicted are the discontented; satisfied are the content. Pessimistic are the discontented; hopeful are the content.

Be content and enjoy the outcome.
Contentment's concerns are few.

JUNE 3

WISDOM AND UNDERSTANDING

And he said to the human race, "The fear of the Lord—
that is wisdom, and to shun evil is understanding."
JOB 28:28

There is no wisdom apart from the fear of God, so a wise person fears God. This means relating to Him on His terms, not yours. When you fear Him, you know Him. You follow Him and you obey Him. Yes, it is a relationship of love, but it is also a relationship of obedience. When you fear God, you never get over the fact that He is God and you are not. There is awe and an extreme reverence toward your Savior. Fear of God pushes you and prods you to remain prostrate before Him. A humble attitude saturates your heart and mind. When you fear the Lord, you do not want to knowingly sin, so you choose not to.

This is why you can be smart and not be wise. You can be rich, educated, and popular and not be wise. Very smart people have been known to make very unwise decisions. Intelligence does not guarantee wisdom. In fact, the higher your IQ, the more susceptible you are to missing the humble access to wisdom. If you are left to your own limited perspective—without God's global view—you become misguided. The more it looks as if you don't need God, the more you need Him. His wisdom steers you through complex and not so complex decision-making. The wisdom of God is your warning not to fall to the flirtations of the world. It is your ability to draw on your moral fortitude with confidence and grace.

Wisdom is what God thinks. God does not dish out commands that are incomprehensible. His ways are the right ways. Wisdom says, "The wise fear the Lord and shun evil" (Proverbs 14:16). That means you are to escape from the appearance, the influence, and the control of evil. Wisdom and understanding says you cannot handle evil's allure. When you get too close, it's like getting sucked into the backside of a giant fan. You feel that you are in control and then get cut to pieces. Therefore, be wise and develop a storehouse of wisdom. Wisdom will come as you experience God and learn of Him from His Word.

Wisdom and understanding are the gold and silver of emotional and spiritual wealth. Therefore, gain them and steward them well. Remember, the fear of the Lord facilitates wisdom and understanding.

TEST WORDS

"For the ear tests words as the tongue tastes food. Let us discern for ourselves what is right; let us learn together what is good."
JOB 34:3-4

Words are to be filtered. If words travel unfiltered through your ears they can clutter and confuse your mind. Mixed messages to the mind are confusing and disconcerting. Some words are bad for your mental health, while others invigorate and energize your thinking. This is why discernment is required with your verbal intake. Your ears are meant to be a checkpoint for truth. If lies attempt to enter, you need to arrest them with your good sense and send them on their way.

Your mind is a product of what comes through your ears and eyes. Train your ears to value the eternal over the temporal; educate them to reject lies and invite truth. Do not allow harmful thoughts into your thinking. Discerning ears automatically drop-kick diseased words away from entering the playing field of your mind. Do not nurse or coddle sick words, for they will only infect you with their adverse effects. Vile and wicked words are normally packaged by hurt and delivered with anger, so mostly dismiss the words of the angry. They are unproductive and hurtful, because words spewed in anger are quickly regretted and deeply damaging.

Digest God's words often through the ears of your heart. Let Him speak to you through times of prayer and reflection. His words are an effective filter for the words of others. Watch for the subtle words that suggest submission to something or someone other than God. Those are the words that tend to look good on the surface but come back to bite you with their hidden agenda. Take the time to test these attractive words. If someone says he wants to help you, it is prudent to wait and get to know his intentions. The words of the wise can be received promptly and embraced wholeheartedly. However, the words of fools need not make it past your ear lobes. If their foolish pronouncements slip into one ear, send them out the other one just as quickly. Post the two sentinels of good sense and discernment at the entrance of your ears. Receive into your mind the best and the brightest in wise thinking. Reject the rest.

It is incredibly wise to test every wooing word with the wisdom of God. Let the intake of your words feed right thinking. Listen only to words that pass God's grade-A standards.

PROSPERITY RETURNS

After Job had prayed for his friends, the LORD restored his fortunes and gave him twice as much as he had before.

JOB 42:10

Sometimes, you have to lose everything in order to find God. It takes becoming broke to experience brokenness. Losing everything is difficult, embarrassing, and life altering. Yet, when you have no one but Christ to cling to, you have what matters most. Other possessions, and even people, can substitute as your savior, but He does not compete with anything or anyone. Money and work will come back to bite you if they are not kept in proper perspective. Therefore, stay immersed in the scriptures. "Keep this Book of the Law always on your lips; meditate on it day and night, so that you may be careful to do everything written in it. Then you will be prosperous and successful" (Joshua 1:8). The Bible is your behavioral baseline.

Robust relationships are fulfilling and necessary. However, people may be ravaging your time and energy while leaving you nothing for Your heavenly Father. He deserves and desires the first fruits of your time and money, not what's left over. He alone desires 100% of your devotion and commitment, so be extremely wise, and be careful that distractions do not contest with Christ. Now is not the time to give up on God, but to look up to God. Look up to the Lord and pray.

Pray for honesty about your own pride and use this time of purging to prepare you for God's goodness. For the first time in your life, you may be poised and in the best position to receive His blessings. He can make you prosperous again. There is no guarantee, but anything is achievable with the Almighty. Repent of presumption, pretense, and pride; God's forgiveness flows freely in a repentant heart.

Prosperity is meant to point you and others to God. Use your next season of success as a kingdom platform. Learn from your past mistakes so you can avoid future failure, and become a facilitator of faithfulness to God. Your life is now a résumé of faithfulness to your heavenly Father.

God may or may not bring you prosperity again, but if He does, never forget where it came from and never forget where you came from. Use prosperity for good before it uses you for bad.

SEASONAL FRUIT

That person is like a tree planted by streams of water, which yields its fruit in season and whose leaf does not wither.
PSALM 1:3

So much of life is seasonal. Relationships are for a season; you experience good and bad for a season; you work a job for a season; you volunteer for a season; you attend a particular church for a season; you live somewhere for a season; you attend school for a season; you live life for a season.

Seasonal assignments in life are as much a part of God's design as the four annual seasons we celebrate. This season of your marriage and parenting will probably not thrive with last season's methods. Your young adult children expect to be treated as adults now, not immature adolescents. This new season in your career requires training and learning, so become a student of innovation, and thrive.

Your greatest challenge during seasonal transition is to stay rooted in God and His Word. Your stability is in the unchanging Almighty. Everything around you may be seasonal and changing, but He is your anchor of dependability. Now is the time to extend the roots of your trust deep into the soil of Scripture. Your level of readiness for the next season is contingent upon your current spiritual preparation. Be sensitive to the things of God now, and your seasonal transition will be more seamless and natural. God is growing you into a mighty oak of influence that bears fruit seasonally. Your attention to simplifying your life, developing a healthy root system of dependency on God, and avoiding sin's dreadful disease all position you for seasonal fruit bearing. "And let us not be weary in well doing: for in due season we shall reap, if we faint not" (Galatians 6:9 KJV).

Your fruit-bearing takes on a different look and feel in each season. This is God's spice for your life. Before, your children may have been your primary ministry. Now, in this new season, it may be mentoring other young men. Before, you were so busy making money; now you have the experience and the capacity to wisely give it away. Before, you were a giver; now you are a receiver. Before, you served many relationships; now you focus on a few. Before, you read more than you wrote; now you write more than you read. But the compelling characteristic is how God is bearing beautiful fruit through you. The fruit is seasonal, but it is sensational because it originates in your Savior and Creator.

Therefore, invite, prepare, and look forward to life's seasonal opportunities. Then, by God's grace, bear bountiful fruit in each season of life He brings your way. Go with the seasonal fruitful flow of your heavenly Father.

FOOLISH DENIAL

The fool says in his heart, "There is no God." They are corrupt, their deeds are vile; there is no one who does good.

PSALM 14:1

Denial can be death to God-awareness and it is death to self-awareness. It causes you to believe lies about yourself and God. Denial of God's existence is the worst kind of denial. It's like refusing to accept a sincere gift from an unconditional lover. Just because you deny the lover's existence does not negate their gift. God is not too good to be true. He is good because He is true. When you accept the existence of God, you accept the reality of His influence over you and His influence over the world.

Denial of deity is like saying the sun is not brilliant in its illumination by day and the moon by its illumination at night. Moreover, it is foolish to deny a grand designer behind the human body. Common sense craves for an acceptance of God as Creator. However, denial's greatest driver may be the desire to behave badly. A fool denies God because he is morally challenged. The thought of God or anyone else telling him how to act is foreign to his foolish heart. Yet, every day, we all have to follow the instruction of some authority. A fool can attempt to remove all authority from his life with denial but he will fail.

Be open to the evidence that points to the Almighty and be intellectually honest about the historic reality of Christ's death and resurrection. Above all else, be honest about your motives for denying God. Is it expedient for your own lifestyle or is it an honest appraisal of the facts? Honesty is the first step in overcoming denial.

God invites all to know and understand Him. Ultimately, He cannot be denied. He may be denied for a season, but sooner or later, His presence will press for a personal acknowledgment. Denial of God's existence is spiritual death, but physical death shatters denial's claims. One second after death, the reality of eternity will ring true. Faithless living has made a fool's bed forever. Now is the time to wake up and embrace Christ's existence. The Bible says, "But everything exposed by the light becomes visible—and everything that is illuminated becomes a light. This is why it is said: 'Wake up, sleeper, rise from the dead, and Christ will shine on you.' Be very careful, then, how you live—not as unwise but as wise" (Ephesians 5:13-15). He cannot be denied, and a fool will deny this to his detriment.

**Denial is death; acceptance is life.
The wise choose life over death.**

JUNE 8

INTIMACY THROUGH BROKENNESS

The Lord is close to the brokenhearted
and saves those who are crushed in spirit.
PSALM 34:18

Intimacy with God goes hand in hand with your brokenness. Do not despise this condition. Rather, delight in its opportunity for closeness with the Lord. A broken and contrite heart delivers intimacy with the Almighty. You may long to know Jesus in the power of His resurrection and the fellowship of His suffering (Philippians 3:10). These prayers are not in vain. Your brokenness can be answered prayer, although the answer may not be exactly what you expected. But the path of personal relationship with Christ is not always easy.

Most of the time, intimacy requires difficulty. It is at this point of pressure and discomfort that some people disembark the train of intimacy. It is much easier to talk about a close relationship with Christ than it is to arrive at this point through brokenness. He stands at the door of our heart and knocks (Revelation 3:20). When you invite Christ into your broken life, He comes in.

Intimacy with God through brokenness is not unlike what you experience in relationships with people. Hardships and brokenness are meant to grow you closer to other people. A crisis will either drive you further away from someone or closer together. God's best for you is to make you relationally stronger with one another during a season of brokenness.

Brokenness, however, is not a one-time phenomenon. It is an ongoing part of the committed Christian's life. It's not as if you swallow this one hard pill and are then set for a lifetime of intimacy with God. Once God has marked you with brokenness, then you are positioned for Him to build on this firm foundation. He will still use mini moments of brokenness throughout your life. These regular occurrences are bricks of brokenness joined by the cement of His grace. Over time, a life of brokenness becomes a stalwart structure of sanctification designed by God.

Your brokenness is meant for your betterment. Indeed, you are much better when you experience a defining moment of brokenness. It deserves your embrace, rather than your rejection. If you fight brokenness, you delay God's best. You circumvent intimacy with Christ if you bypass brokenness. Focus your energies on changing yourself, not your circumstances. Christ will handle the circumstances while you adjust your attitude. A life of brokenness is an invitation to intimacy. His closeness and salvation are worth this time of brokenness.

Don't buck brokenness. Instead, rely on Him and get to know Him at this deeper level of intimacy. You are much better broken because brokenness leads to intimacy with God.

START YOUNG

For you have been my hope, Sovereign Lord, my confidence since my youth. … Since my youth, God, you have taught me, and to this day I declare your marvelous deeds.
PSALM 71:5, 17

Start to learn the ways of the Lord when you are young. This is your wisest and best investment. When you start young, you don't have to wade through the muck and the mire of disobedient living and its consequences. Stay the course of Christ while you are young, and this will develop you into an obedient adult. Youthful dependence on God results in an adult who depends on God. Do not kid yourself into thinking that you can change your ways quickly once unhealthy habits have been entrenched in your life.

Do not despise your youth or let others do the same. Paul exhorted his protégé, Timothy, "Let no man despise thy youth; but be thou an example of the believers, in word, in conversation, in charity, in spirit, in faith, in purity" (1 Timothy 4:12 KJV). Take God at His word. Depend on Him for your confidence, wisdom, and security. God uses youth to accomplish His purposes. Even as those older in the faith falter in fear, your heavenly Father frees youthful hearts to attempt big things for Him. Courage and conviction blossom in a young and hungry heart for God. The Holy Spirit is calling forth faithful young people to further His kingdom. Listen to the heart of your heavenly Father and do what He says. God is calling His youth to something much bigger than themselves. And you can facilitate their faith with prayer, financing, and training.

Help young men and women start early in their engagement with God. Teach them, train them, model for them, and then send them out to serve on the Lord's behalf. Youth do not need to be overly protected but set free to think big for God. The larger their vision, the larger their God. So present them with a God-sized challenge. Expect great things from young people who have a heart to follow hard after God. Do not underestimate their ability to be catalysts for Christ. Youth need not be coddled with the status quo, but challenged to break out of boxes that restrain them. Invest in and equip young people so they can roll up their sleeves and serve others. They can far exceed your efforts with your significant support, and persistent and powerful prayers.

Support the young. For a youthful person, called by God and full of the Holy Spirit, can change the world.

HELP THE HELPLESS

A father to the fatherless, a defender of widows, is God in his holy dwelling.
PSALM 68:5

God helps those who can't help themselves. He is a defender of the poor and needy, for the disadvantaged are on His heart. Jesus came for those who recognized their need for God and He has appropriated His forgiveness and grace. Those who are poor in spirit are candidates for Christ's true riches. It is only when you recognize your spiritual bankruptcy outside of a Savior, that you can receive the right kind of help.

There is also the need to minister to those who have been devastated by difficult circumstances. They are waiting for someone to care. A little bit of healthcare, a little bit of money, and a little bit of time can provide for the poor in ways most of us take for granted. God's heart is to help the helpless. Therefore, pray for the poor and ask God to send you someone who could use your help. Grace is drawn to the needy. Love edifies and kindness cares. Faith flushes out fear, and humility hunts down the hurting. Compassion shows up with resources that resonate where people live, so help the helpless in the name of Jesus.

Perhaps you may find yourself on the helpless half of the equation. We are all helpless to some extent. You may feel helpless in your current situation at work, with a family member, or in your physical condition. Your helpless position is poised for God's helpful position. Engage your heavenly Father in your helpless circumstance. Lean on His love and request His wisdom. You cannot make it alone. There was a day when you may have thought you could make it without the help of God or other people. But rejection of help is not how God works. Refusing help is refusing God's provision. Indeed, you receive the help of heaven so you can help others get to heaven. Help is a gift that keeps on giving. Because someone believed in you and helped you, you desire to do the same for another. So gain fresh perspective by looking to heaven for help. The Bible says beautifully, "I lift up my eyes to the mountains—where does my help come from? My help comes from the LORD, the Maker of heaven and earth" (Psalm 121:1-2). Plead with Him to provide in ways you haven't thought of but then ask others to help. When others are engaged in eternity's agenda, they are happy and content. Blessed are those who become helpers in the purposes of God.

Be a giver and a receiver of help. Above all else, be helpful by giving help to the helpless. Help those who can't help themselves.

JUNE 11

NO STRUGGLES

They have no struggles; their bodies are healthy and strong.
They are free from common human burdens;
they are not plagued by human ills.
PSALM 73:4-5

Having no struggles at all will never happen in this lifetime. A no-struggle existence is not possible until you graduate to heaven. The righteous and the wicked both struggle to varying degrees. No one is exempt. Therefore, don't spend your life trying to insulate yourself. The Bible teaches, "For our struggle is not against flesh and blood, but against the rulers, against the authorities, against the powers of this dark world and against the spiritual forces of evil in the heavenly realms" (Ephesians 6:12).

Envy can erode your eternal perspective by giving you a false impression of others, who seem to live lives without struggles. This is inaccurate and ill-conceived. No amount of money or power can completely drive struggles from someone's life. In fact, it may compound struggles because of the complexity of choices that wealth and power create. Someone's large amount of discretionary time may, on the surface, give the appearance that they are without struggles. Not true. There are still the internal struggles of sin and self against God's best. And there are the external struggles created by other people's choices and circumstances that are out of one's control. You can join in another's struggle through prayer. Paul requested this when he wrote, "I urge you, brothers and sisters, by our Lord Jesus Christ and by the love of the Spirit, to join me in my struggle by praying to God for me" (Romans 15:30).

Struggles are meant to grow you in Him and not drive you away from Him. Use struggles to your advantage, rather than to your disadvantage. Struggles do not mean you are less spiritual. It may be that just the opposite is true. Because of your sensitivity to obeying God, you may struggle. You may struggle over the misunderstanding others have over your love for Christ. You may struggle because of the mistreatment by those convicted by your lifestyle. You may struggle to forgive because of the unforgiveness that is extended back to you. Struggles come in all shapes and sizes.

Go quickly to your Savior, Jesus, with your struggles. Use them as an asset rather than a liability in your relationship with God. Lean on prayer to persevere through this time of struggle, because struggles only strengthen the faithful. You are not alone in your struggle against sin, self, and Satan. Therefore, stay true to the task of disciplined devotion to Christ and be with those who survived their struggles by the grace of God. His grace is sufficient no matter what the struggle.

Don't seek to be struggle free. Rather, accept struggles in stride, with His greater purpose in mind. God uses your struggles for His glory.

JUNE 12

SHEPHERD AND LEAD

And David shepherded them with integrity of heart; with skillful hands he led them.

PSALM 78:72

Leadership requires the gentle touch and persistent persuasion of a shepherd. The wise leader pays attention to how and when to apply each. Shepherding moves people beyond their own needs, to their ability to serve others. It helps people discover a need and then encourages them to engage in its fulfillment. Unafraid to mark a course, true leadership sets the pace as the team embarks upon a new goal. It understands the big picture and then communicates this grander vision in a compelling and consistent fashion. Leadership is anticipating the next step and adapting as needed. Leading implies progress toward a destination.

Good shepherding requires awareness. You are aware of people's limitations of capacity and capabilities. Be careful not to overload them and burn out your best people. You are aware of the training required to get people up to speed in their performance and productivity. You are aware of what motivates certain individuals but not others. You are aware of how to best communicate with, and hold accountable, people according to their style and expectations. You are aware if people around you are happy, sad, discontented, or grateful. You are aware when they hurt and when they cry. You are aware because you care. Shepherding is caring, so take the time to shepherd, and you will increase the probability of retaining your people. If you drive them instead of shepherding them, you will eventually drive them away, so skillfully shepherd and lead the team.

Leaders also give attention to detail and understand its value. However, detail does not derail them from reaching the goal. The analysis of data is necessary to make the wisest decisions possible. But leaders avoid paralysis from analysis, and move forward, testing the waters as they go. Leaders lead, whether they are liked or not. Their motivation is to execute the plan, not to appease the people. Leaders may be branded as insensitive because of their untiring focus on progress, excellence, and execution. But this is the role of the leader. There is no need for leaders to apologize for leading. Leaders shepherd and lead.

If you shepherd with a heart of integrity and lead with your God-given skills, then you are a leader worth following. Aspire to this level of leadership. This is the leadership style of David and Jesus.

JUNE 13

FRESH FRUIT

They will still bear fruit in old age,
they will stay fresh and green.
PSALM 92:14

A fresh heart and mind feed a healthy attitude. Fresh people, like fresh fruit, are appealing, delicious, satisfying, and good for you. No one wants to be around someone who is disengaged. Fresh thinking does not necessarily mean new information. It is, however, the ability to understand and apply truth in a way. Freshness allows you to see things for the first time, as if traveling to a new land.

Make a point to stay fresh in all areas of life. When you stop learning, you stop growing. When you stop growing, you become stale. Take the time to engage with the aged. Maybe calendar a day with a sage who has a proven track record of faithfulness to freshness. Take notes on their thoughts then prayerfully apply them to your stage of life. These wise men and women have aged well. The outward signs of age can belie a fresh heart beating with a youthful attitude. Focus on those who have "fruit that remains" (John 15:16 KJV).

A fresh outlook on life is fed by a mind that devours books, sermons, and small group interaction. You stay fresh when you give yourself the freedom to think outside the box. God stays sacred, but even certain beliefs about Him change for the better around fresh thinking. This discovery of truth in a fresh way energizes and compels you to become better.

Your age is your advantage, so leverage your years for the Lord. Invite people into your life of learning. Allow them to sit on the lawn of your life and learn what works and doesn't work for you. Old age is designed by God to be your home stretch of achievement and influence. Therefore, take care of your body so you can be in a healthy state of mind and heart. Physical fitness is an important part of staying fresh and green for God. You are much better positioned to invest in others when you are not preoccupied with your own health issues. However, even in your weakness of body you can have a fruitful life. Don't let your illness cause you to retreat from people. They may come to bless you, but this is your opportunity to bless them.

You may be frail of body, but let others see the love of God exhibited through your fruitful life. Though your body is fading, your faith is accelerating. So stay fruitful and fresh until you see Him.

WORLDWIDE RECOGNITION

Give praise to the LORD, proclaim his name;
make known among the nations what he has done.
PSALM 105:1

God deserves and desires worldwide recognition. The Holy Spirit ignites revivals in North and South America. He reigns as the Almighty in Australia. His influence reaches Christians in China. He is Lord over Europe, Russia, the Middle East, the Arctic, and Antarctica. There is no corner of the globe that does not display the glory of God. His great works are without boundaries and bring glory to His name. Indeed, His wondrous works include physical healing of cancer, tuberculosis, heart disease, and leprosy. He delivers addicts from drugs and alcohol, and He still makes the lame to walk and the blind to see.

His fingerprints are all over creation. He is the Creator of craters, sunsets, sunrises, and hurricanes. He makes a sedate and silent volcano erupt with hot, orange lava. He creates parrots, monkeys, lions, tigers, elephants, rhinos, and camels. Moreover, He gives a businessman the brains for innovation and creation. He brings a smile to a face and forges forgiveness in a heart. He answers prayer. His works are wonderful and worldwide. God is a doer. He is not stuck in some theological vacuum waiting for things to happen. He makes things happen in accordance with His will. Nations come and go but He remains the same, ever working for His glory.

The world is waiting for a reminder of God. He has put it in their hearts and He has painted it on the canvas of creation (Romans 1:19-20). He has also combed the conscience of man with His moral code and sense of right and wrong. Your role, as a follower of Jesus, is to be Jesus to the nations. As a glorious hymn proclaims, "Bless the Lord, O my soul and all that is within me bless His holy name. He has done great things, He has done great things, He has done great things: bless His holy name." His truth reaches to the vilest of hearts and the remotest of villages. Now is the time to use your discretionary time and money for large doses of global discipleship and evangelism. Leave a legacy for your Lord that engages generations to come and creates cultures of character.

Pray for the nations, go to the nations, serve the nations, teach and train the nations. And say to the nations that God has done great things and will do great things.

MAN OF PRAYER

In return for my friendship they accuse me, but I am a man of prayer.
PSALM 109:4

A man of prayer prays. It is his first line of defense, not an afterthought. It is conversing with Christ and is not just asking God for goodies and guarantees. The man realizes that God is in control and that His wisdom is needed for life and work. He avoids self-inflicted problems because he prays first.

A prayerful person may not have silver and gold to give, but he can give his supplications (Acts 3:6). A man of prayer does not simply talk about praying. On the contrary, with a seriousness of purpose and responsibility, he stops what he is doing and lifts to heaven the concerns of the one requesting prayer. His prayer is not stale but fresh.

Start by getting on your knees for five minutes each morning. Prayerful posture is important. His stature is humble and dependent. Humble yourself daily before your heavenly Father. Lay face down on the floor, if necessary. Then get up and consider making a prayer list.

This role is not reserved for the super righteous. It is for adulterers, liars, and murderers like David (Psalm 51). A man of prayer is still a man in recovery from sin. Sin does not cease to hound the man who prays, but it drives him to pray; then sin's influence is stunted in the face of the man of prayer. It is hard to sin while you pray. There is accountability to God that bolsters the man of prayer in his everyday life.

Being a man of continual prayer is a discreet lifestyle. (1 Thessalonians 5:17). It becomes a habit of life, like eating and sleeping. Prayer is not an elective; it is a required course. Moreover, the man of prayer cannot be pigeonholed as to his behavior and speech. He comes in all shapes and sizes, depending on his God-given temperament. He is humorous and humble; he is loud, and he is quiet; he is spontaneous, and he is methodical; he is creative, and he is concrete; he is eloquent, and he is simple. However, there is one thing he is not: he is neither proud nor arrogant. People are his pleasure and heaven is his home, where he checks in often. Jesus is his "go-to man."

Worship, thanksgiving, praise, and adoration permeate the prayers of a man of prayer. A man of prayer prays.

JUNE 16

WIFE SUPPORT

"Surely all the wealth that God took away from our father belongs to us and our children. So do whatever God has told you."
GENESIS 31:16

Husbands need the support of their wives. Of course, it works both ways, as the wife needs to feel the support of her husband; but for a man, support is huge. A God-fearing husband knows the Lord has placed him in a position of leadership. It is overwhelming sometimes because he can feel squeezed by the pressures of life. The last thing a husband needs to feel is distance or distrust from his wife.

Encouragement may be the only thing that is preventing some men from giving up, so do not underestimate the strength of your wife's support. We are not as self-sufficient as we may seem. On the outside we may seem invincible, but on the inside, we are needy and desperate for recognition and validation. Thank her for her encouraging words that help build you up. Let her know that her affirmation means the world to you.

As a husband, it is imperative in God's sight that you lovingly lead your wife and children. You may feel your wife is more qualified, smarter, and more spiritual. These all may be very true. However, God's plan is for you to take the position of leadership in the home. She is looking for you to do whatever God has told you. Prayer is your mantle of responsibility. See it as a privilege to enjoy and not an obligation to tolerate. She will trust you more and more as you remain trustworthy. It takes time to overcome a track record of distrust. Remain in the process of listening to God, following His commands, and then leading your family to do the same. There are days you don't feel like leading or even listening to the Lord. Life can be overwhelming. It can get you down to the point of wanting to walk away from all your responsibilities. But by grace, you carry on in your commitment to Christ, your wife, and your children.

It is foolish to flee from your responsibilities as a husband and father. Fools give up, but God has you in this position so you can learn about Him and His plan for you and your family. Do what He says with passion and abandon. It may mean moving to another country. It may mean downsizing for a season. It may be organizing a family vacation. It may mean planning the calendar and budget for the upcoming year. Men, love leads.

Love follows God and leads his family. Give your wife the assurance that you listen to and follow God. She will respect you and trust you for this.

HEART TURNER

"He will turn the hearts of the parents to their children, and the hearts of the children to their parents; or else I will come and strike the land with total destruction."

MALACHI 4:6

God is a heart turner. His influence can reach out to and change any hard-hearted person. He can turn the hearts of kings; He can turn the hearts of parents; He can turn the hearts of children. God is a spiritual cardiologist, clearing the arteries of the hard-hearted. His caring ablation can clear the heart of its rebellion. He can even perform a transplant and replace the old heart with a brand new one. This radical surgery is, of course, conversion to Christ. Someone has a good heart if God turns it.

Your heart is in the hand of God. This is the ideal place for it to rest. He guards it. He cleanses it. He turns it. A heart in the hand of God is a defeat for the devil, who has to try to pry back the fingers of your heavenly Father to get to your heart. Give God your heart and watch Him turn it toward Himself and to His will. God's work of heart is beautiful and breathtaking. Whether it's a young, innocent heart or a seasoned, guilt-ridden heart, He makes it into a healthy heart. Give your heart to God and trust Him to turn it into what is best for you.

Trust Him with your heart, for He already knows its intentions. He understands it better than you do, so allow Him to diagnose your motives and prescribe His character. Your heart is stronger in Him. Once He turns your heart toward Him, you are in a position of trust. You can trust Him to turn the hearts of others. A person cannot turn another person's heart, but God can. Pray to God and trust Him to turn the heart of your child back to Him and back to you. The same can be said of your parents' hearts. Trust God to turn their hearts to Him, then watch their hearts long to be with you and your children.

If your marriage is struggling, God can heal your wounded heart and turn the heart of your wife back to God and back to you. If a friend has walked away, He can change the heart of your friend on a dime. The heart of your work associate can soften. Pray for him or her. Trust God to turn the hearts of those who may be miles away. These are the hearts that God turns for His glory.

Trust Him with your heart and the hearts of others. He is a heart turner.

JUNE 18

FAITHFUL FATHER

A father to the fatherless, a defender of widows, is God in his holy dwelling.
PSALM 68:5

Most people long for a faithful father who will feed them when they are hungry, love them when they are lonely, and care for them when they are crying. They long for a dad who will listen to them when they wonder, encourage them when they are discouraged, and discipline them when they do wrong. Some fathers do well at being a faithful father and others do not. Some are extremely successful, and others fail miserably. Fortunately, God is your model of a faithful father. Your heavenly Father fills the gaps left by your earthly father; He is your faithful Father.

Your heavenly Father deserves your respect and commands your love. Jesus said to pray, "Our Father in heaven, hallowed be your name" (Matthew 6:9). God is a father who is totally trustworthy. You never have to doubt God's Word. What He says He means, and what He means He does. Your Father in heaven will not let you down on earth. Now, sometimes it doesn't feel as if He's faithful. There are times you don't have answers for the questions that gnaw at your heart and confuse your mind. It may be that He is speaking but you are not listening. It may be that He is silent because He wants to grow your trust in Him. He will tell you what to do in time, so while you wait, become better.

Be a lifetime learner of faithful fathering. Each season of fathering is different. What worked in the last stage of your child's life needs to be adapted for the next stage. By faith, be flexible. As infants, they need your gentle touch. As children, they need your patient instruction. As teenagers, they need your example of love and forgiveness. As adults, they need your wisdom and friendship. In all seasons, they need your time and trust. Above all else, look to your heavenly Father as the baseline for your behavior. Being a faithful father does not mean perfection, but it does mean you depend on the Perfect One. You lean on the Lord for His loving care, so you can extend the same.

Because of your faithful heavenly Father, you can be a faithful earthly father. Invite Him to love on you and lead you into faithfulness.

PUSH BACK

I was pushed back and about to fall, but the Lord helped me.
The Lord is my strength and my defense; he has become my salvation.
PSALM 118:13-14

Life can be a sequence of pushbacks. People push back; projects push back; progress pushes back; circumstances push back. Sometimes, it seems that everything and everyone is pushing back. How you respond will be the difference between living in peace or turmoil. It is very wise to walk in lockstep with the Lord during a pushback period. Let Him be your help and strength. You will drive yourself crazy trying to determine all the reasons around the pushback. Instead, let God handle the people who are pushing back. They have their reasons, noble or ignoble. God will judge a person's motive, not you.

Pushbacks buy you time to develop a better relationship and to craft a more accurate plan. A pushback is not a failure, but a time to regroup and do better. More often than not, a pushback should not be taken personally. You don't know everything that is going on, personally or professionally. This pushback may be for your own protection; it is what is needed to guarantee God's best for you. He works His will despite—and through—a pushback. It is disheartening and sometimes frustrating when someone close to you goes back on a promise. They were sincere in the moment, but now have cold feet because they truly understand the commitment. You may need to push back on them and ask them to reconsider.

Prayerfully orchestrated pushbacks are powerful ways to progress in God's will. Your "no" may very well be what's needed to transition to your "yes." This is the wisdom of pushing back. It disciplines you to wait on God. Why redo things in the future, when you can push back now and start off on the right foot?

Relationships void of pushbacks are fragile and unpredictable. However, relationships peppered with pushbacks are resilient and authentic. This is how you get to know each other. So receive pushbacks from the Lord. A gentle pushback from the Holy Spirit in the beginning is much better than a shove by the Spirit later down the road. Therefore, be prayerful and discern whether God is pushing back or pulling forward. In either case, Christ can be trusted.

Receive and give pushbacks as part of God's process. He is your help and strength. Above all else, know that God is working during your times of pushback.

INVITE ACCOUNTABILITY

Let a righteous man strike me—it is a kindness;
let him rebuke me—it is oil on my head. My head will not
refuse it, for my prayer will still be against the deeds of evildoers.
PSALM 141:5

Invited accountability is the most effective kind. Accountability is like prayer; many talk about it but few practice it. You know you are accountable when you have submitted to someone about a particular issue.

It is normally better to submit to two or three people so you gain the benefit of diverse perspectives and temperaments. You need some accountability partners who are honest about their own temptations. It is hard to not benefit from the accountability of someone who has been there. Give them the whole truth and nothing but the truth. See their loving accountability as an investment in your life. They are taking the time to walk with you so you can change destructive habits and avoid making harmful decisions in the future. Pray for accountability from smart, discerning people with impeccable integrity. Above all else, remain teachable and do what they say.

There are two forms of accountability: preemptive accountability and deliverance accountability. You may need some of both. Preemptive accountability is protection against pride. It is building an arsenal of actions aimed at avoiding adultery. It understands how to nip anger in the bud before it raises its destructive head. It is developing good financial habits before you are blessed with abundance. Financial accountability keeps you honest with a little so you can be trusted with much. If you don't tithe while earning a small amount, odds are you won't with a large amount. Preemptive accountability is looking ahead at trouble brewing on the horizon and adjusting before it makes landfall. "The prudent sees danger and takes refuge, but the simple keep going and pay the penalty" (Proverbs 22:3). It is proactive in prayer and courageous in wise behavior, which makes adjustments in the face of approaching disasters.

Deliverance accountability, on the other hand, is specific in moving you out of a current crisis. It is action oriented. It is an intervention of tough love. This level of accountability is more than likely your last chance for change. So, wise is the man who invites loving accountability early into their life. Make it a normal part of your life early on, and you will avoid crisis management later.

Better is your accountability to the Almighty when you are accountable to those He trusts. Therefore, send out your accountability invitations today. Some will RSVP and some will not. Go with those God sends you.

JUNE 21

INTELLIGENT DESIGN

He determines the number of the stars and calls them each by name. Great is our Lord and mighty in power; his understanding has no limit.
PSALM 147:4-5

God is the intelligence behind the design of all creation. The creation of space is His design. Every galaxy, universe, star, planet, meteor, and asteroid is a result of His intricate design. He designed the craters on the moon so we could compare it to cheese. He designed the rings around Saturn so we could marvel at its majestic beauty. The tilt of the earth's axis He designed so it would sustain life but not spin out of control. He positioned the sun at just the right distance from Earth so it would warm but not destroy. He knew all the planets' gravitational pull and orchestrated one big simultaneous swirl around the sun. The flickering lights in the sky, the Big Dipper and Little Dipper and the North Star, are all embedded in the intelligence of His design.

Intelligent design is rational and logical. The Lord's intelligence is astounding and all encompassing. It cannot be measured or completely understood, but it can be adored and praised. Intelligent design is proof of His profound power and might. The pure snowcapped peaks of the highest mountains point in praise toward their divine designer in heaven. Their rugged stone faces are a reminder of the rock-solid dependability of your Lord and Savior, Jesus Christ.

Anyone who has ever scaled an Everest-like mountain knows the exhilaration tangibly encountering God's creation. When you engage with the intelligence behind the design of creation, you begin to dance with its Creator, for intelligent design is not meant to be an end in itself. It is not just a lot of impressive scientific facts and statistics, but it is God's communication to us about Himself. Indeed, Jesus was enamored with the intelligence of His father's design as a metaphor for life. He spoke of the birds of the air, the lilies of the valley, and the stature of man. He described the Holy Spirit as a calm and unseeing wind. The new birth was contrasted with physical birth. Above all else, Jesus was the "Word" in the beginning with God, installing intelligent design throughout all creation (John 1:1-3). Intelligent design is God's invitation to faith. Anyone serious about his religion and equally serious about intellectual honesty will trawl the depths of God's design. The sincere search for truth will most likely lead them to Christ. Sincere seekers of a Savior through science will not be disappointed but amazed by engaging with the Creator Himself. Use intelligent design to galvanize your faith and give your evangelistic effort credibility.

The truly intelligent invite Jesus Christ in as the interior designer of their soul. His outward and inward design is matchless and magnificent.

FIRST UNDERSTAND

Fools find no pleasure in understanding
but delight in airing their own opinions.
PROVERBS 18:2

Fools are quick to offer a cure before they understand the illness. That can be a deadly tendency. Offering medicine to someone who may have an allergic reaction could prove fatal. Anyone can offer an opinion, and fools love airing theirs. It is entertaining to them, for they delight in talking about anything, as long as there is an opportunity to talk. However, a babbling fool can get you into trouble; so don't be impressed by his words. Instead, measure his words by making sure he understands you and the topic of your concern.

Look for wisdom from someone who looks you in the eyes with empathy. Take the time to validate their ideas from a variety of respected sources. Invite influence from those who draw their wisdom from the Word of God and avoid people who talk too much. It is impossible to understand without listening, for an unsure heart does not need a quick fix, but a listening ear. Those seeking wisdom need someone who listens with understanding.

So, be very cautious in what you say and how you communicate your care. Ask questions like, "Why do you want to do this?" "What does your spouse think?" "Is this what you really want to do?" or "What do you think God is telling you?" Additionally, you can't go wrong by offering prayer support. The most appropriate counsel for you to offer may be a prayer with the person seeking wisdom. Ask God to give them His divine counsel and directive. The wisdom of God, obtained in prayer, is the most valuable and accurate advice. Your advice may not sound as eloquent as a fool's self-serving soliloquy, but it is much more soothing for the soul.

Lastly, do not seek to impress others with your wise words. Instead, gain their trust and respect by truly seeking to understand their hopes and dreams. Learn what makes them afraid and what gives them peace. Find out where happiness and contentment reside for them. This level of intimate understanding is a microscope that focuses in on the DNA of their personality, temperament, and past experiences that determine present behavior. Wait to offer opinions until you thoroughly understand the person or situation. It's okay to wait. Wisdom comes to those who seek understanding first. Therefore, pray to see others as God does. Look for the good, and don't be naïve about the bad.

But when all is said and done, ask first what God thinks. Listen to Him, for the Lord's insight is the best type of "understanding."

AVOID THE ANGRY

Do not make friends with a hot-tempered person, do not associate with one easily angered, or you may learn their ways and get yourself ensnared.
PROVERBS 22:24-25

Avoid the angry and do not make friends with those who are easily angered. They are undependable and hard to get along with. You may be the object of someone's anger simply because you happen to be around them when they snap. No one can predict what an angry person will do next. The source of their anger may be as simple as not getting their way, or it may be a string of broken expectations all the way back to a wounded childhood.

Your role is not to fix them or to be their therapist. However, the times you do have to associate with them can be an opportunity for you to model peace and calm. But be very careful; do not become like them. Their impatient ways may become your impatient ways. Their rude tendencies may become your rude tendencies. Their sarcasm may become your sarcasm. Their blowups may become your blowups.

Yes, the angry can change, but real change will only occur as God heals their heart. Unless forgiveness penetrates an angry heart, it is destined to remain the same. Hard and stubborn is a heart driven by anger. Unless anger is gently unwound by grace and love, it may unleash its furor suddenly or may constantly simmer just beneath the surface. The heavenly Father can squeeze out the venom of vengeance. The love and acceptance of God can flush out foul language and faithless living. To be loved by God is to not remain angry, for the Lord's love and anger cannot coexist. Unconditional love that is received melts the heart of anger.

Some angry people are hard to avoid because you live with them. What now? You certainly pray for and with them. People driven by anger are never content; nothing you do will make them happy. Their anger may subside momentarily, but you will remain on pins and needles, waiting for them to erupt at any moment. Help them to talk about why they have feelings of anger. What makes them mad at themselves? Unresolved anger is a time bomb waiting to explode.

If you're the one who's angry, a safe environment to talk through your heated emotions is a great place to start on the path to peace. Channel your anger into proper passions that are sanctified by your Savior. Be angry at sin, while forgiving yourself and others. Avoid the angry and relinquish your own anger to your heavenly Father above.

Friendship with the angry creates angst. Friendship with the forgiven—and healed—promotes peace. Go with peace.

JUNE 24

AVOID STRIFE

It is to one's honor to avoid strife;
but every fool is quick to quarrel.
PROVERBS 20:3

Avoid strife. It is a bitter conflict, and it can become heated and violent dissension. Strife results in a struggle, fight, or quarrel. It is the opposite of living in peace. It can also be the result of someone not getting their way or feeling they weren't heard or understood. It may be rooted in old-fashioned selfishness, but strife is more than an occasional disagreement.

A fool looks for opportunities to disagree and engage in conflict. This is one way a fool feels important. He is able to get the attention of another by being a nuisance. A nuisance is in need of recognition. His insecurity finds security in strife. Strife is sport to the foolish. Any fool can find an excuse to engage in an argument.

Avoidance of strife does not mean you should not confront when there are disagreements and concerns. Honesty is important to healthy relational development. Talking through misunderstandings is not strife, but smart. Strife, on the other hand, produces chronic chaos and confusion. There are no moments of peace for the carrier of strife. Life seems to go from one crisis to the next. Foolish strivers position themselves against the world because they don't know how to trust God and others. Their understanding of reality is skewed and jaded. Therefore, remove those who inflict the pain of strife, and then peace and calm will reign in their place. It is honorable to avoid strife. This is especially true for a man. Strife-free living is a badge of honor that most men would enjoy wearing. For a man, avoiding strife is the honorable thing to do. Strife strikes at his manhood and respect. He feels disrespected by the fool who is always discontented, disagreeable, and in disarray. It is all about honor.

You can have mature discussions that address disagreements in an honorable and respectful way. But there is no need to foolishly feed in a frenzy of uncontrollable emotions. Fools jump to conclusions without understanding the context of the discussion. This is dishonoring to those who desire not to flail away in a cycle of strife. Strife can be avoided with patience and prayer. Truly seek to serve and understand the other person, first and foremost. Put others' needs above your hurt feelings or your need to be right. Strife will cease with a humble response, but it will increase in the face of pride. Peace is the fruit of humility, while pride is the weed of strife.

Put strife to rest with radical forgiveness and unconditional love.
Start by honoring the one stuck in strife, for honor reduces a ruckus.

JUNE 25

MIDLIFE CRISIS

"Meaningless! Meaningless!" says the Teacher.
"Utterly meaningless! Everything is meaningless."
ECCLESIASTES 1:2

Midlife is a natural time to do a life audit. This is the season to do a performance review of your passion and your life's productivity. You measure how well you have amassed money and acquired assets. You grade the success of your life on your position in the workplace, your educational advancement, your character development, and the quality of your relationships, especially those in your family. Midlife is a time for reflection, regrouping, and recalibrating big goals. But a midlife crisis comes from meaningless living—from scoffing at God's plan and purpose and replacing it with your own.

Proper purpose precludes meaningless living. Yet, every day, men meander into a midlife crisis. They think midlife is a time for release from responsibility, but it is meant to be a time of terrific transition, not terrible torture. It is created for celebration, not regret. Midlife is meaningful if rooted in the purpose of God and a future hope in Him. "'For I know the plans I have for you,' declares the Lord, 'plans to prosper you and not to harm you, plans to give you hope and a future'" (Jeremiah 29:11).

Maybe you did live the first half of your life without purpose, but you were successful by the world's standards. You may have more wealth than you ever dreamed of, but your spouse and children do not really know you. You are relationally poor. Or maybe you have been a faithful Christian, but you always seem to encounter bad things. Christianity feels like a farce; it is not what was promised to you when you started out in gleeful obedience. But now is not the time to bail on God. Yes, you may be tired, and even sick, but stick with your Savior.

Life will be meaningful if you travel with your Master. Your real midlife meaning needs to come from Him, so surrender and you will see success as God defines success. If adventure is what you crave, then pray. And if the Holy Spirit gives you the green light, then take your spouse overseas and serve the poor. Now, that's adventure. Meaning comes from selfless living. So run toward God and your family, not away from them. Make midlife your best season of life yet. Live it well driven by your God-given purpose and your future hope.

Allow your midlife crisis to draw you close to Christ. Moreover, enthusiastically embrace eternity and enjoy a midlife celebration. Meaningful! Meaningful! Life with the Lord is meaningful!

RESPONSIBLE GRACE

What shall we say, then? Shall we go on sinning
so that grace may increase? By no means!
We died to sin; how can we live in it any longer?
ROMANS 6:1-2

Grace is a gift from God, one that requires responsible and wise stewardship—not a license to sin, but permission to live. Grace is all about living for God and walking with Him. It engages with eternity by approaching God's throne with gratitude, awe, and boldness. God's grace is a guarantee of eternal life. It is absolutely amazing because Christ collateralizes it.

There has never been a shortage of your Savior's grace. No group or individual has ever made a run on heaven's grace account. You can go to the bank with God's grace. It is as everlasting as the Lord. However, though unlimited in supply, it may be the most underused resource available.

People miss grace when they thrash around and stumble about in their own strength. They apply bad theology. They believe in salvation by grace through faith but then drift into living in their own strength. Demons must chuckle when they observe Christians applying dead works. Working to earn God's favor after receiving salvation is as futile as it was before salvation. Do not fall into the trap of graceless living, for grace is God's remedy for the self-indulgent. Grace values community with people and communing with Christ. There is a spirit of acceptance and peace with those who often receive and apply God's grace.

Grace means you have a stewardship of wise choices to manage for the Lord. It gives you permission to be free in Christ, but your freedom is for Him. His kingdom agenda is what drives grace. Grace integrates all of life around faith. Christ does not compartmentalize the sacred from the secular. Grace includes; it doesn't exclude. It discloses rather than hides. Sin is subservient to your Savior's grace. Grace gives you the perspective and power for forgiveness and honesty. It is the delivery channel of truth. Grace is your excuse for extending forgiveness and second and third chances—and more—to culprits. Indeed, as you extend grace, you are more likely to receive grace. Be responsible with grace, and you will be trusted with more.

Grace saved you from sin, so don't go back to your pre-grace condition. Because of grace, you are free from sin, not free to sin. Therefore, be a responsible and gracious follower of Christ.

CHRISTIAN CELEBRITIES

There are quarrels among you. What I mean is this: One of you says, "I follow Paul"; another, "I follow Apollo"; another, "I follow Cephas"; still another, "I follow Christ." Is Christ divided? Was Paul crucified for you? Were you baptized in the name of Paul?

1 CORINTHIANS 1:11-13

Christian celebrities sometimes create quarreling factions. But followers of Christ are not on theological teams competing to win. There is no competition in the kingdom of God, yet human nature yearns for a hero. People want someone they can see who stands for excellence in eternal matters. This admiration for those who are extremely gifted in teaching, speaking, writing, and leadership is not bad in and of itself. But factions occur when people view their leader as superior to all other servants of the Lord. They get caught up in the man and look down on others who are not as "successful." It is immaturity that promotes a person instead of the Lord.

There is an ugly co-dependence that is created by celebrity worship. The line between leader and Lord becomes blurred when followers begin to deify a gifted man or woman. It becomes cult worship when Christian celebrities are not challenged or questioned. A pastor is called to equip the saints and exalt the Savior, while awe is reserved for Almighty God. You help your pastor by keeping him off a pedestal. Pedestals produce pride. Honor him, yes; worship him, no. The accolades of man are cheap substitutes for God's eternal rewards.

Congregants who worship and fear God are to first walk away from Sunday sermons in awe of God, not enamored or entertained by man. If the purpose of worship becomes engagement with a person's personality to the exclusion of eternal accountability, a destructive and dysfunctional environment is brewing. Teaching and leadership are meant to be catalysts for Christocentric living. A wise leader makes sure that worship services become launching pads for truth, as he points people to Jesus. Therefore, do not crave the role of Christian celebrity. It shows a lack of maturity. Maturity means you decrease, and He increases (John 3:30). Deflect any attention that is reserved for the Almighty. Authentic leaders, teachers, and pastors pour themselves out for Christ's sake. They use subtle acts of service—such as feeding the poor—to keep themselves humble.

Your Master is the main attraction, so celebrate Christ through worship, prayer, Bible study, and service. He is your Christian celebrity.

SELF-DECEPTION

If we claim to be without sin, we deceive ourselves and the truth is not in us. If we confess our sins, he is faithful and just and will forgive us our sins and purify us from all unrighteousness.
1 JOHN 1:8-9

Self-deception is scary and subtle, for it can lead people to live a lie. It feeds pride and strokes ego, creating a sense of superiority. You become convinced that you can outsmart others—and even God—because you are more successful, more educated, more experienced, or more winsome and attractive. Self-deceived individuals act as if they listen to the advice of others but, in reality, have already predetermined a course of action. They only listen to what they want to hear, so they deceive and are deceived. Ironically, they do their best work with sincerity and a smile, and there is no remorse, repentance, or any hint of confession.

The self-deceived can justify their ways with the best of them. It's always someone else's fault. The self-deceived look for the "speck of sawdust" in the eyes of others, while ignoring the "plank" in their own eyes (Matthew 7:3). They don't take responsibility for their actions and attitudes. They are motivated by the approval of those in charge, and they get nervous when someone gets close to the leader for fear of losing their influence. Self-deception is a sick condition. It chokes the soul; it quenches the Spirit; it strangles love; it sucks the life from relationships. Self-deception is destined to stay in control unless there is a reckoning with sin. When you face the reality of sin in your life, you take the first step in slaying self-deception.

Confess pride, fear, self-centeredness, or self-righteousness. Start by being honest with yourself. There is a common thread in all of your relational conflicts, so start by looking in the mirror. Ask God to escort self-deception out the door of your mind and heart. Invite the Holy Spirit to reveal anything unclean in your attitude and actions. This is hard and humbling, but it is necessary in order to expose the enemy of self-deception. When you move away from the darkness of self-deception, you move into the light of God's revelation and love.

So, set yourself free from the bondage of sin's self-deception. Confess and repent of your sin to your Lord and Savior, Jesus. Make your confession complete by asking a small community of believers whom you trust to hold you accountable.

Confession allows you to see clearly, and your perception is pure. Best of all, you are free indeed because He has set you free from sin and self.

JUNE 29

LIVE IN THE MOMENT

All generations will call me blessed, for the Mighty One has done great things for me—holy is his name.

LUKE 1:48-49

By God's grace, you can master living in the moment. Mary did it. She trusted God with an impossible outcome. Birthing a baby conceived by the Holy Spirit challenged her categories. It forced her to ponder. She chose to be with her heavenly Father in the here and now. Nothing would keep her from living with the Lord and for the Lord in this defining moment.

She could have lived in the past, worried over the rampant rumors of her perceived unfaithfulness. She was pregnant out of wedlock. She could have lived in the future, paralyzed by fear over what Joseph might do. He might have deserted her. He might have divorced her. He might have denied her. But when all was said and done, she refrained from living in the past or worrying about the future. She chose to live in the moment.

Mary lived in the moment because she trusted her Lord with issues out of her control. She could not control what other people thought or what other people might do. Therefore, she drank in the present like a tall glass of homemade lemonade on a hot summer day. Living in the moment fed her faith and satisfied her soul. Her son, Jesus, would save the people from their sins, and He would also save her. He is with you in the moment too, so you can live in the moment.

Living in the moment is what the Lord longs for you to do. He knows that living in the moment engages you with His will, as it is lived out in the present. So if you are with your children, be with them. Laugh with them, cry with them, listen to them, play with them, and pray for them. Lock eyes with your little ones and be with them. So turn off your phone, shut down the computer, and most important, discipline your mind to be present. Bend your mind to listen well and honor others with your purposeful presence. Your undivided attention in the moment says you love and care. Trust God with all the impossible outcomes that await you. You have this one moment and then it is gone forever. So be engaged today and be with the ones you love. Live in the moment, and other things will take care of themselves. Do this one thing, and you will live the life God intended for you.

Master living in the moment with the discipline and love of your Master. Seize the moment for your Savior, for other people, and for yourself.

PART COMPANY

"Is not the whole land before you? Let's part company. If you go to the left, I'll go to the right; if you go to the right, I'll go to the left."
GENESIS 13:9

Do not be afraid to part company. It may be sorrowful in the short term, but in the long term it's God's opportunity to help you grow and mature. So be responsible. Do not leave them high and dry or burn your bridges. Leave on good terms. You will need each other one day. You want to be able to look each other in the eye and smile at social events.

A healthy organization is unified behind one leader, and only one leadership style can dominate. Disagreements and confusion are inevitable when two people are trying to lead with two totally different philosophies of leadership. These differing styles can complement each other in a positive way, but only one can be in charge. Only one person can ultimately make the decisions or there will be quarrelling and hostile conflict. Arguments will erupt among the leaders and their factions. Therefore, be prepared to prayerfully part company.

You can be proud of your accomplishments in a particular place, but now it is time to move on to God's new assignment. You have developed your role at work into a mature position. Now is the time for a new person to come in and build on your documented processes and procedures. Your service is for a season. Furthermore, there are not enough resources or relationships to support your God-given vision going forward.

Lastly, transition requires trust. Consider embracing change as your friend, not your enemy. Invite in the unknown. See it as God's will to make Himself known to you in a fresh and compelling way. You will get to know Him in ways you've never experienced. Stay unselfish by giving more than is expected. Your attitude of honor will not go unnoticed. Of course, make sure the Lord is clearly calling you to something, and you are not just running away from something or someone. Do your homework. Let this new career opportunity pull you in; don't push to make it happen. Be patient. Prayer and patience are your greatest assets during changing times. Part company and watch Christ work. Part company, and everyone wins. Part company in a process that lets God get the glory.

**Part company with the relationship intact.
Above all else, part company prayerfully,
absent of pride and ego. E-G-O: Edges-God-Out.**

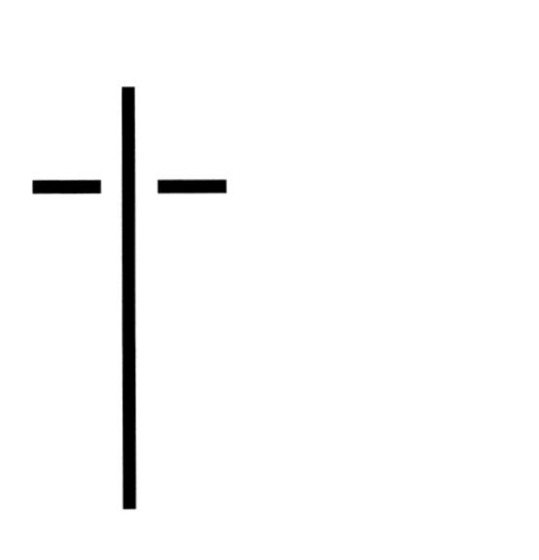

JULY 1

APPOINTMENTS FOR LOVE

Let us go early to the vineyards to see if the vines have budded, if their blossoms have opened, and if the pomegranates are in bloom—there I will give you my love.

SONG OF SOLOMON 7:12

When you make marriage a priority, the other important things that clamor for your attention become secondary and supportive. This is wisdom. Work, children, parents, money, hobbies, friends, volunteering, selfish desires, and life in general can masquerade as marriage competitors. So how can you transform them into complements to your marriage?

A marriage void of calendared appointments is a candidate for indifference with intimacy. If, however, you are intentional in your marriage appointments, your union will flourish with freshness. Coexistence does not create intimacy in marriage, but intentionality—and getting to know one another deeply—does. Romance is the result of regular real time together in communication, care, and understanding.

Therefore, make routine appointments to love your wife. Pull out your calendars and create a time just for the two of you. The best gift you give to your children, next to faith in God, is a healthy marriage. So, make appointments for love. Emotional love may be unfiltered listening; learn about the fears and fantasies of each other. Together you can enjoy a hobby, read a book, or watch a movie together. Love on her relationally with written correspondence and acts of service or demonstrate your love by working on a project around the house. Make your wife feel secure by being trustworthy and respectful and listen intently to her struggles and disappointments.

Yes, even physical intimacy needs to be planned and prepared for; let any spontaneous rendezvous be a bonus. It is part of God's game plan for a husband and wife (1 Corinthians 7:3-5). Romance one another with a date night by dressing up and smelling good, as if it were a grand occasion. Woo each other with the fire and excitement of youth. Make sure to calendar time where you have an occasional overnight together or a week of vacation for just the two of you. Use the calendar to create emotional and physical intimacy. The Bible teaches there is a time for everything, even a time to love (Ecclesiastes 3:8).

Your spouse will love you better if she loves Jesus more than you. Indeed, make appointments for love and you will love!

REBELLIOUS CHILDREN

Hear me, you heavens! Listen, earth! For the Lord has spoken: "I reared children and brought them up, but they have rebelled against me."
ISAIAH 1:2

Rebellious children can drive you to your knees, for they don't seem to care or concern themselves with their parents or the things of God. It is all about them, period. Prodigal young people can keep you up at night with worry and fear. Many were sweet and behaved appropriately. Their compliance was stellar, for the most part, and their hearts were honest and open. Now everything seems closed.

This is not the time to write off your rebellious child. Give them up to God and pray the Lord will use their sin to show them the emptiness of self-centered living, but do not shut the door on the relationship. While pride keeps the relational gap wide, humility builds bridges.

All communication may seem shut down and restricted. Perhaps if they need something, they will break the silence momentarily. Do whatever it takes to initiate contact and communication. Write when no one writes back. Call when no one calls back. Pray for your son when he is hell-bent on going his own way.

Do not fall into the trap of fighting rebellion with rebellion. Hardening your heart is rebellion. Not backing down is rebellion. Rejection is rebellion. Work with God during this rebellious season in your child's life, not against Him. Grow in your dependency on God and avoid blaming Him and others. Do not let yourself become bitter and feel hopeless. Instead, search your own heart.

Build the relationship; do not tear it down. Go as a family to a Christ-centered counselor. Pray for a mentor to influence your young person in wisdom and respect. Pray that God brings your daughter back to Himself, no matter what it takes. This rebellious spirit is probably for a season. Pray for them to come to the end of themselves and turn to Him. Pray for them to be influenced by other God-fearing followers of Jesus.

Be patient. Pray. Accept them where they are and watch God work. His timing may take longer, but His work is thorough and worth the wait. Don't beat yourself up over your children's behavior. Allow God to love on you so you can love on them.

Let go of your anger and accept your heavenly Father's embrace. Acceptance squashes rebellion.

BE DECISIVE

"Make up your mind," Moab says. "Render a decision."
ISAIAH 16:3

Decisions can be as elusive as your shadow. They can haunt you from behind, or they can lead you from out front. God gives you the counsel and the wisdom, but you make the decision. No one else can make the decision for you; God wants you to make it. This is your responsibility and opportunity.

You may be cautious because a similar experience in the past did not work out so well. But decisions are not designed to be delayed forever. They are meant to drive you toward God's purpose and plan for your life. He allows you to make decisions that determine His future for you. Say yes or no, but do not procrastinate any longer. It is not fair to those who depend on you, nor is it fair to those who believe in you. If you delay much longer, you may very well miss a precious window of opportunity.

The bottom line probably might be a matter of trust. Can God be trusted to lead you through the implications of this decision? Can He handle the "what ifs?" The answer, of course, is yes. God will not lead you into a decision that is detrimental to His plan for your life. There will surely be bumps along the way. The bottom may fall out, but He is still faithful. It is better to be in a storm with Jesus, than on the calm shore without Him. You can take this first step and then trust God with steps two and three. Do not become overwhelmed with what might happen tomorrow. Just remain faithful today. Do your best now and trust the Lord with later.

The same holds true for others stuck in indecision. It is responsible for you to give them a deadline. It is bad stewardship for you to linger too long, and so it may be time to move on and "knock the dust from your sandals" (Mark 6:11 KJV). God may very well be shutting the door because of another's inability to decide. This may be His protection, so be grateful for this divine delay. But now move on with Christ in quiet confidence and bold creativity.

A life mired in indecision is messy and going nowhere. A life marked by wise decisions is moving forward with the heavenly Father's help. Be a bold decision maker because you can. Align your decisions with His wisdom, for He has it all figured out.

Get the facts. Review the truth. Get counsel. Pray. Then decide to decide. By faith and by the grace of God, decide. This is the best decision.

BLESSED NATION

Blessed is the nation whose God is the Lord,
the people he chose for his inheritance.
PSALM 33:12

Abraham and his family were chosen by God to be His people. They became a nation through whom God would reveal His glory. We learn from their long history what it means to be set apart and blessed by God. Now, anyone who trusts in Jesus is a part of God's family—God's special people. We learn from Israel and from the New Testament churches that God blesses His people because of their prayers, not their power. He blesses people because of their trust in Him, not their advanced technology. God blesses people because they fear the Lord, not man. God blesses those who love Him and who express that love in caring for the impoverished and diseased and vulnerable.

God extends this blessing to cities and nations because of His people. God blesses a nation when individuals gather corporately in vibrant Christian worship because the church is God's means to awaken a nation. Nations who try to control or hinder the church from flourishing lose God's blessing. Countries that restrict churches and rely on a state-church monopoly miss the mark. The church is meant to confront and restore culture. Christians are "salt and light" (Matthew 5:13-14) in the midst of decayed and darkened nations. When believers gather in a bond of love, they create a thirst for righteousness and shed light on the ways of the Lord.

Wise nations encourage many different congregations and denominations to meet. Freedom of religion feeds faithfulness in God. God expects His church to grow and engage with the culture. This is how He changes a nation. A church that is alive and growing becomes a catalyst for good things.

God blesses those who humbly seek Him. "If my people, who are called by my name, will humble themselves and pray and seek my face and turn from their wicked ways, then will I hear from heaven and will forgive their sin and will heal their land" (2 Chronicles 7:14).

SENSELESS ADVICE

The officials of Zoan are nothing but fools; the wise counselors of Pharaoh give senseless advice. How can you say to Pharaoh, "I am one of the wise men, a disciple of the ancient kings."

ISAIAH 19:11

Be careful where you look for advice; avoid senseless sources. If you want good advice about marriage, then seek out couples with a track record of love and respect for one another. If you want smart advice about business, then seek out someone who builds a business with integrity. If your goal is wise stewardship of finances, then engage with those who are experts in earthly and eternal investments.

Make sure you surround yourself with people who will tell you what you need to hear, not necessarily what you want to hear. People will feed your ego if you let them. You are not God's gift to the world; Jesus is. If you look long enough and hard enough, you may eventually find those who side with your point of view, but agreement does not guarantee wisdom. Instead, invite unbiased, objective, Bible-based advice. Leaders are the products of those by whom they are surrounded. So, look at the character and competence of those who are the authorities in your life, for they are a mirror image of their advisors.

Follow leaders who follow wise advice. Flee from leaders who follow foolish and senseless advice. The principle of "you are who you listen to" is timeless and true. Therefore, pray for your leaders to surround themselves with those who are full of truth and wisdom. Trust the Lord for bold counselors who are not afraid to respectfully speak with courage and conviction. Ask God for advisors who are willing to give up their positions for the sake of principled behavior and beliefs.

Someone who always agrees with you is a dispenser of senseless advice. Instead, gather around you those who ask the hard questions, and then listen with a teachable heart. Be willing to change your mind as you glean more accurate information. Wisdom is the ability to understand differing perspectives and then incorporate them into the best option and solution. This, of course, is all assimilated through prayer and stillness before God. His advice is all-encompassing and eternally motivated.

The Holy Spirit is your highest and best counselor. Go to Him often for validation, revelation, and eternal advice. It makes sense.

A BEAUTIFUL MIND

You will keep in perfect peace those whose minds are steadfast, because they trust in you.
ISAIAH 26:3

A beautiful mind believes God, for faith flows from a mind focused on the Lord. It is steadfast on its Savior because it trusts in Him. An ugly mind is contrary, conflicted, and unsure. Its focus fluctuates between fear and faith. In an ugly mind, there is a battle that fatigues. The mind's eye can become trapped in the temporal and lose its willingness to trust God. This is tragic and terrifying for those whose minds become numbed to the things of God.

The mind is a beautiful thing if it is focused properly, but it can be disturbing and destructive when it loses perspective. The mind can play tricks on you because Satan has his mind games. He tries to draw you in with his allure, but his thoughts lead to faithless living. Therefore, build up your intellectual stamina and trust in God so you can reject Satan's lies. Fill your mind with good thoughts. "Finally, brothers and sisters, whatever is true, whatever is noble, whatever is right, whatever is pure, whatever is lovely, whatever is admirable—if anything is excellent or praiseworthy—think about such things" (Philippians 4:8).

A mind needs to be stretched, as a heart needs to be exercised. An unused mind is a waste; it atrophies and becomes ugly. It is a waste of time to have a disengaged mind. Mindless activity will get you into trouble. Therefore, think. Be a thinker and not just a doer. Engage your mind with large thoughts about the Lord. Reflect on His righteousness and the grandeur of His glory. Get beyond trivial thoughts to thoughts that trust in God. The quality of your life follows the quality of your thoughts. Classical books—along with the Bible—provide fertile soil for great thinking. Great thinkers help you develop disciplined thinking. Make it a goal to read, dialogue, and debate with wise thinkers. This will help you think well. A mature mind is a beautiful thing to behold. Stretch your mind. But keep trust in the Lord top of mind. Trust in God is your catalyst for wise thinking. Legalism leads to non-thinking and little faith. Without trust in the Lord, your mind becomes fertile ground for deception. Therefore, allow trust to become the scope in which your mind's eye gazes, and it will see perfect peace.

The mind of Christ is worth a lifetime of study; it beautifies your thinking. A beautiful mind trusts and rests in the Lord.

UNWISE ARGUMENT

"Woe to those who quarrel with their Maker, those who are nothing but potsherds among the potsherds on the ground. Does the clay say to the potter, 'What are you making?' Does your work say, 'The potter has no hands'?"

ISAIAH 45:9

Do not argue with the Almighty, for it is unwise and unproductive. Debating deity is a vain and proud proposition. How could you know—better than God—what's best? People possess a fraction of all knowledge; He owns all knowledge. Your perspective is limited at best; His view is all encompassing. You are the created; He is the Creator. You are a worshiper; He is worshiped. You pray; He answers prayer. You receive grace; He gives grace. You sin; He forgives. You are human; He is God.

The best way to relate to God is with agreement instead of argument. Agree with Him about who you are, as He has made and gifted you uniquely. You do not need to be anyone else other than yourself. You will stay frustrated trying to fashion your life after someone else's, so be you. Let others inspire you to become better, but do not be overwhelmed by their abilities. God may have given them a greater capacity for activities and relationships. Be who God wants you to be, and don't argue with Him about not having the opportunities afforded to others. He knows what's best for you.

You may argue with God and even get your way, but there is a price to pay. Guilt, broken relationships, hurt, and anger are not worth the trouble. Maneuvering around your Maker to get something may come back to haunt you. Arguing many times means you are not getting your way. Therefore, call a time out. Take a prayerful pause and align your way with His. Arguments can be resolved with alignment of purpose. Stay true to His call on your life, take responsibility, and do not argue with God or blame others. You have an opportunity to deepen your faith during this time of uncertainty. Cling to your Savior for affirmation and direction. Accept the truth instead of resisting reality. God is in control, and He can be trusted. He will send you the relationships and resources needed to accomplish His will. The enemy tempts, so debate the devil with God's word and align with the Almighty's purpose for your life. Choose acceptance of God's will over argument. Acceptance allows you to channel your energy toward eternal matters.

Argue less and accept more. This is wise and acceptable to the Almighty. No need to argue.

A HAUGHTY HEART

Before destruction the heart of man is haughty.
PROVERBS 18:12

"Haughty" isn't a word we often use, and rarely to describe ourselves. Yet in today's culture of self-promotion and personal branding, a haughty heart is more common than we'd like to admit. It sounds like, "Look at me, look at what I've done—I matter." Here's an interesting definition from Merriam-Webster: "Proud and disdainful; having a high opinion of oneself, with contempt for others; lofty and arrogant." Not exactly the kind of person people are drawn to. In fact, a haughty heart leaves others—and even ourselves—relationally exhausted.

Ever noticed how a room shifts when someone walks in wearing their superiority like an invisible crown? Pride doesn't just enter—it struts, silently demanding attention. Everyone nearby begins adjusting, scrambling for footing in the quicksand of subtle comparisons and unspoken expectations. The proud person often doesn't realize they're trapped in performance mode, constantly maintaining an image. Conversations become games of one-upmanship, compliments laced with competition: *"Your lawn looks great—though you should see mine since I started that special fertilizer."*

The tragic irony? Pride promises to elevate but ends up isolating. At day's end, everyone feels drained, and the haughty heart, though unaware, is often the most exhausted of all. Left unchecked, this exhaustion leads to relational erosion. What begins as subtle weariness can morph into deep resentment. Friends and loved ones begin to step back. Invitations stop. Vulnerability is replaced with silence. "Come to dinner" becomes as rare as "Tell me how you really feel." The relationship starts to crumble under the weight of pride.

Here's where humility enters like oxygen into a suffocating room. When someone finally surrenders their need to be impressive and whispers those magic words, "I was wrong" or "I need help," watch how quickly the relational landscape transforms. Humility creates safe landing places for authentic connection. It trades exhausting performances for a refreshing presence. The humble heart asks questions instead of making pronouncements. It listens to understand rather than to counter. It celebrates others' successes without mental footnotes. And most beautifully, it models the vulnerability that invites others to remove their own masks. Relationships don't just survive under humility's care—they flourish, growing roots deep enough to weather any storm.

Let the Lord soften your heart and remove any pride within you. Walk in humility, to serve others with love, and to seek God's will above your own.

THE RIGHT THING

This is what the Lord *says: "Maintain justice and do what is right, for my salvation is close at hand and my righteousness will soon be revealed."*

ISAIAH 56:1

Do the right thing, because you can't go wrong by doing what's right. The right choice may not be the easiest choice, but it will result in what's best. It is tempting to bypass what's right for what's convenient or expedient. However, convenience and expedience can get you into trouble if they become an excuse for not doing the right thing. So do the right thing and trust God with the results. It may very well cost you time and money, but what value can you place on living free of regret?

The right thing may ruffle some feathers and cause you short-term suffering. Some people may reject you for doing what's right. Some people may avoid you because your right choices are a reminder of their wrong ones. Do not be intimidated by others who are uncomfortable with your right choices. Choose right and trust God. Moreover, keep your attitude free from arrogance. Your right choices do not make you spiritually superior.

Doing the right thing is a matter of trust. Can God be trusted with the results of your right decisions? Yes. However, you're on your own when you dismiss the wise counsel of those who really care. If you choose to settle for something less than best, then your outcomes will erode. To choose what's "good" over what's "best" is not the right course of action.

God can be trusted with what happens when you break off a less-than best relationship. He has someone better in mind, who will lift you up spiritually and not drag you down. Investing in unhealthy relationships is not the right thing to do. Your parents and your friends have warned you not to go down this road of relational recklessness. You can still do the right thing by breaking off the relationship and seeking God for His best. His best is a hundred times better than settling for someone who makes you "feel alive," yet has no firm foundation of faith. Be careful with whom you entrust your emotions. Your affections are not to be given away indiscriminately.

The right thing is to first set your affections above, where Christ sits at the right hand of God (Colossians 3:1-2). Then trust Him.

So, do the right thing because it's the right thing to do. And do it with an attitude of humility, grace, and patience. You can't go wrong doing what's right.

JULY 10

DEFINITION AND DIRECTION

LORD, I know that people's lives are not their own;
it is not for them to direct their steps.
JEREMIAH 10:23

A great exchange took place when you first believed in Jesus. What's yours became His, and what's His became yours. The life of Christ became your life. It is not your life to define, but His. He has wrapped a wonderful definition around whose you are in Him. You are a child of God. You are secure because your Savior keeps you. You are valuable because the Lord values you. You are protected because the Almighty owns you.

The Bible is God's glossary of how to define yourself. Scripture gives you a family tree of faith for you to trace your religious roots. It is a mirror of how God sees you. He sees you as accepted in His Son, though you suffer rejection from others. Cherish and enjoy daily the acceptance of Jesus.

Furthermore, He directs His own (Isaiah 48:17). God wants you to understand and follow His plan for your life. Praise God it's a step-by-step process, and He directs your steps! Some days you may feel like it's three steps forward and two steps back, but do not be discouraged or dismayed. God is still directing your steps, though at times they seem tedious and laborious. The Lord leads you in lockstep with His steps. His steps tread the path of wisdom.

Do not run ahead, thinking you have to set a record for speed. In fact, fast steps may cause you to backtrack and relearn what God was trying to teach you. Walk patiently with Him and watch Him work. The Holy Spirit is your step director. You are in His step class for instruction in His Word and exercise in faith. Learn how to let the Lord direct your steps. Prayerfully listen to the quiet prompting from His spirit. Stop when you need to stop. Speed up when you need to speed up. Slow down when you need to slow down. God directs the steps of a submitted and surrendered man or woman.

Stubbornness is hard to direct (Psalm 81:12). Pride resists direction, and independence attempts to self-direct. Listen to your spouse or close friend. God may speak His next steps through them. He gives divine directions that show His will for your life. Step by step He leads you. You can trust that His way is the best way. Be patient. Watch Him work despite adversity and a seeming lack of resources. Avoid a two-step with yourself and stay in step with your Savior.

Allow your Maker to define your moves. Walking with the Lord is the wisest way to go, so resist directing your own steps. Trust in Him and allow His direction to define your steps.

JULY 11

WORTHY WORDS

Therefore this is what the LORD says: "If you repent,
I will restore you that you may serve me; if you utter worthy,
not worthless, words, you will be my spokesman.
Let this people turn to you, but you must not turn to them."
JEREMIAH 15:19

Persuasive people can pour on the words. Like an aggressive avalanche of ice and snow, they bury you with spectacular speech. So be careful with persuasive people. They can talk themselves and others into just about anything. However, their words become worthless when their behavior does not back up their promises. Words become worthless when they are not backed up by noble character.

It is much better to promise little but deliver much. Likewise, it is wise to manage expectations well. However, avoid people who talk a lot and do little. And don't be one of them yourself. Serve others with your actions and let your words become a bonus.

If you have a persuasive personality, be careful. It may be easy to place yourself before others. You will be tempted to manipulate others for your own needs instead of serving them. Be very cautious how you use Christ's name to validate your decisions. Indiscreetly tossing around phrases like, "The Lord said," or "The Lord told me," is treading on the turf of worthless words. Make sure your motive doesn't degrade into using "Godspeak" to get your way. These are the worst kind of worthless words.

Make it your goal to value others more than they value you. Worthy words extend sincere and meaningful compliments for the inspiration of the individual. Worthless words praise others with the goal of getting them to act a certain way.

Check your speech often. People will not receive your words if they cannot overcome the way you give your words. Do an audit of the tone and timing of your truth-telling. Words can become worthless, even when they represent truth. Indeed, be wise to communicate your insights with a gracious tone at a time of high receptivity. Anger is not the best environment to extend new insights. "I told you so," is not an attitude conducive to rapport; it doesn't invite your instruction. Look for teachable and tension-free moments in which to share truth. Be prayerful with your words. Repent of judgmental gestures and ungracious goads.

Let Jesus lead you in what to say and how to say it. Those will be worthy words. Those are words the Lord will use to carry out His will. God persuades people through prayerfully placed words.

SPIRIT RESOURCES

A shoot will come up from the stump of Jesse: from his roots a Branch will bear fruit. The Spirit of the Lord will rest on him—the Spirit of wisdom and understanding, the Spirit of counsel and of might, the Spirit of knowledge and of the fear of the Lord—and he will delight in the fear of the Lord.

ISAIAH 11:1-3

God provides spiritual resources for His children. The same Spirit of the Lord that rested on Jesus is the One who indwells His followers. "You, however, are not in the realm of the flesh but are in the realm of the Spirit, if indeed the Spirit of God lives in you. And if anyone does not have the Spirit of Christ, they do not belong to Christ" (Romans 8:9).

The Holy Spirit provides you with all the spiritual resources needed to carry out His will. You need wisdom; He provides it. You need understanding; He provides it. You need counsel; He provides it. You need power, knowledge, and grace; He provides it.

Every day the resources you need are a prayer away, so don't be so wrapped up in your plan, that you miss God's provision. The same Spirit who empowered Jesus (Luke 4:18) does the same for you. The Spirit of the living God is ready and able to give you good gifts. When Jesus left the Holy Spirit, He left you a Comforter. Jesus is your friend and Savior. God is your Father and Lord. The Holy Spirit is your guide and convincer. He will guide you in truth and righteousness.

The fruit of the Spirit will flow from your life as He gives you life. Love, joy, peace, patience, kindness, goodness, faithfulness, gentleness, and self-control are the fruit of the Holy Spirit. This is where your unremarkable religion can become a rejuvenated relationship. If your relationship with God is in a rut, let the Holy Spirit fall fresh on your life. Fear God and allow the fruit of the Spirit to mold your character. Let the Lord and more mature friends help you purge fruitless attitudes and actions from your life (John 15:2).

As the Spirit bears fruit in your character, allow His gifts to develop and fully ripen. If you are gifted to teach, teach; if you are gifted to write, write; if you are gifted to lead, lead; if you are gifted to give, give.

The Spirit of the Lord that rested on Jesus provides you with every resource you need.

JULY 13

QUIET REST

The apostles gathered around Jesus and reported to him all they had done and taught. Then, because so many people were coming and going that they did not even have a chance to eat, he said to them, "Come with me by yourselves to a quiet place and get some rest." So they went away by themselves in a boat to a solitary place.

MARK 6:30-32

Wise leaders lead others into a time of rest. They find a quiet place and rest together. Rest is required after extreme busyness because of the hustle and bustle of life. The joy you found in service for God may start to fade, and people become a drain rather than a blessing. It might be time to break away to a solitary place. Even Jesus took a break. If you continually push yourself and others, you will eventually lose all energy and perspective.

God gives goals as a guide and motivation, but do not be driven by the goal. Rather, be led by the Holy Spirit so the goal does not become your god. Take time to develop the team and then watch God work through them way beyond your capacity. Some of your team development, however, comes in quiet places.

Find a quiet spot and calendar a time today for you and your team. They may desperately need this enrichment, both personally and spiritually. Some may be on the verge of burnout or they may be ready to quit out of discouragement. Solitary places allow you and your team to recalibrate with the vision, values, and mission of the organization. Quiet times together build camaraderie and trust. A retreat is an investment; by taking time to pause, you are able to continue with more effectiveness and efficiency. A quiet place is where you can get on the same page with God as your soul is refreshed and replenished. The wise words of Scripture leap from the pages and lodge in the crevices of your heart and mind.

A retreat into a place of solitude is an exercise in faith. You trust that routines will be taken care of in your absence. You believe the financial investment will return exponentially with lower employee turnover and increased productivity. A quiet place is the ideal setting for relational vigor to erupt. Smooth relationships go a long way toward avoiding future issues and solving current problems. So retreat regularly for your sake and sanity, and retreat for the morale of the team. You hear more clearly when it is quiet. Your comprehension expands. Your body rests and your soul is renewed. A solitary place provides strength and stamina to finish well.

Sometimes, the most spiritual thing you can do is rest in a quiet place.

REST FROM WORK

There remains, then, a Sabbath-rest for the people of God; for anyone who enters God's rest also rests from their own work, just as God did from His. Let us, therefore, make every effort to enter that rest, so that no one will fall by following their example of disobedience.

HEBREWS 4:9-11

It is hard to rest from work. Some people love their work, enjoy their work, and may even worship their work. Hard, smart, and productive work is good, but worshiping work is bad. It is reckless and leads to ruin. It may be relational ruin, physical ruin, or even financial ruin. God is the only one who deserves worship. It is good to be proud of good work, but do not allow work to become an end in itself.

If you find your identity in your work, you will be positioned for a roller coaster ride of emotion. One day you will feel secure, and another day you will be swept away by insecurity. As a follower of Christ, your identity is found in Him. This is one reason why rest from work is vital. When you work all the time, you tend to drift from your moorings of faith in Christ to faith in yourself. It becomes a trust issue. "Can God be trusted enough for me to rest from my work?" Of course! He divinely redeems the time of your limited work and produces more lasting results. After all, you are His workmanship in Christ Jesus. When you take the time to cease working, God accelerates His work in you. Some of God's best work takes place when you don't work. So, enjoy your Sabbath rest as He works on your heart. Allow Him to draw you to Himself, so when you go back to work you are refreshed and revitalized.

There is a trap to avoid as you take a break from work and enter God's Sabbath rest. You can physically be away from work and still be at work mentally, so free your mind from this split-focus. Rest your thoughts from work, and you will discover your thinking is more robust and innovative when you reengage in your work. During your Sabbath rest, shift your thinking to bigger thoughts of God and His plan. Superimpose simple faith in Him over the complex issues that are assaulting your rest.

If your Sabbath rest from work involves people, let them see the sincerity of your involved presence. Do not act as if you wish you were somewhere else. Your rest is a testament to God's faithfulness. Let others read it up close and personal. Your Sabbath rest can be a catalyst for others to reengage with God. It's not always easy to get to God's rest, but once you arrive, it is well worth the effort.

His rest ignites your obedience and trust. So, rest from work and rest in Him. Then watch your work become better.

SABBATH OBSERVED

"Observe the Sabbath, because it is holy to you. Anyone who desecrates it must be put to death; whoever does any work on that day must be cut off from his people. For six days, work is to be done, but the seventh day is a Sabbath of rest, holy to the Lord. Whoever does any work on the Sabbath day must be put to death."

EXODUS 31:14-15

The follower of Christ is required to observe a Sabbath. This rest and reflection upon God is recognized as Sunday, the first day of the week. It is downtime from work time. God requires it because He knows the importance of your need for Him and your need to take a break from labor.

Obsession with work and making money leaves no time for God and other meaningful relationships. If you spend all your time working, you will become frustrated, and so will those around you. Conversely, if you spend all your time in leisure, you will miss God's best. Work gives you the perspective to appreciate leisure. Leisure without work is like food without hunger. You can't enjoy one without the other. Moreover, either of these extremes—too much work or too much leisure—will lead you to a meaningless life.

God is serious about being the focus of His Sabbath. This is not an option for Christians. But over time, if you are not intentional in your Sabbath experience, it will melt into endless activity or mindless monotony. Indeed, beware of outwardly observing the Sabbath while inwardly neglecting it. If your mind is preoccupied with work that needs to get done, then you are defeating the Sabbath purpose. Do not use this pause in your week to create more work or worry about current work.

Neglect of the Sabbath may at first seem like a small indiscretion, but it ultimately is a matter of trust in God. Can God take care of my work in six days if I choose to aggressively observe His Sabbath? This, of course, is a rhetorical question. So, use your Sabbath time to focus on God; fear Him; love Him; worship and adore Him. Use this time to know Him, learn about Him, and enjoy Him. Sabbath is holy to the Lord. Place Christ at the forefront of your Sabbath experience. Rest in Him, and rest with those who love Him. Break the chains of the bondage of busyness, and replace them with the freedom that comes from resting in Christ.

It is holy to you and it is holy to Him. Therefore, rest with Him and reflect on His faithfulness.

RESPONSIVE HEART

"Because your heart was responsive and you humbled yourself before the Lord when you heard what I have spoken against this place and its people, that they would become a curse and be laid waste—and because you tore your robes and wept in my presence, I have heard you, declares the Lord."

2 KINGS 22:19

God responds well to a responsive and humble heart. It is guaranteed an audience with the Almighty. His heart is drawn to humility. He knows a responsive heart can be trusted with His truth. So when He finds someone responsive to righteousness, He has found someone who can be entrusted with His blessing. A responsive heart is teachable, tender to truth, and quick to obey. It is the opposite of a hard heart. A hard heart stews in the juices of sin, while a responsive heart flees from sin's appearance. Instead of making excuses for unacceptable behavior, a responsive heart seeks to become trusting and forgiving.

God and godly influences are constantly suggesting, teaching, convicting, and prodding you to conform to the character of Christ. God's Word speaks to your heart and then your life responds. Therefore, living for Jesus is an act of worship. Your responsiveness to truth is a testimony to the living God. As you obey God, others are drawn to Him and you.

Remove any affections that compete with Christ. If money drives your behavior, then put it in its proper place through generosity. If work is your worship, then calendar time for rest and find your security in your Savior. If television or the Internet is your obsession, then unplug them for a season. Abstain from e-mail, voicemail, and meetings for a period of time and fill the void with quiet reflection around a responsive heart toward the Lord. Activity and noise can numb your sensitivity to the Holy Spirit's leadership. Therefore, seek to do less, and trust God and others with what still needs attention. Others can take care of these issues, but you are the only one who can manage your heart. An unresponsive heart will suffer from spiritual blockage and eventually shut down. Exercise it well by responding to the things of God. He is looking for humble hearts to invigorate with His wisdom and discernment. Stay responsive to your heavenly Father, and watch in awe as He quietly, boldly, and lovingly responds to you.

A responsive heart to God is quick to obey Him, and slow to sin.

RESTING PLACE

God will speak to this people, to whom he said,
"This is the resting place, let the weary rest"; and,
"This is the place of repose"—but they would not listen.
ISAIAH 28:11-12

Everyone needs a place to rest, a time to rejuvenate and restore their soul. A soul without rest is vulnerable to doubt, disease, and dread. So, allow your soul to catch up with your activity through rest. Stop right now and take an audit of your soul. Is it strung out and anxious? If so, rearrange your schedule for rest before it rearranges you. Without rest, you are going nowhere fast. If you intensify the pace, you are going nowhere, faster.

Rest allows you to recalibrate your priorities and replenish your cistern of creativity. Indeed, each resting place looks different, depending on your needs. For example, your resting place may be the quiet screened porch, where you relax with a cup of coffee and a good book. For someone else, a resting place may be a comfortable couch, where they nap to the steady beat of raindrops pelting the rooftop. It can be the park where you walk with your best friend, a secluded drive in the countryside, or an adventurous exploration of the great Pacific Northwest. Whether your resting place is the beach, the mountains, or in front of a good movie, make time to engage with it. God speaks to you in your place of rest. This is one of His favorite spots to shape your soul.

Furthermore, your resting place allows you to resist temptation. Fatigue causes you to stumble and fall through life. A depleted spirit is not primed for discernment, and decision-making during duress can be dreadful. Therefore, go away to a resting place. Find God and find yourself under the canopy of His creation. A resting place is your protection from yourself, from evil influences, and from lost perspective. Above all else, your resting place reveals God in a refreshing way. Your confidence is resurrected. Your trust takes on a new level of intensity. Your patience leads to a deeper understanding of what it means to wait on the Lord. A resting place is for your sake and His. It is necessary to experience God's very best for you and your family. Discover your resting place in prayer, and go there often. Repentance follows rest, and robust relationships result from rest.

Your best and most creative ideas emerge from relaxed meditation on your Master. Wisdom resides in rest.

CLEAR MINDED

You will keep him in perfect peace, Whose mind is stayed on You, Because he trusts in You.
ISAIAH 26:3 (NKJV)

A clear mind promotes creativity but a cluttered mind clings to the status quo. The mind is like a computer's inbox: It can fill up quickly with annoying spam—the worries of this world—or it can paralyze you with people whose requests exceed your capacity to respond. An unfiltered mind will stress out under the bombardment of information and invitations for action. There has to be a process to offload lingering action items, or you will be crushed under the weight of hyperactivity. Pace yourself, and allow most things to freely flow from your head to a folder labeled "Trust."

Trust that God will take care of those things for which you have neither the time nor the energy to tackle. You cannot be everywhere, do everything, or please everybody. So, be intentional about doing a faith flush on your thinking. Drive away the demons that play mind games of fear and overcommitment. Rely more on the wisdom of God and less on the cleverness of man.

A person who thinks clearly is a strong candidate for peace of mind. A person who gets quiet before the Lord will clear his mind in holy harmony with its Maker. There is a transaction and a transformation that takes place during prayer. There is a transaction of trust that takes the pressure off the one offering the prayers. And the transformation of the Holy Spirit deletes worry and sin from the heavy-hearted and the high-minded. Prayer transforms a racing mind. Prayer reboots your life's operating system to align with His and positions you for a cleansed mind. Priorities come into focus in the presence of Christ. The object of your affection keeps you. The Lord will keep you in perfect peace, because you trust in Him. He will give you the peace of mind to carry on. He will give you the patience to mind your own business. He will give you the courage and the right spirit to speak your mind. Therefore, keep top of mind trust in your Savior and Lord.

Allow His creativity to flood your unfettered mind.
A mind submitted to its Master will serve Him well.
A mind created, crafted, and kept by Christ is free and clear.

COVENANT EYES

*"I made a covenant with my eyes
not to look lustfully at a young woman."*
JOB 31:1

Pure eyes are a priority for a disciple of Jesus Christ. Like a heat-seeking missile, lustful eyes will accelerate their course until they reach their destination of destruction. They can easily choose the path of pornography and become married to their emotional impulses. Misguided eyes can lead a person to be so preoccupied with destructive behavior that he becomes an embarrassment to himself and a disgrace to others.

God takes seriously the stewardship of sight. Do not expose your eyes to everything. Of course, they cannot be sheltered from all sin. Eyes are not designed to be reclusive, purposefully blind to the outside world. However, eyes are meant to be respectful of their Creator. Eyes are avenues for good or bad. Jesus said, "The eye is the lamp of the body. If your eyes are healthy, your whole body will be full of light" (Matthew 6:22).

Like any of His great blessings, eyes are meant for good. It is good to gaze at God's creation in all of its splendor and glory. How beautiful is the rush of a crystal-clear waterfall as it intensely tumbles over moss-covered rocks into a quiet reflecting pool at the bottom of its crashing course. This is a magnificent expression for our eyesight. Eyes are meant to enjoy beauty and not exploit it. If you have an eye for art and interior design, you are blessed indeed. God has given you perspective and creativity that most lack.

When you covenant with your eyes, you covenant with your Creator. He longs to guide your eyes, so trust as you follow God with your eyes. He will guide you toward love instead of lust. He will guide you into contentment instead of discontentment. He will see you through vulnerable times. Moreover, He takes your contractual agreement with your eyes to heart. Your responsibility in this binding contract is to make wise choices. Having a covenant with your eyes liberates you. Make a contract with your eyes and then trust God to guide you away from gullibility into goodness, so you are not blind to the ways of the Lord. Understand and apply the terms of your eyes' covenant. God's terms provide boundaries with radical freedom.

Keep eye contact with God and you will be free indeed.

DRAW NEAR

He said to me, "The room facing south is for the priests who guard the temple, and the room facing north is for the priests who guard the altar. These are the sons of Zadok, who are the only Levites who may draw near to the Lord to minister before him."

EZEKIEL 40:45-46

Draw near to God before you minister on behalf of God. This is the proper sequence for serving the Lord. Otherwise, you serve others in your own strength and limited abilities. You are not meant to serve in the flesh. Draw near to Him.

Some cannot draw near to God because they fear failure and all its embarrassing ramifications, but this means that fear has the upper hand. Hyperactivity drives them because they fear that everything depends on them alone. No one can persevere in ministry or service under this kind of self-imposed pressure. It is up to the Lord whether you reach your goals or not. It may not be His will for so much to be accomplished so soon. A ministry that does not depend on drawing near to God is a ministry that doesn't last. A person who attempts to serve Christ without drawing near to God will become overwhelmed and frustrated. Therefore, draw near and let the Lord whisper assurances—and perhaps whisper some adjustments—into your ear.

Make drawing near to the Lord a holy habit of your life. Change your thinking so that no decision or activity will define your activities until you have communed with Christ. Do not commit to do ministry until you have met with your Master. It is better to have one engaged in ministry who has first drawn near to God, than to have a dozen operating in their own strength.

So, draw near to Him. Draw near to the Lord and let Him touch your lips with life-giving words of hope, encouragement, and rebuke, when necessary. Draw near to God and allow Him to unleash your giving, so you are freed in the Spirit to give with hilarious generosity. Draw near to your heavenly Father and experience His love and forgiveness so you are aptly able to administer the same to your sometime-strained relationships. Draw near to God and rest in His grace and peace. Draw near and dismiss fear. Draw near and give Him your listening ear. His voice is soothing and secure.

Draw near to God and you will minister to others in His power. He is extremely accessible and close by, so draw near now. "Let us draw near to God with a sincere heart with the full assurance that faith brings" (Hebrews 10:22).

DECEIVED PRIDE

[Nebuchadnezzar] said, "Is not this great Babylon I have built as the royal residence, by my mighty power and for the glory of my majesty?" … And those who walk in pride [God] is able to humble.

DANIEL 4:30, 37

Pride is deceived; it walks in deception, believing things that are untrue. It thinks it is in control and is responsible for its own accomplishments. Pride has an inflated belief in itself and a condescending attitude toward others. It is all wrapped up in its own agenda. A prideful man may even mouth the right words, but his behavior betrays him. Pride is a product of unaccountable living

Pride tries to convince you that you are God's gift to the world, but that was Jesus, who God sent to us for the forgiveness of our sins. The reminder of that gift is meant to flush out pride and replace it with humility. Pride and humility cannot coexist. Humility understands and does not forget that God is the author of all good things. His Holy Spirit cuts through pride's deception and replaces it with humility's reality. Without the blessings of God, people are paupers lost in pride.

You know pride is losing its grip when you release control of your life. Humility lets go. You let go of recognition; you let go of hurt feelings; you let go of the past; you let go of judging; you let go of bad habits; you let go of your family, your work, your relationships, your need to be right and to always have your own way. You let them go and you leave them with God. This is what it means to trust God.

Humility and trust go hand in hand, as much as pride and control. It is uncanny how humility and trust lead to more responsibility and power, while pride and control lose it. This is the great deception of pride: pride thinks it is in control, but it is not.

The humble man recognizes God's control and is trusted with more. When you humble yourself in your relationships, you will be given more peace and fulfillment. Stiffen up in pride, and you will lose trust and joy. Therefore, give up your way of doing things and submit to God's way. Do not force your agenda; rather, accept the Almighty's. He will bless you far beyond what you expect or deserve. The benefit of humility far outweighs pride's illusions.

Humble yourself before God does it for you. The Bible says, "Humble yourselves, therefore, under God's mighty hand, that he may lift you up in due time" (1 Peter 5:6).

PRAYER AND PETITION

So I turned to the Lord God and pleaded with him in prayer and petition, in fasting, and in sackcloth and ashes.
DANIEL 9:3

Prayer and petition are privileges of Christ-followers. They are the means of solemn supplication to your superior authority and Savior, Jesus. When all is said and done, your hope for relief or answered prayer rests with your heavenly Father. It requires faith in the Almighty who absolves us of sin and melts our fears. Indeed, fasting and prayer bring your privileged position of access to the Almighty into sharp focus. He is great and awesome and worthy of worship. He has established a covenant of love with His children, a covenant which is engaging and eternal. He is high above us in heavenly holiness, but not so detached that He cannot hear the pleas of His people.

He is without sin, but He forgives sin. He judges, but He extends mercy. He is grieved over disobedience, but He rewards obedience. He is the God and Father of our Lord, Jesus Christ. Scripture reveals Him in all His majesty and regal righteousness. No other gods of this world come close to the God of creation. Idols are deaf and dumb, unable to respond to prayer. But prayer is precious to the Prince of Peace. This is His mode of communication and communing with His highest order in creation. Nature is unable to nudge God's heart in prayer—but you can. Animals have no comprehension of how to make an appeal to the Almighty—but you do. By faith, you are privileged people because you can petition and pray to your heavenly Father.

So, go to the Lord in prayer and petition. Often and boldly confess your sins and keep short accounts. Ask often for the peace of Christ to engulf your heart and mind. Pray regularly that God's love will transform your enemies. Pray boldly for great and mighty things on His behalf, whether healing from cancer or healing of relationships. Lift up to the Lord petitions for the salvation of friends and family members. Prayer is your first line of defense, not your last resort. Prayer means you care, and most will invite prayer, even unbelievers. Prayer to God is potent, and your willingness to pray for others will impact the proudest of people. Prayer brings you to your knees in humble gratitude and shows you the need for God and His wisdom.

Be an example of prayer by praying for others. The Bible says, "And pray in the Spirit on all occasions with all kinds of prayers and requests. With this in mind, be alert and always keep on praying for all the Lord's people" (Ephesians 6:18).

SECRET TO SUCCESS

[Uzziah] sought God during the days of Zechariah, who instructed him in the fear of God. As long as he sought the Lord, God gave him success.

2 CHRONICLES 26:5

It should come as no surprise that success, as God defines it, comes from seeking Him. For the follower of Jesus, doing the will of God is the highest degree of success. You have already achieved success if you are walking in step with your heavenly Father. Therefore, seek Him just as aggressively during the calm as you do in the chaos. Seeking God is to know Him. Seeking God is to love Him. Seeking God is to praise and worship Him. Seeking God is confessing and crying out to Him. It is enjoying the comfort of your heavenly Father. You seek God at church, at home, at work, and with your friends.

There is no place where He is not sought, other than in hell itself. What a privilege and perk for Jesus people, anytime, anywhere, and for any reason, to be able to seek God. Jesus doesn't want to just be your crisis manager; He wants to be your Lord, who leads you into wise living. The Bible says, "Seek the Lord your God, you will find him if you seek him with all your heart and with all your soul" (Deuteronomy 4:29).

You cannot seek God in isolation. Pursuing God involves the counsel and advice of those much the wiser—godly and mature believers in Christ. You learn to fear God from those who fear God; you learn to love God from those who love God; you learn to forgive from those who forgive; you learn to pray from those who pray; you learn to serve from those who serve. Hang out with those you want to be like. This is why church and community is vital to seeking God. You cannot seek God while not seeking out the right people. Scripture teaches, "The heart of the discerning acquires knowledge; the ears of the wise seek it out" (Proverbs 18:15).

Seek God in His Word. The Bible is God's anthology, and it is the revelation of Jesus Christ. Scripture is the first and last word on God. It defines Him, so it can define you. Know His Word, and you will know Him. Read it. Memorize it. Meditate on it. Learn it. Above all else, apply it.

Success is a result of seeking God. Therefore, seek Him more often than not. "Seek the Lord while he may be found; call on him while he is near" (Isaiah 55:6). Seek God in the scripture and you will be successful.

JULY 24

RIGHT MOTIVES

"Ask all the people of the land and the priests, 'When you fasted and mourned in the fifth and seventh months for the past seventy years, was it really for me that you fasted? And when you were eating and drinking, were you not just feasting for yourselves?'"

ZECHARIAH 7:5-6

Right motives can be illusive. One minute you can be pure in why you do what you do, the next, you can subtly slip into suspect behavior. Therefore, be relentless and regular in reviewing your motives. Pride is always looking to pounce on your purposes, so ask the Lord to cleanse your motives and mark them with His purposes.

You can make faith in Jesus a filter for right motives. "Why would Jesus do this?" is a wise question that helps you get to the heart of the matter. The why question reveals intent and encourages honesty. Regularly asking, "Why?" addresses your motives. You may want to give to someone, but why? You may want to serve someone, but why? You may want to sacrifice an opportunity, but why? You may want to perform a religious duty, but why? Where does your devotion reside? What drives you to do good things? If your reasons are self-serving, then you have failed to manage your motives for eternal purposes. Your motive may be to use religion and the church to promote your profession, but God does not like to be used for anything other than His glory (John 2:14-16).

If you serve because it makes you feel better or because it feeds your ego, your motives are dysfunctional. If you are trying to make up for your shady past or you are driven by guilt, not only are your motives wrong, you are a good candidate for burnout. As a consequence, your misguided motives will cause others discomfort, for it has a ripple effect on relationships and organizational dynamics. Unhealthy motives that seek attention and credit will compromise principles and values in an effort to reach the desired results. It is driven by whatever means necessary to justify worthy results, but lasting fruit results from the seeds of pure motives.

Jesus said, "You did not choose me, but I chose you and appointed you so that you might go and bear fruit—fruit that will last—and so that whatever you ask in my name the Father will give you" (John 15:16). Therefore, do an audit of authenticity and stop doing acts of righteousness that draw people to yourself instead of to your Savior. Fast and pray but do so with discretion; give anonymously (Matthew 6:5-6). Do everything for the glory of God so your love for the Lord and for people lifts your motives to a grace-filled level.

Continually allow the Holy Spirit to scrub your motivations. Ask often, "Why would Jesus do this?" Model His motivations, for right motives reap God's rewards (1 Corinthians 3:10-15).

LAUGHING JESUS

"He will fill your mouth with laughter and your lips with shouts of joy."
JOB 8:21

Laughter is from the Lord. It is His medicine for the mind and therapy for the soul. Indeed, He knows laughter is one way to get us through life's intense moments. God is not so serious that He cannot smile and laugh. How could Jesus have been 100% human if He hadn't experienced an old-fashioned belly laugh? Just hanging out with impetuous Peter would be reason enough to giggle under your breath, or even burst into raucous, roaring laughter. Indeed, God has a sense of humor. You don't have to look beyond the mirror to verify this fact. A world without laughter would be like a joke without a punch line, so look to the Lord of laughter and smile; He does.

God has given you permission to laugh. In fact, He has put joy in your heart and laughter on your lips for a purpose. When you laugh, you relax. When you laugh, the cares of this world shrink and the Lord looms larger. When you laugh, you learn to enjoy life and the Lord Himself. When you laugh, you look like the Lord. Laugh loudly and laugh often. Moreover, generosity will fuel your laughter. It is cheerful giving that brings joy to the soul (2 Corinthians 9:7). Generosity ignites joy and laughter. No wonder the greedy frown and fret; there is no freedom to let loose and laugh. Laughless living is for losers. They are bound up in boring behavior. If you are too serious to laugh, you are too serious.

You may be more serious than God. Instead, throw your head back and begin by laughing at yourself. Take yourself less seriously and God more seriously. A good laugh lends itself to longer and better living. A scowling face seems to rush quicker to the grave. Lean on the Lord for your laughter and make His joy your strength. Laughter infuses your faith with mercy and hope. You are not a naïve laughing fool, but a joyful follower of Christ. Take time each day to laugh at yourself and to laugh with others. Recognize laughter as the Lord's way of leveraging a balanced and healthy life. Life without laughter is dull and mundane. Therefore, choose to lift up others and yourself with a good laugh. There is a time to laugh, so do it often and do it well.

The Lord may be laughing right now. He certainly is smiling. The Bible says, "He will fill your mouth with laughter and your lips with shouts of joy" (Job 8:21).

ATTITUDE ADJUSTMENT

For seven days they celebrated with joy the Festival of Unleavened Bread, because the Lord had filled them with joy by changing the attitude of the king of Assyria, so that he assisted them in the work on the house of God, the God of Israel.

EZRA 6:22

Attitude is everything; it can lift you up or bring you down. If your attitude is negative, then your words and your behavior will be too. There is a difference between being a realist about negative circumstances and living with a chronic bad attitude. A positive attitude, however, will eventually outlast and overpower a negative one.

Do not allow others' bad attitude to influence yours. Be the attitude influencer instead. Greet a frown with a smile, crush criticism with affirmation, and listen patiently until fury loses its steam. Most of all, pray for those who thrive on negativity. Pray for them to be set free from their hurt, anger, guilt, and insecurity. God has you in their lives to reflect the Almighty and to encourage an attitude adjustment through Him.

Each day, your attitude gets knocked around and abused by life. If left unattended, your attitude will drift into wrong thinking, harsh words, and bad behavior. Self-pity and anger can begin to replace selflessness and forgiveness. With just a little bit of daily tweaking, your attitude stays in line with His. It is subtle, but sometimes attitudes need to be adjusted moment by moment.

God is the genesis of a right attitude, and He is the right attitude sustainer. He wants His attitude to be our attitude. The attitude that Jesus exhibited was one of humility and servant leadership. His attitude reflected submission to His heavenly Father, which resulted in service, generosity, and love for people. Jesus was joyful and hopeful, because He rested in the will of God.

Slow down and pray when you feel your attitude eroding. When you're in the midst of a bad attitude, don't make important decisions; the time isn't right for that. You will regret every decision you make during a time of emotional upheaval. Be patient, and wait until your anger has subsided, your heart is cleansed, and your attitude is objective. Almighty God is into attitudes that trust Him and reach out to others with compassion and understanding. Anyone can be negative; so don't be anyone, be different. Allow God to shape your attitude on the anvil of His heart.

An attitude molded by God is infectious and transforming. Allow Him to change yours and then trust Him to change another's. The Bible says, "Have the same mindset as Christ Jesus" (Philippians 2:5).

DESERT EXPERIENCE

At once the Spirit sent him out into the wilderness,
and he was in the wilderness forty days, being tempted by Satan.
He was with the wild animals, and angels attended him.
MARK 1:12-13

Sometimes the Holy Spirit sends you into a desert experience. The purpose of this hard time is not punishment, but purity. God wants to purify your faith and grow your dependence on Him. Your desert experience may involve a child who is away from God and away from home. It may be that your health is failing quickly, and you are on the fast track to heaven's gates. Your desert experience may encompass loneliness and a Lord that does not seem to answer prayer. Heaven may be silent during this time of stress and distress. Your marriage may be in the ditch and even on the way to divorce court, so be careful not to make a dumb decision during your desert time. He will carry you through. His angels are not passive to your plight but present to minister to your needs.

Times of trial are full of temptation from Satan, for he appeals to your pride, your physical appetite, and your spiritual vulnerability. He wants to bring you down when you are at your weakest. He sees you alone and ready for the kill. Satan smells blood, but the blood he smells is not your demise, it is your salvation. It is the blood of Jesus Christ that covers you during this crisis time in your desert of life.

The promises of God rain down like manna during desolate desert times. Feed your soul with Scripture, and you will have strength to make it through this time of turmoil. Look to the Lord, for He cares. He is willing to make you whole and to walk with you through this desert of distress. Do not attempt to gut it out without God and people. Your heavenly Father is sending reinforcements for your faith, so stay immersed in the Word of God because His Word is your anchor during this troubling time.

This desert experience will pass, so don't waste this pain and discomfort but use it to go deep with the Divine. Turn the tables with trust, for your faithfulness inspires others to remain faithful. The irrigation of God's love, grace, and forgiveness will flood your desert with new life and will be beautiful to behold. Jesus creates a paradise of character where once existed a desert of temptation.

The Bible says, "Then will the lame leap like a deer, and the mute tongue shout for joy. Water will gush forth in the wilderness and streams in the desert" (Isaiah 35:6).

FEAR REPRESSES FAITH

Yet at the same time many even among the leaders believed in him. But because of the Pharisees they would not acknowledge their faith for fear they would be put out of the synagogue; for they loved human praise more than praise from God.

JOHN 12:42-43

How can you be a quiet Christian? If fear is your reason, then you are wrong to continue down this road of cultural conformity. Where are the leaders who will live by principle even when it may mean losing power? Don't use your faith just to get a following, and don't compromise your convictions just to please a group that refuses to respect your values. Fear-based decision-making has no place in the lives of Christ's disciples.

Covert confession is not an option for a follower of Jesus Christ. Yes, in some parts of the world you have to remain under the rule of atheistic authorities. Discretion is both wise and responsible, but there is no doubt where bold believers stand. Faith is not motivated by fear of man, but by love of God. Believers who confess their faith in Christ are set free from fear. Confession is freeing, while repression is constraining. You may currently be flailing away on the battlefield of fear. You fear how others may perceive you if they know you fear God. They may label you as weird, narrow-minded, or judgmental. Yes, public confession of your faith may cost you. Leaders especially have a lot to lose by laying their beliefs on the line. Do the right thing, even though it may cost you votes, a job, a raise, a promotion, praise, or opportunities. In turn, you gain the confidence of Christ.

When you give up something because of principle, you gain His praise. When fear becomes your fortress, you fight a losing battle, for fear is indefensible. There is not enough you can do to defend its exposed flank. Therefore, fight fear with a consistent and compassionate confession of Christ. Trust God to use your public confession for His cause and glory. Confession gives confidence and calm. It agrees with and proclaims the ways of God and builds your faith.

Fear melts under the heat of confession. Public confession of Christ refreshes faith and overcomes fear. The Bible says, "Through Jesus, therefore, let us continually offer to God a sacrifice of praise—the fruit of lips that openly profess His name" (Hebrews 13:15).

CUT TO THE HEART

When the people heard this, they were cut to the heart and said to Peter and the other apostles, "Brothers, what shall we do?"
ACTS 2:37

The Holy Spirit cuts to the heart and, with laser-beam precision, He probes and penetrates and prescribes truth. He claims your conscience for Christ. Your heart is the seat of your emotions; when your heart is convinced, you are convinced. He is quick to deliver truth with clarity and conviction.

A divided heart will not stand under the scrutiny of the Spirit of God; so keep your heart for Christ and Christ alone. Cut free any other competitors for Christ's affection. Money, homes, success, children, work, travel, and hobbies are all means to the end: glorifying God. The heart is heaven's home, not hell's playground. Therefore, do not hesitate to expose your heart to eternal purposes. Lay your heart before the Lord and ask Him to mold it with His almighty agenda. Listen and apply truth to your heart. Invite the Holy Spirit's awakening of your slumbering soul, for He is God's change agent.

Action accompanies a heart cut by Christ. There is a humility that cries out, "What am I to do?" A hungry heart responds with an appetite for the Almighty. Everything else pales in importance when compared to obeying God. A heart engaged by the Holy Spirit longs to love the Lord by obeying the Lord. There is a direct correlation between obedience and a heart cut by the Spirit; self seduces a disobedient heart.

The Holy Spirit is committed to conforming you to the image of Christ. The fruit of His work transforms you into a faithful spouse, engaged parent, loyal friend, wise mentor, loving leader, and caring colleague. His inner conviction leads to repentance of sin, faith in Christ, and community with believers. This is His mode of operation. Never numb your conscience to Him. Rather, seek Him out. Christ left you His Spirit for the specific purposes of convicting, comforting, and counseling. Pray for His power to permeate your feelings, thinking, and behavior. He cuts to the heart because He cares.

"Very truly I tell you, it is for your good that I am going away. Unless I go away, the Advocate will not come to you; but if I go, I will send him to you. When he comes, he will prove the world to be in the wrong about sin and righteousness and judgment" (John 16:7-8).

PERSEVERING PURPOSE

"Therefore, in the present case I advise you: Leave these men alone! Let them go! For if their purpose or activity is of human origin, it will fail. But if it is from God, you will not be able to stop these men; you will only find yourself fighting against God."
ACTS 5:38-39

The purposes of God cannot be stopped. No king or catastrophe can conquer Christ's will or ways. He is specific in what He wants done, as the Almighty accomplishes what He desires. Man may get in the way momentarily but, over time, the Lord's lasting purpose prevails. Resistance sometimes comes from religious leaders whose control is threatened. They drift into bad theology that equates time-bound methods with timeless truth. Religion, if not kept relevant, can become its own worst enemy, limping as it maintains the status quo.

God's good news is Jesus Christ, period. He does not have to be enhanced or embellished. You do not have to apologize for who He is or what He stands for. When you lift up Jesus with your life and lips, others are drawn to Him. Causes and people who are not of God will fail. You do not have to plan their demise; it will happen in the course of Christ's good timing.

Each generation seeks to define itself through music, art, technology, sports, economics, leisure, and yes, religion. Nevertheless, the Lord is large enough to apply His purposes in each of these environments. Music is His universal language of praise and worship to Himself. He is more concerned with the outcomes of awe and obedience than He is with style and rhythm. Art is His expression of Himself in human beings, nature, and architecture. Artistic creators of beautiful design and geniuses of expression point to a much greater Designer. Modern technological advancements have accelerated our ability to communicate the Gospel of Jesus Christ around the world. Sports testify to our Creator's intrinsic intellect behind the pinnacle of His creation, the human body. The best economic systems in the world execute commerce on principles found in the Word of God.

The church has persevered because it is the bride of Christ, the hope of the world, and God will carry out His purposes through the Body of Christ. He is not bound by time or tradition. His purposes persevere because He perseveres. Your role is to align with His purpose and trust Him with the right outcome.

"In him we were also chosen, having been predestined according to the plan of him who works out everything in conformity with the purpose of his will" (Ephesians 1:11).

DRASTIC MEASURES

We took such a violent battering from the storm that the next day they began to throw the cargo overboard. On the third day, they threw the ship's tackle overboard with their own hands.

ACTS 27:18-19

Some situations call for drastic measures, such that you cannot continue as usual, or you will miss an opportunity to make major adjustments. Figuratively speaking, your boat needs to be lightened for you to stay afloat. This may apply to finances. Because of your increase in debt and your decrease in income, your spending must be drastically curtailed. Your lifestyle cannot continue to rise on the back of credit cards and equity lines. This straw house of credit will collapse one day under the weight of one small crisis. One misstep can cause everything to quickly tumble down.

God's best is not for you to live on the verge of financial frustration and failure. Start now and pay down debt while you can. Your next job may not be as financially friendly. Prepare today for tomorrow's turmoil. It is not a question of if things can go wrong, but when things will go wrong. Adversity has a way of revealing bad habits. Success can mask mistakes, but failures bring them up, front and center. Don't risk your relational wellbeing for the sake of stuff. "Simple" equals "freedom," but "complex" can be "bondage." Maybe you need to lower your stress by lessening your commitments.

Each season of life calls for re-evaluation of what's needed. The needs of an empty nest marriage are much different than when the children scurried all through the house. This is especially difficult for a wife who has drawn emotional strength and security from the love of the children. She feels insecure and less significant when the kids are no longer under the roof, waiting to be mothered. Yes, she needs the love of her heavenly Father, but she desperately needs the love of her earthly husband. It is during this season of major transition in motherhood that a wise husband loves more. It may mean taking drastic measures in how you love your wife.

You may need to give up a hobby or ministry role for a season. Margin may be the best medicine for your marriage right now. Don't ignore this need for major adjustments in how you love and respect your spouse. Take initiative to avoid becoming another divorce statistic or just apathetically coexist.

The Bible teaches, "Do not deprive each other except by mutual consent and for a time, so that you may devote yourselves to prayer. Then come together again so that Satan will not tempt you because of your lack of self-control" (1 Corinthians 7:5).

GOD'S TIMING

There is a time for everything, and a season
for every activity under the heavens.
ECCLESIASTES 3:1

God's timing can be frustrating, but it eventually leads to freedom. Perhaps you strongly desire something or someone. The timing is not right, for whatever reason. It may not be right for you, and it may not be right for the other person. However, God may be protecting you from failure because you are not ready for the grueling responsibility that lies ahead. He has your freedom in mind.

There are still valuable lessons to learn where you are. It's like your last semester of school. You are way past ready for graduation, but there were still final exams to study for and pass. You need to do your best where you are before moving on to God's next assignment.

Timing is everything. Perhaps you have a son who really needs you right now during a challenging stage of his life. Perhaps you have teenagers with insecurities that are eating them alive. They need extra attention and time from you to navigate through this uncertainty. This is a season, a season that will not be repeated. Your career can wait; children can't. The security and confidence you sow into your children will stay with them for a lifetime. Your absence will stick with them as well. Fearful and insecure adults were once fearful and insecure children. So, allow this season of life to build bridges rather than barriers between you and your children.

Learn to celebrate various seasons of life. Do not resist them; embrace them. Join the wonder of their realities. Perhaps you have a son or daughter getting married. Celebrate with them. Do not let the stress of the details and the outlays of cash rob you of the joy connected to this momentous occasion. As the father of the bride or groom, learn how to let go and allow them to become one flesh.

You can rest in the fact that God has answered your prayers concerning your child. You have prayed for their marriage into a God-fearing and Christ-honoring family. You have prepared them the best way you know how. Ultimately your child is in God's hands. Your relationship with them will look different going forward. This is a new stage of life, so do not try to control them. Your ability to adapt and adjust to new seasons of life has a direct correlation to your joy and happiness. Jesus understood this when He said to His mother, "Woman, what does your concern have to do with Me? My hour has not yet come" (John 2:4 NKJV). His perfect timing will be evident in your children's lives too.

God's timing can be a surprise.
It is rarely early and never late.

BOLD GOING

Then I heard the voice of the Lord saying, "Whom shall I send? And who will go for us?" And I said, "Here am I. Send me!"

ISAIAH 6:8

Bold going is responding to God's invitation to join Him in unlikely places. These are places that need the love of Christ, places that smell different and look different. Places where people talk differently, and act differently. All these places have the same need for a Savior. These places have people who are waiting for someone to tell them the truth about Jesus.

Cross-cultural encounters are not always romantic or noble. Sometimes they are hard and grueling. They are difficult for missionaries whose bodies reject the local food and water, but the salvation of souls is worth discomfort. The joy of seeing others come to faith in Christ and grow in their faith often causes Christians to forget any temporary ailments they may be suffering. The beauty of missions is that it transforms people to become like Christ in the context of their own culture. You are not there to make them like you. You have the great privilege of leading them to be like Jesus.

Jesus instructs His followers to make disciples globally. You may be called to a short-term or long-term mission trip overseas. Either way, engage with God in this great adventure. Give money to missions, but don't stop there. Show up on the ground with the Holy Spirit in your heart and the Word of God on your breath. Find those who are teachable and teach them the Word of God. Train them to be servant leaders. Seek out the evangelists and help them to evangelize. Build buildings, create jobs, birth businesses, start ministries, feed the hungry, clothe the orphans and widows. Do whatever it takes in the name of Christ to bridge the cultural gap with God.

Do not feel like you have to have all the answers. Do not be afraid of the unknown or of illness. Do not be shy but be bold in the power of the Holy Spirit. Jesus said, "But you will receive power when the Holy Spirit comes on you; and you will be my witnesses … to the ends of the earth" (Acts 1:8). This is God's opportunity to grow your faith and perspective to another level.

God wants you to partner with Him to unleash your faith and, by doing so, unleash the faith of others.

TOTAL TRUST

"Surely God is my salvation; I will trust and not be afraid. The Lord, the Lord Himself, is my strength and my defense; he has become my salvation." With joy you will draw water from the wells of salvation.

ISAIAH 12:2-3

Total trust in God is available to every blood-bought follower of Jesus Christ. Trusting Him fully means you give up total control, and the Lord's assurance replaces your fear with peace.

If God is who He claims to be, He can be trusted. God is trustworthy, so He can be trusted. The well of His salvation is infinitely deep. If you can trust Him with the eternal salvation of your soul, you can trust Him with the temporal control of your life. His character and resources are unlimited. You have limited capacity to bear burdens. Without the support of a sympathetic Jesus, you will be immobilized, even crushed under the weight of worry. Jesus understands and offers to take your yoke.

His part is provision and your part is trust. He can be trusted to lead you even before you put a prayerful plan into motion. If you can trust Him with the big things, you can trust Him with the small things. If He led you to the right spouse, He will give you the opportunities to provide. If He led you to a new career, He will give you the wisdom, finances, and relationships to be successful. If He led you to be a missionary, He will build bridges across the cultural barriers that allow you to engage with the people. If He led you to have children, He will provide for the needed resources to be successful parents. What God initiates He completes.

Distrust in God is distasteful and an insult to His integrity. He is offended if you do not trust His support. Don't fall into the trap of trusting Him with some things and not trusting Him with others. How can God not be big enough to handle any situation? Health, war, teenagers, money, conflict, prosperity, relationships, and people can all be placed into His hands. There is no need to root around and search for answers when He already has it figured out. There is no need to sacrifice your health in worry and overwork when He offers peace and options you have yet to discover. There is no need to rush through life and then ask Him to bless your efforts after the fact.

Trust in God means you patiently walk with Him in your decisions and choices. The Bible says, "Trust in the Lord with all your heart and lean not on your own understanding; in all your ways submit to him, and he will make your paths straight" (Proverbs 3:5-6). Trusting God does not mean you act irresponsibly and seek forgiveness later. Partial trust leads to frustration and worry. Total trust in Jesus leads to contentment, joy, and peace.

Slow down, look up, trust Him, and watch Him reap extraordinary results.

SHARPENED SKILLS

*If the ax is dull and its edge unsharpened,
more strength is needed, but skill will bring success.*
ECCLESIASTES 10:10

Life is not meant to be full of endless activity and busyness. Without pause it loses its edge. A life worth living is one that takes the time to sharpen its skills. As you sharpen your skills, you are moving forward. Skill-sharpening is an investment that will serve you well the rest of your life. Wisdom says, "Do you see someone skilled in their work? They will serve before kings; they will not serve before officials of low rank" (Proverbs 22:29).

Your commitment to sharpen yourself is much like that of a farmer. A wise farmer will use his seasonal down time to upgrade, replace, and repair his equipment. He literally sharpens the tips of his plow, rebuilds the tractor engines, and upgrades and cleans his equipment. A prepared farmer will not only survive but will thrive with this type of motivation to always improve. In the same spirit, there is a time to execute and a time to regroup and sharpen yourself for the next initiative.

A person with sharpened skills is an effective tool in the hand of God. He wants to use you to your full potential. Your activities and work will produce more lasting results when you take the time to hone heaven's gifts. Steward God's talents and gifts to their fullest. Swinging at issues with a dull life will lead you to the brink of giving up. God wants to use your life to cut through life's issues the way a sharp knife slices through a juicy, ripe tomato. Stay sharp, and your skills may swing open some impressive doors.

A skilled concert pianist practices the piano. A skilled writer searches out new words and becomes engrossed in sentence structures. A skilled speaker learns how to understand his audience and communicate one point in a variety of ways. A skilled golfer continues to hit balls way after the tournaments end; he smashes the little white objects into the night. So, seek out new ways to keep your mind sharp and engaged in new ideas.

Use a variety of tools to stay sharp. Learn from wise leaders of the faith whose writings have stood the test of time. Books are tremendous skill-sharpeners. Join a book club to ramp up your commitment and accountability. You can attend seminars or pursue a graduate degree. Discover your skills through assessments and the counsel of others.

Nothing sharpens a mind like wisdom from above. Sharpen your mind with the Word of God. God's principles are like a whetstone on a battered blade. He smooths the jagged edges of your roughed up life. Like an axe that has become chipped and blunted over time, your life is refurbished by God till it regains its radiant and shiny silver edge.

**Do not settle for mediocrity; by God's grace
seek to be the best in your life roles.**

RADICAL ROMANCE

Let him kiss me with the kisses of his mouth—
for your love is more delightful than wine.
SONG OF SONGS 1:2

Romance is not just for the young. It can become more robust with age. This is one of God's ways of keeping your heart youthful. The excitement of wooing your wife is an important part of God's plan for marriage. There is nothing more boring than a marriage that has gone stale. Like an old and moldy piece of bread, the relationship becomes crusty and distasteful without the freshness of romance. Sparks fly because passion is aflame for each other. They don't take each other for granted when romance is robust. Romance is a combination of spiritual, emotional, and physical dynamics. All three of these ingredients contribute to a romantic rendezvous.

Firstly, the spiritual element keeps God in the forefront. Love the Lord first, and you will love your wife well. This love triangle is healthy since you worship God, not your spouse. God and His word keep your motives pure. The Bible teaches, "The husband should fulfill his marital duty to his wife, and likewise the wife to her husband" (1 Corinthians 7:3). The motive to serve each other and speak each other's love language is important in God's design for marriage.

Secondly, romance involves your emotions. Your best friend is your wife. She is where you make your primary emotional investment. Romance thrives on friendship because transparency is a bridge to laughter, tears, and comfort. Share the depths of your heart, your fears, your failures, and your dreams with each other. Friends do not have to fix things, but they are there for support and encouragement. Friends forgive freely and often. Friendship fuels the flames of romance.

Lastly, romance is physical. Make sure you are easy on the eyes for your spouse. Remember how you gussied up for her when you were dating? Some things need to never change. Your pre-marriage strategy—smelling good and looking good—still applies. So take the time to clean up and dress up.

Once you catch your life-mate you have to keep her. Make radical romance a regular routine in your marriage. Plan a weekly date night or an occasional overnight away. Communicate during the day with texts, calls, or emails. Take her shopping for a new outfit. Surprise her with a romantic dinner. Mow the grass for her. Hike with her. Romance is planned and very practical.

There is nothing more exciting than a husband and wife who never get over pursuing one another.

SORROW REMOVED

[The Lord Almighty] will swallow up death forever. The Sovereign Lord will wipe away the tears from all faces; he will remove his people's disgrace from all the earth. The Lord has spoken.

ISAIAH 25:8

Sorrow is the fruit of sin in a fallen world; it has liberty to inflict pain. No one is immune from sorrow. Sorrow is created by sin, death, divorce, selfishness, poverty, rejection, loss, and fear. Sorrow is all around, and it circles its prey like vultures around a carcass, ready to pick away at the meat of your soul. Sorrow does not discriminate among races, gender, social class, or stage of life. It causes a weepy heart and a weary mind. It never goes away in this lifetime.

Your sorrow may be overwhelming to the point of anguish and despair. The hurt is about to drive you crazy. You feel you can't handle it. You have lost perspective, and God seems a million miles away. Things have gone from bad to worse; you have nowhere to turn. You have hit a brick wall, and life seems to be crumbling around you. Sorrow is like a ball and chain around your joy, and you live in the regret of the past rather than the hope of the future. Your current circumstances and worries are crushing down on you to the point of claustrophobia.

You may not know how to put your sorrow into words, but Jesus still comprehends. Jesus was acquainted with grief. Sorrow is not foreign to Him. He was a man of many sorrows. He was inflicted with not just one but multiple sorrows. Nothing is beyond the omniscience of your Sovereign Lord. Others may not understand, but He does.

You do not have to stay in this state of perpetual sadness. Jesus is the Savior of your sorrows. He is the way out, and in Him, there is hope. There is a balm for your scarred soul; you can be rescued from drowning in your sorrows. So, ask Him to dive in and rescue you from thrashing about in the deep waters of your sorrows.

Sorrow removal is His specialty. Let God remove your points of sorrow one by one as if they were trees downed by a storm's horrific winds. He will lift them individually from the objects they have crushed. He will replace hurt with healing. Sorrow is temporary with God; His joy is permanent. He wants to gently wipe away your tears. Let Him remove your sorrow, and you will be glad you did.

He wants you to experience His abundant life. The Scripture is majestic: "Those the Lord has rescued will return. They will enter Zion with singing; everlasting joy will crown their heads. Gladness and joy will overtake them, and sorrow and sighing will flee away" (Isaiah 35:10).

He is a sympathetic Savior waiting to soothe your pain.

HOW TO KNOW

But Abram said, "Sovereign Lord,
how can I know that I will gain possession of it?"
GENESIS 15:8

How do you know what God has for you? If assurance of knowing what God was saying came easily, you would be tempted to take the credit for your accomplishments with the Almighty. He wants you to know what to do, but on His terms.

You will know all you need to know, as you get to know Him. Knowing Him is your passage to knowing what to do. God does not leave you in the dark to grope around in unbelief. He wants you to go to Him for discernment and understanding. The Bible says, "I keep asking that the God of our Lord Jesus Christ, the glorious Father, may give you the Spirit of wisdom and revelation, so that you may know him better" (Ephesians 1:17). Engage with Him in your crisis of belief. When you are ready, God will allow you to understand how to know you can have something.

He constantly communicates with His children through Holy Scripture. He may speak to you in a dream. He may be shouting at you through friends and foes. Search God's Word and the advice of those who know you best and who hold you accountable.

Many times, knowing what to do follows belief and obedience. It may mean extending kindness to a nemesis at work or praying more for your teenage child and saying less. Be faithful with these small steps. Trust God with this one thing and ask Him for discernment on the next steps. Resist the temptation to rush to the next big thing. Be patient.

For example, do not let your drive for possessions paralyze you from trusting and obeying. Be faithful with your finances. Personal debt can short-circuit God's work, so rely on Christ, not credit. So, take a financial reality check and start by paying off the credit card with the lowest balance. Money can draw you closer to your Master or drive you further away. You can know you are positioned to buy something if you have the cash for the purchase. Cash collaborates with the future, but debt presumes on the future. Paying as you go helps you to know the Lord's leading. So, follow the Lord by faith.

The Lord loves you too much to leave you in the lurch. There are a lot of little miracles yet to be encountered. The lion's share of your vision may happen after you are gone. The continued execution of "how to know" may follow you into eternity. So set the table now for those who will feast on the results of your faith after your exit.

Take God at His word today and be faithful to His instructions.

GOD'S SENSE OF HUMOR

Sarah said, "God has brought me laughter,
and everyone who hears about this will laugh with me."
GENESIS 21:6

God has a sense of humor, and to walk with the Lord means to laugh with the Lord. He makes you laugh because He has a sense of humor. Heaven is not humorless; it's full of joy and laughing out loud. The Lord laughs with you. He gives you laughter to remind you of His sense of humor. He gives you laughter to unleash joy, and He enables you to relax in Him. God is in control, and you have His permission to laugh. It is tragic when there is failure to receive heaven's humor. It is a false belief that a smile is not spiritual; piety produces joy.

Awe and laughter are not mutually exclusive; they go together. You laugh out loud when you have a child, especially when the little one is unexpected. You laugh when you land a job or deal that was totally unexpected. You laugh when the Lord loves you beyond your wildest dreams.

Celebrate God's sense of humor with others. Do not hold back your laughter with those you love and respect. It is an elixir for evangelism and discipleship. It is a marinade for mentoring. Don't wait only for special occasions like weddings and birthdays to laugh. Laugh in between those times. It may be at a child's performance at school or a church play. Laugh with them at their risk of being vulnerable and expressive. Laugh when things don't go just as planned at work and home.

Laughter links people to the Lord and each other. Laughter keeps you from taking life and yourself too seriously. Your laughter gives others permission to laugh. You love on someone when you laugh together. Christ gives laughter as solace for your soul. You miss experiencing an important part of Christ's character when you choose not to laugh.

Let go and laugh. Let go of anger and laugh. Let go of hurt and disappointment, false humility and pride, and laugh, for He has done great things. Reminisce on those prayers that seemed almost irresponsible, yet He answered them in the most unlikely way; He smiled and said yes. Think about the last time Jesus surprised you by joy. Did you take the time to laugh out loud with the Lord?

Our mouths were filled with laughter, our tongues with songs of joy. Then it was said among the nations, "The LORD has done great things for them" (Psalm 126:2).

SELF-ANGER

"And now, do not be distressed and do not be angry with yourselves for selling me here, because it was to save lives that God sent me ahead of you."
GENESIS 45:5

Self-anger is self-destructive. Self-anger is a symptom of insecurity, unrealistic expectations, and unforgiveness. It happens when we get mad at ourselves and do not forgive ourselves. We get hot-headed over missed opportunities. We boil over into anger when we overcommit and are unable to follow through with excellence. We kick ourselves when we are unkind to others, and we regret after the fact that we lost our temper. We beat ourselves up for dumb decisions that penalize our family with financial stress. We quickly snap at others because of unmet expectations, and we can't even meet the unrealistic standard we hold over ourselves.

Anger soars when there is no context for Christ-centered living. Therefore, take self-anger to your Savior before you self-destruct. Jesus wants to work with you. Take a deep breath of trust in Him and exhale a prayer of gratitude and thanksgiving. Come under the yoke of Jesus and allow Him to bear your burden of pain. God can use the sins of your past to carry out His plan in the present.

You cannot undo a divorce, but you can apologize, make restitution, and be forgiven. You can forgive yourself and you can ask forgiveness from those whom you severely mistreated. You forgive yourself when you see yourself as God does. He sees you as a needy soul incapable of forgiving yourself without first receiving His forgiveness. Forgiveness first comes from your heavenly Father. God forgives you so you can forgive others and yourself. It is a chain reaction of grace.

This is how far-reaching the forgiveness of the Lord extends. His forgiveness flows to the most significant and insignificant of hurts. Your self-anger will subside in the face of forgiveness, so let go of your resentment and embrace forgiveness. Jesus has already paid the price for your misdeeds and sins.

You do not have to stay simmering in your anger over guilt. You are set free from self-anger because of our Savior, Jesus. Replace resentment with acceptance, pride with humility, and self-anger with your Savior's unconditional love and forgiveness. Give yourself permission to weep, for tears heal a torn heart. Warm weeping dissolves self-anger like hot water over ice. Forgive and be forgiven. Because the Almighty accepts you just as you are, so can you.

"Accept one another, then, just as Christ accepted you, in order to bring praise to God" (Romans 15:7).

GRANDPARENT'S BLESSING

"They are the sons God has given me here," Joseph said to his father.
Then Israel said, "Bring them to me so I may bless them."
GENESIS 48:9

Grandchildren are certainly a blessing; who can argue this? Their smiles bless. So does their laughter. Their creative and passionate conversations bless. Their infant coos and twinkling eyes, their honesty and love, their trust and imagination all bless. Grandchildren are a blessing without a whole lot of effort. Grandchildren are a grand gift from God.

God's gift to grandchildren is their grandparents' blessing. It is significant for grandsons and granddaughters to receive this grand blessing. It's invaluable to the spiritual, emotional, and physical well-being of children. There is a greater family purpose beyond their immediate relationship with mom and dad. Grandparents are there to bless with kind words and understanding ears. They model good money management and teach their grandchildren everything from how to whittle rough sticks of wood into smooth works of art, to how to eat peanuts from a soft drink bottle. Blessings of confidence, courage, and candor come from being around grandparents who care.

Therefore, position your family to interact and engage with grandparents. Visit them often. Invite them over at holidays and on the spur of the moment. Create environments for your children in which they can be blessed by their grandparents. Grandparents are not competition, but agents of Almighty God. Do not deny them the opportunity to be blessed and to bless.

Grandparents, bless your grandchildren with a legacy of love for God and people. Do not become the center of attention. Instead, lead your grandchildren to fall in love with Jesus. God will live in your grandbabies beyond your life. Bless them with Bible reading and prayer. Bless them with worship at church. Bless them with stories and adventure. Bless them with generosity. Bless them with obedience to God. Bless them with a life worth emulating. The Bible says, "The glory of young men is their strength, gray hair the splendor of the old" (Proverbs 20:29).

You invest in eternity when you bless your grandchildren.

AUDACIOUS ASK

The Israelites did as Moses instructed and asked the Egyptians for articles of silver and gold and for clothing. The LORD had made the Egyptians favorably disposed toward the people, and they gave them what they asked for.
EXODUS 12:35-36

Giving is a God thing. Once God paves the way, it is time to ask. You may have to ask many times, but do not give up on the generosity of others. Oftentimes, asking is how the Almighty wants us to access His provision. He is pro-vision. Vision is His vehicle for mighty works. He is the one who instills His fear and faith.

We limit the Lord when we fail to ask others to participate in His almighty acts. Our procrastination may prevent others from experiencing God. It is not about our limited abilities; it is about Him and His works. It is freeing to ask of God and watch Him work. Pride tends to paralyze bold requests. We don't want to look foolish or irresponsible. We place ourselves—instead of God—at the center of our request. Asking is all about the acts of Almighty God, not our lowly limitations. Reject excuses to slither out of your responsibility to show up and present your case to Christ. Do not limit the Lord's provision.

Money is not an issue to your Master. Your obedience to audaciously ask may be the only limiting factor. You are God's broker. Therefore, do not hold back; ask audaciously. Your ministry and your business are His. He wants His work to be more successful than you do. You may need ten times the cash and resources you have needed in the past. Do not allow the largeness of the vision to scare you away.

Asking is not always easy, but it is most beneficial. The number one reason people do not give is that they are not asked. You may need to solicit donations for your ministry. If so, proceed with determined dignity and quiet confidence. Paul understood the principle of asking when he wrote, "Confident of your obedience, I write to you, knowing that you will do even more than I ask" (Philemon 21).

Prepared people are expecting an "ask." God has already prepared their hearts. They are favorably disposed to you and your God-given vision. It may come from the most unlikely places. People you have never met before may want to purchase heaven's stock for the sake of His cause. Do not be overwhelmed by the number of zeros needed on their check. Trust Him to touch the hearts of those to whom you propose His plan.

It is time to move out of the bondage of visionless and limited living and ask audaciously of the Almighty.

SIN'S REMEDY

Moses said to the people, "Do not be afraid, God has come to test you, so that the fear of God will be with you to keep you from sinning."
EXODUS 20:20

Sin has a feared enemy: the fear of God. The fear of God is not only a remedy for sin, but it is a potent vaccine. Sin and the fear of God cannot coexist for long. The fear of God extinguishes sin's combustible character.

When you focus on your heavenly Father in worship and prayer, you can't help but fear Him. When we fear God, we love God and He loves us. When we fear God, we understand that some things are off limits, and we avoid them. When we fear God, we trust God. When we fear God, we run toward God in worship and away from sin in disgust. The fear of God is our friend, and it enhances our friendship with our heavenly Father. Fear Him and you will be set free from sin and self.

This is why the devil attempts to devalue the fear of God. He knows if we do not take seriously the fear factor of our heavenly Father, then we are exposed to sin's influence. Without the fear of God, we are set up for serious sin problems. Cultures crumble without a moral fabric. Families fall into severe dysfunction when the fear of God is not lived out or understood. Individual lives lose their meaning and purpose when the fear of God is placed on the shelf.

The Ten Commandments are rules for how to express our fear of God. An adulterer sins because somewhere along the way, the fear of God did not matter to him anymore. The idols of materialism can consume us when we forget to fear God and instead, worship at the altar of financial gain. The fear of God encourages children to honor their parents, and it positions parents to lovingly raise their children. The fear of God is our fortress against the devil's onslaught. We are motivated to put on the full armor of God, knowing we are no match in our own strength to defeat the devil.

The trials and tribulations you may be facing are not meant to create an unhealthy fear that cringes before Christ, but rather a healthy fear that trusts Him despite this test of your faith. Do not allow the sorrow of loss or the success of gain to keep you from fearing God. The fear of God is not a mindless and cold obedience. On the contrary, it is thoughtful, prayerful, and full of joy. It sees the opportunity to obey God as an honor. We can dismiss it as an old-fashioned doctrine (it has been around since Adam and Eve), or we can embrace it as necessary for successful living.

Wisdom says, "To fear the LORD is to hate evil; I hate pride and arrogance, evil behavior and perverse speech" (Proverbs 8:13). Therefore, do not be afraid to fear.

AUGUST 13

GOD JOURNAL

When Moses went and told the people all the LORD's words and laws, they responded with one voice, "Everything the LORD has said we will do." Moses then wrote down everything the LORD had said.

EXODUS 24:3-4

It is wise to journal for Jesus, for it captures the thinking of an ever-communicative Christ. When you take the time to write out what God is saying, you see His fingerprints all over your life. You understand more clearly, and you remember more robustly. His words are more penetrating and meaningful when you filter them through your heart and mind into words on paper.

A dull pencil that writes is much better than a sharp mind that forgets. Writing out words and wrestling to define what you feel crystallizes your thinking. A diary deals primarily with horizontal relationships; a God journal engages with eternity. The world makes more sense when you see it from God's perspective.

A God journal allows you to chronicle what Christ is doing in and through you. It is an immediate reminder of His faithfulness. It can be a time to celebrate answered prayer. It can be a time to release your struggles and anxieties to your loving heavenly Father and think through His will and plan for your life. It can be a time to unleash your frustration on an absorptive white page.

Journaling for God reminds you that He owns everything, including you. You are His representative to a lost and dying world. You are reminded of right when you choose to write. Like an alert secretary, you are to listen intently to dictation from deity. God speaks through Holy Scripture. He speaks through your body, soul, mind, and spirit; He speaks through people, both friend and foe; He speaks through money or the lack thereof; He speaks through circumstances and in quiet prayer.

His words do not wander far away when you write them down. Therefore, find a quiet corner with a hot cup of coffee, tea, or hot chocolate. Open the best-selling book of all time and meditate on God's timeless truth. Ask Him to apply His wisdom to your mind and heart. It may be one sentence, a paragraph, or a page. The length doesn't matter. Your words may be misspelled and your sentences fragmented. Your goal is not journalistic excellence. What matters is capturing your meditative moments, so you can decode Christ's heart for you.

God can take broken phrases and heal fractured faith. The Bible says, "Then the LORD said to Moses, 'Write this on a scroll as something to be remembered and make sure that Joshua hears it'" (Exodus 17:14). It will one day bless those who may wade through your writings.

Slow down, listen, and pen the heart of God.

GOD CHOSEN

Then the Lord said to Moses, "See, I have chosen Bezalel son of Uri, the son of Hur, of the tribe of Judah, and I have filled him with the Spirit of God, with wisdom, with understanding, with knowledge and with all kinds of skills."

EXODUS 31:1-3

When there is a vision to be cast, a mission to be accomplished, or a task to be completed, Christ calls specific people for a specific purpose. God uses whom He chooses, and He equips whom He calls. The call of Christ is humbling, but His call is real, nonetheless. It is a call to obedience, first and foremost. God chooses those who have been faithful with what may seem like small gifts so He can bring on bigger abilities.

He will grow you into the leader you need to be, and the Holy Spirit directs an obedient follower. Your Lord is not slack in anointing and equipping you for the task. There is no vision that overwhelms your Father in heaven. God emboldens your faith and consecrates your character. Watch in wonder as He hones your skills. His desire for your next season of service is that your knowledge and abilities be elevated to a whole new level. This may mean more formal education or informal mentoring from more experienced men and women. It may require self-education and on-the-job training. Or it may require a combination of all these initiatives and more.

You can be sure that your faithfulness in managing His giftedness matters. He fills with His Spirit those who surrender to Him and His calling on their life. When you submit as His chosen one, His Spirit indwells and empowers you for His assignment. Therefore, let the Lord drive your spiritual development. Submit your parenting skills, your leadership skills, and your spiritual know-how to Him. Stay submitted, surrendered, and obedient, and He will fill, anoint, and baptize you in His spirit.

Above all else, stay in Christ's school of prayer. The lessons learned in your prayer closet will instruct you way beyond what you can ask or think. Prayer is an exchange of the natural with the supernatural. Prayer takes your finite understanding and empowers it with eternity's infinite knowledge, wisdom, and discernment. Prayer prepares your heart and mind to receive and apply the wisdom of God. There are no insignificant assignments from the Almighty, so tackle your new role with faithful prayer.

Accept this fact: You are His choice. Jesus summed it up the best. "You did not choose me, but I chose you and appointed you so that you might go and bear fruit—fruit that will last—and so that whatever you ask in my name the Father will give you" (John 15:16). He has prepared you for this season; so don't look back. Just look forward to the Lord by faith.

Be humbled. Be grateful. Be obedient. Be trusting.
Will you say yes to the Lord's call?

IMPATIENT ACTIONS

When the people saw that Moses was so long in coming down from the mountain, they gathered around Aaron and said, "Come, make us gods who will go before us. As for this fellow Moses who brought us up out of Egypt, we don't know what has happened to him."

EXODUS 32:1

We become impatient when things don't go our way or when uncertainty looms over our life like a dark cloud. We become impatient when time seems to be running out or when people don't act as we think they should. We even become impatient waiting on God. We all wrestle with impatience from time to time. Hopefully, you are not chronically impatient. If so, there is a good chance you are discontented and even miserable. Impatience can be good if your house is on fire, but in the normal course of life, it is not the best choice.

Impatience can cause you to do things that are totally uncharacteristic of your normal behavior. You are prone to deviance if others prod you on, for impatience does not like to be alone. Its emotions are fueled by the discontent of a group. Somehow, the voice of reason suffocates in a crowded room full of discontent. Its words become garbled by intense grumbling. Even level heads become unbalanced when intoxicated by impatience.

The timing of impatience can be uncanny. God could have just performed a beautiful act such as childbirth, when suddenly we become impatient with meeting the needs of the totally dependent baby. We forget the joy of birth and revert to the burden of bringing up a child and complain about the inconvenience of infants. We become impatient with their cries that started out as cute.

What you do while you wait determines whether you are patient or impatient. First, use this time of waiting to ratchet up your service to others. Service to others on behalf of Christ keeps you from being impatient around your own expectations. It diverts idle minds from believing Satan's lies; you avoid playing foolish mind games when you are engaged in unselfish acts of service.

Second, seek the Lord in worship and thanksgiving, because that's how you facilitate patience and contentment. You can't contemplate the goodness and greatness of your heavenly Father and not be touched with patience. Worship feeds trust, and trust is the parent of patience. Worship recalibrates your reasoning to reflect on the character of Christ.

Third, pray for those who have not met your expectations. They may be spiritual leaders who seem to be ignoring you. It may be a wife who is in a self-absorbed season. Your boss may be demanding and unreasonable, your children uncommunicative and uncooperative. You can battle impatience with Christ's unlimited patience.

"But for that very reason I was shown mercy so that in me, the worst of sinners, Christ Jesus might display his immense patience as an example for those who would believe in him and receive eternal life" (1 Timothy 1:16).

AUGUST 16

CARELESSLY COMMIT

If anyone thoughtlessly takes an oath to do anything, whether good or evil (in any matter one might carelessly swear about) even though they are unaware of it, but then they learn of it and realize their guilt.

LEVITICUS 5:4

Be careful with your commitments. Keeping commitments gives you credibility, and without credibility you are a mere shell of sincerity. Simple living creates margin, which helps you to fulfill commitments. With margin in your life, you can calculate your commitments prayerfully and practically. Does the Lord want me to be part of this initiative, organization, or relationship? A pause to pray protects you from overcommitting. Does this commitment align with your purpose, calendar, and budget? If it crowds out a priority on your calendar or blows up the budget, it is not necessary.

Forgotten commitments cause us the most frustration. Forgetfulness may be a reason, but it is not an excuse. These commitments may be the worst kind because if you don't even know you have let someone down, there is no opportunity for restitution. Foolish is a man or woman who continues to commit with a debt of unexecuted obligations mounting up on their credit card of commitment. Therefore, stop the crazy cycle of commitments before your word becomes bankrupt. Go to those who are still waiting in confused silence and ask them for more time or ask them to let you out of the commitment. Ignoring them is not an option.

Above all else, make sure you keep your commitments to Christ. He does not take commitments cavalierly. A commitment to Christ is bound by heaven, so it is never to be entered into carelessly. All other commitments flow out of your submission to your Savior. Your "yes" to Jesus is not sentimental, but sincere and even sacrificial. His Spirit leads your conscience to commit. It may be a big thing like salvation, for at conversion you committed to believe in Jesus as your Lord and Savior. Your commitment to Christ goes way beyond conversion, to our growth and maturity. As followers of Jesus, you commit to follow Him in trust and obedience. You stay true to this commitment to follow Him even when it is not convenient, or when it may cost you something. You commit to the church because it is the bride of Christ. We commit where Christ commits. The Bible says, "So then, those who suffer according to God's will should commit themselves to their faithful Creator and continue to do good" (1 Peter 4:19).

Are you engaged in His best or have your commitments become a snare to kingdom productivity? Do not commit to any more than you have in time, money, and character.

Make Christ-centered commitments your filter of choice.

SUCCESSION PLANNING

"The priest who is anointed and ordained to succeed his father as high priest is to make atonement. He is to put on the sacred linen garments and make atonement."
LEVITICUS 16:32-33

Succession planning is about stewardship. By God's grace, you built a good reputation, and your enterprise is one people trust. You want to make sure that what you have been blessed to build is managed well after you leave.

Smooth succession requires you to define and document what you do. Make your job description up to date and clearly defined. Codify the processes, policies, and procedures that sustain the work. Make sure the systems that are run are defined, decentralized, and do not depend on you. Succession planning is a natural time to get the spotlight off you and onto the team. This needs to happen sooner rather than later. Wise leaders build teams that carry on the work long after those leaders are gone.

Leaders who plan for a successor succeed, but leaders who hang on past their prime hold back the enterprise. The lack of succession planning can mean a slow death for the leader, his team, and the organization. Therefore, pray for your replacement, for someone with a passion and calling for the mission of your business or ministry. Successors are not to be considered lightly. If they are not called and energized over the culture you have created, they are not a right fit. Don't just look for those who are convenient, but trust God for someone who believes he is led by the Lord to engage with the vision.

Begin to think and pray about what type of person needs to eventually replace you, and when this needs to occur. What is God's perfect timing and what is your role, as the leader, to execute its fulfillment? Talk with your board, investors, or trusted advisors regarding your intentions. Ask them to begin to think and pray about the process. Everyone is replaceable in time, and your service is for a season. Trust God with His business or ministry, for He wants it to succeed more than anyone. Almighty God is the owner, so look to His Spirit to lead the succession process. The Bible says, "By the grace God has given me, I laid a foundation as a wise builder, and someone else is building on it. But each one should build with care. For no one can lay any foundation other than the one already laid, which is Jesus Christ" (1 Corinthians 3:10-11).

Be prayerful, intentional, and trust Him with the successor.

AUGUST 18

FOLLOW UP

Moses inspected the work and saw that they had done it just as the LORD had commanded. So Moses blessed them.
EXODUS 39:43

Follow-up is necessary for effective leaders at home and at work. It is necessary as you hold others responsible. Follow-up means you care about the person, and you care about the work being done. It is necessary in your work and family. You follow up with your children because you care for them too much not to stay involved in their lives. They may seem distant and disinterested, but you still follow up.

Effective follow-up is as much an art as a science. Yes, have a systematic style to your communications, but do not badger people by bombarding them with too much, too often. People do better when you "inspect what we expect." So, take the time to inspect. Create margin for inspection and accountability. Frequent inspection leads to clarification and correction. Small adjustments along the way defuse frustrations and avert subtle surprises down the road.

Do not assume that someone understands the first time. Make sure everyone is on the same page and that there is a coalition of efforts and resources. Also, be willing to adjust, as thinking and engaged people will reveal a better way of doing things. Encourage and reward their wise and resourceful innovation. Follow-up frees people to give much needed feedback.

Above all else, make sure your projects and processes revolve around God's principles of work and relationships. It is imperative that everyone be aligned around the Almighty's agenda. His way is the best way, so do not compromise the non-negotiables that define the values and mission of the enterprise. Follow-up keeps a focus on the purpose of glorifying God.

Use your frequent follow-up as a way to bless the other person. Make the follow-up of the transaction or task a small percentage of the conversation. Use this excuse for relational engagement to find out about the person. Listen for their fears, their frustrations, and their dreams. People want to know they are cared for, before they care to listen. Use your faithful follow-up as an opportunity to bless others on behalf of God.

Paul wrote out expectations and then followed up in person. "Although I hope to come to you soon, I am writing you these instructions so that, if I am delayed, you will know how people ought to conduct themselves in God's household, which is the church of the living God, the pillar and foundation of the truth" (1 Timothy 3:14-15).

**Follow-up enables wise stewardship,
excellent communication, and affirming accountability.**

SIN OF SILENCE

"If anyone sins because they do not speak up when they hear a public charge to testify regarding something they have seen or learned about, they will be held responsible."
LEVITICUS 5:1

Responsible people speak up when necessary. Sometimes, it is easier to remain silent, but God has not called us to a path of least resistance. Suffering in silence is not God's design. He wants us to speak up under the influence of His Spirit. Even if the words are hard and direct, God's Spirit can deliver them in a loving manner. When you speak up, it means you care. We love other people too much to allow them to hurt themselves with inappropriate actions.

This is especially hard for men. Pride and ego keep us from being vulnerable to rejection or relational controversy, but we owe it to God, to others, and ourselves to "speak the truth in love" (Ephesians 4:15). Love compels you to take a relational risk and say something.

Furthermore, make sure to speak up and defend those who are defenseless. Rise to the defense of widows, orphans, and the poor who are crushed under the weight of the world's injustice. The Bible says, "Religion that God our Father accepts as pure and faultless is this: to look after orphans and widows in their distress and to keep oneself from being polluted by the world" (James 1:27). You may not have to look very far. There may be family members who need your attention.

We must also speak up for those who need another chance. Second, third, and fourth chances are called for to model Christ's attitude of acceptance. Your reputation may become soiled because you choose to speak up on behalf of a seedy soul, but trust God. We can relate best to sinners because we suffer from the same temptations and sorrows. Christians are sinners saved by the grace of God, and no one is beyond God's reach.

Lastly, speak up for and serve the poor. The poor need a person they can trust. The poor need us to give them a voice against the greedy souls who seek to take advantage of them. They need financial training; they need medical supplies and education; they need nutrition; they need jobs; they need indoor plumbing; they need shoes on their feet and clothes on their backs. Mostly, they need a growing relationship with Jesus Christ. The poor are drawn to Jesus when they see God's people stand up for them. They are attracted to those who care enough to sit in their homes and drink coffee, create jobs, and speak up on their behalf. It is time some of us break out of our bubble of affluence and expose ourselves to the sufferings of the poor.

You sin if you remain silent over those who are defenseless. Be faithful to speak the words and then trust God with the results.

STUBBORN PRIDE

"I will break down your stubborn pride and make the sky above you like iron and the ground beneath you like bronze."
LEVITICUS 26:19

Everyone has to be careful of stubborn pride sneaking into his or her beliefs and behaviors.

Stubborn pride creates hardened hearts. It is shortsighted and insecure in its aggressive attempts to control. Stubborn pride acts as if it has everything together and doesn't need the help of anyone, even God. The demands of stubborn pride are unreasonable, and its perspective is skewed toward itself. Stubborn pride resists change and misses out on improvement for the sake of the project, the team, or its family. Stubborn pride rejects relational engagement that requires confession and forgiveness. Stubborn pride will dig itself into a deeper hole of distant living before it takes a risk of being found out.

Humility can help someone sucked into the seduction of stubborn pride; that stubborn pride melts under the heat of humility. Discerning people already understand the charade and the manipulation of a man or a woman who is unable to admit faults. Humility means you fight fair together. You truly listen to the perspective of your spouse or coworker, without reacting defensively or judging too quickly. You are willing to change for the greater good and for the sake of pleasing your Savior.

The Lord loves us too much to stand by while we struggle under the influence of stubborn pride. Like wild stallions with lots of willpower and energy, we need brokenness and training. Almighty God uses whatever means necessary to get our attention. His Holy Spirit is assigned to break our will and align our spirit with His. He breaks us from the power of ourselves. He breaks us to be bold for Him. He breaks us and molds us into reasonable people who honor the views of others.

God is the one trying to get our attention. We may be mad at others, but our case is against Christ. The Spirit's conviction is what causes us to cringe and shrink back from stubborn pride's relational poison.

The Bible says, "The eyes of the arrogant will be humbled and human pride brought low; the Lord alone will be exalted in that day" (Isaiah 2:11). Do not negotiate with stubborn pride but break it under the hammer of humility and replace it with love, respect, and forgiveness.

God's brokenness brings down pride.

HIGHER STANDARD

"[Priests] must be holy to their God and must not profane the name of their God. Because they present the food offerings to the Lord, the food of their God, they are to be holy."
LEVITICUS 21:6

Ministers of the Gospel submit to a higher standard and answer to a holy authority. There is something special and fearful about being a vocational servant of Jesus Christ. This is not a role to be undertaken lightly or to be chosen casually, as some do secular career paths. God places eternal expectations on priests, pastors, and ministry leaders.

Leaders in the church have the Lord as their baseline for behavior. Deviant behavior is unacceptable for those who lead on behalf of the Lord. The leader's character is his greatest asset. How hypocritical and foolish to think leaders can flaunt immoral behavior when church members are disciplined for the same sin. Double standards may be for the uninformed and the unaccountable, but not for faithful followers of Christ. How surreal to have to declare that character in the church matters!

There is a holy obligation for leaders to model and teach holy living as defined in God's Word. A church or ministry leader cannot practice immoral living and still lead the bride of Christ. They cannot practice homosexuality, adultery, stealing, or lying. They cannot practice unfaithfulness in any of its destructive forms. Holiness is defined by God. Leaders of God's church and ministry are to be holy as He is holy. Therefore, you can't say you are a leader on behalf of Jesus Christ if you embrace and endorse the very sin for which He died on the cross.

Do not use the Bible to defend your sinful living or use the church as a crutch for crude behavior. If someone is bent on breaking 2,000 years of church tradition and 4,000 years of biblical teaching, then he should do it in the name of another religion, not on behalf of Christianity. Wake up to the fact that you have a heavenly Father to whom you will one day answer. Yes, He loves. Yes, He forgives. But above all else, He is holy.

The Bible is clear: "Be shepherds of God's flock that is under your care, watching over them—not because you must, but because you are willing, as God wants you to be; not pursuing dishonest gain, but eager to serve; not lording it over those entrusted to you, but being examples to the flock" (1 Peter 5:2-3).

Holy leaders make people thirsty for God. Be a leader whose character aligns with Christ's and who models faithfulness, not perfection. Do not conform to this world but be transformed by God's truth.

If anyone is hell-bent on hellish living, the church cannot condone it, for doing so causes the church to lose its saltiness and dim its light.

NON-VICTIM MINDSET

No, in all these things we are more than conquerors through him who loved us.
ROMANS 8:37

Followers of Jesus are not victims, they are more than conquerors. You have overcome because Christ has overcome. There is no need to give in to the temptation of victimized thinking.

A "woe is me" attitude places the focus on you instead of your Savior. Victims seek out sympathy from unsuspecting souls. Their desired outcome is you feeling sorry for them. Ironically, their goal is to make you feel guilty for their sorry state of mind. They want someone else to fix their circumstances. Meanwhile, the victim remains immobile while stuck in a fear-based quagmire. Victims refuse to take responsibility. People who languish in a victim mindset do not last very long. Their life's inertia gets them nowhere, and they finally experience the self-fulfilling prophecy of failure.

On the contrary, Christ frees you from the vicious cycle of victimized living. Christ is your confidence and the object of your faith. He gives you the security and strength to carry on even when you feel misunderstood, marginalized, or rejected. When you take responsibility for your choices and your circumstances, you cease to be a victim. People who embrace victimless living get on with life. They shed feeling sorry for themselves and begin to serve others. They lift their discussions from the depths of despair to the heights of hope. Therefore, do not allow your circumstances to define you. Christ has already defined you as more than a conqueror through Him. You are victorious in Him.

Moreover, help those seduced by and stuck in a victim mindset. Be patient while they process what possesses their thinking. Help them break what may be a family trait of defeatist living. Their parents may have been victims. Their grandparents may have been victims. For generations back, their legacy may have been marred by a victim mindset. Through Christ, lead them to break the chain of this corrosive thinking. Help them discover that they need people to pray for them, not to feel sorry for them. They need the power of God to prevail in their lives; they don't need the manipulation from man.

Because Jesus has overcome, you have overcome. The Bible says, "The Lamb will triumph over them because he is Lord of lords and King of kings—and with him will be his called, chosen and faithful followers" (Revelation 17:14). Jesus has overcome pain, suffering, and death. He transforms His children from victims to victorious followers. Therefore, be authentic in your adversity, honest about your fears and frustrations, and offer solutions, not complaints.

Pray for the power of God to fall fresh on you, for by faith, you can go from victim to victor.

ANGRY OBEDIENCE

Moses raised his arm and struck the rock twice with his staff. Water gushed out, and the community and their livestock drank. But the Lord said to Moses and Aaron, "Because you did not trust in me enough to honor me as holy in the sight of the Israelites, you will not bring this community into the land I give them."

NUMBERS 20:11-12

Angry obedience is not the best obedience. It has its positive results, and it has its negative consequences. It does get results, but it does so at the expense of dishonoring God and people.

It's like a frustrated husband who lashes out at his wife yet shows that he loves her through his provision of her food, a home, a car, and clothes. The facts of his provision are true, but there is something ominous about the omission of love and respect in the tone of his defense. In this angry reaction, God is not glorified.

Anger drives this type of response. It may be anger from the grumbling of ungrateful people; it may be anger at others whose capacity for work and activity does not meet your expectations; or it may be anger at oneself for not preparing others to do their own planning and implementation. True obedience is going through the right motions with an attitude that acknowledges God as the source of provision and trust.

Appropriation of God's grace infuses graciousness. His grace enables you to trust in the Almighty's agenda. You can trust Him and rest in His provision, instead of rushing into angry reactions. You can get right results without being driven by anger. Ask God to replace your anger with His understanding. Submit to the conviction of the Holy Spirit. Your submission to your Savior positions you to walk in humility and not in pride. Humble people are patient and self-controlled. They are as concerned about the means as they are the ends. Unfortunately, at any given moment, anger can push humility out and replace it with pride. It is a Christless coup of the heart. Praise God there is a remedy to anger-driven living.

The remedy is living at a pace governed by grace. Living without margin pushes out grace and incubates anger. Therefore, create more time for people and prayer. Pray without ceasing and ask the Holy Spirit to douse any fluttering fires of anger that pride tries to ignite. Grace-filled living is more relational and less transactional. Relationally motivated people ask caring questions instead of engaging in angry accusations. Their obedience to God is motivated by their fear of God. This honors Him, which in turn extends love and respect to others.

Pray as the psalmist: "Give me understanding, so that I may keep your law and obey it with all my heart" (Psalm 119:34) and replace anger with peace and patience.

PRIDE FORGETS

Your heart will become proud and you will forget the LORD your God, who brought you out of Egypt, out of the land of slavery.
DEUTERONOMY 8:14

Pride forgets where it came from. It is forgetful either intentionally or unintentionally. Pride may get promoted, but it forgets those who contributed to the process of success. Pride gives too much credit to self and too little credit to others. Pride forgets its family. Pride takes family for granted and ignores their needs. It is selfishly wrapped up in itself.

Pride forgets others, while humility includes others; pride takes all the credit, while humility shares the credit; pride discourages, while humility encourages; pride pontificates, while humility prays; pride talks too much, while humility listens liberally; pride blames, while humility takes responsibility; pride is oblivious to good manners and courteous conduct.

Above all else, pride forgets God. It may talk about God but only as needed to rubber-stamp its plans. Pride subtly uses God to carry out its agenda, and it forgets to see God for who He is. Pride forgets that God governs the universe and all its inhabitants. God is engaged with you up to the smallest of details, and He knows where you are and where you need to go. He wants you to remember His pristine track record of faithfulness. His past provision is a predictor of His future provision. Pride forgets this; it has amnesia to the things of the Almighty. It is too busy to create margin for its Master.

Therefore, it is imperative you allow Christ to keep your pride in its place. Pride can only be conquered with humble dependence on God and obedience to His commands. The Bible says, "Seek the LORD, all you humble of the land, you who do what he commands. Seek righteousness, seek humility" (Zephaniah 2:3). Humility displaces pride and bows down before divinity in prayer. Humility remembers God's faithful deliverance from darkness into light. It remembers God's salvation from sin and self to grace and service. Humility remembers to love God and people first and subjugates its needs so that they are second. It has tremendous recall for good because God is its leader. Humility remembers how generous God is and it is generous in return. Humility remembers to thank others and to pray for them. It understands and remembers what's important to the Lord and then invests its energies toward His initiatives.

Humility remembers.

ACTIVITY WITHOUT REALITY

For I can testify about them that they are zealous for God,
but their zeal is not based on knowledge.
ROMANS 10:2

Activity without a sense of reality leads to futility. For example, finances are a reality check, for they are an indicator of God's will. God speaks through money, or the lack thereof. You can sincerely spend yourself into a false affluence. Reality is that you have to pay for the assets that have been obtained by debt. Credit may cause you to check out of reality, but its consequences will roar back in real bills. Reality is that you cannot continue spending more than you make. The only way for the math to work is that income must exceed expenses. Debt may suspend reality for a time, but it will eventually come crashing down from the overwhelming weight of credit's pressure. Do not be afraid to wait and save before you spend. For example, take a low-cost vacation you can afford instead of an extravagant one you can't.

So go with God's definition of reality, as He defines reality in His Word and validates it with His will. The most effective way to remain in touch with reality is to stay connected with Christ. Confessing your sin and receiving Christ into your life is the only way to begin a relationship with Him.

Alignment with the Almighty ensures reality. His perspective positions you to engage in reality with an eternal mindset. He is a reality check, along with wise counselors. This is why a humble and teachable spirit is a prerequisite to understanding reality. Do not allow your experience, success, and intelligence to blind you from reality. Go to God often for His reality check. Let Him define your need for change and maturity. Ask Him to use the realities of your situation to make you more like Jesus.

Make sure your church activity is grounded in the reality of a relationship with God. Religious activity does not equal relationship. Spirituality without faith in Christ skirts the reality of the need for repentance and redemption. Sincere spirituality based on wrong assumptions will get you into trouble. No amount of good deeds can substitute for your need for a Savior. Prayer is your guide to what's real. Ask questions and really listen for a reality check of where you are and where you need to go.

Jesus stated this reality: "I have told you these things, so that in me you may have peace. In this world you will have trouble. But take heart! I have overcome the world" (John 16:33).

Instead of denying or rejecting reality, embrace it. Reality is the reason for dependence on God. By faith, accept the Lord's reality check and rely on His grace.

Activity grounded in reality is rewarding,
so thank Him for keeping you in a place of blessing.

AUGUST 26

DISCIPLINE INVITES RESPECT

Moreover, we have all had human fathers who disciplined us and we respect them for it. How much more should we submit to the Father of spirits and live!
HEBREWS 12:9

Discipline invites respect, whether it's your children or your coworkers. Your children may not like it, but they will respect you for taking the time to correct their behavior. Discipline is an application of accountability and is a consequence for unwise actions. Wise discipline means you define clear expectations and reasonable rules. Delayed discipline dilutes the dangers of bad decisions. This is why it is wise to discipline our children sooner rather than later.

For example, your son or daughter needs to know in no uncertain terms that they will be disciplined for a disrespectful attitude, disobedient actions, or dishonest speech. Write it down, have them repeat it back to you, and then enforce it consistently. If they suspect they can slip by with undisciplined living, they will. Better to engage in conflict today than to watch them destroy themselves for lack of discipline tomorrow.

Discipline is not a club of correction, but a laser of love, so discipline with loving patience. Discipline done well creates discipline in the recipient. Those who are tuned in and discerning will apply loving discipline soon after the offense. Wise discipline includes instruction. You show and tell why and how to live better by God's grace. You lead your children to be responsible adults. They learn discipline by being disciplined.

Above all else, receive the discipline of your heavenly Father. The Bible says, "Blessed is the one whom God corrects; so do not despise the discipline of the Almighty" (Job 5:17). He disciplines because He loves. Because God cares, He disciplines. You cannot hide from the long, loving arm of the Lord. He will expose deeds done in secret. You cannot ignore God's principles and escape the ramifications of His discipline. He disciplines for your own good, as it is protection from further harm. His discipline stokes the fires of fear for Him.

The Almighty uses different avenues to deliver His discipline. It may come through finances, relationships, or health. Don't despise His discipline or be surprised by it. How you handle God's discipline can weaken or strengthen your faith, for the fruit of God's discipline is intimacy. Closeness to Christ and others comes as a result of discipline. Furthermore, divine discipline is training in peace. His peace dwells in the hearts of those who receive well the discipline of their heavenly Father. There is no greater peaceful, easy feeling than knowing your Lord loves you.

Respect for God follows discipline from God.

AUGUST 27

FACE TIME

I have much to write to you, but I do not want to use paper and ink. Instead, I hope to visit you and talk with you face to face, so that our joy may be complete.

2 JOHN 12

Some things are best communicated face-to-face. A proposal for marriage, a job interview, a discussion with a mentor, and a deep conversation with family members are all things that thrive in a one-on-one relational environment. Fear tends to force us away from direct engagement with people. We sometimes avoid human contact because of overwhelming insecurity, fear of rejection, or busyness.

The season of face-to-face time with family evaporates unwittingly. Soon kids are off with friends, attending college, and then married. Just as Harry Chapin's song says, "The cat's in the cradle and the silver spoon. Little Boy Blue and the Man in the Moon. When you coming home, Dad? I don't know when, but we'll get together then. You know we'll have a good time then." Therefore, reserve time daily, weekly, monthly and yearly with those you love. Invest time and money in face time with your son, your daughter, your wife, your parents, and your friends.

Face time allows your smile to shine a ray of hope across a discouraged heart. Face time is your opportunity to discuss those hard issues and to be sure the sincerity of your love is not missed. So, show up and love on them in person.

Most important, you need face time with your heavenly Father. The eyes of our soul need to gaze, by faith, at God. If we chronically miss coming alongside Christ, we burn out in our own strength. We desperately need "face time" with Jesus. We need His affirmation and love; we need His instruction and correction; we need His discernment and wisdom. He can give us all of these at any time. Our Savior is spontaneous for our sake. Christ is on call for His children, but we still need structured time with Him. It is imperative that we instill in our lives the discipline of daily face time praying and grafting God's Word into our minds and hearts.

You can tell when someone has been with Jesus. They have peace that brings calm; they have patience that extends a second chance; they have boldness based on wisdom; they have love that forgives; they have service that is relentless; they have faith that is strong; they have a hope that perseveres. People who have regular face time with Jesus are unique and pleasant. Therefore, linger with the Lord, face-to-face. Invest time in your relationship with the Almighty. Keep an eye on eternity.

Moses experienced this. "The Lord would speak to Moses face to face, as one speaks to a friend" (Exodus 33:11). Faithfulness in face time leads to robust relationships. Therefore, enjoy the joy of being with Jesus and friends.

A GOOD IMITATION

Dear friend, do not imitate what is evil but what is good.
Anyone who does what is good is from God.
Anyone who does what is evil has not seen God.
3 JOHN 11

Imitation of good is good, but imitation of evil is bad. So, look for the good in others and compliment them with imitation. When you copy another's character, you extend an affirmation of who they are. You validate them when you follow their example. They are encouraged, and you are equipped to live a better life. Everyone is happy when imitation of good is applied.

When you discover a good person, you have a gift. Honor them with respect and recognition and give God the glory for their goodness. If you want to grow as a giver, pray for generous givers whom you can follow. If you want to grow in your marriage, be around married people who put God first and their spouse second. You are wise to imitate the healthy habits of good people because you can't be good alone.

But also be discerning in your imitation of others. A smile does not guarantee that someone is good. People may be friendly only for their own sake. A religious person may or may not be a good person to emulate. Probe their motives for being good and beware of self-righteousness and performance-driven living.

Authentic goodness is from God. The Holy Spirit produces godliness in the heart of Christ-followers. Goodness without God is sentimental, shallow, and has no eternal consequences. It is only when your goodness promotes God that you are genuinely good. The God factor is what gives goodness depth and breadth. His goodness travels from one generation to the next. The goodness of God penetrates hard hearts and evil circumstances.

Imitation of good begins by receiving Christ into your heart by faith. The Bible says, "So then, just as you received Christ Jesus as Lord, continue to live your lives in him, rooted and built up in him, strengthened in the faith as you were taught, and overflowing with thankfulness" (Colossians 2:6-7).

So, above all else, imitate the goodness of God. Look at the life of Christ and, by God's grace, seek to imitate Him. Jesus is your model for goodness. "Taste and see that the Lord is good" (Psalm 34:8). The goodness of God satisfies your hungry heart. Be cautious not to do good deeds without first receiving the goodness of God in Christ. Godly goodness flows from the inside out. It is an internal imitation with eternal outcomes. Therefore, imitate God, so when others imitate you, they imitate a good thing.

When you imitate goodness given by God,
you embrace a life with positive eternal consequences.

AUGUST 29

ETERNAL GIFT

And this is the testimony: God has given us eternal life, and this life is in his Son. Whoever has the Son has life; whoever does not have the Son of God does not have life.

1 JOHN 5:11-12

The most significant gift we can receive is the gift of eternal life in Jesus Christ. This gift cannot be bought with money and is received by faith. God's greatest gift to the human race is His son, Jesus Christ. His birth, His life, His death, and His resurrection were all gifts. God gave His son because He loved you. Christ was born for you. He lived for you. He died for you. He rose for you. He wants to be your life. What an extraordinary gift God has bestowed upon you by grace.

Jesus says, "Now this is eternal life: that they know you, the only true God, and Jesus Christ, whom you have sent" (John 17:3). Eternity is a gift that keeps on giving forever and ever. Your eternal gift to someone could take the form of a Bible, a book, a sermon, or a conversation explaining the gospel of Jesus Christ. If you are a believer in Jesus, He lives within you. When you give yourself, you are giving Jesus. You can give yourself in service on behalf of Jesus; you can give money on behalf of Jesus; you can give a listening ear on behalf of Jesus.

When all is said and done, people around you will wonder about this gift. Deep down they desire God's gift. He has created us all to want His eternal gift. Give it away with grace, and trust God that others will receive it by faith. Believers bear the beautiful gift of Christ.

God's part is to give; your part is to receive. Your heavenly Father patiently offers His Son Jesus as your gift of eternal life. You can receive it by faith, or you can reject it as unimportant or irrelevant. The best thing you can do is to accept God's gift of eternal life in Jesus. An unopened gift communicates rejection to the giver. Without Christ becoming real and personal, you are destined for a life lacking proper purpose and a death with dreadful eternal consequences. But eternal life with Him is His expression of love and forgiveness.

Receiving God's gift of eternal life has its benefits. Christ exchanges your old life for His new life. He lives within you and through you. His character compels you to live life to its fullest. He forgives you of past, present, and future sins. He leads you, guides you, and directs you. He comforts you when you hurt; He affirms you when you are right; He convicts you when you are wrong; He brings a smile to your face and a bounce to your step; He replaces greed with generosity, anger with forgiveness, pride with humility, and gloom with gladness.

There is no disappointment after opening God's eternal gift, only joy unspeakable.

SERVANT LEADERSHIP

"Whoever wants to become great among you must be your servant, and whoever wants to be first must be your slave—just as the Son of Man did not come to be served, but to serve, and to give his life a ransom for many."
MATTHEW 20:26-28

Servant leadership is service. It is not jockeying for position, nor is it politicking for power. Instead, it is posturing for the opportunity to serve. Servant leaders avoid the limelight and serve in ways that many times go unnoticed. The little things make a servant leader. It may be taking out the trash at home or making the coffee at work. No task is too menial to the servant leader.

There is something bigger than behavior that distinguishes a servant leader. It is an attitude of how to make others successful. He knows that if those around him are successful, then there is a good chance he will experience success. Servant leadership is not caught up with getting the credit, for the servant leader has put to death the need for recognition. The attention and credit can easily flow to others, which is where it belongs. Instead, the servant leader may give away opportunities that come his or her way. They know titles will come in God's timing, so they seek to serve, letting status find them.

Self-service, on the other hand, builds a culture of mediocrity. It is all about taking care of one's own little world and not giving any thought to the needs of other team members. The unspoken rule is: survival of the fittest. This self-service contributes to a scarcity mentality. If I serve you then you may look better than me. You may get all the credit. This fear factor facilitates competition instead of cooperation.

Jesus was the servant leader of all servant leaders. He boldly confronted the sins of the religious hypocrites but washed the feet of His disciples. He ran out those who commercialized the temple, but He had time to allow children to sit on His lap. He questioned the motives of threatened leaders of the day, while taking the time to feed and teach thousands of people. Jesus did not cower to the power brokers on the left or the right. Instead, He challenged their theology and questioned their character. Jesus served quietly on most occasions and boldly as needed. No sincere seeker was neglected, and His motive was to serve for the glory of God. His ultimate service was laying down His life for the human race. Consequently, as a follower of Christ, you can become a better servant leader because Jesus seeks to serve through you. Submit to Him and watch Him use you to serve. Quietly volunteer for the next lowly task. Set up others to succeed. Give away your life and you will find it.

This is the example of Christ. This is the model of serving and leading in the way of the Holy Spirit.

CONFLICT RESOLUTION

"If your brother or sister sins, go and point out their fault, just between the two of you. If they listen to you, you have won them over."
MATTHEW 18:15

Christians tend to be too nice and skirt conflict. However, Jesus teaches that healthy conflict is necessary for relational and spiritual growth. It is required to keep clean accounts with others and stay focused on kingdom priorities. Conflict resolution may be uncomfortable, but if an issue or offense is ignored it can become ugly and even explosive.

There are two roles in the beginning stages of conflict resolution. One role is the confronter; the other role is the receiver. If you are the confronter, it is critical to communicate the facts of the situation. If you are loose with the truth and cavalier in your confrontation, the situation will worsen. You probably need to have the details documented and verified. The second critical aspect of the confronter is the spirit in which he directs the conversation. Do not use an accusatory tone of voice. You are there in a spirit of reconciliation and healing. Avoid a condescending attitude, as you are a candidate for the same concerns you are bringing to your friend. Confront in a spirit of humility and grace, with the truth, in love.

The receiver, on the other hand, needs to be wary of defensiveness, denial, and defiance. When confronted, the receiver needs to listen carefully and avoid interrupting with petty excuses. After hearing the accuser, the receiver can correct any misconceptions and inaccuracies. His spirit of correction is mature and levelheaded. Moreover, in most cases the receiver needs to apologize.

Nine out of ten times a sincere apology from the one receiving the rebuke remedies the situation. If there is not a private resolution, then there is the option of mediation. If mediation doesn't bring unity, it might be time for church discipline. In the worst of cases, this may result in publicly expelling from the fellowship someone who is obstinate and determined to remain in sin, while still claiming to be a committed follower of Christ.

The Bible says, "Brothers and sisters, if someone is caught in a sin, you who live by the Spirit should restore that person gently. But watch yourselves, or you also may be tempted. Carry each other's burdens, and in this way you will fulfill the law of Christ" (Galatians 6:1-2). The mature follower of Christ seeks to lovingly warn others of the consequences of unwise decisions. When you take the time to confront another, you could save them from humiliation and disgrace. Grace gives them an opportunity to change.

Praise God for those who have offered grace to you through confrontation.

SWORN FRIENDSHIP

Jonathan said to David, "Go in peace, for we have sworn friendship with each other in the name of the Lord."
1 SAMUEL 20:42

Sworn friendship in the name of the Lord is serious and based on faith. When Jesus Christ is the central figure in a friendship, there is fidelity. Loyalty based on the Lord is an extremely strong bond for friends. A friendship based on the Lord takes on the Lord's attitude toward friendship. He sticks closer than a brother. He never leaves or forsakes His friends. Jesus personified friendship as He served His friends, forgave His friends, loved, taught, rebuked, prayed, and gave to His friends.

Sworn friendship is committed, especially during dire circumstances. There is a commitment to always be there for the other person. It seeks out the very best for a friend during hard times. This is when friendships require an exorbitant amount of time, money, and effort. They become high maintenance when they become caught in a crisis. It may be a situation of the friend's own doing, or a result of forces outside of his control. Your friend may be on the brink of bankruptcy because of poor financial decisions. You serve him even though he suffers from self-inflicted wounds. Your friend's health may be going downhill fast; if so, be there to listen.

Sworn friendship in the name of the Lord defends you to the point of risking a right standing with other respected relationships. Faithful friends will stand up for you even when it costs them. It may cost them misunderstanding. It may cost them a promotion. It may cost them financially. It may cost them their job.

Because they are invested in you unconditionally, they are honored to defend you, especially in your absence. They ask questions of your unseen critics such as, "Have you talked to them about this?" or "I'm surprised by what you say. There must be more to the story." Friends stick up for each other in the face of caustic critics. Love is not silent; it speaks up.

Above all else, cultivate your friendship with Christ. His model of friendship will raise the quality of your friendships. His friendship is forever. His friendship is immediately accessible. His friendship is honest and loving. His friendship is faithful. Jesus spoke eloquently about friends: "Greater love has no one than this: to lay down one's life for one's friends. You are my friends if you do what I command. I no longer call you servants, because a servant does not know his master's business. Instead, I have called you friends, for everything that I learned from my Father I have made known to you" (John 15:13-15).

Be intentional in your investment of time with sworn friendships in the name of the Lord. Do not take these special friendships for granted. Pray for them aggressively.

NONLINEAR ROUTE

So David inquired of the LORD, and he answered, "Do not go straight up, but circle around behind them and attack them in front of the poplar trees."
2 SAMUEL 5:23

God's will is not always a straight line and, many times, it requires a change in direction. His plan is an adventure that cannot be confined to "point A to point B" thinking. God is so much more creative than to give us a predictable path that we can control. His will keeps us trusting and praying. It keeps us looking to the Lord for direction and discernment. This is why we get confused at times. We strike out in one direction and then feel led to move in a different direction. Sometimes He leads us down an entirely different path than where we started. The adventurous part of us likes this, while our cautious and security-seeking part grows fearful.

So what is God up to? How do we experience the Spirit of the Almighty leading us into His great adventure? It is imperative that we listen intently to the Lord. We are compelled to follow Christ, thus we desperately need His marching orders.

But the noise of life can easily drown out the Lord's tender call. His voice will not compete with cluttered living that gets in the way of listening. His voice is pure and plain, and He longs for our undivided attention. He wants us to turn down the racket of modern day conveniences and come to Him. When we're stuck in one of life's traffic jams, and the voice of the Lord is drowned out by the noise around us, He's right there with us—inviting us to listen.

He knows you can't handle His entire plan at once, so go with what He gives you. Go with what you know today, and trust Him with what you don't know about tomorrow. He blesses obedience and trust. God's work is in the here and now. Reality is where you passionately pursue Him. So don't be shy to go where God says to go, even when it doesn't make sense. He is positioning you for success.

Lastly, do not be afraid of the enemy as you follow Christ, but confront him in prayer. Fight the unseen forces of evil by faith. The devil will try to distract you from following God's will. He will tempt you with the allure of wealth, women, and wine. Do not become sidetracked by Satan. Put on the full armor of God. Lean into the Lord and listen to His trusting voice. Dismiss the sultry voice of self-deception. The enemy is the great imposter. He disguises his voice to sound like God's. Indeed, be so in tune with the voice of Jesus that a counterfeit sounds like a shrill fire alarm you want to avoid. Jesus says, "My sheep listen to my voice; I know them, and they follow me" (John 10:27).

Follow the Almighty even when it seems like you are going in a big circle.

VISION COMPLETER

"He is the one who will build a house for my Name, and I will establish the throne of his kingdom forever."
2 SAMUEL 7:13

God has used you way beyond what you could have ever imagined. He has given you extraordinary opportunities, and you have been a good steward of them. But God may have someone else in mind to complete your vision.

It may be hard to understand why you can't be the one to see the culmination of a lifetime of work, but in reality, His vision is always clearer than ours. Others should be able to build upon what you have labored over. Don't worry; your work has not gone unnoticed. Be willing to share its fruits with other faithful followers of Christ. A vision is meant to be built upon and expanded by younger, bold visionaries.

This does not mean you should be any less sold out to the Almighty's agenda. Attack your God-given goals with gusto. Support the one He has chosen to complete your work. This process of entrusting the vision to a leader God has chosen is exciting. You can prepare for the transition by bringing to bear the resources and relationships needed to increase his chances for success.

Pray about how you can serve the next generation in a way that increases their probability of successfully executing God's vision. It may be your son or daughter who needs your training and instruction in leadership and money management. The lessons you have learned—and are still learning—are invaluable. Slow down long enough to mentor. These skills are necessary for your progeny to see God pull off this bigger-than-life vision. Your faith in God will be a foundation upon which they can build. Teach them how to pray to God and trust His truth. Be a model of extravagant generosity and show them selfless service.

Your vision-completer needs your confidence and support. Do not smother him with your well-meaning micromanagement. Instead, let him craft the vision around his personality and preferences. His methods will probably be a modification of yours, if not entirely different. It is when your vision becomes another's that you know God is at work. Let go of your vision and let someone else run with it. This person will complete it better than you because he was the one called to complete it.

God has it under control, and what He starts He completes.

EDICT TO ENCOURAGE

Therefore encourage one another and build each other up, just as in fact you are doing.
1 THESSALONIANS 5:11

Do not underestimate your ability to dispense courage. Your kind word is encouraging. Your warm smile is encouraging. So is your generosity, your presence, your listening ear, your investment of time, and your wisdom. Your encouragement builds up others. People die a thousand deaths of discouragement because daily life saps courage from the human heart.

What Satan tears down, you build up. His goal is the demolition of faith, hope, and love. Your God-given mandate is the building up of faith, hope, and love. Like an opponent in a chess match, he is trying to deceive others into thinking they are trapped with no way out. He plays for a checkmate of discouragement, but you have courage and hope in King Jesus. Jesus already has the devil checked, and there's not even the possibility of a stalemate.

Discouragement needs courage, first from the resurrected life of Christ. He is our hope. He is our Savior. He is our Lord. He is our life. Because Christ is in you, you may be just the dose of courage needed for a friend to make it through another day. Take courage from God, so you can give courage to others. Lead others to this same fountain of eternal encouragement so they can drink when no encouragers are around.

Courage to the soul is what food is to the body. It is filling at the time but exhausts itself quickly, so dine at the table of God's encouragement regularly. His Word is sumptuous, satisfying, and encouraging. Dispense His Word to others in doses of daily encouragement. Human words are hollow compared to the meaty words of Scripture.

It is not possible to consistently feed on the Bible and not be encouraged. Believe His Word, and you will be encouraged. His promises are true: He has forgiven you, He has accepted you, He loves you, He walks with you, and He desires you. This is encouraging! Be encouraged so that you can encourage others. It is encouraging to encourage. You see a person breathe a sigh of relief, and you are encouraged. You see them do the wise thing, and you are encouraged. You train a child in the way that he should go, and when he lives for God, you are eternally encouraged. Choose the high road of encouragement over the low road of discouragement.

"'Rise up; this matter is in your hands. We will support you, so take courage and do it'" (Ezra 10:4).

SUCCESS & FAILURE

If either of them falls down, one can help the other up.
But pity anyone who falls and has no one to help them up.
ECCLESIASTES 4:10

Your role as the leader is to provide coaching, resources, relationships, teaching, and training to the team. If the team is successful, the leader is successful; so it is imperative that the team succeeds, or the leader won't. Help them craft their strategic plan and then let them execute the plan with excellence.

There needs to be periodic assessment and feedback around the mission and objectives. And don't forget to set aside time of accountability for alignment and encouragement. The team wants to succeed, but they need to be assured that they are succeeding at the right things. Provide feedback, resources, and training by investing in their personal development. Promote team members by giving them the opportunity to replace or surpass you.

If your team is unfocused and ineffective, start by looking in the mirror. The leader sets the pace for focused, diligent, creative, systematic, and wise work. Don't hold team members back, but free them around their passions, skills, and gifts. You want the team to surpass any results you could accomplish alone. So allow the team to succeed by coaching them, not micro-managing them.

Here's another tip for becoming a wise leader: Failure is an option. God fosters faith out of failure. Some of your best lessons are learned through failure. It is imperative for the leader to give team members permission to fail or even encourage them to fail. Team members who never fail are team members who need to fail. Without failure, there's no innovation or creativity. Small failures lead to big successes, for this is the process for improvement.

The secure leader knows how to manage risk. When team members do fail, the leader is there to infuse them with courage and perseverance. This gives them the respect and responsibility needed for a willingness to fail. Allow them to craft their own plans. This ensures their ownership with passion around execution. Invite them to continue taking risks. Wisdom says, "For though the righteous fall seven times, they rise again" (Proverbs 24:16).

Our heavenly Father knows we will fail, but He is there to pick us up and encourage us to move forward by faith. He celebrates with us on the mountaintops. He comforts us in the valleys. We lose not when we fail, but when we give up. So persevere, as you are a success in the eyes of your Savior.

Carry on with Christ through the ups and the downs.

CHALLENGE THE PROCESS

Certain people came down from Judea to Antioch and were teaching the believers: "Unless you are circumcised, according to the custom taught by Moses, you cannot be saved."
ACTS 15:1

Everything has a process, good or bad. A good process provides wise checks and balances and makes for a best decision, a quality product or service, and excellent execution. A bad process rushes through an inferior design or a half-baked decision and impedes progress. So, a wise leader allows all processes to be up for debate.

No process is immune to questioning, but the discussion is to be done with dignity and respect. Keep the conversation focused on processes, not personalities. personalities. Anyone can complain, so challenge the process with thoughtful solutions, not mindless meandering. You respect others when you listen to their ideas without defensiveness. This is why everyone should hold process with an open hand. If you become a rigid proponent of your pet process, then there is a good chance you will take any criticism of your process personally. Process, by design, is what's best for the entire organization, not just a convenience created to accommodate someone's preference. Therefore, do not overprotect process with smothering ownership.

Healthy organizations require everyone to think. Collaborative thinking facilitates teachability, teamwork, and responsible stewardship. No one's ideas are unimportant. From the mailroom to the boardroom everyone can come up with better ways to do their job.

Practically speaking, think of creative processes that save time and money and utilize technology. Incorporate research and document your processes. Within a growing enterprise, the processes that worked last year will probably be lacking this year. Pilot new processes before implementation, because this enhances quality. If a process does not propel progress, then it needs to be replaced with a results-driven model.

God is into process, and His will is process-driven. Look at His will for Noah. He gave him a process: "So make yourself an ark of cypress wood; make rooms in it and coat it with pitch inside and out. This is how you are to build it: The ark is to be three hundred cubits long, fifty cubits wide and thirty cubits high. Make a roof for it, leaving below the roof an opening one cubit high all around. Put a door in the side of the ark and make lower, middle and upper decks" (Genesis 6:14-16).

**God is ultimately in control of every process.
You can trust God, His timing, and His processes.**

BE HONEST

"I know, my God, that you test the heart and are pleased with integrity. All these things have I given willingly and with honest intent. And now I have seen with joy how willingly your people who are here have given to you."
1 CHRONICLES 29:17

Be honest with yourself and be honest with others. Honesty with others admits and exposes what they already feel and know. It is a natural application of integrity and is one of the top reasons people stay around for any length of time. It creates an environment of trust, which is a safe place to work and live. Honesty puts rumors to rest and is as quick to communicate the negative, as it is to promote the positive. Honesty is secure enough to apologize to the team and come clean with a bad decision or an awful attitude. Honesty is the best policy because everyone is free to be truthful.

Be honest with yourself and be truthful about your strengths, your weaknesses, your limitations, your personality, and your character. Be who you are and who you can become with God's transforming power, and do not become an imitation of someone else.

Be ever vigilant in your self-awareness. Take a variety of self-assessments. Open yourself to a regular review from your supervisor and other team members and open yourself up to scrutiny and feedback from your family and friends. Self-honesty comes from a teachable heart that listens to—and learns how to improve from—the perspective of its peers. Honesty means you confess what you don't know. You don't pretend to have all the answers, but you humbly seek to define the right questions.

Validate with others who know well what you do best. Is it analyzing data, writing, leading, strategic thinking, networking, communicating, recruiting, managing, nurturing relationships, supporting, planning, or implementing to name a few? Discover what you do best and in what area you have the most passion and then focus your time and attention there. It takes honesty to refrain from doing those things you like when your results are only average in their outcomes. Putting your courage and trust in others to carry out these interesting tasks will bring about the best results for everyone. So, focus on what you do best. This leverages your time and promotes the best stewardship of your skills, gifts, talents, and abilities.

Cover-ups and blame kill the spirit of a caring culture, but honesty breathes life, loyalty, and professionalism. Be honest with others by caring enough to confront, for this keeps accounts short and cultivates trust. Be honest by confessing your mistakes, for this frees others to do the same and builds respect. Lastly, be honest by communicating the good and the bad, for this keeps everyone engaged. Christ's mode of operation is honesty, and He expects us to strike from our vocabulary the dishonest habit of saying, "I'll be honest with you." Authentic honesty does not require a disclaimer. It is the natural response of someone who is honest with God, themselves, and others. Therefore, be honest and watch God bless you with joy, peace, love, and respect.

"An honest answer is like a kiss on the lips" (Proverbs 24:26).

STAY FOCUSED

"I have brought you glory on earth
by finishing the work you gave me to do."
JOHN 17:4

Focus is the fuel to productivity, and it frees you to stay on task. Focus facilitates God's will, and it has the ability to bring intensity to a situation, problem, or opportunity. There is a sense of urgency that pushes out distraction and brings clarity back to the matter at hand. Focused individuals understand that some things naturally drift out of focus, so they intentionally refocus. "Mission drift" ensues when the leader becomes distracted and unfocused, as well-meaning activities can distract the team or the individual from the original purpose.

The opposite of focusing on a task is to ignore or disregard it. We lose focus when we lose interest or assign a lower value to a person or opportunity. We lose focus when something else more attractive draws us away and, like a moth toward a candle, we can get burned if we are not careful. We are forever fighting to stay focused because of bad distractions and good attractions. But we don't have to remain unfocused or get focused on the wrong things. When we stay laser-beam-focused on the Lord, important things become priority, and our minds become centered on Christ.

Whether we realize it or not, we focus all the time. We may not focus on our most important options, but we focus. We focus on sports. We focus on having fun. We focus on finances. We focus on fitness. We focus on frustrations. Indeed, your mind and your heart tend to follow your focus. Your life aligns around where you focus, so, by God's grace, stay focused on Him and His will for your life. Focused faith goes a long way toward experiencing God's very best. Focus brings freedom to do His will without reservations; so stay focused on the one thing He has called you to do, and you will be amazed at the results.

One idea is to focus on your family. Focus more intently on your family than you do your work or your hobbies. Put a puzzle together, take scuba diving lessons, plan a family reunion, organize a trip, or take care of a pet. Intentionally focus on your family now, while you have the opportunity and while they are interested. Your children deserve your intense focus. They will be gone soon, so zero in on them. Finally, focus on God in prayer. Prayer brings into focus what matters most.

Above all else, become an intensely focused person of faith and character. Your character determines your credibility with people. Jesus says, "But seek first his kingdom and his righteousness, and all these things will be given to you as well" (Matthew 6:33). Your influence grows as your character grows; so stay focused on becoming more like Jesus.

Prayer dismisses distractions and invites priorities.

SEPTEMBER 9

CONFRONT WITH TRUTH

Instead, speaking the truth in love, we will grow to become in every respect the mature body of him who is the head, that is, Christ.

EPHESIANS 4:15

You confront because you care about the circumstance, the person, and the organization. Non-confronters are driven by fear, not care. They are fearful of rejection, of hurting someone's feelings, of losing their position, even their job. Fear drives out care and replaces it with delayed dysfunction. A non-confronting culture is filled with fear, gossip, and resentment. A confronting culture, on the other hand, is safe, secure, and rewarding. It praises people for speaking their minds. Authenticity is encouraged, and they speak up because they strongly believe in the values of the organization. They are compelled not to compromise excellence by expedience and not to value results over relationships. So they take the time to speak their mind with respect.

When you confront because you care, you confront often. This keeps any wrongs from turning into resentments. Confront caringly, for this shows respect and that you want what's best for everyone. Confront calmly and attack the issue, not the individual; this invites dialogue. The spirit of confrontation defines its effectiveness.

It is also important to get the facts before you confront. Take the time to understand the situation and the people involved. Clarification around the truth avoids misunderstandings and many times prevents major blow-ups. Without confrontation we assume inaccuracies that come back to bite us; phrases like, "I didn't know you meant that," or, "I didn't understand, so I assumed ..." Factfinding keeps us from wrongly accusing or, at the very least, wrongly assuming.

Teachable hearts accept truthful speech when it's delivered in love. So, honor the person, as this increases their receptivity. Apologize for your insensitive or inappropriate actions, for this disarms the other person and promotes trust. In the same way, receive those who confront you.

Christ is the master of confronting with truth; so confront in the spirit and clarity of Jesus. "The third time he said to him, 'Simon son of John, do you love me?' Peter was hurt because Jesus asked him the third time, 'Do you love me?' He said, 'Lord, you know all things; you know that I love you.' Jesus said, 'Feed my sheep'" (John 21:17).

If someone takes a chance to speak the truth in love, you are wise to receive it in humility. Truth is your friend, not your foe. The more you appreciate and comprehend truth, the more you value confrontation and its delivery of truth. Security in Christ invites confrontation wrapped in truth. Truth keeps you out of trouble and discerns the best options. Create environments that encourage this by being an example. Your willingness to receive truth and change transforms others. Reward those who receive the truth properly, as this motivates authentic behavior.

Surround yourself with those who speak the truth in love and those who humbly receive the truth.

SEPTEMBER 10

STRENGTHS AND STRUGGLES

We have different gifts,
according to the grace given to each of us.
ROMANS 12:6

Know and understand your strengths, for it is best to invest in the talents God created you to have. By God's grace, He places within you giftedness to carry out His plan. You may be a gifted leader, so lead. You may be a gifted coach, so coach. You may be a gifted counselor, so counsel. You may be a gifted administrator, so administer. You may be a gifted networker, so network. You may be a gifted writer, so write. You may be a gifted teacher, so teach. You may be a gifted servant, so serve. You may be a gifted artist, so create. You may be a gifted communicator, so communicate. There is a long menu of gifts, and you probably resemble several of them. Study your gifts, and you will discover your strengths.

Become comfortable with and accept the one thing you do naturally. This one thing is effortless because God has engineered you for it. He gave you the skills and abilities to innovate, create, and produce these desired outcomes. However, make sure you do not confuse passion with strength. If you have the passion to speak, it is imperative you at least have the raw skill for speaking.

Embrace and celebrate your struggles. They keep you humble. Accept your struggles; embrace them. Make your struggles your servant by allowing others to do much better than what you can't do. It is okay not to like details, but value them and those who manage them well. Your struggles beg the need for a team. It is in your struggles that you depend more on God and others. So, be honest with yourself about what you don't do well. Accept the fact that even though you want to do something, you don't need to if others can do it better. They can free you to do only what you can do. Release your areas of mediocre effectiveness, as this gives others opportunities for excellence.

Take the time to understand what you do best and where you have the most energy and then position your responsibilities at home and work to mirror that ideal. Ask those who know you well to affirm where they see your passion and strengths come together. Then, prayerfully align around both. You can know and understand your strengths by taking a spiritual gifts test, as this helps you define your God-given disposition. Take a personality assessment, for this helps you understand your temperament. Lastly, consider taking a psychological test, because this reveals your emotional intelligence and your leadership style. Discovering your gifts, passions, and strengths allow you to serve God's kingdom to the best of your ability. You are a valued member in the Body of Christ.

"Just as a body, though one, has many parts, but all its many parts form one body, so it is with Christ. For we were all baptized by one Spirit so as to form one body" (1 Corinthians 12:12-13).

PLOTTING EVIL

The Lord said to me, "Son of man, these are the men who are plotting evil and giving wicked advice in this city."
EZEKIEL 11:2

The sun never sets on evil, and alarmingly, there are people as intent on evil actions as there are those committed to good ones. The worst kind of evil is disguised in the robe of religion. In the passage above, Ezekiel is told to warn the priests of Israel that God sees their corruption, and He will not let them continue to harm His people. Wickedness disguised as piety is abhorrent to God, whether it is coming from within the community of His people or as an attack from outside. Sadly, there is no reasoning with people whose thinking is so warped that they believe their corruption or violence are justified—or even virtuous. These religious fanatics are, of course, deceived and delusional.

Satan smiles at acts of atrocity aimed at innocent people. What better strategy for hell than for sin to be promoted by religious people and for evil to happen in the name of religion? We can act as if we are isolated from it, but we are not. We will be affected as long as evildoers plot evil acts. Beneath religious violence, there is an unseen battle raging. It is the battle for the souls of men and women.

Prayer is the primary weapon for fighting spiritual warfare. Heaven's call is for followers of Jesus Christ to rise up in a powerful proclamation of prayer. We are the body of Christ. When one member of the body suffers, the entire body suffers. Evil plotters are no match for persistent and pure prayers. Pray for God's kingdom to come on earth as it is in heaven.

Until evil is totally defeated by the grace of God, we have an opportunity to invest our hope and confidence in eternity. The Bible says, "But mark this: There will be terrible times in the last days. People will be lovers of themselves, lovers of money, boastful, proud, abusive, disobedient to their parents, ungrateful, unholy ... having a form of godliness but denying its power. Have nothing to do with such people" (2 Timothy 3:1-2, 5). We must examine the evidence we see in the lives of people to determine whether they are advancing faith in Jesus or undermining it. Humbly and persistently, we must present Jesus in our own behavior and beliefs. He is the answer to atrocities hatched in hell. Pray every day for Christ to triumph in your life and in this world.

Heaven trumps hell because Christ is preeminent.

SAVIOR SATISFACTION

Simon Peter answered him, "Lord, to whom shall we go? You have the words of eternal life. We have come to believe and to know that you are the Holy One of God."
JOHN 6:68-69

Jesus satisfies. He is all we need in life, death, and in-between. However, there are competitors with Christ that try to get in the way of our contentment in Him. Fear, envy, and regret attempt to wedge themselves between our Savior's satisfaction and us.

We forget that we have all we need in Him. He has the wisdom we need for smart decision-making. He has the grace we need for love and forgiveness in relationships. He has the discipline we need to manage money effectively. When we deviate from the divine, we become discontent.

Discontentment can look many ways. Worry is a wart of discontent. Anxiety causes it to grow and disfigure your faith. Fear is seedy and seductive, and it leads down the path of anxious living. Fear and contentment cannot coexist; they are mutually exclusive.

Contentment comes from Christ, for in Him there are no regrets from the past, no fears of the future, and no envy in the present. Regrets can come in many forms: disappointment from a vanished youth, embarrassment from a busted marriage, or guilt over obsession in career advancement. But in Christ's economy, regrets are not meant to remain. He wants our past regrets to transform our relationship with Him into one that is more robust, because His forgiveness has freed us from our worldly weights of the past.

Jesus is the Alpha and the Omega, and contentment comes from trusting Him with your future. He knows what lies ahead for you and, because He is your Creator, you can be content in Him. The future is His invitation to trust Him, and it is meant to inspire hope, not fear. The Bible says, "May the God of hope fill you with all joy and peace as you trust in him, so that you may overflow with hope by the power of the Holy Spirit" (Romans 15:13). You will eagerly anticipate what the future holds if you are aligned with the Almighty. Your life is not an accident waiting to happen, but Almighty God's orchestration. Christ is your conductor, so look to Him by faith, and your life will sound beautiful, as it harmonizes with heaven and engages on earth.

Lastly, contentment in Christ has no room for envy in the present. All you have or enjoy is a gift from Him: your health, your family, your freedom, your friends, your faith, your finances, your mind, and your heart. They're all gifts from above. Envy flees in the light of eternity. Your Savior satisfies, and after Him there is nowhere else to go. He has the words of eternal life, and He is your life.

Embrace Christ, and you will become rich in contentment.

SPIRITUAL PREPARATION

Then Esther sent this reply to Mordecai: "Go, gather together all the Jews who are in Susa, and fast for me. Do not eat or drink for three days, night or day. I and my attendants will fast as you do. When this is done, I will go to the king, even though it is against the law. And if I perish, I perish."

ESTHER 4:15-16

Spiritual preparation is necessary for divine guidance, and the Lord leads those who take the time to listen. Common sense does not need to be the final answer, as engagement with eternity is essential for the best decision. You have the resources of heaven at your disposal. Spiritual preparation invites God's blessing and people's participation.

Prepare by putting pride in its place. It is unwise and a waste of time to tackle terrific problems in your own strength. Instead, pray and fast. Pray and ask others to pray before you challenge the system or call into question a long-standing tradition. People are open to listen when our pride is in check.

Prepare with a heart of gratitude. On your knees, you can thank God for the trials you are experiencing. He comforts like none other, and conflict causes you to cry out to Christ. You can thank Him that in your adversity, you feel the need to be loved by your heavenly Father.

Prepare by asking others for prayer support. Prayer and fasting along with others aligns our hearts and minds with the Almighty's. It is not only your own heart that needs cleansing and healing, but also the hearts of those who support you. We are the body of Christ; we anguish in each other's pain and celebrate in one another's gain. But if you remain silent in your hurt, no one knows how to pray for you. They may assume that everything is okay, when in reality you are dying on the inside. Therefore, take a chance and speak up. People are willing to give up food and pray for you, because they love you.

God has prepared you for a purpose. Do not waste His preparation. Once you have solicited the prayers and support of people you trust, be bold to follow through by faith. Steward well your preparation and watch Him bless with bountiful results. Courage and confidence converge around a prayerful process.

You can be bold now because you are spiritually prepared. You lifted up your own fears and frailties, and He heard your humble plea. Stay humble, trustworthy, and prayerful, for God knows your heart.

"Brothers and sisters, pray for us that the message of the Lord may spread rapidly and be honored, just as it was with you" (2 Thessalonians 3:1).

SEPTEMBER 14

HURTING SPOUSE

If one part suffers, every part suffers with it; if one part is honored, every part rejoices with it. Now you are the body of Christ, and each one of you is a part of it.

1 CORINTHIANS 12:26-27

Sometimes, our spouses experience hurt. It may be for a moment, for months, or in some chronic situations they may hurt over years. Hurt can come from a variety of sources. Busy parents who don't take time to demonstrate love cause hurt, disappointments deposit hurt, lack of control contributes to hurt, shattered dreams hurt, and health issues exacerbate hurt.

Hurt may linger on the surface of your spouse's heart, or it may have inflicted deep wounds into the soul—a soul that desperately needs God's healing hand. Sadly, the scars of hurt can disfigure her countenance. So be aware, because your insensitivity can compound the hurt, or your sensitivity can cure the hurt.

When your wife hurts, you hurt. You may hurt because of the empathy you feel for her pain, or you may hurt because of the pain she has knowingly or unknowingly imposed on you. Hurt cannot be ignored, as it will expose itself mildly in public and wildly in private. Hurt will not go away unless there is healing.

Your tender touch brings healing. Your extra patience eases the pain. Your kind words are an ointment that soothes anxiety. Your gracious attitude is a legion of love ready to recapture your spouse's heart. Don't give up reaching out to your hurting wife. Yes, it's inconvenient, and your goals may be on hold for now. You are in survival mode. Do not grow weary in doing good, for in due season you will reap God's blessings (Galatians 6:9).

If you are the one who is hurting, go to your heavenly Father for healing. Let Him love you through this. Lay down your burden before it crushes your spirit. Jesus said to go to Him for rest in your weariness and for wholeness for your heart. "Come to me, all you who are weary and burdened, and I will give you rest" (Matthew 11:28). You cannot bear this burden by yourself or fix this alone. Your loving Lord wants to lead you into forgiveness and freedom. Release your regrets and disappointments to Him and let go of your need for control. Remember that Jesus can be trusted during this time of turmoil. Take your Savior's advice and experience His healing for you and your spouse.

Healing is the outcome from applying the outrageous love and forgiveness of God.

SEPTEMBER 15

LIFE LOATHING

"I loathe my very life; therefore I will give free rein to my complaint and speak out in the bitterness of my soul."
JOB 10:1

Some people loathe life, as it is a chore just to exist on earth. It is a burden to get out of bed and face the day. There is an overwhelming feeling of dread and disappointment. With a jaded perspective they say, "People are out to get me, and they don't care about my despair." The glass of hope is half empty, as is their soul. There is an aversion to the Almighty, their spiritual vibrancy has long since passed, and they feel punished by pain. The Lord seems unsympathetic, as if He were a million miles away.

Loathing is exhausting, as it requires more energy to intensely dislike than to forgive and accept. Loathing speaks from the bitterness of its soul. For loathers, there is no security in Christ, only confusion and complaints. Complaints from people who loathe life become contagious to others who will listen to their unfounded fears. Loathing leans its ladder against a wall of worry. Those who loathe embrace the worst case. Loathing is a killer of creativity and compassion, and it sucks the life out of relationships.

Jesus, on the other hand, gives life. He offers an abundant life, built on trust in Him. Jesus said, "The thief cometh not, but for to steal, and to kill, and to destroy: I am come that they might have life, and that they might have it more abundantly" (John 10:10 KJV).

The Lord loathes sin and all its destructive ways. It is okay to loathe those things that are disgusting to Him, but do not loathe what the Lord loves. He loves us. He loves us despite ourselves. He loves us in the middle of our messy circumstances. He loves us in our anger and apathy. He loves us in our fear and faithlessness. He loves us in our discouragement and dislikes. He loves us too much to let us loathe our lives.

The love of God overcomes loathing. Loathing and love cannot coexist, for love conquers all. "In all these things we are more than conquerors through Him who loved us" (Romans 8:37). So, allow Christ to convert your complaints into compassion. He can replace what you lost with something better.

People can relate to you when you admit your struggles and suffering. It is in your pain that your faith becomes credible to those who want to know Christ. When the weak in faith see you love the Lord and love life, even in your adversity, they are drawn to Jesus. When you choose love over loathing, you vote for vitality in your relationships. Love soothes your soul, seeks to be a blessing to others, and is a testament to trust in Him.

Quit loathing life, for it is a poor reflection on the Lord. Instead, accept life with all it has to offer, and see the good and the bad as part of God's plan.

SAFE ENVIRONMENTS

"Your brother has come," he replied, "and your father has killed the fattened calf because he has him back safe and sound."
LUKE 15:27

Our soul seeks out safe environments. We are attracted to people we can trust, who accept us for who we are instead of who we need to be. Safe environments give us security and peace. We can bare our souls because we know we are in a place of confidentiality, and do not fear rejection. A business meeting with a rigid agenda, pretense, and pride is not a safe place in which to be yourself.

Those who foster safe environments seek first to understand, not to judge. In safe environments, we're still loved, especially when we are unlovely. Parents have the privilege of providing a safe environment for their teenagers transitioning into young adulthood.

Safe environments are also necessary for Christ-seekers. People in a search for authentic faith need someplace to ask questions without being rebuffed for their elementary inquiries. More mature believers have the opportunity to be there for those on their faith journey, but judgment is a juggernaut against safe environments, as it crushes with condescending attitudes. So, be careful not to impose your high standards on a person or situation, endangering the safe environment. Share your own failures and struggles, as this builds bridges to the heart. Consider hosting a Bible discussion in your home and follow it up with a fun activity. Make Christianity attractive, not boring. Safe environments draw people to Christ.

Above all else, seek out a safe environment with your Savior. Your Lord longs to linger with you. He deeply desires to listen to your dreams and fears. In your safe place with Jesus, you are loved completely. Your heavenly Father feels your pain. In your safe place with Him, you are positioned to receive His love and blessings. Your safe environment with God may be early in the morning with a cup of coffee, the Bible, and your journal. It may be late at night before your head hits the pillow. It may be on your lunch break in the shadowy sanctuary of a tree. It may be a walk in the woods, a jog on a treadmill, or a run across a maze of sidewalks. It may be a quiet occasion in the mountains or an engagement with eternity at the beach.

God gives you safe environments for your soul's refreshment. It is there you can cry, laugh, complain, thank, create, give, listen, and ask. Christ celebrates when you go to Him and He receives you just as you are, needy for love and acceptance. Safe environments are necessary for communication and trust. Therefore, create and enjoy safe places, and go there often for your sake and the sake of those you love.

"'You will be secure, because there is hope; you will look about you and take your rest in safety'" (Job 11:18).

FIRST GO BACK

"Therefore, if you are offering your gift at the altar and there remember that your brother or sister has something against you, leave your gift there in front of the altar. First go and be reconciled to them; then come and offer your gift."

MATTHEW 5:23-24

Christ commands us to humble ourselves and go back to seek reconciliation of fractured relationships. The flesh wants to forget without addressing the real issues that divide, but this is not the Jesus way. Disappointment with your parents may have severed communication. Go back before you move on, or you will drive a relational wedge. You may have harbored resentment toward a friend. Go back and make things right relationally. It's hard to serve heaven while in the midst of broken relationships on earth. In fact, your worship reminds you of where you need to restore relationships.

It is not a good thing to offer a gift to God while there are still grudges in your gut. An unclear conscience is unable to authentically associate with the Almighty and others. When you go back to the point of offense, you better understand the reason for the hurt; here is where healing begins.

When you go back, make sure you are prayed up. A gentle and humble attitude goes a long way toward avoiding an altercation. Take more than your share of the responsibility by apologizing and making restitution (compensation for loss), as it enhances reconciliation in relationships. Use the right words in the right way. Right words, delivered without pride, bring healing and wholeness to the ruptured relationship. Deposits of gentleness, humility, and unselfishness move the relationship in the right direction.

Jesus is all about relational reconciliation. His mission on earth was to reconcile man to God. His goal was to dissolve the distance between His holy heavenly Father and sinful man. This was the purpose of His death on the cross: reconciling relationships.

Moreover, your ministry from God is reconciliation (2 Corinthians 5:17-19). How can you be reconciled to God in heaven and not to people on earth? The Bible says, "Whoever claims to love God yet hates a brother or sister is a liar. For whoever does not love their brother and sister, whom they have seen, cannot love God, whom they have not seen" (1 John 4:20-21). God's expectation for His children is to come clean with those between whom there is division. This is the normal Christian life and is consistent living for the Lord.

However, you cannot accomplish this countercultural commission by yourselves. The power of the Holy Spirit humbles your heart and heals. Forgiveness forgets and moves on only after reconciliation.

You are not to move on in your generosity and service to God until you first go back to the point of offense and make amends.

SEPTEMBER 18

SMALL THINGS

"Do not despise these small beginnings, for the LORD rejoices to see the work begin, to see the plumb line in Zerubbabel's hand."
ZECHARIAH 4:10 (NLT)

Small things are big to God, so they are not to be discounted or despised. After all, our Savior is in the small things. Our pride wants to get on to the larger and more important opportunities. It dismisses the mundane or the monotonous. But success and significance are also found in the small things.

A quiet smile to a restaurant server is small, but significant. A little gift to an unsuspecting sanitation worker is small, but significant. Learning the children's names of a fellow employee, and occasionally joining him for lunch is small, but significant. Attention to small things makes people big. Celebrate an office friend's birthday over breakfast, or an important personal milestone over lunch or dinner. When we give attention to small things, we say we care. Private acts of love foster public loyalty and long-term commitment. It is the attention to small things that builds great people and grows great companies.

This is also true with our children. If we want influence with them when they face big issues as teenagers and adults, it is imperative we show interest in the small things of their childhood. Parental investment in ballgames, recitals, school plays, scouts, church camps, outdoors, homework, shared hobbies, and church all add up to an invitation to big things. Little things like tucking them in at night will one day give them the trust to invite us into the dark night of their soul.

How much is it worth for your spouse to become your best friend? It won't happen overnight, but faithfulness to the small things will facilitate the reality of your hopes and dreams.

Therefore, do not despise this season of small things. The small things are like seeds that eventually grow into grand and glorious opportunities of influence. Your Savior is into stringing together a sequence of small activities that lead to larger outcomes. So stay with the small things, for in due season you will reap the harvest. God may allow you to harvest far beyond what you could have imagined in the beginning.

The small things you do honor God: bowing a head before a meal, showing up early for an appointment, memorizing a brief Bible verse, or giving a small anonymous gift. Any small expression with the Lord in mind goes a long way.

The small things are big, they matter, and they may matter most.

SEPTEMBER 19

TESTING PURIFIES

*"But he knows the way that I take;
when he has tested me, I will come forth as gold."*
JOB 23:10

Testing purifies, as it brings out our worst and preserves our best. It is not always easy or enjoyable, but it is necessary to stay solid in our faith. Tests are not meant to be torture, but a time that we can claim the promises of God. Testing purifies your faith to a higher level of trust in the Lord.

Tests come in the form of people we may not understand or have yet to totally appreciate. God uses people every day to purify our hearts from pride. Tests also come in the form of taking on more responsibility at work. We have never done what we are doing, and we feel inadequate and desperate to learn. This new assignment has us crying out to God for wisdom and discernment. God may be asking you to give up something, so He can give you something better. This test is meant to prepare you for God's very best. We fail the test if we give up. But if we persevere, we will make progress and eventually reach the goal.

In some sense, your life is one big test, but its intensity is temporary. Sometimes you feel trapped by tests, as they can be smothering and discouraging. Your career transition is a test of whether your security is in prestige or in Christ. You struggle with, "What will people think?" or "Will they believe less in me, because I took a lesser role?" But the truth is, God's will is always a step up, and this may be a test of your motives.

Tests come down to trust. Can God still be trusted during this severe trial? You believe in your head that He can, but your heart needs to commit without reservation. How can you trust Him when circumstances seem to be swirling out of control? You trust Him one day at a time, and you trust Him with the authorities in your life that still have questions and concerns.

Truth is designed as our survival kit during times of testing. Truth is terrific because it reminds us of the bigger picture of God's faithfulness and plan. He allows us to experience difficulty in order to build our dependence on Him. Therefore, it is imperative that we drink daily from the fountain of God's Word. The Bible is our baseline for belief and behavior. Indeed, testing brings truth front and center. It turns our focus away from our pain to our hope and provision in the Lord. We long for and receive God's love in the heat of our testing. We see Him clearly in our crisis of faith, as testing turns us toward truth and into the arms of Jesus. By faith, value this time of testing, and embrace it as an opportunity to be loved by your heavenly Father, for tests turn you to Him.

"'Do not be afraid. God has come to test you, so that the fear of God will be with you to keep you from sinning'" (Exodus 20:20).

SEPTEMBER 20

VISION REGAINED

I answered them by saying, "The God of heaven will give us success. We his servants will start rebuilding."
NEHEMIAH 2:20

Sometimes we lose the compelling nature of our vision. Your opportunity to trust God has been severely limited, and a magnetic vision needs to be regained.

Maybe your vision's cutting-edge intensity became dulled. You became attracted to other good opportunities, while in the meantime the original vision lost its luster. A dull vision demands that you regain a resurgence of energy and fire in the belly. Maybe you became bored because you met your goals and there were no next steps to a greater vision.

You need a new vision that challenges your dependency on God and stirs your emotions. So pray for a vision that gets you out of bed in the morning, one that easily engages your mind and your heart.

Try going back to the original vision. What elements of the vision drew you in and upward to God? Was it the size? Was it the results? Did it align around your passions? Was it bold and unpredictable? Hold the tired vision with an open hand and watch God inject it with new enthusiasm and extreme possibilities. Regain the vision by going to God and by approaching those who have yet to engage enthusiastically.

Convene with your leadership team or your family to pray. Pray for a revitalization of God's vision for your life, enterprise, and family. Do not limit God by expecting anything less than the grandeur of how His vision may unfold. If you're a leader praying for a new vision for your team, ask for your team members' input. Take some crayons and a sheet of paper and ask each team member to privately and creatively illustrate the vision they sense God is giving. It's uncanny what Christ can do through such a simple, but profound process. Share the results with each other and notice how He aligns your hearts.

There are new people waiting to join in with the regained vision. They may be notable leaders who are waiting for your invitation. You need a new crew of faithful leaders who will show up and do their part. Go after extremely ordinary people who, because of their focused passion, get extraordinary results. Don't waste time with flashy talkers. Move past their pretentious noise and invest in the quiet, faithful ones who get the job done. The God of heaven will give you success; so regain His vision for His glory.

"After this, the word of the Lord came to Abram in a vision: 'Do not be afraid, Abram. I am your shield, your very great reward'" (Genesis 15:1).

HUMAN BEINGS

"Be still, and know that I am God; I will be exalted among the nations, I will be exalted in the earth."
PSALM 46:10

God created us as human *beings*, not human *doers*. Yet everything—from our culture to our career—defaults to doing. We are taught by western society that if we are not busy, we must be lazy. We are so intent on getting things done that we forget why we engaged in the process to begin with. It's all about progress and seeing it through to the end. It's all about the results, making the grade, and exceeding the earnings estimates. After all, if you are really important, your cell phone will constantly vibrate and your email will seduce you 24/7. This is the sad state of those of us who are trapped by doing.

Our ego glosses over the need for God, as we justify driven behavior with bad theology. We act like the Almighty's hands are tied and it is up to us to make things happen. But God is not limited by our low view. He still governs the universe and our lives. Kings, presidents, and dictators are still accountable to the Almighty and His agenda. CEOs, entertainers, and athletes still have a higher power in Jesus Christ to whom they must answer.

Therefore, it is wise to get off our high horse of self-importance and be still before God. If we continue to race through life at a breakneck pace, we will break. Our health, finances, and relationships are fragile, and eventually they will fracture under the pressure of habitual doing.

Indeed, we are humans in need—in need of being who God created us to be. Our God-given roles in life are a great place to cultivate our human being-ness. For example, when we take the time to be a respectful child who honors his parents, we are being. You honor God when you honor them.

Above all else, be with God. There is a knowing and understanding of God that comes only from spending time with Him. In-depth knowledge of God is not derived from service only, but in sitting and reflecting on the Holy One being served. It is in the stillness beside the waters of worship that you feel His presence (Psalm 23). In stillness, you see God. In stillness, you feel God. In stillness, you worship God. In stillness, you receive from God. In stillness, you are loved by God. In stillness, you love God. In stillness, you believe God. In stillness, you see and know God. Allow your "doing" to flow from your "being." The equation is simple: "stillness" plus "being" equals dynamic "doing" for the glory of the Lord.

"'The Lord will fight for you; you need only to be still'" (Exodus 14:14).

FEAR OF DEATH

By his death he might ... free those who all their lives were held in slavery by their fear of death.
HEBREWS 2:14-15

Jesus has conquered death; therefore, followers of Jesus need not fear death. You may have a fear of dying, but not of death. For the believer in Christ, death is a pass through, a transition from this life to the next. Death is not final, for it is the doorway to eternity.

Indeed, it is the beginning of an eternity in the physical presence of Jesus. Everything we have experienced with Christ on earth is an appetizer of what is to come. Our faith can only digest a mere morsel of what God has in store for those who love Him. Do not let the prospects of death get you down, as it is a commencement to be celebrated. You have remained faithful in this school of life, and now God has a glorious graduation in store for you.

Yes, there is some fear of the unknown, but there is a lot we do know that keeps fear in check. We know that death, for the followers of Christ, places them in an environment of sinless bliss. Death releases you from the pain of your current suffering. You will live and breathe in a place without the pain of AIDS, murder, adultery, homosexuality, lying, cheating, pain, hunger, abortion, or poverty. Your suffering perfects your character and faith in Christ. You will be ready to be received back home.

The fear of death creeps in where there has been no preparation. You can ignore its reality, but you will still die. You can deny death, but not its consequences. You may have a chance to repent on your deathbed, but why wait? Why take the chance of choosing hell over heaven? Death is not a lottery ticket, so don't gamble with your soul. Go with God's sure thing, faith in Jesus Christ. He has died and risen from the dead, so He can be trusted. He has dealt with death and reigns over all in heaven.

Moreover, love on those who are dying. Reach out to those closer to death's door. The wisdom that comes from the dying has the aroma of heaven. That which is important falls from their lips, as priorities are aligned and lived. Being with the dying prepares you for dying. Death is an absolute. It may come suddenly or at the end of a long process, but either way, God can be trusted.

Thank God for every breath you take. Enjoy and celebrate death's release. Because Jesus died and rose again, you will do the same. Fear only God and enjoy the benefit of death's freedom.

"'Death has been swallowed up in victory.' 'Where, O death, is your victory? Where, O death, is your sting?' The sting of death is sin, and the power of sin is the law. But thanks be to God! He gave us the victory through our Lord Jesus Christ" (1 Corinthians 15:54-57).

PATH OF LIFE

You make known to me the path of life; you will fill me with joy in your presence, with eternal pleasures at your right hand.
PSALM 16:11

God set us on a path when we surrendered by faith to our Savior, Jesus. His path is not without bumps, but it is by far the best path. It is an inviting path because Christ accompanies us.

Wherever Jesus walks, we want to walk. Where He goes, we want to follow. When He is out front, we have confidence in the direction He leads us. When we run ahead, we lose the advantage of Christ's compass. When we lag behind, we lose perspective. God's path is the most productive because it's where we walk with Jesus. Along the path with Christ, we hear His voice, and He guides us. When we started out, we were determined to go in one direction. But over time, He has a way of revealing to us a better way.

Therefore, stay on the path with Jesus. Our direction determines our destination. We can be full of good intentions and still be on the wrong path. The road we are on determines our route. We can pray about visiting Washington, DC, and even plan a trip there, but if we strike out due west from Atlanta, Georgia, we will not arrive at our desired destination. The path you choose carries you toward or away from your goals. A loving and respectful spouse is on a path of understanding and accountability. An excellent employee is on a path of doing what he does best with diligence. A fulfilling friendship is on a path of service and unselfishness. Those who enjoy financial freedom are on a path of generosity, saving, and wise spending. Paths have predetermined outcomes, so make sure to go down the God-honoring ones.

Therefore, do not be led astray down destructive paths. Addictions to work, drugs, alcohol, and pornography lead us down the path of death. Leading an out-of-balance life is traveling down the wrong path toward a wreck. Get off, go back, or start over; just don't be naïve and keep going. Things can and will get worse unless you make a change of direction.

Ask godly counselors to set your true north toward truth. God's truth will set you free from flailing around on an unproductive path. So, walk in the truth (3 John 3) and walk with Jesus, as He is the way, the truth and the life (John 14:6). Our spiritual, emotional, financial, relational, and vocational directions need to converge into Christ's personal path designed just for us. Remain on the path of faith in Christ.

Are you walking on Christ's path?

SEPTEMBER 24

WARNING AND REWARD

By them is your servant warned;
in keeping them there is great reward.
PSALM 19:11

The Word of God is our warning and our reward as we travel through life. When driving down a highway under construction, we may see signs warning us of a rough ride, closed lanes, or a bridge that may be out. We do not ignore these signs, because we value our life, time, and automobile. So it is as our body, soul, and spirit make their way through this life. The Word warns us of impending danger, and by simple faith, we listen and become wise. Obedience to God's precepts is fundamental to successful living, and it is sin to know what to do and not do it.

God may be trying to speak to you through your spouse, a friend, or even an enemy. So, do not allow pride to deafen your heart. God's principles barricade you from the exits of unwise decision-making. Therefore, do not force down a door that does not freely swing open on the hinges of God's grace. The cavalier foolishly continue on.

The Bible is our mentor, our monitor, our reminder, and the keeper of our conscience. Though the brilliant white from a freshly packed snowfall causes blindness to the skier, God's Word has the opposite effect. Its application to our lives lifts the natural blindness of our soul. The Bible disperses the fog of our confused minds and replaces it with focused and clear thinking. His truth makes our heart right and then gives it joy.

There are rewards to those who remain faithful and follow God's instructions. His grace is His grandest reward. He gives us grace to become His child. He extends us grace to be a faithful husband, an engaged parent, a loyal friend, or a loving leader. We receive grace every day to forgive more and resent less.

There are also the rewards of God that transcend this life. He is all about eternal rewards. If heaven's outcomes are important to Christ, they are important to His followers. Christ will crown His children for cleaving to His service, whether in success or difficulties.

Your faithfulness with His stuff determines your eternal rewards. What you do on earth with your time, talent, and treasures defines the quality of your experience in heaven. Jesus says, "So if you have not been trustworthy in handling worldly wealth, who will trust you with true riches?" (Luke 16:11). This is His warning and His reward. Therefore, heed His warnings, and send as much ahead as possible in saved souls and financial leverage for the Lord. Keep enough now to shine the brightest for Christ but invest the rest in eternity.

How can you invest in Christ's eternal reward today?

TAKE AND GIVE

"So take the bag of gold from him and give it to the one who has ten bags."
MATTHEW 25:28

God has the prerogative to take and give. He can take what He has given you and give it to someone else. He can execute this transaction with or without your knowledge or understanding. Just because you enjoy His blessing today does not guarantee His blessing tomorrow.

There is a direct correlation between your faithfulness and His blessing. However, your relationship with Him does not always operate as a cause-and-effect process. For example, "in Christ" you are always accepted, and He gives you His unmerited grace. So, your role is not to strive and strain to please Him. He wants you to wait on Him and to walk with Him. He invites you to rest in Him and to serve Him (albeit with gladness!). Obedience and faithfulness determine your level of responsibility within God's kingdom.

You have been blessed with resources, relationships, opportunities, and skills. God has given you much, so this responsibility of managing His blessings is not to be taken lightly. What is not used for God's purposes could very well be lost for good. To do nothing, when He has said to do something, is not acceptable. If you remain in a state of denial and defiance, you may very well lose an opportunity. He can take what He has given to you and entrust it to another. If this happens to you, do not get mad at God or be resentful. Rather, learn from the situation and become better, not bitter. Let God restore you to a position of blessing. God can restore the joy of His salvation. David cried out in brokenness, "Restore to me the joy of your salvation and grant me a willing spirit, to sustain me" (Psalm 51:12). What He took He can give back.

This is not a reason to live in fear. God is not a cruel taskmaster waiting to crush you over one little misstep on your part. He does not impose unrealistic expectations on you to frustrate your progress. His will is doable, and His plan is discernible. He has given His children everything for life and godliness. Do not believe the lie that God is trying to catch you in a misdeed so that He can bring swift and unfair judgment. On the contrary, His patience affords you many opportunities to get it right.

Time proves your ability to execute His will. Excuses are not acceptable. Only Spirit-led risks are needed to explore options and test the waters of His will. After He gives you an assignment, look around for the relationships and resources to accomplish the task. Look to God for wisdom and look to others for validation and counsel.

Faithfulness allows you to enjoy God's blessings.

BEAUTIFUL MEMORIAL

Aware of this, Jesus said to them, "Why are you bothering this woman? She has done a beautiful thing to me. ... Truly I tell you, wherever this gospel is preached throughout the world, what she has done will also be told, in memory of her."
MATTHEW 26:10, 13

How do you want to be remembered? The memory of your life will linger beyond your death, so how will your obituary read? Will it point to God and people or to you?

We will all have a memorial that reflects our life. It may be pigmy-sized because it was built around us, or it may be bigger than life because it was built around Christ. Your defining moments are building a memorial that will extend into the future. There are spectators watching you assemble your life memorial. Your family is watching, friends and acquaintances are watching, and the world is watching, but most important, God is watching.

Some of your heavenly-minded friends and family will do more than watch. Their memorials will intertwine with yours, creating a beautiful tapestry of God's faithfulness. Your memorial may be more a collaboration around community accomplishments. No matter, stay in the process of keeping your life aligned with eternal purposes.

Others may try to dissuade you from a lifetime commitment to seek God's best. They may define God's will differently and have "a wonderful plan for your life." But you have your own life to live. God's best for you may not be God's best for another, so take what God has given you and completely dedicate it to Him. Your commitment to Christ is compelling. It provides the wet cement that bonds together the bricks of your life experiences.

As you construct your life memorial, consider a few things. Ponder what if means to make God your foundation. When He is your foundation, your memorial will stand for eternity. The memory of your lifelong acts of service for Christ and others may fade over time, but your God-based foundation will remain. Build eternal financial investments for Jesus into the architecture of your beautiful life memorial. Leverage your resources for God's kingdom. Your memorial may be bricks and mortar that represent churches, schools, hospitals, businesses, community centers, or homes. Whatever you build, build for the glory of God.

Your memorial may consist of paying for the Christian education of your grandchildren. It may be funding initiatives and projects that leverage evangelism and discipleship in a country outside of yours. Whatever you do, do as unto the Lord. Resist the critics, embrace Christ, and be ever mindful of beautiful kingdom memorial-building.

"I will perpetuate your memory through all generations; therefore the nations will praise you for ever and ever" (Psalm 45:17).

SEPTEMBER 27

SICK SINNERS

When the teachers of the law who were Pharisees saw him eating with the sinners and tax collectors, they asked his disciples: "Why does he eat with tax collectors and sinners?" On hearing this, Jesus said to them, "It is not the healthy who need a doctor, but the sick. I have not come to call the righteous, but sinners."

MARK 2:16-17

Sick sinners need a Savior. Sick sinners are perishing all around us. Some are sick and don't realize their spiritually terminal state. Those dying in darkness do not know any difference and they are content to languish outside the light.

However, we who are children of the light know better. If not for the grace of God penetrating our hard hearts, we would still be severely sick in our sins. Followers of Jesus have seen the light, and it has illumined our souls and healed our sick hearts. We have been saved from sin and from ourselves. The Bible says, "Since, then, we know what it is to fear the Lord, we try to persuade others. What we are is plain to God, and I hope it is also plain to your conscience" (2 Corinthians 5:11).

Yes, there will be those who deny their sinful condition. They will avoid a spiritual doctor like the plague. One of Satan's schemes is to keep the healthy saints from the sick sinners. They are dying by the droves and entering into eternity without Christ. Sick sinners need a Savior.

But with grace, humility, and prayer we can pursue them and pray for them in their sick spiritual state. Some physical illnesses cannot be cured, but sin's sickness can be cured in Christ. Care for the spiritually sick where you work and live. Use your home as a haven for them. You can become their heavenly hospice. Watch God raise them up from their sin-sick bed. You may not feel qualified to practice spiritual medicine, but by God's grace you can be a soul caregiver.

You have the cure, so live authentically and engagingly among sick sinners. Perhaps you need to recalibrate your calendar to include time with sick sinners because the sterile saints are consuming most of your time. Do not underestimate the potency of Scripture, especially texts you consider elementary. An aspirin of John 3:16 provides relief and hope for a sick soul.

Moreover, your own story of righteous recovery provides hope to the sickly sinner. Others gain hope that God can do the same for them. There is nothing quite as compelling as someone "working as unto the Lord." Your testimony may be the faith stretcher that carries them to Jesus. Your story and Scripture shared in a timely fashion are healing.

Time is short, and people need a Savior.
They need a Savior for eternity and for now.

ACCOUNTABILITY'S CONSEQUENCES

"If your hand causes you to sin, cut it off. It is better for you to enter life maimed than with two hands to go into hell, where the fire never goes out."
MARK 9:43

Accountability without consequences is powerless and ineffective. It is like a lion without teeth. It performs like a car engine without oil. Only the uninformed or foolish would drive a car without oil. The engine, of course, would burn up. The same can be said of a life. A life lived without the oil of accountability will burn up or burn out.

You can say you are accountable and not actually be. You may be going through the motions and getting nowhere fast. You may have been accountable at one time, but do not kid yourself. When the smoke of activity cleared, you may realize you have not changed. You may have even regressed in your behavior. The most dangerous person may be the one who thinks he is accountable and is not. He talks it, but does not walk it. There is a disconnect between his words and his actions. Is there a need for an accountability audit of your life?

For accountability to work it has to cost you something, otherwise it is just a masquerade. Think about it. The reason you are cautious and don't exceed the speed limit is because of the potential consequence of a wreck or a speeding ticket. Do you have similar consequences in place for running too fast through life? Your body may be screaming for attention, and it may be writing you multiple warning tickets to exercise and eat right. Be careful not to mistake today's mild consequences for tomorrow's severe ones.

Accountability starts with your time with God in prayer and Bible study. If this is currently difficult for you, then implement a meaningful consequence. You may need to write out a contract between yourself and God. Outline in this covenant agreement what you are committing to do in your relationships, finances, and time management. State clearly the positive and negative consequences associated with each area of accountability. Ask accountability partners to sign the document as witnesses. There is something about defining the consequences of your accountability in writing. If it is stated in black and white, there is little room for interpretation.

This may seem like overkill, but few people are overly accountable. Start by submitting to God and His authorities in one area of your life. You will learn to trust them, and then you can begin implementing consequences of accountability in all areas of your life.

"Therefore, it is necessary to submit to the authorities, not only because of the possible punishment but also as a matter of conscience" (Romans 13:5).

SEPTEMBER 29

TEACHABLE HEART

"Well said, teacher," the man replied. "You are right in saying God is one and there is no other but him." ... When Jesus saw that he had answered wisely, he said to him, "You are not far from the kingdom of God."

MARK 12:32, 34

Jesus affirms a teachable heart, for He knows it has potential to learn and understand the things of God. Wisdom comes from God, and a teachable heart learns the ways of God.

A teachable heart is positioned to receive truth, and it is an attitude with more questions than answers. It invites truth in to be examined, understood, and applied. Truth invigorates the teachable heart, and there is a rush of spiritual adrenaline when truth intersects with an open mind and heart. Pride plateaus in its learning, but a teachable heart continues to scale the mountain of truth.

Change doesn't come easily, even as you understand that God has your best interests in mind. Most of us don't like to be told what to do. But the transformation that comes from God's truth is telling. Your character and behavior fall more in line with Jesus; your spouse and children notice something different. Your patience, rather than your intimidation, becomes dominant; your bad beliefs will be replaced with good ones, so let your teachable heart start first with God. Truth facilitates this change in behavior and attitude.

Let your teachable heart root itself in these solid truths about God: God is one. He is not many gods, but one God. He is not a mini-god, but the great and glorious God of the galaxies. God the Father, God the Son, and God the Holy Spirit are all one God. His oneness is to be worshiped and celebrated. Any acceptance of other gods is unacceptable to God. He is jealous for you. To love God is to make room for God in all aspects of your life. Love is action, therefore love Him and allow Him to love you.

Let His truth mold your heart, because what God thinks trumps any other thinking. The Holy Spirit within you has the answers to the questions that consume your thinking. Follow His internal promptings, not the external clamor. Know God, love God, and learn of Him. Stay teachable in your understanding of God.

"'Assemble the people—men, women, and children, and the foreigners residing in your towns—so they can listen and learn to fear the Lord your God and follow carefully all the words of this law'" (Deuteronomy 31:12).

SEPTEMBER 30

MONEY'S DISTRACTION

Jesus looked at him and loved him. "One thing you lack," he said. "Go, sell everything you have and give to the poor, and you will have treasure in heaven. Then come, follow me." At this the man's face fell. He went away sad, because he had great wealth. Jesus looked around and said to his disciples, "How hard it is for the rich to enter the kingdom of God!"

MARK 10:21-23

Billions of people wake up every day to make money, but are they making money for wise use or is money using them? It is easy for money to become a distraction. Yet money becomes a subtle master if it is not held in check. We think about what we love, so if the majority of our waking moments are consumed by the thought of making more money, then we are distracted.

You may think that your current obsession with making money is for the long-term purpose of autonomy. This thinking is flawed, because the follower of Jesus Christ is never really autonomous. Time and energy for others become scarce in the wake of compulsive money making. Even a wealthy believer is still tethered to God's will. They are still expected to submit to community and Christ for accountability and service. Yes, finances afford you options, but only options that are under God's will. He may free you up to serve Him and others, but not to sit and soak. Too many options can be a distraction to God's best.

When you allow money to love on you, you feel a debt to money. If your love quotients are currently met by stuff, then your affections will gravitate in that direction. This is a subtle but effective tool in the enemy's arsenal. Without a love relationship with your Creator, you will become sad, even in the midst of more stuff than you ever dreamed.

So how can you avoid money's distraction? Let the Lord love you into heavenly investments instead. Let Him love you away from the seduction of possessions. By faith, regularly look into the loving eyes of Jesus, and you will feel led to love Him. Money's distraction is derailed by a love relationship with Jesus.

Love Him wholeheartedly and leave no room for money to distract. Love Him and build your treasure in heaven and not on earth. You cannot love God and money at the same time. Receive His love and give generously, especially to the poor. Then you can enjoy your citizenship in His kingdom with community, accountability, and authentic love.

"Whoever loves money never has enough; whoever loves wealth is never satisfied with their income. This too is meaningless" (Ecclesiastes 5:10).

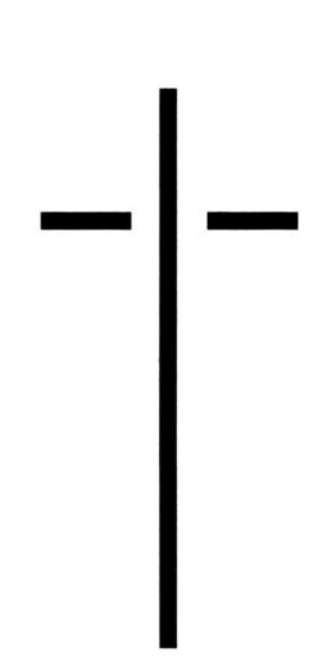

LISTEN THEN ASK

As they talked and discussed these things, Jesus himself suddenly came and began walking with them. But God kept them from recognizing him. He asked them, "What are you discussing so intently as you walk along?"
LUKE 24:15–17

Have you ever tried sharing your troubles with someone who jumped straight to solutions? Even well-meant advice can fall flat when it comes too soon. It's not always wrong—it's just mistimed.

I'm struck by Jesus' approach on the road to Emmaus. The risen Savior—Truth Himself—walked beside two grieving disciples. If anyone had the right to interrupt with, "Let me explain what really happened," it was Jesus. But instead, He chose to listen first. "What are you discussing as you walk along?" He asked, even though He knew the answer. Imagine the restraint: the Creator allowing His creatures to explain creation to Him. The Author of the story lets others interpret His plot. Why would Jesus do this? Perhaps because He knew something we often forget—people need to be heard before they can hear. A friend of mine heard a young person say recently, "I wish the Church would stop answering questions we're not asking." That's stayed with me. How often do we offer spiritual fixes for wounds not yet revealed? How often do we interrupt stories still unfolding?

Jesus models a better way. He walks with the disciples. He listens first. Only after they've poured out their pain does He gently begin to speak truth. And what happens? "Stay with us," they urge Him. His patient listening invited deeper relationship. In our fast-paced world, listening seems inefficient. We want to explain, solve, and move on. But love is patient—it listens before it speaks. It walks alongside rather than rushing ahead.

True listening requires humility—acknowledging we don't fully understand. It calls for patience—letting others process at their pace. It cultivates curiosity—asking questions that deepen, not end, the conversation. Tomorrow, try walking like Jesus did in Emmaus. When someone shares a burden, resist the urge to teach or fix. Simply say, "Tell me more." Watch what happens when someone feels truly heard. Sit in prayer to listen to the Lord before walking with others to share the Lord. Before you pour out, be filled. Before you speak, hear. People don't need our wisdom nearly as much as they need what God has whispered to us in stillness.

Listen with a humble heart before you speak.
Be patient to hear fully, have wisdom to respond gently,
and grace to reflect the Lord's love in every conversation.

TIME FOR TRANSITION

Moses my servant is dead. Now then, you and all these people, get ready to cross the Jordan River into the land I am about to give to them—to the Israelites.
JOSHUA 1:2

Death is hard and it is a time for pause. Death is a time for transition, and grief is a bridge to that transition.

Your struggle may be the death of a vision or a plan that you prayed over. You may have thought you were a lifer in this particular career, but things change, and people change. Have you been neglecting family time for the sake of your career? Perhaps your family needs a break from your breakneck pace, and now is the time for you to go out at the top of your game. Do you feel God tugging at your heart toward a career transition? It is up to you to walk by faith through the Lord's open door into this new opportunity. Don't wait until you are asked to leave your current role but choose to leave so another leader can build on your good work with his new and much needed leadership style. Everything is for a season. Your winter of discontent is about to bloom into a spring of contentment.

Your struggle may be putting to death past ways of living. You may need to preside over a funeral of bad habits. Bury them deep into the soil of your Savior's love and forgiveness. Let the strong hand of the Lord lay them to rest; make His confidence your confidence. His transformation of your character is a terrific transition. It requires a lifetime of surrender and obedience to Him. Receive God's encouragement as your strength for life's journey. God is walking with you on this path of change; so do not fear, because your heavenly Father is not far away.

Your struggle may be the death of a close friend, a parent, or a grandparent. Be very strong and courageous in Him. Although He has graduated your loved one or friend to heaven, He has left you behind on earth to carry out His mission. Your intimacy with Almighty God is your energy for living. Tap into His truth often—especially during transition—and trust Him with this life change.

Let your life of transition point to trust in God.

DEVOTED THINGS

But keep away from the devoted things, so that you will not bring about your own destruction by taking any of them. Otherwise you will make the camp of Israel liable to destruction and bring trouble on it.
JOSHUA 6:18

God is honored by our devotion. We hold Him in high esteem when we devote our marriage, our children, and our friends to Him. Devoted things are sacred to Jesus. A meaningful routine or a worshipful ritual may represent our devotion to Him. We may have devoted money or relationships to Him. Things devoted to Him cannot be tampered with for our own selfish desires. He delights in devoted things and is jealous over their ownership.

He desires devoted things, especially those things that bring Him the most glory. Your devotion is a reflection of Him. Think about things in your life that need to be devoted to the Lord.

A good starting point is to devote your entire being to God. This does not mean you have to move to a foreign land and live in poverty (though it might); this does not mean you have to quit everything you are doing and go to seminary (though it might); this does not mean you have to speak in a religious gibber jabber, act strangely, and draw attention to yourself. But it does mean you glorify God in your speech, attitude, and actions.

Devote your home to Christ. Use it for Him openly and freely. Create a home that exudes warmth and hospitality. See your living quarters as a sanctuary for seeking souls. People long to be in an environment that extinguishes loneliness. Though it is not a conflict-free zone, a devoted home is a shelter from the storms of life. Refrain from just using your home for yourself and see it as a God-spot for weary wanderers. Encouragement explodes in a home dedicated to the Almighty.

Devote your family to your heavenly Father. There is so much you cannot control as it relates to family. Your best strategy is to lay them at the feet of our Savior. Jesus takes your devotion to family and sets you free from having to make them into something that you think is best. You can trust your spouse and children to Christ. They are His devoted possessions.

Lastly, devote your work and career to Christ. Give your job to Jesus. When you give over your occupation to Him in sweet surrender and devotion, you are freed from preoccupation with "what ifs?" such as "What if I lose my job?" or "How will I take care of my family?" The psalmist says, "Guard my life, for I am faithful to you; save your servant who trusts in you. You are my God" (Psalm 86:2). Therefore, do not hold onto for yourselves what you devote to heaven.

Your Savior secures devoted things.

OCTOBER 4

PROCESS DISAPPOINTMENT

Cast your cares on the LORD and he will sustain you;
he will never let the righteous be shaken.
PSALM 55:22

Process disappointment or you will remain in a disappointed cycle. If disappointment is not processed, it harms our heart. It builds up like emotional plaque that blocks the flow of the Holy Spirit between Almighty God and us. Disappointment is meant to drive us toward God and not away from Him.

Unprocessed disappointment leads to angry reactions. Whether it leaks out gradually or explodes unexpectedly, it is ugly. It causes others to ask, "Where did that come from? Is he okay?" Disappointed people become dreadful to be around.

Disappointment may come in the form of a broken promise or an unmet expectation. You may find disappointment when you look in your checkbook, flip through your calendar, or step on the scale. Most likely, your disappointments revolve around people. They let you down, they don't act right, they don't give you the respect you deserve, or they don't seem to care.

Since disappointment is a fact of life, how can we process it in a healthy manner? How can disappointment work to our advantage instead of our disadvantage? Processing disappointment properly begins with seeking God's perspective. We can begin to align with His view on the matter with questions like, "What does God want me to learn from this disappointing situation?" "How do I need to change?" "How can I be a blessing to others in the middle of my extreme disappointment?" "How can I shift focus from my disappointment to His faithfulness?" These questions, and others like them, help us process disappointment in a way that makes us more dependent on God and less dependent on circumstances.

God understands our disappointment and wants to meet us in the middle of our hurt. But He meets with us to move us beyond our disappointment into the satisfaction of our Savior. Make regular appointments with your heavenly Father to process your disappointment. Flood your soul with His grace and forgiveness. There, you can find hope. The Bible says, "And hope does not put us to shame, because God's love has been poured out into our hearts through the Holy Spirit, who has been given to us" (Romans 5:5). Therefore, cast your cares on Christ and receive God's care so you can care for the disappointed.

Process your disappointment by the grace of God,
for His hope overcomes disappointment.

FEAR HIM

The Lord's love is with those who fear him.

PSALM 103:17

Fear of God is access to the love of God. On the surface, this doesn't feel right. But we discover the truth to this when we dive deep into God's character.

His righteous attributes compel us to fear Him. We cannot contemplate, for very long, our awesome Almighty God and not be struck with awe. His goodness and holiness require our unrivaled worship and devotion. He is mighty to save and worthy is His name. Fear of God flows from our innermost being when we realize He alone is the Holy One. The degree to which we understand the character and nature of God is the degree to which we fear God. The larger the Lord is to you, the greater your fear of Him.

The degree to which you fear God directly affects your capacity to receive His love, as the Lord's love follows fear of Him. So when we choose to fear God, we choose to be loved by God. The Bible says, "Let those who fear the Lord say: 'His love endures forever'" (Psalm 118:4). He intently loves those who fear Him.

The fear of God will lead you to understand His calling on your life. Therefore, fear Him and be loved and led by Him. Fear of God positions you to experience His very best. Yes, it is an attitude of dependence, but also one of tremendous freedom, because you can trust Him. Fear of God does not thrust you into a corner to quit. On the contrary, it compels you to persevere in doing right. It takes you on an adventure with the Almighty. Fear of God is freedom to do His will with abandon, and it is fueled by His love. Freedom is the fruit of the fear of the Lord.

Stubbornness and pride do not fear God, nor does unbelief. Disobedience is fearless of God, and in these places void of fear, love is lacking. Sincere and lasting love is embedded in the fear of God. Love is shallow and conditional when motivated by sources other than God. He is love, He is holy, and He is to be feared.

Fear of God will bring back your sense of shame in not doing nice things or honest activities. Fear of God will bring dignity to all human beings, especially those who have no voice. Fear of God will remind you of what's important: purity, peace, hope, forgiveness, faith, honesty, holiness, generosity, and above all else, love. He is waiting for God-fearing people to take Him at His word. His ways are not your ways, but His ways are the best ways. Therefore, follow Him in fear and receive an abundance of His love.

God's love is looking to partner with God-fearing followers, so fear Him and be loved by Him.

OBEY HIM

Son though he was, he learned obedience from what he suffered and, once made perfect, he became the source of eternal salvation for all who obey him.
HEBREWS 5:8-9

Obedience to God is the heartbeat of Jesus. He learned and modeled obedience, even in the midst of suffering. Anyone can obey when it is easy, but in the fire of adversity and pain, our obedience is put to the test. Will we obey even when it hurts, even when it costs us dearly, even when we don't want to, even when we are uncertain of the outcome? Obedience's tests unmask our motives. Be prepared to obey, just because you know it is the right thing to do. God is watching to see if we will obey Him when no one else knows.

The Bible says, "See, I am setting before you today a blessing and a curse—the blessing if you obey the commands of the LORD your God that I am giving you today; the curse if you disobey the commands of the LORD your God and turn from the way that I command you today by following other gods, which you have not known" (Deuteronomy 11:26-28). God expected obedience from the Israelites, and He expects it from us.

Jesus knows from first-hand experience that obedience is what makes us more like Him. We experience Him in our acts of obedience; He assures us in our obedience; He loves us in our obedience; He empowers us in our obedience; God shows up in the middle of our obedience. It is so important to Him that He makes it a priority to bless our obedience. His blessing may not be recognized immediately. It may take months or years before we enjoy the fruit of our obedience.

Obedience to prayer can be hard. It's especially difficult when things are going well. Success reveals a different type of suffering. We suffer from isolation, greed, and pride. Without obediently seeking God, we fail where it matters most. It seems like we don't need God when we are fine. We unwisely drop our prayer guard and are exposed to a punch in the face by our adversary, Satan. The reality is that success and prosperity need to propel us to pray more. Progress demands prayer. How can we maintain this level of achievement or move forward to conquer new horizons without obedience in prayer?

We obey God because He gave us new life. When we passed from death to life, from darkness to light, we became a new creation in Christ. Our names changed from self to selfless, we went from control to trust, from disobedient to obedient. As Jesus-followers, we represent heaven on earth; we are the face of our heavenly Father. We obey Him because there is a higher purpose in life. We are ambassadors for Almighty God, hosts for heaven, and greeters for God.

You obey Him because you are His.

OCTOBER 7

GOD'S QUALIFICATIONS

But the Lord said to Samuel, "Do not consider his appearance or his height, for I have rejected him. The Lord does not look at the things man looks at. People look at the outward appearance, but the Lord looks at the heart."

1 SAMUEL 16:7

Sometimes we use a wrong measure of what is meaningful to God. What means most to our Master is what's in our heart. A heart after God has unlimited upside potential. Heaven hunts down a heart hungry for God to accomplish its purposes. We can wait for the right opportunity because He is in control, or we can spend an inordinate amount of energy arranging our lives, when ultimately God is the one who opens or shuts doors. God chooses who He wants to carry out His causes, and He first looks inward for a pure heart.

Why we do what we do incubates within our heart. This is why it is imperative that the Holy Spirit works in our heart. He massages away toxic motives and keeps us honest. He calls us to place the welfare of others above our own needs.

Sometimes we attempt to compliment people by saying they have a good heart. However, in some cases, our comments carry a tinge of condescension. We add a "but." "He has a good heart, but he gives no attention to details." "She has a good heart, but she is not good with follow-up." "He has a good heart, but he cannot think strategically." "He has a good heart, but he is not an effective leader." So, what do we really mean when we say someone has a good heart?

A good heart does not guarantee success in a certain skill set, but it does position us for success. Indeed, both character and competence are necessary for success. A superb salesman without a good heart should be shunned. A dependable manager without a good heart will bring you grief. A leader who gets results without a good heart will run off good people. Make sure to align goodness of heart with goodness in skill, otherwise this disconnect will erode your work or family culture.

Goodness of heart comes from God. It is His gift not to be taken for granted. Learn to diagnose the heart. Outward trappings can fool you into recruiting or relying on the wrong person. The heart is the best long-term indicator of dependability. Skill can be taught, but character is confirmed by a heart enamored with Christ. Allow the Spirit to keep your heart healthy for Him, and qualify others based on God's qualifications. Good hearts attract and keep good-hearted people.

"Now that you have purified yourselves by obeying the truth so that you have sincere love for each other, love one another deeply, from the heart" (1 Peter 1:22).

OCTOBER 8

ONE IN SPIRIT

After David had finished talking with Saul, Jonathan became one in spirit with David, and he loved him as himself.
1 SAMUEL 18:1

Being one in spirit means you have reached a level of relational intimacy that few obtain. The loyalty, generosity, love, service, and depth of communication reach levels that are rare in relationships. You know the other accepts you and they love you as they love themselves.

Relationships that are one in spirit go beyond the surface of self-indulgence and move toward selfless acts of service. People become one in spirit when there is no scorekeeping. One in spirit means you are comfortable with one another's company. There is a peace that penetrates in the presence of one another. There is an unspoken loyalty that leavens the relationship of those who are one in spirit. When one or the other is caught in the crossfire of life's events, each knows his friend is close by to help. Oneness in spirit means you hurt when your friend hurts. When he feels the barbs of rejection, you feel rejected; when she is the brunt of another's anger, you are taken back by the anger; when he is jarred by jealousy, you feel the pain of jealousy; when she is suffering from disease, you are available any time.

Jesus is the best facilitator for real relationships. He is the glue that brings hearts together in oneness for what's best for God's kingdom. Christ is the catalyst for unity around what's really important. Oneness around our one and only Lord and Savior, Jesus Christ, brings us close together. As we grow closer to Christ, we grow closer to Christ's followers. We are able to have oneness in relationships with those who are one with Christ. The unity we share from the Spirit of God is the most meaningful.

Moreover, stay one with your Savior. Oneness with the Lord means we are prayed up, confessed up, and cleaned up. We have abandoned ourselves to the Almighty in anticipation of His wants and desires for our life. There's oneness with Christ because we sincerely seek to serve Him out of love and gratitude. Unity with the Unifier compels us into oneness of spirit with others who are unified in Christ. Therefore, pray for those God brings your way. Pray for them to experience oneness with the Lord and, as He leads, oneness in spirit with you. Get beyond the surface with your spouse, family, and friends. Go after God and each other in oneness of spirit.

Jesus prayed, "Holy Father, protect them by the power of your name, the name you gave me, so that they may be one as we are one" (John 17:11).

OCTOBER 9

HIGHLY MOTIVATED

When the attendants told David these things,
he was pleased to become the king's son-in-law.
1 SAMUEL 18:26

Motivated men are persistent to produce radical results. With them, there is no lack of confidence or determination. They are on a mission, and they will not be denied. By God's grace, they will get to the goal because they are motivated by a greater call.

Discover what motivates you and then position your life and work to be motivated by these desires and outcomes. Money, results, and accomplishing excellent work may motivate you. Working with a team, a loving leader, the approval of others, winning, and your family may be compelling motivations in your life. Good health, exercise, sports, travel, or a number of other good things may get you up in the morning. However, be wise and make sure your motivations align with Almighty God's.

Just because someone invites you into a role does not mean God has called you to that position. Pray about it and make sure you are motivated for the right reasons to engage in this new endeavor. Hold out until you are highly motivated because there is no need to attack an opportunity if you lack motivation to persevere. If you get in because it looks good, but you lack motivation, you will struggle.

God-given motivations are for the good of His kingdom. As followers of Jesus, we have been called to His greater purpose. This is why our motivation is not just to get rich. Most of us will live in frustration and disappointment if becoming wealthy is our primary motivation. However, if the true riches of experiencing God are our motivation, then there is an excellent chance we will enjoy the wealth of God's grace. Its supply is endless, and its applications are abundant. It provides momentum for living and dying. This level of motivation allows us to live a focused life by faith.

Above all else, be motivated by engaging in God's will. Do not hold back, for He has you here on behalf of heaven. Jesus said, "I will not say much more to you, for the prince of this world is coming. He has no hold over me, but he comes so that the world may learn that I love the Father and do exactly what my Father has commanded me" (John 14:30-31). Follow Jesus' footsteps and be motivated by God's commands. You can be proud that you are His representative. Be who you are for Him and do what you do for Him. Execute His game plan with excellence and live like a man on fire for God.

Be patient, align your motives
with God's, and obey His commands.

PROCESS ANGER

Saul tried to pin him to the wall with his spear, but David eluded him as Saul drove the spear into the wall. That night David made good his escape.
1 SAMUEL 19:10

Anger is a self-fulfilling prophecy of destruction. It destroys peace and quiet and ravishes relationships. Anger is acidic, for it eats away at your credibility, your health, and eventually your ability to function successfully in life. Anger is an ugly emotion, as it easily embarrasses itself and humiliates others for sport. It has a way of expressing itself at the most inappropriate times. Process your anger, or it will control your attitude and your actions.

Work environments build walls of distrust because of seething and unresolved anger. Relationships never get beyond the surface because of the fear of anger's rejection. No one wants to be around an angry person. The Bible even says, "Anger is cruel and fury overwhelming, but who can stand before jealousy" (Proverbs 27:4). It also says, "Fools give full vent to their rage, but the wise bring calm in the end" (Proverbs 29:11).

Where does anger come from? There are probably a variety of sources. When a heart is perpetually unloved, it has a void that is first influenced by—and then filled with—anger. Anger incubates in a hurting heart. A heart raw with emotion is a candidate for anger. Suffering may be hurting your heart, and you can't take it anymore. Your heart is crushed and wrung out by pain.

On the contrary, a heart full of love has no room for anger. Love melts anger. Cold anger is no match for the warm flames of love. Love responds with understanding, instead of seeking to argue or defend itself. Love learns to forgive instead of storing up resentment. Love moves on instead of seething in the stew of what should have happened. Love matures over mistakes made, while anger whines in immaturity.

Reflect on God's love for you and then process your pain in prayer. Listen intently to the Lord, for He really does care. He loves you right in the middle of your mess. Invite the love of Jesus to do surgery on your soul. After the Almighty has loved on you, let others love on you.

Perhaps your own anger is not the problem. You may be the brunt of another's angry outbursts. Do not take their anger personally. See those people as Jesus sees them and extend forgiveness. Anger may be the defense mechanism another uses to keep you at bay. Initiate forgiveness seven times seventy and pray for this person to be loved by God and by you. Anger is an ugly mask, so unveil it with acceptance.

Anger is your excuse to love and accept, not fight and flee.

OCTOBER 11

PRODUCTIVITY FOLLOWS PREPARATION

Put your outdoor work in order and get your fields ready; after that, build your house.
PROVERBS 24:27

Our activities need to be more than just going through the motions without any meaningful results. God blesses prayerful preparation and uses it to accomplish His purposes. In other words, preparation leads to productivity.

Farmers understand how preparation leads to productivity. They show up for a massive amount of pre-work. Their preparation of soil makes way for God's sun and rain do the rest. Their ongoing care contributes to the end results. So it is as we prepare our heart, our home, and our work.

First, prepare your heart. A clean heart has high leverage in the hands of the Lord. Therefore, we must ask God daily to prepare our hearts so that He can use us well (Psalm 51:10). A cleansed heart gets righteous results. We must go to God daily and offer our lives as living sacrifices to Him (Romans 12:1-2).

Second, prepare your home. By doing so, you will have a higher probability of watching your family flourish. It is in your home where faith is your first line of defense. A home built on the solid rock of your Savior will stand when the winds of adversity reach gale force (Matthew 7:24). So, make sure to invest relational and emotional capital in your family first. Do not wait and give them the leftovers of your life. Prepare your family by giving them the very best of your time and attention. Prepare your wife and children by leading them in the ways of the Lord. Your model of love and obedience to God will give them the motivation and courage to do the same. Teach them how to know God and why it is wise to obey Him.

Lastly, once you have prepared your heart and home, you are positioned to prepare for productive work. Take the time to listen to, understand, and plan with those whom you serve. Steward your time, resources, and relationships around robust planning, process, and accountability. Make meetings meaningful by engaging the participants in planning the agenda beforehand. Ask for ongoing feedback on how to improve processes and future projects. Wise work preparation results in accomplishing what's best for the organization.

"Stand firm then ... with your feet fitted with the readiness that comes from the gospel of peace" (Ephesians 6:14-15).

OCTOBER 12

STRENGTH IN GOD

And Saul's son Jonathan went to David at Horesh and helped him find strength in God.
1 SAMUEL 23:16

Strength in God is significant. It is our stronghold when we are in serious trouble. It is our source of encouragement and our motivation to persevere. It is easily accessible and always available. His strength is an unlimited reservoir of resolve. It may see us through the death of a loved one. It soothes the grief of our heart and keeps us from total despair. The Lord's strength is what gives us hope when our financial fortunes are tentative at best or have been swept away altogether. But

The sovereign strength of God is strong, unbending, and unyielding. Our confidence may be crumbling, our health may be declining, or our relationships may be a complexity of confusion. Perhaps you discovered someone is not who he claimed to be. He lives two lives and now the truth is unfolding and it is not pretty. Pray for this man. Lean on the Lord and draw your strength from your Savior. Prayer to the Almighty positions you to receive His power. Make faith-filled prayer a purposeful part of your life.

Moreover, God's instruments for infusion of His strength are His people. They are His ambassadors of goodwill. These are the special friends in your life who strengthen you in the midst of challenging times. Stick with the ones who stick with you and do not be embarrassed to lean on them during these lean times. Like a transfusion of blood, you may need a transfusion of faith. Your ability to pray is nearly obliterated. Ask for others to pray that God would strengthen you and keep you focused in the middle of your own gnawing needs. Ask for prayer that God would use you to encourage those who have encouraged you. Do not deny others the opportunity to strengthen you with their presence and prayers.

Lastly, be quick to strengthen others in the name of the Lord. Write a note of encouragement to a friend or leave an encouraging prayer on a coworker's voicemail. In some creative way, let those who are struggling know you are thinking of them. Prayer retains employees and engages friends. People will never forget those who reached out to them in their time of need. Each day, seek someone you can strengthen in your Savior's name.

In a sense, you are a strength coach for those you come in contact with on behalf of Christ. Your goal is to get others to God, and His strength will stretch their faith way beyond your initial encouragement. Strengthen your family in the Lord and you will be strong. Strengthen your peers in the Lord and you will find eternal energy. Strengthen friends in the Lord and you will find strength for your soul.

"'Wealth and honor come from you; you are the ruler of all things. In your hands are strength and power to exalt and give strength to all'" (1 Chronicles 29:12).

EVIL FOR GOOD

David had just said, "It's been useless—all my watching over this fellow's property in the wilderness so that nothing of his was missing. He has paid me evil for good."
1 SAMUEL 25:21

Sometimes, we receive the opposite of what we expect. Our good deeds shouldn't encounter an evil response, but sometimes they do. Sometimes those we have served seem to have forgotten our faithfulness, and gratitude has faded from their memory. They forgot the fantastic fruit from our labors, and it has become all about what might inconvenience them. You were there for them at their point of need but now in your need, they reject your request. It seems like a cruel joke. Yet, this export of evil is just what you are experiencing. There is a relational trade imbalance. You are the brunt of an evil inequity.

So what do you do when you are repaid evil for good? What is your response? This is a test of our dependence on God. Our flesh screams foul and our anger wants to attack. We want to instantly repay their ingratitude by inflicting some type of loss or pain. Anyone can act like a Christian as long as everything is going his way. It is easy to be nice when everyone else is nice. However, when supposedly mature leaders let us down and even respond to our requests with hostility, what we do next defines our true self. How you respond in moments of deep disappointment will reveal your true character.

We cannot lower ourselves to this kind of schoolyard revenge. The question is not, "What is the right thing for them to do?" The question is, "What is the right thing for me to do?" The Bible says, "Evil will never leave the house of one who pays back evil for good" (Proverbs 17:13). You can reverse the force of the verbal jabs by returning good for evil. When you choose not to fight false accusations by accosting your accusers, you repay good for evil. You trust the truth will come out at the right time, in the right way. When you choose to forgive the malicious actions of insecure and mean men, you repay good for evil. When you pray for ungrateful souls to see God, you repay good for evil.

Above all else, anchor your hope for justice to be done through Almighty God. The Lord can take care of the business of dealing with evil people and their actions. Wait on the Lord to settle matters as He sees fit. Trust Christ to take evil men down in His timing. Your window of reprieve is their opportunity to repent, so be patient. You would want this same grace extended to you. Evildoers may never change, but they might. In the meantime, when you encounter evil, repay it with good, and then trust God.

Thank God that His goodness trumps evil, for evil is no match for good.

TOO EXHAUSTED

Then David came to the two hundred men who had been too exhausted to follow him and who were left behind at the Besor Valley. They came out to meet David and the men with him. As David and his men approached, he asked them how they were.
1 SAMUEL 30:21

Sometimes, you are too exhausted to take one more step forward. Your faith is fatigued, and your energy is sapped. It is not because you are unspiritual, but because you are spent. It is time for a rest, otherwise you are a prime candidate for burnout.

Exhaustion is God's warning to slow down and His appeal for you to adjust. You can choose to slow down, or your Savior will help you slow down, sometimes with sickness. Do not think you have to keep up with others who have a greater capacity. God has a place for you to perform within your passion, skills, and giftedness.

Be willing to humble yourself and do something different. Following God does not mean you cannot vary your responsibilities. Variety is the spice of serving Christ. You may be surprised to see new enthusiasm erupt like a brilliant Roman candle on the Fourth of July. Pray for your work and the people around you, as prayer is the Lord's lever to move past persistent problems. Prayer brings peace, calm, and clarity.

Some may see your exhaustion and may criticize you as weak or unspiritual. They might talk behind your back in resentment, but you cannot control the reactions of such people. They are probably feeling the effects of exhaustion themselves. Fatigue makes everyone feel a little fearful. They are venting their frustrated feelings that are rising from weakness, and you happen to be the most convenient target for their complaints. So pray they will have the courage and trust to rest in God at the right time, for the right reasons.

In the meantime, take the time to recover from your exhaustion. Trust God with the results of your work, and trust that you will receive what's fair. You may need an extended sabbatical or a vacation to properly extinguish your exhaustion. Use emptiness to enhance your relationship with the Lord.

Slow down and be with your Savior. By God's grace, you will overcome exhaustion, but it takes time and faith. Trust Him and trust others to get the job done. The work will be there when you get back, so be patient. Take time for your healing, and He will make your relationships whole again. His grace and forgiveness cannot be exhausted. Therefore, overcome your exhaustion with His inexhaustible grace.

"He gives strength to the weary and increases the power of the weak. Even youths grow tired and weary, and young men stumble and fall; but those who hope in the Lord will renew their strength" (Isaiah 40:29-31).

OCTOBER 15

TEARS OF GRIEF

So David and his men wept aloud until they had no strength left to weep.
1 SAMUEL 30:4

Tears of grief are given to us by God to express our larger-than-life losses. In the Lord's mercy, He allows us to weep. Tears of grief transcend our normal emotions, for they come from deep within our heart and can erupt in uncontrollable crying. Tears of grief can flush out our fears and foster our faith, as they represent a cleansing process.

In our loss, we need the Lord. We need the comfort of Christ to wipe away our tears and replace them with His hope. We need Him to be our comfort and caregiver. God shows up in our tears of grief through sympathy and soul care. God is not passively dispassionate about your despair; He cares. Our tears of grief elicit our Savior's tender touch.

Your loss may be that of a loved one who voluntarily disassociated herself from your family. She grew tired of your influence and authority and wanted to see the world for herself. Her departure may have been sudden and unexpected. You weep because you wonder if she will ever come back the same. Pray that Christ will change her on that journey to find herself. Pray she finds Him and embraces the good values you have instilled in her character. Present your tears of grief as a humble offering to Him.

Your loss may be material. Lost mementos and photos may still be framed in your mind's eye, though now absent from their frames. Thank God you still have the ability to remember. Do not allow the physical loss to rob you of treasured memories. Moreover, do not focus on fleeting financial losses. Your grief will never subside if it depends on dollars.

Lastly, let the Lord and others love on you through your tears of grief. God grieves with you. He gave His Son; He understands loss. Jesus weeps when you weep; so you are not alone in your pain and suffering. Tears are a liquid bridge to the Lord. Grief is meant to lead you to the Lord. Therefore, receive the warm embrace of your heavenly Father and invite His children to pray and care for you. Use grief to leverage your life for the Lord; the Bible says, "We can comfort those in any trouble with the comfort we ourselves receive from God" (2 Corinthians 1:4). Your weeping washes your soul for service, so you can tenderly engage with others in their tears.

**When your tears subside,
stay at the side of your Savior, Jesus.**

SHOW GOD'S KINDNESS

The king asked, "Is there no one still left of the house of Saul to whom I can show God's kindness?"
2 SAMUEL 9:3

God's kindness is unconventional. It extends to the unexpecting and to the undeserving. God's kindness has no bounds and it is not limited by past disagreements or conflicts. His kindness does not cower in a corner for fear of being taken advantage of. The kindness of God gets over grudges and reaches out to the unreachable. It transcends times of confusion and misunderstanding, and its design is to be distributed indiscriminately.

For the sake of Christ, God extends His kindness to Christ's friends. The Bible says, "And God raised us up with Christ ... in order that in the coming ages he might show the incomparable riches of his grace, expressed in his kindness to us in Christ Jesus" (Ephesians 2:6-7). Our affiliation with Jesus opens wide the door to our heavenly Father's kindness. Love Jesus and the kindness of the Lord will flood your life.

We can be kind because the Lord has been kind to us. His kindness is our unlimited reservoir of kindness. Without our Savior shedding His kindness on us, we have little capacity for kindness. It is because we have been blessed by the kindness of King Jesus that we are able to extend His eternal kindness to others. We don't deserve it, but He allows us to feast with Him by faith. His blessing is bountiful to those who love His father. So, unleash the kindness of God on others.

Who are candidates for God's kindness? Everyone with whom we come in contact on a daily basis is a kindness candidate. The cashier at the retail store needs a kind smile. The server at the restaurant needs a kind commendation and a generous gratuity. An angry child needs kindness and love. A discouraged spouse needs kind words of understanding, not a speech on what to do next. Employees need kind instruction, and employers need kind feedback. Friends need kind accountability, and extended family needs your kind presence. The poor need kindness and care, and the afflicted, suffering, and rejected need a boatload of kindness.

Therefore, do not grow weary in being kind. The kindness of God kills critical spirits and overcomes uncaring attitudes. Indeed, the kindness of God treats others as it wants to be treated, so don't be surprised that in the long run, your kindness generates kindness. God designed His kindness to be deployed as soon as it's received.

Who can you show Christ's kindness to today?

OCTOBER 17

POSITIONED FOR TEMPTATION

One evening David got up from his bed and walked around on the roof of the palace. From the roof he saw a woman bathing. The woman was very beautiful.
2 SAMUEL 11:2

The allure of temptation has a lot to do with proximity. If we position ourselves to be tempted, there is a high probability we will drift toward its deception. It is unwise to be out of position and enjoy the cheap thrill of temptation. Our eyes can be sentinels for our Savior or they can be seducers of Satan. Beautiful people are easy on the eyes but they are not meant to mesmerize us into wrong thinking and, eventually, bad behavior. Temptation's immediate gratification seems harmless, but once it has us in a vulnerable position, it pushes for more ground until it captures our heart. If we discover ourselves in the wrong place at the wrong time, we are at high risk for temptation. This is why we do not position our eyes in ways that lead to wayward behavior.

God has given us His Holy Spirit to check our wrong positioning. Following the Lord does not free us from temptation, but He empowers us to flee when we encounter its pull. The Bible says, "There hath no temptation taken you but such as is common to man: but God is faithful, who will not suffer you to be tempted above that ye are able; but will with the temptation also make a way to escape, that ye may be able to bear it" (1 Corinthians 10:13 KJV). We properly position ourselves toward God and away from temptation by prayer. It purges pride and our tendency to take temptation lightly. Discipline deteriorates without the forging fires of the Holy Spirit.

It is also wise to position ourselves under the accountability of people. We cannot stand up to the seduction of temptation if we are secluded. Left to ourselves, we flirt with the fun that temptation offers at the outset, then get stung by its humiliation and hurt. Do not depend on yourself alone. We all do much better when others are watching us. We have all discovered that we do better when those around us remind us of the obvious.

Stay positioned to serve others and fear God. Otherwise, you are tempted to leverage others for yourself. People become expedient for your own selfish desires, and your temptation to live for the moment becomes master. Use power for people, instead of using people for power. Persons are meant to be blessed, not abused by power. So, use your influence for the sole benefit of others, while trusting that God will meet your needs.

What steps can you take today to position yourself wisely?

KINGDOM CITIZENSHIP

But our citizenship is in heaven. And we eagerly await a Savior from there, the Lord Jesus Christ.
PHILIPPIANS 3:20

Followers of Jesus Christ are not citizens of this world. This life is a pass-through, as we are on temporary assignment as agents of God. We serve on foreign soil, for heaven is our home. Kingdom citizenship is easy to forget; we sometimes begin to act as if this is as good as it gets.

The best this world has to offer is of no consequence compared to even the least of what heaven has to offer: A sumptuous meal here is much better there. Wonderful worship here is no comparison to the chorus of angels there. Raving relationships here cannot hold a candle to the absence of sin and sorrow there. The beauty of God's creation here merely foreshadows the incomprehensible glory He has prepared there. The enjoyment of stuff here is laughable in comparison to the value of His heavenly rewards, and the comfort of the Holy Spirit here is but an appetizer before the fullness of God's presence that is to come. Things are much, much better back home in heaven.

Heaven is where our hope lies, ultimately and fully. Do not become enamored with, taken in by, or too comfortable with this world. It is passing by, and we are passing through. We can hold our head high because our King Jesus rules in majesty, holiness, and grace.

Furthermore, you are an ambassador for Christ, so it is necessary for you to remain on earth for now, for the sake of the gospel. You represent your Lord for others; so do not take your ambassadorship lightly or flippantly. Keep top of mind your responsibility to be a good citizen in the kingdom of God. You can constantly be aware of opportunities to represent God's concerns and draw others into His kingdom.

The kingdom of heaven will not arrive until battles are won, so fight the good fight for the glory of God, and for the souls of men and women, boys and girls, and the unborn. Christ is already victorious over sin, so let others know they do not have to remain prisoners of sin. They too can become kingdom citizens right now. While you remain on earth, invite as many others as possible to submit to the Almighty's reign. Be humble, bold, and joyful of the fact that your citizenship is in heaven.

People are attracted to God when they see Christ manifested in your life. They want to apply for citizenship in the kingdom of God. Their visas from this world are torn, tattered, and limited to the temporal. This is not the case for those with passports to heaven. Their papers are good for eternity because they are citizens of an everlasting kingdom.

"But you have come to Mount Zion, to the city of the living God, the heavenly Jerusalem. You have come to thousands upon thousands of angels in joyful assembly" (Hebrews 12:22).

RELATIONAL STALEMATE

And King David longed to go to Absalom,
for he was consoled concerning Amnon's death.
2 SAMUEL 13:39

A relational stalemate is separation from someone with whom you have enjoyed good times in the past. You once loved each other with a rare level of relational understanding. You both have a lot invested, yet there is no communication from either of you. In whatever circumstance you find yourself, it is not worth maintaining relational separation. The distance needs to be dissolved.

So where do you start? Your first step of acceptance will at least breach the wall of communication. If you are the one in authority, you should make a genuine gesture toward reconciliation. You may want to invite your estranged friend or relative into your home for a meal and conversation. Reach out to this person without any expectations other than to accept and love them at their point of need. Leave any behavior and attitude change to the work of the Holy Spirit. It takes time for relational stalemates to become resolved, so don't stop initiating.

The second step is to be open to a mediator. Wise and discerning friends—or even strangers—can be facilitators of rational thinking. God can use a third party as a catalyst to break the chains of relational resistance. Prayerfully choose someone both parties respect and will respond to willingly. This unbiased individual can be an instrument of healing sent by heaven. Pray for someone with a spirit of gentle boldness who can keep you focused on facts and on the character of Christ. This godly bridge builder may be just what's needed to break the relational logjam.

There is something bigger at stake than just an estrangement on earth. Your Savior, Jesus, knows that your relationship with Him will be impeded until you can come clean with your parents, your child, your employee, your employer, your wife, or your friend. Relational blockage with people contributes to blockage of intimacy with the Almighty. Ask God to give you grace so you can extend it often to the estranged. Then be quick to apologize, and even quicker to love. Receive His forgiveness and extend it to the other. Trust God to begin breaking the relational stalemate and pray for healing. You owe it to each other, your family, the Christian community, and you owe it to God.

"When the Lord takes pleasure in anyone's way,
he causes their enemies to make peace
with them" (Proverbs 16:7).

PROFITABLE PATIENCE

Wait for the Lord; be strong and take heart and wait for the Lord.
PSALM 27:14

Life is normally lived waiting. We wait in lines; we wait for job promotions; we wait for news from the doctor; we wait for the next meal; we wait for our future spouse; we wait for a lawsuit to be settled; we wait for a meeting to conclude; we wait for those who have yet to keep their commitment. Every time we turn around, we have an opportunity to wait. Why wait? Because most of the time, it's what's best and most beneficial.

A vegetable gardener is a prisoner to waiting, but this is an asset, not a liability. A tomato is much tastier when it is red, large, and juicy, rather than green, small, and hard. The smart gardener will wait for the vegetables to ripen, though he will nurture the soil along the way and keep out the weeds.

There is a waiting cycle that must be completed before there is worthwhile fruit. If you didn't have to wait, you may have been satisfied with how things have always been done. When you are forced to wait, you have the opportunity to think differently. Maybe there are other people or resources that can contribute to your project or plan. So, when things do not go as planned, see it as an opportunity to improve the plan.

Through this, God teaches you how to wait for Him. What a valuable asset to wait upon. The Lord God Almighty is worth the wait. People camp out to wait and see a rockstar or to pay big bucks to wait and meet the President, so waiting on God should be a cinch. Waiting is fundamentally being patient with God. He is running the universe, He knows what is going on, and He knows what is best for you. You can trust Him in your waiting.

Use this sabbatical-like time to get to know your heavenly Father more closely. Use this time to love on your family and others, like no other time in your life. Allow Him to mold your character so that others will comment to themselves that you are somehow different. You are different because you have been with Jesus. Waiting is not just a passage to God's blessing. It is God's blessing.

It is worth waiting for His joy, because it comes to uplift you, and bring a smile to your face; it is worth waiting for His peace that calms your soul and allows you to sleep at night; it is worth waiting for His wisdom that provides discernment in the middle of conflicting options; it is worth waiting for His strength that propels you through adversity and gives you confidence and perseverance for life's journey; it is worth waiting for His hope that lifts you up and out of your despair and depression.

"Lord, I wait for you; you will answer, Lord my God" (Psalm 38:15).

INFLATED VIEWS

When Ahithophel saw that his advice had not been followed, he saddled his donkey and set out for his house in his hometown. He put his house in order and then hanged himself. So he died and was buried in his father's tomb.
2 SAMUEL 17:23

It is tempting to have an inflated view of our own views. We think our opinions are extra special. We expect everyone to believe that what we think is most important or even preferred. What started out as humble recommendations for others to consider grew into mandates, from our point of view.

Unfortunately, this type of conditional counsel and authoritative advice is driven by pride. The Bible says, "The way of fools seems right to them, but the wise listen to advice" (Proverbs 12:15). The gift of discernment and wisdom is a great stewardship that requires a spirit of humility and graciousness. Otherwise, no one will be able to hear our insights over the roar of our arrogance. God does not need more self-appointed gurus; He desires humble servants who will submit to Him as vessels of truth.

We set ourselves up for rejection and unreasonable expectations if we rely on the affirmation of others for our validation. If we are not careful, we tie our value to the degree to which our views are accepted. Acceptance becomes a barometer for our self-worth. This is dangerous because our views, of course, are flawed. We are ever growing in our understanding and learning of God's expansive truths.

If we are teachable and maturing, our views from the past will become more accurate in the present. For example, we will probably be less judgmental and more motivated by mercy. We will most likely take ourselves less seriously and God more seriously. And as we grow in grace, our words will build up more than tear down. Patience will become preeminent and our inflated views will deflate, as we depend more on God.

Healthy perspectives are born out of dependence on God. Your belief about God determines the way you approach life. If you get this right, everything else comes into alignment. It is wise to be close-minded around your convictions, just make sure they are convictions from God, and not just personal preferences. One truth you can depend on is that God is engaged in everyday life. The Almighty is not absent but is alive and well.

Therefore, seek to lead others to see a grander view of God. Keep Christ the centerpiece of your counsel. If you lead people to be accountable to God, you are wise. If they ignore this insight, they miss their Master's best. His view is the most valuable, so steer them toward the Almighty's perspective.

Make the Lord the beginning and the end of your advice.

RETAIN RELATIONSHIPS

"Now go out and encourage your men. I swear by the Lord that if you don't go out, not a man will be left with you by nightfall. This will be worse for you than all the calamities that have come upon you from your youth until now."

2 SAMUEL 19:7

Encourage your best people and be careful not to take them for granted. It is tempting to give all of your attention to problems and leave nothing for those who have stood by your side. Someone who seems okay may be suffering in silence; they may not want to be a burden, so they keep quiet. They know you are busy with bigger matters, and they don't want to be a bother. But this lack of attention can only last for a short season. Everyone needs personal care and encouragement. The Bible says, "But encourage one another daily, as long as it is called 'Today,' so that none of you may be hardened by sin's deceitfulness" (Hebrews 3:13).

Make it a priority to praise those who have been with you the longest. We all know our most fulfilling relationships are the ones that have stood the test of time. Something special happens relationally when you endure hardships together. There is a bond built that is hard to break, but even this quality of relationship needs nurturing. Old relationships become cold relationships if they are not given attention. So take the time today and thank God for your most loyal friends and work associates. Pray specifically for their personal and professional needs.

This line of thinking and encouragement especially applies to your family. Go out of your way to be with your spouse and children. Love and respect your spouse in a large way, as a child's love and respect for mom or dad will not rise any higher than the level they observe between their parents. Furthermore, make sure not to neglect your less needy child in favor of your needy one. Your compliant child still needs encouragement and reassurance. He or she needs to know they are doing well. Take the time to encourage all of your children; just as they need food and rest, they need encouragement; it's energy for their souls.

Lastly, retain relationships by encouraging others in their faith. Jesus will be there for them when you are not. Eternal encouragement is the most meaningful and long lasting. He is the greatest encourager. He understands when you don't. He loves when you lack love. He listens when you are preoccupied with your problems. Encourage others in the Lord, and they will be on board. Take the time to sincerely give much needed encouragement so others can continue.

Who can you encourage today?

OCTOBER 23

BATTLE FATIGUE

Once again there was a battle between the Philistines and Israel. David went down with his men to fight against the Philistines, and he became exhausted.
2 SAMUEL 21:15

It is imperative that in our exhaustion, we recognize and receive help from others. We cannot continue alone in our exhaustion. Our body and soul cry out for care. If we ignore exhaustion's warning signals, we will probably fail. Our health may fail; our judgment may fail; our faculties may fail; our faith may fail. Exhaustion increases our probability for failure. We are unwise if we think we can do everything. This overwhelmed state compromises the quality of our work. Things that would otherwise be taken care of slip through the cracks. It is in our exhaustion that excellence exits our work and life.

Moreover, our character becomes fragile under the weight of exhaustion's pressure. Our patience becomes thin, and we lash out at undeserving souls. What would never bother us during times of rest soon becomes stressful and an exhibit of embarrassment. Meaningless arguments begin to fill our minds, so there is no room left for pleasant thoughts. Exhaustion pushes us to the edge and makes us prone to relax our convictions, so make sure you confide in your spouse, not someone else's. Intimacy is meant for marriage, so leverage exhaustion for a deeper relationship with your wife.

Exhaustion is also God's way of getting your attention. You cannot continue to run hard in life and leave out the Lord. He wants much more than surface acknowledgment on Sunday. Exhaustion is meant to engage you with the eternal. You are reminded, in your weak state, that God is your rock. He is your fortress, your deliverer, your shield, your stronghold, and your salvation. Because God is your refuge, you can rest in Him. The Bible says, "Yes, my soul, find rest in God; my hope comes from him" (Psalm 62:5). You do not have to strive in your own strength. You can be infused with the Almighty's eternal energy and everlasting love.

So, let go and let Him. Let go of your unrealistic expectations that wear you down. Let go of your way of doing things. Let go of your timetable. Let go of the relationship that is wearing you out. Engage in activities and relationships that energize you. Yes, you need to be available, but rest in Him. Invite the Holy Spirit to fill you up by faith; allow God's grace to flush out your fears. Rest in Him and leave the rest to Him.

Your gracious heavenly Father is the answer to your battle fatigue.

JEALOUSY DESTROYS

And from that time on Saul kept a close eye on David.
1 SAMUEL 18:9

Jealousy is destructive. It can destroy your reputation, your relationships, your health, and your favor from God. Jealousy is insidious, as it gradually creeps into your life over time. Slowly and surely, it inflames your anger and squelches your joy. Instead of celebrating the success of another, jealousy resents not being the center of attention. A relationship that started out as supportive and encouraging can turn 180 degrees to one of criticism and betrayal. Insecurity feeds jealousy, for there is a sense of not experiencing God's blessing in the same way another is experiencing God's blessing. "Therefore, I must be inferior," is the lie that is tolerated. If you believe this deception long enough, it becomes a self-fulfilling prophecy, because jealousy feeds inferiority.

Jealousy is truly a green-eyed monster seeking to destroy everyone in its path. It does not discriminate. Jealousy drives the poor to bad mouth the rich because of their wealth and opportunities. The wealthy can become jealous of the less successful because of their simple and carefree lives. Women are jealous of women, and men are jealous of men. You can become jealous of another's spouse, children, or career. The Bible says, "You are still worldly. For since there is jealousy and quarreling among you, are you not worldly? Are you not acting like mere humans?" (1 Corinthians 3:3). You can even be jealous of another person's relationship with God.

Jealousy is a game that no one wins, and it makes Satan smile. If jealousy is directed toward you, seek to disarm it with confrontation and grace. Jealousy needs to be extracted from the heart, as if by a skilled surgeon. Ultimately, only God can perform the procedure. But you can be God's conduit to bring the issue to the surface and urge the offender to come clean. The person may not respond immediately, but at least you have planted the seed.

Do not make room for jealousy's accusations. Deflect attention from yourself to others and God. Don't have a false humility, but an authentic humility that communicates grace and truth.

Lastly, if jealousy haunts you and you are enamored with its seduction, admit it, and confess it as sin. Do not be deceived any longer. Learn to celebrate the successes of others and let gratitude be the driving force of your life. Be content with what you have, and trust God with what you don't have. Disciples of Jesus are to rise above immature and worldly ways.

Spend time in prayer asking God to reveal any jealousy in your own heart.

CHRIST CONFIDENT

With your help I can advance against a troop; with my God I can scale a wall.
2 SAMUEL 22:30

In Christ we are confident. We do not have to waver in fear or regret if Jesus is with us. We are always welcome to lean into the Lord in prayer and renew our confidence in Christ. This places our trust back on our unshakeable Savior.

Doing so fixes your perspective and reminds you to ask the right questions: Has God called me to this current circumstance? Is He with those who have answered His call? Can I be confident in Christ and continue? The right perspective also offers the right answers. You can advance in your adversity because the Almighty is not against you, but for you. You can scale your wall of worry by faith.

Confidence can be crushed under the weight of cruel people. You may know people right now who are intimidated by your life. Instead of praising your good deeds, they are repulsed by righteous acts. Your life reminds them of how they once were or how they need to be. Your character makes them uncomfortable. They want you to change and relieve their pain of conviction. They want you to worship with them at the altar of mediocrity. People who are comfortable in their sin do not want to be reminded of their selfish motives. They instinctively attack anyone who is confident in their walk with Christ.

So, how does Christ want you to respond? In your confidence, you need not be combative. Your attackers are lost and hurt. What they need is the love of God to fill their heart and soul. You must stay confident that you are Christ's conduit for His love. Respond to rejection with acceptance and extend compliments to criticism. Reach out and love those who love to hurt.

Confidence in Christ cannot be shaken because Jesus is alive and well. So, stand firm by faith. Move forward on your knees in prayer and dependence on God. Confidence in Christ is bold but humble. It is engaging but calm. It is quick to ask questions but slow to answer in judgment.

The Bible says, "Being confident of this, that he who began a good work in you will carry it on to completion until the day of Christ Jesus" (Philippians 1:6). So, in your home be confident that Christ is growing the faith of your family. In your work be confident that Christ is developing your team's character and competence. In your own life you can be confident that Christ is in control.

Your confidence is not based on your bank account, your clothes, or your looks. It is not contingent on where you live or what you drive. It is based on Christ alone.

OCTOBER 26

BEST EFFORT

"She did what she could. She poured perfume on my body beforehand to prepare for my burial."
MARK 14:8

God expects your best—nothing more, nothing less. Your best plus God's best is a productive combination. Be careful that you don't fall into thinking you can take the stress of everything on your shoulders without inviting the God component. Be careful not to do the opposite and fall into the false belief that God will take care of everything without your efforts. Neither is healthy nor right. God simply expects your best and He understands your limitations. Your best is a valuable resource, so use it for others and to serve God's kingdom.

There will always be opportunities, so consider each activity alongside your ability to give it your best. Your stage of life, giftedness, experience, availability, and wisdom all determine your capacity. The capacities of others will be more or less than yours; so do not make them your standard. Instead, steward extremely well what God has given you.

On the other hand, do not become puffed up over your best. Don't leave room for feelings of superiority. There is always another person who has done or will do better. Do not commit when you know your ability to deliver is sorely limited. Instead, have confidence in God to say a no now in preparation for a yes later. Don't let perceived underachievement lead to discouragement. Your best might seem to be in the shadow of someone else's, but self-flagellation will not gain you points with God or people.

Your best mixed with God's best is dynamic. Yes, you have limitations and you can only do what you can do but with God, all things are possible. He can arrange circumstances, relationships, and resources that intersect with your best. Your best plus God's best plus the best of others leverages outcomes you never dreamed could happen. Your $1,000 gift will yield one result, but that same gift combined with $100,000 will far exceed a one-hundredfold result. Why settle for the wilderness of simple addition when you can celebrate the promised land of complex multiplication?

The more you exercise your best, the better you become. Your best may become the best; by God's grace you can be a genius in your field. You can become an expert at what you do, so do what you can, and devote your best to the Lord.

"'The soldiers took sheep and cattle from the plunder, the best of what was devoted to God, in order to sacrifice them to the Lord your God in Gilgal'" (1 Samuel 15:21).

DUE DILIGENCE

With this in mind, since I myself have carefully investigated everything from the beginning, I too decided to write an orderly account for you, most excellent Theophilus, so that you may know the certainty of the things you have been taught.

LUKE 1:3-4

Simply put, due diligence is a process of gathering the facts. Due diligence is necessary for wise decision-making. It is designed to validate assumptions and expose wrong thinking.

You go through due diligence when you buy a house. You explore comparable home prices in the neighborhood and hire a home inspector to check out the nooks and crannies. He is an objective third party that looks for roof leaks, foundation damage, electrical hazards, safe plumbing, and the overall sound structure of the home. His harvesting of information is vital to the final decision of the home purchaser.

In some ways, you apply due diligence to a prospective wife. You observe her attitude toward her parents. You look for love and respect. The same can be said for her reverence of God. Is she submitted to Christ and in love with Him? First impressions may be positive, but more is required to be a wise decisionmaker.

Due diligence is required in life to be a wise steward. So, what has been the extent of your due diligence regarding God? God deserves a thorough investigation, and your intellectual integrity requires due diligence. Then you can have peace of mind knowing you objectively examined all the facts that relate to God. You may read books that document struggles discerning the truth and lies surrounding God. The life experiences of others may become a road map for your own search. More important, however, is to read and research the Bible. Let the Scriptures stand alone. Do not depend on the conjecture and assumptions of people. Read the Bible with an open mind and ask God to speak to your heart through His Word. Use sound rules of interpretation and become a good student of the Bible.

In your due diligence of the Bible, explore the prophecies of the Old Testament. Consider the predictions that occurred hundreds of years before Christ and were fulfilled with mind-boggling accuracy. His place of birth, His method of death, and His provision of salvation are all embedded in the text. Study closely the life of Christ and continue your due diligence in the book of John. Jesus claimed to be God and the only way to God. If that is true, then it holds life-altering implications. Your due diligence may very well lead you into a divine encounter.

"'For day after day they seek me out; they seem eager to know my ways'" (Isaiah 58:2).

WELL SPOKEN

Woe to you when everyone speaks well of you,
for that is how their ancestors treated the false prophets.
LUKE 6:26

A result of following Jesus is that not everyone will speak well of you. This comes with the territory when you commit to Christ. It should not alarm us. This is how people treated Jesus.

The crowds would praise Jesus for His authoritative teaching but there always seemed to be a jealous group lurking. There were those in need of anger management who despised Christ's good works. His authentic living condemned their hypocrisy. His clear teaching made the teaching of the religious leaders look complex and controlling. To be a disciple of Christ is to know that we will not be well spoken of. If we try to please everyone, we will end up letting down more people.

People intimidated into pleasing people become anxious, fearful, and exhausted. They cannot do enough to satisfy some people, because there will always be something else that needs attention. Others are wounded and hard to help. Their hurt has caused them to lose perspective and, unfortunately, those around them may receive the brunt of their frustration. But by God's grace, you can love wounded people. You can give them the care and respect they likely deny you. Patience and forgiveness will go a long way to loving them to Jesus.

There is one who you do want to always speak well of you, your heavenly Father. It matters what God thinks about you. You want to hear from Him the tender words, "This is my Son, whom I love; with him I am well pleased" (Matthew 3:17). Of course, your acceptance is a done deal, because He loves and accepts you in Christ. However, your ongoing maturity in the faith is a concern of His. He does expect you to trust Him more and fear man less. He desires for you a love relationship with Him that is seamless and sure.

When God affirms you, then you can rest assured. Do not waver when the conflicting opinions of others seek to urge a certain way. There is a good chance someone will not understand your faith walk and maybe even give you a hard time. Your stability is in God. He is your rock and refuge. His validation matters most, so rest in Him and do not react to the unrealistic expectations of others. Only the Holy Spirit's leading can define God's expectations.

Doing the right thing may cost you a relationship or financial remuneration. Your obedience to Christ may draw a firestorm of criticism from some, or it may receive a subtle rejection that stings. Either way, pray for your opposers and love them regardless of their unfounded words. God knows, and that's all that really matters.

"May integrity and uprightness protect me,
because my hope, Lord, is in you" (Psalm 25:21).

LOVE MUCH

"Therefore, I tell you, her many sins have been forgiven—as her great love has shown. But whoever has been forgiven little loves little."
LUKE 7:47

The depth of your love reflects the breadth of your forgiveness. A person who is forgiven much loves much. Outside of God's good grace, we all have the same wall of sin between Christ and ourselves. We are separated from God by our sins, but the cross of Christ tore down sin's barrier. By faith, we are forgiven of our sins and adopted by God as His children. By receiving the grace of God, we transition from the rags of this world to the riches of heaven.

Forgiveness is cause for gratitude and thanksgiving. Our sin debt could have been more serious than we realized or were willing to admit. The lust in our hearts was addictive, and anger in our attitude was caustic. But God forgave us, and He still forgives us.

Not only has Christ forgiven us of past sins, His grace also cancels out present and future debts of sin. This is another reason for love to resonate in our heart. The massive coverage of His forgiveness is pervasive. You can run but you cannot hide from the love and grace of God. If you are depressed, He loves and forgives you. If you are frustrated, He loves and forgives you. If you are confused, He loves and forgives you. If you are lost, He loves and forgives you. If you are afraid, He loves and forgives you. If you fail, He loves and forgives you. If you are unfaithful, He loves and forgives you. Nothing can separate you from the love and forgiveness of God.

Therefore, you can love much because you have been forgiven much. Gratitude explodes from your heart when you ponder the depth of His forgiveness. The guilt is gone. The shame is erased. Your conscience is clear. You are freed up from sin to love. Your gratitude toward God compels you to love Him and people.

You are a new creation in Christ. It takes a little getting used to, because of the sinful habits attached to your past life; but you are a new person. Christ became your life. Christianity was not added to your life like an appendage. Now you live from the inside out. You love continually and passionately because He has loved you with an everlasting love.

Meditate on and measure the extent of your forgiveness from God. Thank Him often for His forgiveness. Show your appreciation by loving others unconditionally. Love the undeserving. To be forgiven is to love. You can love much because you have been forgiven much.

"We love because he first loved us" (1 John 4:19).

ATTENTION TO DETAIL

"Are not five sparrows sold for two pennies? Yet not one of them is forgotten by God. Indeed, the very hairs of your head are all numbered. Don't be afraid; you are worth more than many sparrows."

LUKE 12:6-7

Attention to detail means you care. When you show intimate interest in something or someone, it means you value them. This is the nature of your heavenly Father. No concern misses His interest. God knows every bird. He cares for each cardinal, sparrow, blackbird, vulture, robin, eagle, condor, bluebird, hummingbird, wren, dove, and quail.

Yet, the cost of a bird, compared to the cost of you, is incomparable. It is like comparing the value of a sliver of glass to a radiant diamond. It is analogous to comparing a bicycle to a Mercedes. It is like setting a nest and a mansion side by side. It is laughable to surmise any kind of similarity in value. Yet God values you as we would the jewelry, the automobile, and the home. You are the prize of His portfolio.

You are His most valued asset, as He knows and understands the details of your life. He, of course, is more intimately involved with you than you are with you. This is reassuring. You may be right in the middle of a maze of uncertainty. Life could not be more confusing. Your marriage is in chaos. Your career has hit a dead end. Your finances are at a new low. Your motivation to move forward is like walking through a marsh of molasses. Life is not fun right now, but the one with His eye on the sparrow has His heart on you. His care is beyond your comprehension. He is relentless and reassuring in His compassion. Let Him into the details of your life. He already knows and He has your best interest in mind.

His attention to detail invites you to trust and lean on Him. The Bible says, "We wait in hope for the LORD; he is our help and our shield. In him our hearts rejoice, for we trust in his holy name" (Psalm 33:20-21). You cannot cover all the details; only God has that capacity. You will go to an early grave if you stay on an obsessive trajectory. No need to fear; God is as near as prayer. God gives affectionate attention to the details surrounding your life, so replace fear with faith and hope in Him.

If details are important to God, then they should be important to us. Be aware of the overall details and give close attention to the ones only you can manage, then delegate other responsibilities. Surround yourself with people passionate about areas in which you are not. This will free you up to give overall vision and leadership.

Trust God and others with the shepherding of details.

OCTOBER 31

PRINCE OF THIS WORLD

I will not say much more to you, for the prince of this world is coming. He has no hold over me, but he comes so that the world may learn that I love the Father and do exactly what my Father has commanded me.

JOHN 14:30-31

The prince of this world is alive and well. His methods are fear, intimidation, and deception. He flaunts his pretentious power over a decaying world. He maneuvers around in a spiritual disguise. His desire for you is partial obedience to the commands of Christ, so that your love for Christ is sentimental and shallow. Then when pain and suffering grow in intensity, you will lose confidence in the Lord. Satan wants your love for the Lord to be conditional on everything being okay. Adversity is the adversary's most intense weapon of distrust. He tries to extract your joy in Jesus with jealousy over the good fortune of others and a jaded belief that God is distant and disinterested. He demands you to believe that death is the end and that no good can come out of your grief and loss.

But followers of Jesus do not have to believe his half-truths. You are free to instantly, willingly, and completely obey God's commands. Doing so is the evidence of your love for the Lord. Love is where joy gestates. Obedience to God makes you an overcomer. There is nothing the devil can demand of you without first going through God. He tries to make you think you are eternally exposed, but you are safely strapped in by eternal security. Christ is in His Father, you are in Christ, and Christ is in you (John 14:20). The enemy is no match for the Master. The enemy tries in vain to recruit those who have drifted behind enemy lines. The prince of this world is powerless to pry you from the Prince of Peace.

The Prince of Peace is large and in charge. He has taken the temptations of the tempter and transforms them for His own good use. Christ stands greed on its head and transforms it into generosity. The Lord arrests lust and rehabilitates it into unconditional love. The temptation of resentment and bitterness is trumped by everlasting forgiveness.

Jesus is all about calm in the middle of confusion; He is light in the middle of darkness; He is peace in the middle of war; He is joy in the middle of sadness; He is acceptance in the middle of rejection; He is love in the middle of hate.

The Prince of Peace has formed an army of the faithful. Hear His voice, learn of Him, and obey His commands. Fight the good fight. Rescue the perishing and care for the dying. The battle is not yours, but the Lord's. Surrender is what we signed up for. The enemy shudders when you surrender to your Savior and not to him. The unseen war was fought and finished at the cross. The Prince of Peace rules eternally.

"He seized the dragon, that ancient serpent, who is the devil, or Satan, and bound him for a thousand years" (Revelation 20:2).

NOVEMBER 1

GODLY GOAL SETTING

He replied, "Go tell that fox [Herod], 'I will keep on driving out demons and healing people today and tomorrow, and on the third day I will reach my goal.'"
LUKE 13:32

Jesus was a focused individual with specific goals in mind. Jesus' goal, first and foremost, was to do the will of His heavenly Father. This is the goal that got Him out of bed in the morning. It was a joint mission with the Holy Spirit. His goal was also to serve the people. He cast out demons, healed, and taught.

His example is a model for goal setting. Like Jesus, keep God and people as priorities. When you set goals, you will reach some, modify others, and miss a few. For the extremely thorough and cautious temperament, it is hard to plan toward something, and then not see it accomplished. However, this is part of trusting God to help you meet the necessary goals and wait on the others.

On the other hand, there are some personalities that set too many unrealistic goals. Yes, all things are possible with God, but not to the point of irresponsible planning. Too many goals can overwhelm you and water down your effectiveness in reaching the right ones. This is where prayer is critical in goal setting.

Ask God what His best is for your life. Goals are a guide to be adjusted daily, weekly, monthly, and annually depending on their nature and the timing of their necessity and implementation. There is a logical flow in goal setting. Make sure your goals flow out of your God-given purpose. If your purpose is to glorify God by being a faithful husband, an available father, a loyal friend, and a loving leader, then start there. Let your purpose statement be a filter for your goal setting. If a goal does not align with your purpose, then omit it and move on.

Goals are not meant to be barnacles that slow down your life ship. Goals are meant to free you up to focus on God's will. Goals are like billowing, white sails powered by the winds of the Holy Spirit. The Spirit's empowerment moves you forward by faith. Daily time with God is a good goal. A regular marriage conference and marriage teaching with your spouse is a good goal. Giving 10% and saving 10% is a good goal. Using your work as a platform for ministry is a good goal. Exercising three times a week and eating a balanced diet are good goals. Write down what God is putting in your heart. Set a timetable that is not so rigid that it cannot be adjusted.

God works through goals, so be a prayerful goal-setter, and watch Him work. The Bible says, "In their hearts humans plan their course, but the Lord establishes their steps" (Proverbs 16:9). You may be surprised what He can accomplish through you. Simply writing down your goals may give you just the needed inspiration and accountability to attempt great things for God.

Take time today to prayerfully set goals and watch Him work.

FINISH WELL

"Suppose one of you wants to build a tower. Won't you first sit down and estimate the cost to see if you have enough money to complete it? For if you lay the foundation and are not able to finish it, everyone who sees it will ridicule you, saying, 'This person began to build and wasn't able to finish.'"

LUKE 14:28-30

To finish well is to plan well; to plan well is to understand the cost of commitment. The commitment to follow Christ is not an added luxury but standard requirement for the Christian. It means following Christ daily in humility and sacrifice. Finishing well does not imply a perfect life, but it does require a submitted life. This is a life that is under the authority of Jesus Christ.

You can start the Christian life ablaze with the zeal of your salvation. However, if the fuel of understanding and applying God's Word is not added to your initial enthusiasm, you will burn out. You will not finish well. People may even observe, "I thought you were a Christian. Didn't you used to attend church?"

Finishing well is about joining with God to accomplish His will. It is daily discerning God's best and then following Him wholeheartedly. Finishing well is a process that over time begins to take shape. You are more likely to finish well when you are pouring yourself into others, as it provides accountability. Your faithfulness gives you credibility to invest in others with what you have learned. You share with them, out of brokenness, what works and what doesn't work.

You may have children or grandchildren who are looking to you for leadership. You are one of their role models. Don't take this lightly. It is imperative to stay in the race until you make it to heaven. Finish well by becoming wiser today than you were yesterday. Love and forgive more today than you have in the past. This is the essence of finishing well. It is becoming more like Jesus in your attitude and actions.

This race of righteousness sweats out our sinful acts. Unrighteous anger is replaced by patience. Fear is replaced by trust. Pride is replaced by humility. Be encouraged. If you are growing in Christ and building a life of obedience, you are finishing well.

Lastly, you can finish well despite a soiled track record. God loves to take your false starts or your backsliding ways and place you on the road to finishing well. Stop today, turn from yourself and turn to Christ. By God's grace, plan to finish well, and you will.

Forget what is behind and press forward for the higher calling in Christ.

SELF-RIGHTEOUSNESS

To some who were confident of their own righteousness and looked down on everybody else, Jesus told this parable.
LUKE 18:9

Self-righteousness is ugly. It is ugly to God, and it is ugly to others. Self-righteousness is a blind spot of the worst kind. Everyone is offended by it except the one exuding its offensive odor. It is really sad and a little pathetic, but many of us have been down this harsh and critical road ourselves. We have been the culprits of caustic and unfair judgment toward others.

Conversations inevitably degrade to a tone of "us" versus "them." It is a slippery and seductive slope that sucks one into a nauseous cycle of one-upmanship. It becomes a competition between who is the "most spiritual." Religious activities become a parade of people hungering and thirsting for the accolades of others. Pleasing and sucking up to people replace passion for God.

It is a sad state of affairs when the self-righteous become the influencers. Sincere Christians become confused, and non-Christians are repelled. The heart of Jesus is riled by the self-righteous. It is not acceptable to Him, nor should it be to us. Pride is the driver behind self-righteousness.

Self-righteousness hijacks a good discipline like prayer and turns it into a sideshow of sorts. Ironically, what God meant for good is twisted into evil. A self-righteous person who prays draws attention to himself rather than God. God must shudder when He witnesses the feeble attempt of a self-righteous prayer. Prideful prayer is not pleasing to God.

This is why it is imperative for God to uproot pride in our lives on a regular basis. Pride never goes away. Pride lusts after God's job. Pride is not content in the role of a humble, submitted, and obedient follower of Christ. Pride puts others down to build up its own ego.

Humility, in contrast, is quick to build others up and bridge them to God. The humble are quick to confess their sins and shortcomings. The Bible says, "If my people, who are called by my name, will humble themselves and pray and seek my face and turn from their wicked ways, then I will hear from heaven, and will forgive their sin and will heal their land" (2 Chronicles 7:14). Humility is the remedy for self-righteousness. Humility launches prayers to heaven and attracts the ear of God. He pours out His grace on the humble. His grace purges self-righteousness, so prayers are heard and answered for Christ's sake.

Root out sin in your own life and watch the righteousness of Christ shine through you.

NOVEMBER 4

HONOR GOD

"Whoever speaks on their own does so to gain personal glory, but he who seeks the glory of the one who sent him is a man of truth; there is nothing false about him."
JOHN 7:18

God is easy to honor because He is the most honorable. His position is without comparison. His role of King of kings and Lord of lords is matchless. Nothing can compare with the God and Father of our Lord Jesus Christ. He is high and lifted up, never to sin and always to forgive. He is not always understood, but He can be trusted exclusively. Honor and glory goes to the One who can be thoroughly trusted. His word is His bond; it is never broken.

Therefore, God solicits honor by His very nature. He is the most deserving of honor. His character calls for it and His holiness demands it. Foolish and unwise are we when we honor ourselves. Self-honoring is about as awkward as the physical act of patting yourself on the back. It looks strange for one thing and secondly, it draws attention to the wrong person. Honor is to be given, not taken. It is to be bestowed, not withheld.

The act of honoring God facilitates authenticity. Honor means you are about truth and you flee from what is false. There is a divine dignity in your behavior and speech. It is a privilege to honor God because He has honored us with His presence. Do not substitute God's place of honor with anyone or anything, especially yourself.

Honoring God starts with attitude. Honor, by definition, means you revere, respect, and fear God. You hallow His name and speak it with humility. There is God and there is none other besides Him. Your words are a reflection of your attitude, therefore they are honorable and you esteem Him by the way you live. The bottom line is you honor what God honors, and you dishonor what He dishonors. You do certain things—like honor others—because you honor God. You do not do certain things—like abuse your body—because you honor God. You recognize your body as the temple of His Spirit; therefore, you honor Him with clean living. Your speech is free of obscenities because you honor God. You love your wife because you honor God. You respect your wife because you honor God. You honor your parents because you honor God. This is why you embrace righteousness and abhor sin. Honor is what God desires and what He deserves. Honor Him first, and it becomes natural to honor others. If you reverse the order, it is impossible to honor Him with a whole heart. Your true life in Christ flows out of honor for God.

A life of honoring God and others means you graduate to heaven with honors. Honor Him with your time, treasures and talents.

NOVEMBER 5

MUCH FRUIT

"I am the vine; you are the branches. If you remain in me and I in you, you will bear much fruit; apart from me you can do nothing."
JOHN 15:5

Fruit bearing glorifies God because He is the source of life for the fruit. No fruit can be produced without God. The branch is intrinsically dependent on the vine. Therefore, we as followers of Christ cannot take credit for the fruit. Jesus is the source, and we are the distributors. The fruit remains luscious as the Father prunes back unproductive branches. We do not always invite pruning, as it is painful and disfiguring in the beginning. But over time, submission to painful pruning produces beautiful and long-lasting fruit. Trust your heavenly Father with the pruning process, and you will be much better off.

So, what is the nature of this fruit He is creating and nurturing through us? It is the fruit of Christlike character. As we abide in Christ, we become more like Christ. This is a natural result of remaining in Him. We start to love more unconditionally because God is love. We experience a fullness of joy because the joy of the Lord becomes our strength. A holy contentment flushes our countenance because the peace of Christ reigns over our hearts. An unselfish servant spirit fills our heart because Jesus set the ultimate example of servanthood. The fruit Christ produces in us is godly character and faithful service that glorifies God and draws others to Him.

Therefore, it is imperative you remain in Christ for maximum fruit-bearing. This is the position from which God leverages His greatest works. It is from here that much fruit is produced and where the results remain with eternal consequences. You remain in Christ by faith. It all comes back to trust in Him. You take Him at His word. You believe His word. You obey His word. Remaining in Christ is not an onerous task. It will be painful at times, but not burdensome.

You also remain in Him as you live in community with other believers. They become God's encouragers and pruning shears as well. Men need to get real with men. Relational honesty and unity are God's way. Learning, growing, and applying God's truth automatically default to remaining in Him. Be a model of remaining so others will be inspired to do the same. Branches do not thrive in isolation, but in the orchards of evangelism and discipleship. As a result, we remain in Christ. Then the fruits of character and souls are harvested on an eternal scale, all for the glory of the great gardener, God.

Much fruit is the result of God working through a humble, obedient, and submitted life for His glory.

IGNORANT ACTS

"Now, fellow Israelites, I know that you acted in ignorance, as did your leaders. But this is how God fulfilled what he had foretold through all the prophets, saying that his Messiah would suffer. Repent, then, and turn to God."

ACTS 3:17-19

Ignorant acts can hurt deeply and unwittingly harm others. These sins of ignorance are blind culprits. If those who sinned in this way were aware of the suffering they caused, they would be miserable. They would be furious with themselves because of the costly consequences of their ignorance.

Loved ones may suffer in silence. Nonetheless, they are still wounded, and the wound has festered over the years. It has gotten worse to the point where the anger lashes back unexpectedly. It becomes a chore to give and receive love all because of an ignorant act that injured them as a child.

Is this your story? You never felt like you measured up to your dad's expectations. The more you excelled, the higher he raised the bar. Your father followed the wrong example of his father. There were no parenting seminars; just do the best you can. Your mom may have smothered you with her well-meaning nurturing, but to the point of building resentment in your independent heart. The culmination of these ignorant acts has caused you to become overly sensitive and underconfident, so repent from your resentment and let God heal your heart.

Jesus felt the brunt of ignorant acts. He suffered immensely because people acted ignorantly. They did not understand they were bruising and beating up a good man. They did not realize they were bringing great hurt and suffering to the Son of God. They had not thought through the consequences of their actions. This is why His parting words included forgiveness for their ignorant sin: "Father, forgive them for they do not know what they are doing" (Luke 23:34).

On an even greater scale, God used the sin of humankind to forgive humankind. This is the wonderful work of God's grace. This is why your wound is not the final act in your life's drama. He is drawing you to Jesus in humility and forgiveness. He has already died for your sin and the sins of your ignorant inflictors. You can let go and let God restore you and them. They may never change but you can. The consequences of ignorant acts need not be forever, so cease the perpetual hurt and suffering. Stop beating yourself up. Today's forgiveness brings tomorrow's healing.

Write out how God loves you and watch Him heal your wound. Your confession and repentance apply doses of healing to your heart.

INFLUENCE INFLUENCERS

He had been quarreling with the people of Tyre and Sidon; they now joined together and sought an audience with him. After securing the support of Blastus, a trusted personal servant of the king, they asked for peace, because they depended on the king's country for their food supply.

ACTS 12:20

How can we be an influence? You may not have access to the person at the top of the organization, but you may be able to build a relationship with someone who does. Do not get discouraged over the aloofness of the leader. Seek rather to influence those who influence him. You can remain stuck in your critical cycle, or you can get to work at getting to know an influencer. This is the realism good leaders recognize. It may take time, but over the course of months and years you can build trust and credibility.

This is the process of influencing. Instead of staying discouraged in your present predicament, seek to influence your way forward. Start by serving others because you influence through serving. Others value you when you sincerely value them. This is the crux of service. When you value them and what they stand for, you want to serve them unselfishly for God's glory. Over time, those you serve will be attracted to your character and will solicit your opinion. People trust sincere and serving hearts. Before you know it, your servant leadership has opened doors of influence you never dreamed possible. CEOs of very successful companies ask for your opinion and accountability. Influential leaders begin to seek out your wisdom and advice. But it all starts by first effectively influencing those in your immediate circle of relationships.

There is one more prerequisite to influencing influencers, and this is foundational. Your influence will extend the furthest when you are perpetually and passionately influenced by God. Being influenced by God qualifies you to properly influence others. When you come under the influence of the Holy Spirit, you become a viable candidate for influencing influencers. You can boldly influence because you have been humbly influenced. You have submitted to the influence of God, godly mentors, and a discerning spouse. You are a steward of influence, so do not waste it or take it for granted. It is a gift of God that can literally affect nations for Christ. As you influence, seek God's best for the other, not what you can gain.

Do not sell godly influence short. It gets behind enemy lines. It moves the hearts of kings, queens, moms, dads, pastors, and business leaders. By God's grace, your shadow of influence could linger longer and more fully than you can imagine.

God is preparing your heart to influence influencers.

A TRANSFORMING TENSION

My prayer is not that you take them out of the world but that you protect them from the evil one.
JOHN 17:15

On His final night—just hours before soldiers arrived with torches and chains—Jesus could have prayed for anything. He could have asked His Father to remove His followers from the danger and darkness ahead. But He didn't. Instead, He prayed: "Don't take them out of the world, but protect them from the evil one." This wasn't a prayer of retreat—it was a prayer of purpose. Jesus knew that light belongs in the darkness, salt belongs where decay threatens, and seeds must be planted in soil to bear fruit. Love heals a broken world—but only when it steps into that brokenness.

I think of this whenever I'm tempted to isolate myself spiritually—to separate the "Jesus me" from the "world me." But Jesus invites us into something braver: to live in transforming tension. To be close enough to love the world but anchored enough not to drift with it. That's why He didn't pray for our escape, but for our endurance—because real witness doesn't shout from a distance; it whispers in the trenches.

There's another layer to Jesus' prayer: the tension between staying and going. Like Paul, we feel it—"to live is Christ, to die is gain." Some days, the pull of heaven feels stronger. When you're weary from ministry. When the diagnosis is grim. When prayers feel unanswered. In those moments, it's tempting to say, "Lord, I'm ready—take me home." But perhaps Jesus foresaw that tension too. Maybe His prayer includes: "Father, when the suffering deepens, when the prison walls close in, when loneliness overwhelms—don't let them surrender too soon. Give them strength to stay."

Because the battle matters. Your presence here matters. Every day you choose to stay engaged, hope pushes back despair. On those mornings when getting out of bed feels like climbing Everest, whisper this: "Today, I choose to stay in the fight. Not because it's easy, but because someone needs to see You in me." Start a "God Glimpses" journal. Write down moments where heaven brushes earth—a kind word, a small miracle, a breakthrough. Remember: hard soil often yields the most surprising harvests. Longing for heaven isn't weakness—it's homesickness. But your willingness to remain? That's holy strength. It's a grace-filled transformation, found in the sacred tension of living in this world while longing for the next. Pay attention to the tension!

Live in this world with a heart anchored in Jesus.
Be holy yet compassionate, set apart yet engaged,
reflecting the Lord's light without being shaped by darkness.
At the same time, paying attention to the tension.

THE LORD IS THERE

Whereas the Lord was there.
EZEKIEL 35:10

Our family has walked through seasons when the presence of the Lord became unmistakably clear. The enemy tried to invade our home with lies, temptations, and division, but God was our rear guard. The Holy Spirit stood on watch, shielding us from the fiery darts of the deceiver. He renewed our faith and extinguished the lies meant to destroy us. Even family members questioned our convictions—urging Rita and I to live together before marriage "just to make sure we were compatible." No thank you. Their relational wreckage was all the evidence we needed to trust God's way instead. We consecrated our home as the Lord's dwelling place, and anything opposed to Him had no authority to enter.

Ezekiel 35 paints a powerful picture. The Edomites—descendants of Esau—seized an opportunity when Jerusalem fell to Babylon. Rather than helping their distant relatives, they sought to claim the land for themselves. But they misunderstood the nature of that land. It wasn't ordinary real estate—it was sacred, because the Lord was there. Edom's mistake wasn't just territorial greed; it was a failure to recognize divine presence. Through Ezekiel, God reminded them—and us—that His presence makes a place holy. In trying to take what belonged to God's people, Edom invited judgment. They weren't merely claiming land; they were confronting the authority of the Almighty.

Is your home under siege by lies or division? If so, reclaim it by inviting Christ to reign over every room, every conversation, every decision. A Christ-centered home reflects humility, grace, truth, and selfless service. Humility chooses to admit wrongs, ask forgiveness, and place others first. Grace forgives quickly and loves generously, even when it's hard. Truth grounds your family in God's Word and opens the door for honest conversations. Selfless service shows up in the little things—doing chores without being asked, offering encouragement, or sacrificing comfort for someone else's good.

Let Christ reign not just over your home but over your heart and mind—the primary battleground where the enemy aims his attack. The Lord is there, ready to drive out fear with love, silence lies with truth, and plant beauty where chaos once ruled. When the Lord is present, wisdom guides your decisions. Mercy strengthens your relationships, and beauty flourishes. People will notice something different—something lovely—because the Lord is there.

Be present in Christ's constant presence. No matter where you go, He is there. Ask the Holy Spirit to fill your heart and home with peace, love, and guidance. Trust in the Lord!

CHRISTIAN MEDIATION

Therefore, if you have disputes about such matters, do you ask for a ruling from those whose way of life is scorned in the church?

1 CORINTHIANS 6:4

Christian mediation is a much better option than a lawsuit for followers of Christ who are locked in a relational crisis. Pursuing mediation rather than taking someone to court over a disagreement matters. Your family is watching; your friends are watching; your foes are watching; God is watching. In the middle of conflict and disagreement, it is of great consequence that you remain true to the process of mediation.

Do not be discouraged or downtrodden. God can be trusted to work it out. Yes, it takes time, and it is painful at times, but this is only worsened by not dealing with issues in a timely fashion. Early on, if you are mad or disagree with a decision or behavior, talk it through. If you wait for the misunderstanding to fester, the foundation of trust begins to crack. Communication ceases, and lies begin to creep into your thinking. Before long, there becomes a standoff, and both parties feel hurt and disrespected.

A situation calls for Christian mediation when a severe disagreement has occurred. Hurt hovers over the relationship. It is extremely critical to check your hurt and anger at the door before you enter the room of mediation. Make it your goal to restore the relationship, rather than getting what you feel you deserve; the relationship is what's most important. What you think you deserve may be inflated compared to what you really deserve. This is why a trusted, fair, and wise mediator is invaluable.

Whatever the mediator decides must be accepted by both parties. The mediator will verify the facts and listen objectively to both sides. After processing the information, the mediator will offer a solution that is beneficial and fair to both parties. At this point, you can choose to forgive, trust, and move forward, or you can choose to stew in your self-pity.

Everyone wins when everyone chooses to grow through this process. If you listen intently with a heart to learn, you will come away a better person in Christ. It is through conflict that pride and arrogance either flame up or fizzle out. The goal is the latter.

Die to your expectations and watch God work; His mediation is masterful.

PATIENT LOVE

Love is patient
1 CORINTHIANS 13:4

Love, by nature, is patient. This is why those couples who are "in love" in the beginning exhibit an inordinate amount of patience. Lovers believe, "I will let you down. You will let me down. I will act immaturely. You will act immaturely. I will struggle with fear. You will struggle with fear. We both need patience, for love is patient." If there is no evidence of patience in a relationship, then there is a love deficiency.

Love expresses itself in patience. For example, you serve your children because you love them. They are sometimes silly and are prone to foolishness, but you still love them. Because you love them, you are patient with them.

This may become more of a challenge when you relate this thinking to relationships outside of your family. A work associate or a stranger, especially someone outside the faith, is harder to love. You barely know them. Therefore, how can you love them? The most difficult person to love is someone who has offended you. We tend to lose our patience with those who are offensive.

So, here is an important distinction to make. You love someone not because they necessarily deserve it, but because they are created in the image of God. Jesus loved them so much He died for them. You can disapprove of their behavior and still love them. Your willingness to tolerate delay may keep the relationship intact. This is love. This is patience. Your calmness and self-control may be the very thing needed to stabilize the situation. Wake up loving, go to bed loving, and love in between. This environment of love will nurture and produce patience—lots of it.

God understands this because He is love. Therefore, He is the epitome of patience. If anyone has the right to lose His patience, it is God. Every day He deals with billions of sinners, many of whom are demanding their way. Some are oblivious to God. Some are harsh and angry toward God. But because of His great love for humankind, His long-suffering love endures rejection and apathy. He feels compassion, not defiance, toward someone lost in his sin.

Followers of Jesus have the Holy Spirit dwelling within them to love through them. Thus, you have the potential for a higher degree of patience. Allow Christ to love through you, and watch your patience grow and expand. You still confront, but in the right timing and in the right way. Invest in patience and the payoff is exponential. Love the unlovable. Love the undeserving. Love the impatient.

"Jesus looked at him and loved him" (Mark 10:21).

COMPOUNDING COMFORT

*Praise be to the God and Father of our Lord Jesus Christ,
the Father of compassion and the God of all comfort,
who comforts us in all our troubles, so that we can comfort those
in any trouble with the comfort we ourselves receive from God.*
2 CORINTHIANS 1:3-4

Comfort is not a one-time act, but rather it is recurring and compounding. It is a gift that keeps on giving, as it can cut through any calamity and bring healing and peace. God is the God of all comfort, and there is no trouble looming that can outpace God's comfort. If you slow down and listen, His comfort will catch up and cover you.

Life may currently have you in a very uncomfortable place. You might feel a little embarrassed and a lot unsure of yourself, but one thing you can be sure of is the comfort of God. Your situation is not unique, and God has been there before. Let Him in, and do not continue to wrestle alone in your discomfort. You were made to be comforted. It is not a sign of weakness to be comforted by God. On the contrary, it is strength and wisdom.

No matter how terrible your circumstances, His comfort has you covered. The Bible says, "I will fear no evil, for you are with me; your rod and your staff, they comfort me" (Psalm 23:4). His comforter of compassion and love compensates for adversity. It is a warm, soft, and soothing comforter that is tailor-made for your bed of life. Do not toss off its warm embrace; it is for your benefit, not your harm. Yes, you must slow down so you can receive His calming comfort. You must trust Him. Rest and relax in the arms of your heavenly Father.

Lastly, He comforts you so you in turn can comfort others. You can express your comfort without even saying you have been there. Handling yourself with grace and concern speaks to the comfortless friend to whom you extend a helpful hand. The small things inject comfort. Take care of a stressed-out mom's child so she can relish a much-needed break. Pay someone more than they deserve so they can feel some financial comfort. Leave a pertinent prayer on a friend's voicemail so they can hear your comforting intercession on their behalf. Write an encouraging note of concern and love to bolster a comfortless heart. The comfort God gives you can become a means by which you bless someone else.

You are a facilitator of God's comfort. You are not responsible for the recipient's response. Their anger may blunt their gratitude. But keep in mind that your motive for extending comfort is your own gratitude to God for His comfort in your life.

**Give comfort because God has comforted you.
Who can you comfort today?**

LEADERSHIP MATURITY

He must not be a recent convert, or he may become conceited and fall under the same judgment as the devil.
1 TIMOTHY 3:6

Leadership in the world does not automatically guarantee leadership in the church or ministry. In fact, if you are a new believer, you need not sign up for leadership in church. Take your time and get to know the current leadership. Serve them and allow them to get to know you.

It is tempting to jump right in soon after becoming a Christian. After all, you are so grateful and energized to do good works. Perhaps you have business experience that seems fitting for service on the board of a church or ministry. But this may be the worst thing for you. There is a very real chance that a premature elevation to spiritual leadership will lead to pride and conceit. Why put yourself in a position to fail?

Be patient and let leadership opportunities come to you. Serve in the nursery, park cars, write a check, volunteer in the kitchen, greet people, or help stuff envelopes. The point is to crawl before you walk. Develop a reservoir of humility that can douse any flames of conceit. Leadership in the church and ministry requires much more than passion and availability. It requires a seasoned walk with Christ that leads with grace, truth, and wise judgment.

This is also a warning to those who are responsible for recruiting and placing leaders in roles of responsibility. Do not do a disservice to someone by assigning responsibilities to them when they are not ready. There is always room for growth and learning, but in situations requiring mature faith and character be very prayerful and patient. It is better to have an empty leadership position than to have the wrong person filling a slot.

Pray for God-called leaders to lead. Pray for leaders who understand the grace of God and the judgment of God. Pray for leaders who lead by example. Pray for leaders who lead by serving. Pray for leaders who point people to Jesus and not to themselves. Pray for leaders who will challenge people to look to the Holy Spirit for their direction and confirmation.

Hold the qualification bar high for leadership in the church and ministry. Trust God for quality leaders who are faithful and lead by the Holy Spirit. Keep developing and apprenticing those with potential but let God grow them. A good rule is to know someone at least a year before you entrust them with significant leadership. Mature leaders are patient. Mature leaders are worth the wait. Mature leaders wait for mature leaders. Wait on God to send them your way.

Pray and ask God to raise up mature leaders in His timing.

GODLY TRAINING

Train yourself to be godly. For physical training is of some value,
but godliness has value for all things, holding promise
for both the present life and the life to come.
1 TIMOTHY 4:7-8

Godly training is profitable now and for eternity. Godly training does not make you into some super spiritual person who cannot relate to others. On the contrary, *godly* means you have the character and sensitivity of Jesus. Thus, you understand and relate to people very effectively. It is not all about you, but about others and their needs. You encourage when there needs to be encouragement. You rebuke when you need to rebuke. You teach when there needs to be teaching. The godly man knows how to laugh, cry, pray, hope, work hard, and trust in God.

Every temperament can express godliness. If you are an extrovert, your godly expression may come in the form of humor or encouragement. Your ability to make people laugh (not at the expense of someone else) is godly. Your passion to encourage and build up others is godly.

Godliness is behaving as Jesus would behave. It is not a certain voice inflection or body language, because those can be pretentious and ungodly. It is having a heart and mind that express as Christ would. True godliness points others to God. It provides value for all things: body, mind, soul, and spirit.

Godliness, however, does not happen accidentally. Just as the body benefits from physical training, so the mind, soul, and spirit benefit from training in godliness. The most effective training comes with consistency and repetition. It is not a complicated process, but it is exercising faith. The muscles of faith expand and contract when engaged in everyday life. Training involves prayer instead of worry. Praying works on your heart. It is your spiritual cardio workout. It helps you keep your focus on the Lord.

Training in godliness means the Word of God becomes your spiritual diet. Snubbing God's word is like substituting chips for chicken. This cheap imitation of spiritual nutrition eventually disables your godly maturity.

Lastly, training in godliness requires service to others. You work out your faith in good deeds. You serve others for the glory of God. This has tremendous value now and forevermore. Train well, and you will be transformed. Over time, when you look into the mirror of your soul you will see Jesus.

"Know that the Lord has set apart his faithful servant for himself; the Lord hears when I call to him" (Psalm 4:3).

A PROMISE TO LOVE

Love does not delight in evil but rejoices with the truth.
It always protects, always trusts, always hopes, always perseveres.
1 CORINTHIANS 13:7-8

When my wife, Rita, and I "fell in love," it was like igniting an emotional flame. All of our senses seemed to be captivated by one another. We couldn't get enough time together. We hung on each other's words. Being in each other's presence was energizing and mesmerizing. But we soon learned that for our flame of love to continue to burn brightly, it required the promise to love in marriage as the relational engine to sustain us over life's ups and downs. "Being in love" was just the beginning of learning how to truly grow in oneness over a lifetime of keeping our promise to love, even when our feelings of love retreat. The promise to love embraces the attributes Paul outlines in 1 Corinthians 13: Forgiving love, trusting love, hopeful love, persevering love, and love alive. A loving relationship built on a promise to each other and to the Lord ... lasts.

Marriage and being in love are much more than an emotional high ... it is a promise. Love is a promise to be committed to the Lord and your spouse when feelings of love fly away like a distracted bird. Love is a promise to stay submitted to the Lord and your spouse when suffering brings pain and strain to the relationship. Love is a promise to the Lord and your spouse when financial pressures squeeze the joy out of your carefree circumstances now that the responsibility of children blesses your home. Love is a promise to the Lord and your spouse when emotional hurt from the past exposes itself in unhealthy ways toward the one who knows you the best and loves you the most. Promises rooted in righteous love fight for the relationship for Christ's sake. Love works to change itself, not the other, while passionately pursuing the Lord and your spouse.

Promises without play can grow cold and rigid, so make sure you embrace the playful aspect of keeping your promise to love. Yes, there will always be the logistics of calendar coordinating, financial management, and serious life issues. But in the middle of doing life, keep a playful life in your promise to love. Collaborate and dream as you walk together, dine together, and take trips. Instead of chastising each other, laugh at yourself when things do not go as planned. Learn how to communicate better as you seriously play together so fun intimacy replaces dull intensity. Your promise to love buys time for the feelings of love to catch up. Being in love excites for a time, but a promise to love gives sustaining peace!

Thank God for His promise to love you, His beloved child, and out of the Lord's love for you love your wife, as Christ loved the church and gave Himself up.

NOVEMBER 16

EXCEED EXPECTATIONS

Confident of your obedience, I write to you,
knowing that you will do even more than I ask.
PHILEMON 21

Exceed expectations because God has done the same for you. He has done what He said and more. There is nothing halfway about God. He does things right and then throws in a little bit extra and even overwhelms us with His grace. Therefore, when God or others ask something of you, go for it with gusto.

Exceed expectations in your prayer for others. Make it a goal to bring more value to a relationship than you receive. If someone asks for prayer, then pray right then and there. Make it a habit to pray regularly for those in need, especially those who request prayer.

Exceed expectations in your work. You work to not just get by with the minimum requirements, but to give glory to God. What better way to make Christianity attractive than to work with excellence? When you exceed expectations, you open the door for others to inquire about your motivation, the Lord Jesus. Exceeded expectations may facilitate advancement in your career. People want to work with and for someone who goes the extra mile. They want to reward and hang out with someone who exceeds expectations.

Exceed expectations with your attitude. A positive and "can do" attitude goes a long way toward making relational deposits. There are a lot of things we cannot control, but our attitude is one we can. Go over the top with an attitude of gratitude and generosity. Go more than one mile for another by giving others what they don't deserve. Be exceedingly grateful!

Exceed expectations in your marriage. Serve beyond what is expected. Make it a goal to outserve your spouse. Marriage is an opportunity to give respect. No one in marriage has ever complained of too much love and respect. Look for creative ways to love and respect her beyond her expectations.

Exceed expectations in your home. When you do, you'll make it a place of harmony and contentment. The home is all about others, not you. It is not a game of keeping score of who has done the most for the other lately. Rather, it is dying to your own expectations so that you can exceed the expectations of your wife and children.

Exceed what God expects of you. Why just get by with God? If God asks for one day of Sabbath, give Him daily mini-Sabbaths. He asks for your heart and your life. Give it all to Him.

Exceed expectation for the sake of God's kingdom.

NOVEMBER 17

FLAWED LEADERS

He himself is subject to weakness. This is why he has to offer sacrifices for his own sins, as well as for the sins of the people.
HEBREWS 5:2-3

Jesus Christ was the only flawless leader to ever live. The rest of us operate in the flawed category. Even the best leaders are flawed. The wise leader will acknowledge this and use his flaws to facilitate a closer walk with Christ. The leader who fails to flush out his flaws into the open is pretentious and positioned for a fall. Flaws can only hurt you if they remain concealed. Exposed flaws wither in their influence under the heat of confession and repentance.

The adversary will accuse you of your flaws, so use your flaws as an asset rather than a liability. Flaws revealed lead to freedom, but flaws concealed lead to bondage. This is when you go to your flawless heavenly Father and ask for His forgiveness and grace. Ask Him to use your flaws to further His kingdom. Lay bare before Him your fears, insecurities, weaknesses, and flaws. Watch Him do a beautiful work of transformation. Your weaknesses become His strengths that carry out His purpose.

Your honest feedback to others about your flaws frees others to do the same. Pretension crumbles and honesty flourishes in a culture of self-awareness of—and openness to—one another's flaws. Therefore, be patient with the flaws in others. Normally, what ticks you off the most are your flaws exhibited in the life of another. Cut them some slack and learn how to use their flaws to facilitate God's will.

Allow flaws to promote relational intimacy rather than relational hostility. Flaws are friends who can lead us closer to God and closer to each other. Flaws remind us that we are a work in progress. Flaws make us better, if they lead us to give our brokenness to God.

The world is made up of flawed people. Those who recognize and accept this use it to their advantage. Leaders have a unique opportunity to set an example in this area. Your ability to be honest about your own flaws sets the course for those you lead. Season your language with, "I am sorry that is a weakness of mine." Or, "Please be patient with me; I am a work in progress. Details are not my strength." Or, "Help me not to overcommit. I can say yes to too many things and fail to do any of them well." Or lastly, "I was wrong. Please forgive me." This honesty and transparency will create a safe environment for the authenticity of everyone. Do not project a flawless image, but one of learning, growing, and many times struggling. Make confession and repentance a normal part of your vocabulary and behavior.

Focus on the flawless leader, Jesus. He will never let you down.

GOD'S PAYMENT PLAN

For we know him who said, "It is mine to avenge;
I will repay," and again, "The Lord will judge his people."
It is a dreadful thing to fall into the hands of the living God.
HEBREWS 10:30-31

Someone may be in debt to you. They may owe you money, a reputation, an apology, a job, or a childhood. But God is asking you to let go and let Him handle this. Your role is to forgive and to trust God with the proper judgment and consequence.

God has a payment plan for those who are in debt to His children. It may mean He takes their debts on Himself. It may mean their stiff necks force Him to bring them to the end of themselves through trials and tribulations. Or, it may mean that what awaits them is an eternity of reaping in hell what has been sown on earth. But God's position is one of judge and jury. You do not have to carry this burden or responsibility.

Life gets complicated and draining when we take on the responsibility of making sure a person gets what he deserves. This is arrogant and unwise on our part. How can we know what others deserve? Our role is not to play God, but to serve God.

Playing God is a never-ending disappointment. We were not made for that role. Only the Almighty can fill these shoes. And He does have it under control. There is no indiscretion or blatant injustice that is off His radar screen of sensitivity. He picks up on every "little" sin. So, rest in the assurance of knowing God will pay back in His good timing and in His good way. Do not bear the responsibility of executing payback time.

Your role is to forgive and let go. God's role is to establish justice. Perhaps your parents may have blown it through their own selfish tirades. The results of their wrongs catch up with them. They need your grace and forgiveness. Trust God with your parents. Let Him worry about what they deserve.

You can bring reconciliation to a fractured family relationship by forgiving. Once you have forgiven, trust God to administer whatever punishment He sees as fitting. He may see a broken and contrite heart in your offender that leads to their salvation and freedom in Christ. Your forgiveness and unconditional love may be the very thing God uses to illustrate what they can experience up close and personal.

Forgive and give. Forgive them of their hurt, insensitivity, and selfishness, then give them over to God. Trust Him with His repayment plan. He owns the payback process. His vengeance may be swift, it may be delayed, or it may be dissolved. Regardless, you do the right thing, and trust God to do the same. Vengeance is His, not ours.

Pray for yourself and others to avoid falling into the hands of the living God, for it is a dreadful thing.

HEAVENLY HEROES

Therefore, since we are surrounded by such a great cloud of witnesses, let us throw off everything that hinders and the sin that so easily entangles, and let us run with perseverance the race marked out for us.

HEBREWS 12:1

Dead heroes inspire you to live life to its fullest. Those who have endured hardship and were treated unfairly inspire us through our current tests and temporary trials. Most of us have not suffered to death because of our faith in Christ. But some have. Others have been down the road that denies earthly wealth, only to receive heaven's riches. Heroes of the faith knew this better way. Theirs was the way of faith in God and obedience to His expectations. No temptation of the world was strong enough to pull them away from the moorings of their walk with God.

Heavenly heroes do not languish without hope on the eve of their homegoing. Instead, they are busy bestowing blessings to those who will be left behind. These heroes of the faith have an eye on heaven in worship, while they quietly wind down for the conclusion of their earthly assignment.

Look for heavenly heroes who may have lived across your lineage. You may be surprised to discover the faith of former generations was robust and alive. Let them motivate you to live a life worthy of God's calling. Let their past faithfulness propel you to do the same in the present. We all need heroes who have overcome adversity by faith in God and who knew how to enjoy Him whether in times of difficulty or times of peace.

Your heavenly hero may be a godly grandparent who walked faithfully with the Lord and is now peering down from heaven's portal. It might be someone you watched persevere through adverse conditions. They kept a relationship with God that flourished and grew, up to the very end of their life on earth. Relationships are what mattered the most to them. They always seemed to have time for you. Phone conversations never seemed rushed and their door was always open. In their presence there was a serenity and stability that had heaven as its origin. You experienced a little bit of heaven each time they graced your presence.

Let their going home galvanize your faith. They remained faithful to the end, even though they did not receive their full reward in this life. Their life of perseverance with God is a tremendous motivation for you to do the same. Ask God to graft their passion for His Word into your heart and mind. Remember their words of encouragement and become more secure and confident.

Your greatest hero is Jesus but be encouraged to remain true to the faith by these lesser heroes who reside in heaven.

THE ART OF RAISING SONS

As a father deals with his own children, encouraging, comforting and urging you to live lives worthy of God.
1 THESSALONIANS 2:11-12

Josh is a father of three sons whom I deeply admire. For fourteen years, I've had a front-row seat watching him parent with grace and intention. Two of his boys are now in college, the youngest still in high school. Their bond is strong in love and respect, yet pliable enough to give space for each to grow into his own. They do life together. House projects become natural openings for conversation. Men often talk best shoulder to shoulder—no eye contact required! Whether buying an old boat and restoring it together or coaching their teams, Josh stays engaged by simply showing up. My friend Bill is equally intentional. In his workshop, the scent of sawdust lingers as he and his teenage son build more than furniture—they build trust, one dovetail at a time. The magic isn't in formal talks but in side-by-side moments: tinkering with engines, casting a line, or driving in silence with music humming in the background.

Wise fathers understand that masculine connection often unfolds in shared activity. That boat project? It's really a floating confessional—where life's deeper questions surface between sandpaper strokes. When you coach his team or chaperone that youth trip, you're telling him, "You matter enough to rearrange my world." When you ask about his interests—even if you don't fully understand them—you build bridges to his reality. Beyond "I love you," sons long to hear: "I see you," "I enjoy you," and "I'm interested in the man you're becoming."

The most powerful spiritual legacy a father leaves isn't found in lectures about faith but in the quiet authenticity of a life lived before God. Sons watch how you handle disappointment, how you treat their mother, and how you apologize when wrong. They're measuring your Monday-through-Saturday faith against your Sunday pronouncements. Create sacred rhythms together—perhaps blessing them before sleep, reading scripture around campfires, or serving alongside them in community. These moments become anchors in storms to come. Ask questions that matter: "What are you grateful for today?" "Where did you see God working?" "What's weighing on your heart?" Then listen—not to fix, but to understand. Pray with them and for them, by name and specifically. Let them catch you on your knees sometimes. The goal isn't raising sons who merely follow rules, but men whose hearts beat in rhythm with their Creator's—just as yours is learning to. Your imperfect journey, honestly shared, becomes their map to follow Jesus.

**Love your son with the Lord's wisdom and grace.
Teach him to bless others with encouragement, patience, and faith, guiding his heart toward Jesus in every season.**

NOVEMBER 21

INCREASING MEASURE

For if you possess these qualities in increasing measure,
they will keep you from being ineffective and unproductive
in your knowledge of our Lord Jesus Christ.
2 PETER 1:8

The Christian who is vibrant and alive is a maturing disciple. As a growing believer in Christ, you are in the process of adding to and developing your character. Your faith is not static; rather, it is dynamic and nimble. You are building a life of character that can stand against the winds of adversity and enjoy the blessings of prosperity.

As a conscientious character builder, you are to possess these qualities of Christ in an ever-increasing measure. "For this very reason, make every effort to add to your faith, goodness; and to goodness, knowledge; and to knowledge, self-control; and to self-control, perseverance; and to perseverance, godliness; and to godliness, mutual affection; and to mutual affection, love" (2 Peter 1:5-7). So, your process of character development is a conscious effort. It starts with faith and ends with love. These are the bookends of God's expectations for your character.

Faith is how you approach God and how you appropriate His virtue into your life. Faith allows you to find your heavenly Father and learn from Him. Faith gives you ears to hear and a heart for change. So, start by asking God to increase your faith. An expanded capacity for faith and trust opens the door for life transformation. Faith is focused on God, and with it comes a relentless resolve to understand Him and His Word. The Bible is a treasure trove of truth that leads to understanding the character of God and ignites your faith. Do not underestimate the potential of increasing your measure of faith by knowing and applying God's Word.

Love, on the other hand, deals with motive. Everything you do needs to be inspired by love for God and people. From the trilogy of faith, hope, and love, the greatest is love! Love understands honoring a relationship over being right. Love motivates faith and is motivated by faith. Your love gives you permission into the life of a person—to influence his life. If he knows he is loved, then your influence is trusted.

People want what you have when they are unconditionally loved. So, make sure what you are offering them is authentic. Seek God even more humbly and aggressively now to increase your measure of character. Keep adding His character to yours; this is effective and productive.

Keep your life book between the bookends of God's character. Your life then becomes an attractive read.

HATE IS CONFUSION

But anyone who hates a brother or sister is in the darkness and walks around in the darkness. They do not know where they are going, because the darkness has blinded them.

1 JOHN 2:11

Hate confuses. It confuses the giver, and it confuses the recipient. Hate corrupts our character and corrodes our faith. Left unchecked, it will damage or destroy everything in its path. This is why it is critical to address hate before it becomes all-consuming.

Hate is deceptive in its origin and insidious in its application. It is an argument waiting to happen. It is bred in the womb of unresolved anger. It lashes out unexpectedly and unfairly. Hate has a chip on its shoulder that carries the weight of the world. Nothing seems right to a person controlled by hatred. They disagree, just to disagree. Hate is always inviting others to join the company of its misery. It is a sad and shameful place to live. Deep down, the person driven by anger is desperate, but the desperation has not yet driven them to God.

Thus, the fruit of hate is confusion and blindness. There is no way out for the one who stays in the perpetual place of hate. Hate emits an intense dislike and animosity toward others. And, ironically, this is the behavior from others that comes back to haunt the hater. Those dispensing hate become hated. Eventually, the hostility and the animosity will kill. It kills relationally, emotionally, spiritually, and physically. Hate spins your life out of control. You end up hating life and everyone who comes in contact with you. Sad but true, a hate-motivated person hates himself. So, how can hate be combated and expelled from a person's life?

You fight hate with love. God is love. He is the lover of your soul. He can cut through a hardened heart that harbors hate. His love illuminates. Receive the love of God and you will be loved. You will be loved purely and unconditionally. The warm glow of God's love melts away the fear that hides behind hate. Let God in on your heartache. Let God in on your hurt. Let God in on your hate. He can love you through this. He will meet you right where you are. It is the love of God that will see you through this maelstrom of malevolence.

Let go of hate and grab hold of God. Hate kills, but love lives; hate resents, but love forgives; hate is harsh, but love is kind; hate confuses, but love clarifies; hate is darkness, but love is light. So, begin to walk in the light of Jesus Christ. By faith, receive His love and forgiveness; then do the same for others. Life is too short to miss God's best, so come clean in confession to God and those you've offended. Allow God and others to love you through this time of torment.

Love God and hate sin. Direct your hate toward evil and become a generous giver of love.

STEWARD SUCCESS

Watch out that you do not lose what you have worked for, but that you may be rewarded fully.
2 JOHN 8

God has blessed you for a purpose, and success may be part of His purpose for you. However, if you do not steward wisely and responsibly the blessing of His success, you may very well lose it.

Success means you have the attention of your peers and others in your industry and community. Your success over the years may have even gained the respect of many you have never met. Your family respects you; your church respects you; your friends respect you; your work associates respect you.

But success is not designed to lull you into apathetic work and lazy living. Success is meant to drive you to your knees in gratitude to God. Success is an opportunity to seek God for His wisdom regarding a new set of problems and opportunities. Accountability and wise counsel are also big parts of stewarding success. Perhaps you have fared well until now without a structured board of directors or advisory board, but because of your level of success, one or both of these may be necessary.

Even after you have enjoyed some level of success, you do not have to prove yourself. By God's grace, you have earned the right to serve in the role of influencer. You can prayerfully set trends and experiment with new processes and products. But develop these new initiatives from the platform of prayer. Do not take unnecessary risks. Conserve your successful results and build your organization from a position of strength. Use success as a springboard for innovation and excellence.

Success can cause you to run ahead of relationships and resources. You can avoid this trap of over-subscribing to activity by staying regimented with a process that leads to thorough execution. You have worked hard for the success you are experiencing, so be even more accountable in your life and work. Make sure your character keeps up with your success. You will maintain success if the depth of your character supports the breadth of your success. If you, as the leader, do not model this, you will lose. You will lose your best people, you will lose new opportunities, and you will lose your success. The stewardship of success is daunting without God's wisdom and the godly counsel of others. Slow down and be coachable. Look into the mirror; ask what needs to be changed and then change. Do not lose what you have worked for. His reward is your greatest success.

"His master replied, 'Well done, good and faithful servant! You have been faithful with a few things; I will put you in charge of many things. Come and share your master's happiness!'" (Matthew 25:21).

THANKSGIVING TO GOD

You will be enriched in every way so that you can be generous on every occasion, and through us your generosity will result in thanksgiving to God. … Thanks be to God for his indescribable gift!
2 CORINTHIANS 9:11, 15

Gratitude to God is a natural overflow of generosity. Stop and think about the gift of salvation in Christ. He gave when we did not deserve. He still gives, even though we are undeserving. Gratitude explodes from our hearts when we are reminded of His generous gifts which are incomparable and incomprehensible.

Thanksgiving to God is a tremendous opportunity to unleash joy. This is one of the fruits of gratitude. "Joy, joy, joy, joy down in our hearts," because He came down to earth and into our heart. The Bible says, "Give thanks to the LORD, for he is good; his love endures forever" (1 Chronicles 16:34). This is an occasion for a raucous but righteous celebration.

Gratitude to God can be a moment-by-moment expression. Even in the middle of the worst of circumstances, your thanksgiving to God is appropriate and needed. Look beyond your current condition to your heavenly hope. God has prepared a place for you, and His preparations are not lacking. They are just what you need and desire. God's generosity is without competition. You can be very, very grateful for this. Let thanksgiving escape from your lips often. Use it to put out the fires of fear and worry before they spread too far. Thanks be to God, for you are made rich. Yes, in Christ you are made rich. You have everything needed for this life in Christ.

The natural result of thanksgiving is ridiculous generosity. Because of your deep gratitude to God, you are called and compelled to give. Gratitude invites you to generosity. It is a beautiful process: because God has given to you, you give to others.

This expression of gratitude results in action. Those who act out of gratitude tangibly and regularly give to people for whom Christ died. Opportunities abound that invite your generous expression of gratitude. Gratitude is one of God's prescriptions for discontentment. The two cannot comfortably coexist. Thanksgiving gives the credit for your accomplishments to God and others. Gratitude is generous. Gratitude is content. Thanks be to God for His indescribable gift.

Thank God for what He has done in the past, for His current provision, and for that which He has prepared for you in the future.

GREATER JOY

I have no greater joy than to hear that
my children are walking in the truth.
3 JOHN 4

Great joy comes when our children walk in the truth. Parents are joyful; grandparents are joyful; mentors are joyful. Children are joyful. So guiding children to walk in truth is an excellent goal for parents. In the meantime, walk in the truth yourself. Truth-walking is joyful living.

This begs the question, "What is truth?" Truth is what God defines as truth. When we examine and learn about Jesus Christ, we begin to know and understand truth. Once Christ enters your life, you have an uncanny capability to embrace truth because truth resides within you.

You can point your children to Jesus. Your belief points them to Jesus; your behavior points them to Jesus; your words point them to Jesus; your note of encouragement points them to Jesus; your decisions point them to Jesus. Every day you have the opportunity to point your children to Jesus.

As a parent, make it a priority to teach your children truth. Make sure their education is based on the truth of Scripture, for there is no other truth. Lead them to Jesus so they can fall in love with Jesus. Yes, challenge them to be intellectually honest with the premise that Jesus is truth and that the Holy Spirit will guide them in all truth.

This is a gift that keeps on giving. When you give your children the truth, you give them the way to live an abundant life. Your parental heart swells with pride when you see your children choose truth over a lie. The by-products are numerous. Not only does great joy come from truth-living, there is also freedom, peace, security, and productivity for the kingdom of God.

Walking in truth is not always easy; it requires the ability to stand alone. Even when your closest friends choose to reject or ignore truth, you must embrace it instead. Walking in truth is not a trouble-free life. It may lead to conflict, but you remain steadfast in your commitment to truth-living, and truth-telling. The truth is, when you and your children walk in truth there is no greater joy.

Be careful to make sure your feelings are not accepting a facade of truth. When you believe a lie in the guise of truth you will suffer relational friction and joyless living. Expose those who peddle deception disguised as truth. Look to the truth-giver, Jesus Christ, for the final word. The Bible is crystal clear in all matters related to living out truth. Its application may be hard or fuzzy, but His truth is transparent, timeless, and not trendy. God's truth is clear.

Truth is not illusive. So, live it, seek it,
and pass it on to your children and others.

NOVEMBER 26

UNHEALTHY COMPETITION

I wrote to the church, but Diotrephes,
who loves to be first, will not welcome us.
3 JOHN 9

Normally, it is good to strive for excellence in innovation and execution, but there is a dark side to competition. There is a competition that is unhealthy. If being number one puts ego above relationships, then there's a problem. If your drive to excel beyond competitors causes you to act unethically or immorally, you have crossed the line from competitiveness to compromise. Long-term superior service will not happen without competition that has a greater purpose.

This is why it is important to periodically examine your drive to achieve. Is it for your kingdom or God's kingdom? Is it for the praise of man or is it for the pleasure of God? Is it to crush the competition or is it to be an enterprise of excellence? Is it out of jealousy or is it to do your very best? Are you a more passionate follower of Christ today than you were yesterday? Unchecked competitiveness will isolate you from the realities of developing yourself, your business, your ministry, and your family.

In some ways, there is no competition in the kingdom of God. On the other hand, there is, in reality, a good competitiveness. You can strive for excellence without compromising your walk with Christ and your care for people. Becoming the best is a result of right priorities, not the reason for right priorities. There is a healthy and productive competitiveness. It is one that constantly calls the organization and the individual to improvement in effectiveness, efficiency, and execution. In some ways, you are competing with yourself. You are seeking, by God's grace, to better who you are and what He has called you to do. You are allowing Him to transform you from the inside out. Thus, you are becoming better because of the Lord working in and through you.

Do not compete with God because you will lose every time. This is the essence of an ego-driven life. An ego-driven life challenges God. It seeks to suppress (consciously or unconsciously) the will of God. An out-of-control ego runs way ahead of God and later asks Him to bless the mess. You cannot rival God, so do not ask Him to join your team; rather, humbly enlist on His.

Satan is the most vicious competitor, and he is your true rival. Every day he is vying for your heart and mind. His competitive methods are fiendish and unfair. He contends utmost for your soul. The only way to crush this unholy competition is through Christ. This is your competitive strategy and eternal edge.

You win when you die daily to self and live for Christ.

FAITH FAKERS

These people are blemishes at your love feasts, eating with you without the slightest qualm—shepherds who feed only themselves. They are clouds without rain, blown along by the wind; autumn trees, without fruit and uprooted—twice dead.

JUDE 12

Faith fakers are active within the community of faith—for themselves. They are not true members of the faith. If so, they would be bearing fruit that remains, rather than plastic and unproductive fruit. Their misguided motives wreak havoc, like an unsuspected stealth bomber. They speak the right words and are persuasive, but their behavior is inconsistent and untruthful. Faith fakers are tireless troublemakers. There is no follow-through, and no give and take.

We all struggle at times to be the faithful Christ followers God wants us to be. This is okay and normal. Without struggle there is no growth. However, faith-faking is an entirely different issue. It is using God and others for selfish and non-Kingdom outcomes.

Do not waste your time or money on those with unholy ulterior motives. What they claim is too good to be true. It is only expedient for the moment. It is all about making them look good. Do not be naïve, for faith fakers will seek to infiltrate your church, your family, your ministry, and your business. Nothing is truly sacred for those who prostitute faith for their own purposes. If you are currently engaged with a faith faker, challenge their behavior. Wise and discerning people will expose faith fakers. They have no patience for shenanigans. Deal with the facts only, because faith fakers are illusive and ambiguous with the truth. If your attempts to corral them have failed, take someone with you to help clarify the severity of the situation.

If you are a faith faker, you can change. You do not have to live behind this facade and fantasy of faith. You can experience the real thing. Faith comes by hearing, and hearing from the word of God (Romans 10:17). Study the lives of Ananias and Sapphira (Acts 5:1-11) and see the demise of those who lied to the Holy Spirit. Study the life of Simon (Acts 8:18-24), and see a leader who attempted to use the Holy Spirit for unholy personal gain. Their fates were final. Their influences ceased because their faith faking caught up with them.

If you have become trapped in faith-faking, you can stop playing the game. You can wave the white flag of submission to God. You do not have to be in control. Capitulate to Christ and exercise authentic faith in Him. Make your motive and goal to serve people, not use people. If your disruptions have been public, then seek public forgiveness and retribution. If they have been private, then seek out the offended parties and offer sincere confession and repentance. Rest in God, for the depth of stamina He provides is inexhaustible. Simply follow Christ with an unfeigned faith and love.

"The goal of this command is love, which comes from a pure heart and a good conscience and a sincere faith" (1 Timothy 1:5).

NOVEMBER 28

OPEN OR SHUT

"These are the words of him who is holy and true, who holds the key of David. What he opens no one can shut, and what he shuts no one can open. … See I have placed before you an open door that no one can shut."
REVELATION 3:7-8

The doors God opens cannot be shut, and the doors God shuts cannot be opened. So, you approach a shut door or an open door the same way—by faith. It is by faith that you walk through an open door, and it is by faith that you walk away from a shut door.

Do not let a closed door discourage you. This just means God has something better in store for you and your family. If you get impatient and try to force open the door, then you may spend the rest of your time in this new situation forcing things to happen. Instead, you want to be invited in. If you have to barge your way into a circumstance, then you are asking for trouble. Many times, a closed door can be the best thing for you.

If a relational door is not open, then grow deeper with God during this time of transition. A wrong relationship can lead you away from God rather than toward God. Trust that He has someone just for you, for He has your best interest in mind. And don't be afraid to revisit a closed door. What He closed today, He may open tomorrow.

Maybe a door was open for a season and now it is closing. A career door has closed. It was a great run. You contributed mightily to the enterprise. The organization is much better off than when you first came. You can be proud of your accomplishments. God used you for His glory, so don't overstay your welcome. Use this transition to execute God's will and encourage others by your obedience.

There may be an open door that is inviting you, but an open door does not require you to pass through. It can be a passage into the adventure of following Christ or it may be a test of patience. If a brand new initiative is inviting you in with energy and enthusiasm, this is excellent. Take the open door seriously. Go off and pray about it. Seek godly counsel without positioning the facts in favor of your feelings. After your prayer and due diligence, if the open door still stares at you with peace and affirmation, follow through by faith.

God opens and shuts doors according to His will. His doors swing on the hinges of providence. He is a wise and kind doorman. See the door, then walk through or walk away, but whichever you choose, do so by faith. Always look for the doors of God, for they represent His best. His are doors of destiny.

"And pray for us, too, that God may open a door for our message, so that we may proclaim the mystery of Christ, for which I am in chains" (Colossians 4:3).

NOVEMBER 29

DIVINE DESIGN

They lay their crowns before the throne and say: "You are worthy, our Lord and God, to receive glory and honor and power, for you created all things, and by your will they were created and have their being."

REVELATION 4:10-11

God is the architect of the universe and the engineer of life. His design of creation is not only intelligent; it is good. Because He is the wisdom behind the world, He did it right. The soft, pinkish blue sunset, He did it right; the brilliant, bold, and bright sunrise cascading over the treetops, He did it right; the pure snow-capped mountains projecting toward heaven in reverence, He did it right; the luscious green and gorgeous vegetation, He did it right; the deep blue seas and the baby blue sky, He did it right. He is the good designer of earth and its inhabitants.

He has given us intelligence to understand that He is the intelligent designer. It takes more arrogance than faith to believe otherwise. If we cannot accept that God is behind intelligent design, then we are not being intellectually honest. The evidence is overwhelming. Its affirmation quietly rests within our hearts, its confirmation floods our minds, and its declaration explodes from out of our mouths. He cannot be ignored.

Ironically, some who claim superior intelligence reject God as the Intelligent One. This is the pitfall of pride. Pride blinds us to the simple truth that we are not the smartest. Intellectual snobs conjecture, contrive, complicate, and compromise Christ as God and Creator. It is hard for some to accept that they are not at the center of the universe.

Because of God's vastness that is validated by His intelligent design, He deserves your utmost for His highest. He is worthy of your praise, adoration, and all glory. It is no accident that heaven is full of hallelujahs directed toward God the Father, God the Son, and God the Holy Spirit. In heaven there is no debate over who reigns over heaven and earth.

The object of our affection and all gratitude and praise will be Jesus. Anything good that God has accomplished through you will be laid at the feet of Jesus. Your crown of rewards will not be proudly worn on your head; rather, it will be placed before the lowest spot in front of Christ. Heaven is all about Him. Worship of Him on earth is but an appetizing morsel of what you will have to feast upon when you gaze upon His face in heaven. Therefore, worship Him now in preparation for worshiping Him later.

Praise, honor, and all power and glory go to God. He deserves it and He desires it, and we have the wonderful privilege to express it.

MULTICULTURAL HEAVEN

After this I looked, and there before me was a great multitude that no one could count, from every nation, tribe, people and language, standing before the throne before the Lamb. They were wearing white robes and were holding palm branches in their hands.

REVELATION 7:9

Heaven is multicultural. Representatives from all over the world will populate heaven. The people are almost as diverse as the numbers are uncountable. There will be no racism, no castes, no poverty, no bad boundaries, or social barriers. Heaven is made up of a variety of people worshiping one God.

However, even though heaven is multicultural, it still has its distinctions. Heaven is a distinct place (Christ's domain), populated by a distinct people (followers of Christ), who are worshiping a distinct God (the Father of our Lord Jesus Christ). It is diversity with definite distinctions. Heaven without diversity would be like a man-made club. It would only be a place to gather with others like you. It invites anyone in the world who has faith in Christ. It excludes, worldwide, those who remain in their sin of unbelief. So, with these diversities of culture, there is one focus, and that is the worship of Christ.

We have unity in heaven because of the shed blood of the Lamb, Jesus. But we do not have to wait until heaven for our reunification. As followers of Jesus, we have each bowed our head, heart, and knees at the foot of the cross. The ground is level at the foot of the cross. Believers in Jesus are on the same playing field, with the same trajectory toward heaven. Therefore, we can serve God and each other with no fear of prejudice or pride.

It is out of humility and gratitude that we love God and each other. Our time on earth is but a prelude to heaven. All that matters is Jesus. He compels you to unify around Him with other believers. They will know we are Christians by the love we have for one another. Christianity is multicultural because heaven is multicultural. It is something to enjoy now because we will enjoy it for eternity. This is the spice of life and the spirit of heaven. Multicultural Christianity has been, is now, and is forevermore. Enjoy the full experience of Christ's multicultural family. It is preparation for heaven.

"Clap your hands, all you nations; shout to God with cries of joy" (Psalm 47:1).

DECEMBER 1

GOD'S MESSENGER

David said to Abigail, "Praise be to the LORD,
the God of Israel, who has sent you today to meet me.
May you be blessed for your good judgment."
1 SAMUEL 25: 32-33

God dispatches His messengers daily. You can expect a regular word from the Lord through others. They may represent His envoy of much-needed encouragement, or they may engage you with a regiment of rebuke. Whether He sends His messengers with a positive or a negative word, it is critical that you concur with their instruction. Your emotions may be driving you in one direction, but God's messenger may be imploring you to take a more reasonable road.

It is easy to ignore, reject, or argue with God's messenger, but think twice before you debate with God's representatives. They are ambassadors of heaven, reaching out to you on earth. He has things under control and desires His very best for your life. So when God's messengers tell you to leave your transgressors in His hands, do it. Let the Lord deal with them in His timing. Your pride and ego have nominated you to the task, but you know in your heart it is not the wise thing to do. Listen to God's messenger and avoid a year of regret.

Many times, God's messenger comes in the form of a friend who knows you all too well and has seen some of your destructive patterns over the years. He has your best interests in mind. His desire is for you to learn from your unwise decisions of the past and flourish in the future. He is taking a risk with his friendship because he cares. If he was self-serving, he would shut up. So, listen to God speaking through your friend, especially when it is not what you want to hear.

He also speaks, frequently, through your spouse. She loves you, and she doesn't want you to miss God's very best. Do not allow ego and pride to blind you to her warnings and concerns. She may not understand all of the ins and outs of business, but she does understand the Holy Spirit's promptings. There is a level of discernment which God has wisely given to her as your gift. Make sure you receive it and use it well.

Reward God's messengers. Their behavior deserves recognition and appreciation. You reward the behavior you want repeated, and you rebuke or ignore the behavior that you want to cease. Do more than say you agree. Instead, make a big deal over their determination to deliver the truth. Instead of blowing off messengers of goodwill, invite them into your circle of influence. Promote those who persist in pitching the facts. God's messengers can be trusted because they bear news from your heavenly Father. Therefore, take seriously their words, and act accordingly.

Listen actively to God's messengers, and in turn, become one.

HE CARES

Cast all your anxiety on him because he cares for you.
1 PETER 5:7

God cares about you. He cares about your job; He cares about your fears; He cares about your spouse; He cares about your children; He cares about your parents; He cares about your worries; He cares about your finances; He cares about your car and your house. God also cares about your character, and He cares about you caring about Him and caring for others. He is a caring God.

You cannot out-care God. His capacity to care is infinite and His competence to care is matchless. You can care because He cares. There is no care of yours that God does not care about. If it is important to you, then God cares about it. Yes, you will experience misdirected cares, but God's desire is to come alongside you and realign your cares with what He cares about the most. He cares enough to bear your anxieties and to replace them with His peace and assurance.

When you give God your worries you, in turn, receive His calming presence. God transforms your cares into what He cares about, so cast your cares on Christ. Equally spiritual people may cast their cares on God in polar opposite ways. One may find release in a quiet written prayer, while another may feel cared for by God through raucous worship. Let another's processing of anxiety be a guide, not a guilty comparison.

Do not wait until matters get worse before you offload on the Lord. Go to God first, because He cares the most. Let bad news travel fast, because He already knows. Jesus said it well: "Do not worry about your life" (Matthew 6:25). The more you trust Him with your worries, the less you have to care.

You know God cares immensely. Therefore, allow Him to do what He does best. Allow Him to care for you. This takes humility on your part. You are acknowledging a desperate need for God. Your declaration of dependence is two-fold. You admit that you are anxious and can't handle your worry alone. Secondly, you submit to the fact that only God can handle this level of concern. Hence, your submission to God allows His care to consume your anxieties.

Over time, He helps bring your feeble faith and misguided mind into focus on Him. What started out as a burden, He transforms into a blessing. Your pain becomes productive. You become free to care for others, because He has freely cared for you. You can focus your care on eternal issues. You can lead others to your all-caring Christ. Care for them as Jesus does. Your care will lead to His care. This is the beauty of the circle of care. You do it right, and they will want your God. Keep your caring Christ-centered.

Do not grow weary of caring; God doesn't.
Therefore, give Him your cares and experience His care.

DECEMBER 3

JOYFUL STRENGTH

Nehemiah said, "Go and enjoy choice food and sweet drinks, and send some to those who have nothing prepared. This day is holy to our Lord. Do not grieve, for the joy of the LORD is your strength."

NEHEMIAH 8:10

God's joy is free and available for all who will receive. The joy of the Lord is limitless. It is like a wellspring of living water that flows forever. You cannot pump it dry, even if you wanted to. No thirsty soul who has ever tasted God's joy has been dissatisfied. Natural resources deplete over time, but the joy of the Lord is infinite.

The weak soul is rejuvenated under the influence of heavenly joy. An athletic victory is fleeting, to be enjoyed only so briefly. But the joy of the Lord penetrates the depths of who you are. God's joy wells up to provide resilience during times of testing. This is the result of tapping into His divine resource. The joy of the Lord also travels way beyond happiness. Happiness is based on your circumstances; joy is based on your faith in God.

God never changes. Therefore, the chances of losing your joy are nil if you are focused on Him, the joy-giver. Just as you depend on the local power company to provide your home with electricity, so the wise follower of Christ looks to God for His provision of joy. God's joy is ready and waiting to be deployed into your heart. He is not stingy. Go to the eternal dispenser of joy and receive what the world cannot sustain, and money cannot buy: the joy of the Lord.

The joy of the Lord comes through the Word of God. It does not come from a cursory reading of God's Word, but rather a reading for understanding, application, and transformation. Joy explodes from the pages of Scripture as you understand your utter dependence on God and His tender compassion and mercy. Your mind is washed of the sin-stained lies of the world, and you begin to believe the truth that you have great significance in God's eyes. Your exposure to the repetition and teaching of the Bible garners understanding. Your understanding of God and what He has done—and is doing—for you, will cause joy to explode in your heart.

Furthermore, He works through the people already in your life to bring you joy. When you witness a young believer growing in the faith as a result of discipleship time, it brings joy. "I have no greater joy than to hear that my children are walking in the truth" (3 John 4). When a husband experiences unconditional love from his wife as a result of a divine encounter, it brings joy.

Lastly, joy comes from celebrating God's faithfulness. Regularly recall the goodness of God. Once you were blind, but now you see. Your family, your health, your friends, your career, your opportunities, your joy, and countless other blessings are all gifts from God. These precious memories are cause for celebration.

This is the joy of the Lord. This is the source of your strength. Be joyful in Jesus, so you can be strong in your Savior.

WICKED PROSPERITY

"Why do the wicked live on, growing old and increasing in power? … They spend their years in prosperity and go down to the grave in peace."

JOB 21: 7, 13

You can live a life of prosperity without God. People die with stuff but without a Savior. It seems that God's blessing does not always discriminate between good and evil. A dedicated Christian can live in the most difficult circumstances, while a vile person lives a life of ease and luxury. There are times when criminals prosper while law-abiding citizens suffer. This injustice rubs us the wrong way. We become angry when it appears that the evil are better off than the good. It messes up our neatly organized categories and our foolproof theology. This may be the reason you gave up on God. You could not accept this unfairness.

God's allowance of free will permits the wicked to get ahead. Someone may go through his or her entire life without God, make money, and enjoy the good life. God may not always immediately punish men who manipulate or strike down those who steal, but their demise awaits them. If people choose to live a Christless life now, then they have prepared themselves for a Christless life for eternity.

It may look like wickedness wins, but it doesn't. It's a dead-end street. It is a fast track to nowhere. Even in this life there are consequences to wrong choices. A wicked lifestyle may lead to premature death, rebellion, or bankruptcy. So what if some have made it to the top but crushed people along the way? There may be a few insecure "yes men" who are impressed, but only because they fear losing what they have.

In the life to come, the wicked lose eternity with God and His saints. The Bible says, "Therefore the wicked will not stand in the judgment, nor sinners in the assembly of the righteous" (Psalm 1:5). Do not let the pseudo-success of the wicked disillusion you. Pray for them and become a magnet of grace to which they are drawn. If you are encamped with the wicked, surrender to Jesus. Evil eventually loses the war, so come over to the winning side before it's too late.

God is at work creating a bigger story, a larger life, and a plan much more elaborate than we could ever envision. There is an unseen world beyond this world. This life is but an introduction to a greater documentary called God's story. This life is but a preamble to coming face to face with the One who is the Word. This life is but a blink of an eye, compared to having our eyes wide open in worship for eternity. This life's pleasures are but a taste to the tip of the tongue, compared to reveling in the glory of God and enjoying each other without sin.

Take time to pray for God to transform the hearts of the wicked.

DECEMBER 5

TEMPORARY SETBACKS

They went immediately to the Jews in Jerusalem and compelled them by force to stop. Thus the work on the house of God in Jerusalem came to a standstill.

EZRA 4:23-24

Don't give up. You may be facing a temporary setback, but God's purposes will not be thwarted. It may seem as if life is on hold and everything has come to a standstill. You have worked so hard to get to a certain point, and now it looks like the opportunity has vanished. Hold your goals with an open hand, as God might have something better for you instead.

Times of setback are not times to get mad, but times to be glad. What God initiates, He accomplishes. He hasn't forgotten about you or your circumstances. He is on top of the situation. Times of temporary setback are good times for you to catch your breath and reflect on the great things He has done so far. Pause and prepare for the next stage of personal and professional growth. You do not need to venture into opportunities for which your character is not ready. The last thing you want is to move forward without the depth of wisdom, patience, relationships, and operational skills needed to complete a project.

The unfair criticism of others is a cheap distraction, so ignore their insults. Immature people act immaturely. Do not lower yourself to their level of behavior. Otherwise, you may never get out. You'll spin your wheels and become defensive; you will get stuck. Focus on God, not your distractors. He is the one who has led you this far and He is the one who will lead you through to completion. If everything were easy, we might take God's blessings for granted or we might forgo gratitude to God.

Don't forget that the Lord knows what is best. He knows how to align everyone's hearts involved in the project. He may eventually use the endorsement, resources, and relationships of your biggest critics. The ones who rolled a boulder onto the road may be the very ones who remove the obstacles and provide you fuel for the journey. Isn't it just like God to turn the tables? With God, obstacles become opportunities; adversaries become advocates; critics become cheerleaders; enemies become emissaries; setbacks become a tremendous springboard for God's will. Take heart and keep your head up. It is darkest before the dawn. Hang in there with Jesus, and He will hold you up. God's purposes will not be thwarted, so believe Him, and watch Him work.

"Now finish the work, so that your eager willingness to do it may be matched by your completion of it, according to your means" (2 Corinthians 8:11).

MODEL THE WAY

"I have set you an example that you should do as I have done for you."
JOHN 13:15

We model with our attitude. Attitude is everything. It is the difference between goodness and greatness. It separates the mature from the immature. Attitude is what causes people to give up or persevere. Indeed, leaders have a responsibility to inspire hope with an optimistic attitude. This is the attitude God blesses. He dispenses more opportunity to one whose attitude is aligned with His agenda. The attitude God honors is humble, unselfish, and hopeful in Him.

Proper attitude alignment requires a prayerful attitude. This attitude depends on God and seeks out His wisdom. Prayer creates a positive attitude that always looks for the good in an individual or situation. Prayer also develops an appreciative attitude that rarely complains. Attitudes aligned with prayer are attitudes that are infectious.

We also model with our actions. Behavior validates our beliefs. If we say one thing and do another, we are dishonest with others and ourselves. Actions are a barometer of our character. Appropriate actions earn us the right to influence and lead. Consistent actions facilitate faithfulness in followers. The Bible is our baseline for behavior. Respectful behavior is illustrated with collaborative discussions over strategy and execution.

Wise actions then become the pattern of an effective and efficient culture. Wise actions align around follow-through. We do what we say and say what we do. Wise actions also solicit feedback from everyone. We rely on the wisdom of the team over our own perspective. The Bible defines right actions, so while everyone on the team may not believe in Jesus, they all agree to act like Jesus.

Lastly, we model with our words. Words can build up or tear down. Our words can be pure and encouraging or poisonous and discouraging. Moment by moment, we have the opportunity to inject courage into our colleagues with truthful, kind, and caring words. A good rule of thumb is to measure words prayerfully and patiently before speaking. Do not allow anger and harshness to dominate delivery. Words are a reflection of the heart. A healed heart produces healing words. Therefore, speak with a spirit of compassion. Speak to build up rather than tear down. Speak the truth in love. Choose caring conflict over insensitive passive aggression. Words matter, so model your speech well.

Above all else, model the way by following Jesus' way. As He stated, "I am the way and the truth and the life" (John 14:6).

DECEMBER 7

THINK THE BEST

"Do to others as you would have them do to you."
LUKE 6:31

Think the best of others because this is what you want them to think of you. Give them the same benefit of the doubt you desire. Believe that they have your best interests in mind. There's a temptation to default to cynicism and be suspect of others' motives, but leave your fears with God.

You cannot judge a man's heart. One role of the Holy Spirit is to convict and lead others to a higher level of Christian maturity. Our role is to trust the good will of those God has placed in our lives. It is especially important to think the best of those closest to us. Husbands, think the best of your wives. If they love God, they want His very best for your life. Their questions are not meant to be critical, but to bring clarity, connection, and accountability.

Beware of pride. Pride does not want to think the best of others. Pride would rather not have to listen to the loving counsel of those who care. Remember when you were a teenager? You wanted to figure things out on your own, without anyone telling you what to do. Wise is the man who instead thinks the best of the authorities in his life. Wise is the man who doesn't let pride get in the way of leaning on the support and advice of mentors.

You can think the best of others because God does. When God looks at His children, He sees Christ. He doesn't look at them as sinners stuck on themselves. The Lord looks at His followers as full of potential for Him. His children are still rough around the edges in sin, and the world does roughen them up at times, but beyond the fear and the sorrow He notices hearts that want to move forward with their heavenly Father. He reaches out to His children and offers opportunities for them to give Him their best.

It is easy to get into the eternal family of God; you believe. God does not disown you for your dumb mistakes. He forgives you and thinks the best of you.

So, trust in God and extend trust to others. Trusting the intentions of others does not mean you are irresponsible. You still follow up, verify facts, and ask questions. You still hold them accountable, but your defining attitude is trust. This is harder as you get older, but let your Savior put your suspicions to rest. Choose to think the best of people and circumstances. It is much more than just being positive. It is a deep-seated trust in the core of your being, given to you by God.

Think the best of yourself, your spouse, your friends, and your work associates. After all, this is how you want others to treat you.

OUTSERVE

"Now that I, your Lord and Teacher, have washed your feet, you also should wash one another's feet. I have set you an example that you should do as I have done for you."
JOHN 13:14-15

To outserve yields an outstanding outcome. An outserve attitude is other-focused and Christ-centered. Make it a lifetime goal to outserve all you come in contact with, especially those closest to you.

Outserve your wife. This is not natural to our selfish self, but outserve your spouse, and you will start to see positive differences in both of you. Service makes her feel cared for and makes you feel fulfilled. Service may be unloading the dishwasher, taking out the garbage, mowing the lawn, maintaining the house, or taking care of the cars. Serving your wife may include showing up for dinner at home, being on time, keeping a calendar, or planning a trip. If you are unsure, ask her how she prefers to be served. Serve your wife out of gratitude to God for giving her to you.

Furthermore, carry this attitude of outserving into your occupation. Be one who serves in the workplace, especially if you are a leader or manager. Quietly clean up the breakroom, even wipe out the gooey microwave. Service from a sincere heart values and respects others.

Our Savior modeled service. He did not come to be served, but to serve and to give His very own life as the ultimate act of service (Matthew 20:28). When we enlist in the service of God's kingdom, we become His full-time servants. Service for our Savior is a thread that runs through the life of everyone who is led by the Lord. If Jesus is your model for leadership and living life, you serve. He served the least and the greatest. He served sinners and saints. He served the rich and the poor. He served when He was tired and when He was rested. You cannot outserve Jesus.

Ironically, Jesus served others even at the point of His greatest need. When engulfed in His own personal crisis, He chose to serve others instead of being served. The night before facing imminent death, He served by washing feet. His service was motivated and fueled by His heavenly Father.

Intimacy with the Almighty compels you to serve too. Use this same selfless strategy of service, and watch the world run to Jesus. In the middle of your own crisis, serve. When you are rejected, serve instead of retaliating. When you are forgotten, serve instead of feeling sorry for yourself. When you are hurt, serve instead of allowing your heart to harden. Serve for Jesus' sake and not your own.

You can't outserve Christ, but you can be a conduit of service on His behalf. Seek to outserve others for your Savior.

EMBRACE AND CELEBRATE

Cherish her [wisdom], and she will exalt you; embrace her, and she will honor you. She will give you a garland to grace your head and present you with a glorious crown.

PROVERBS 4:8-9

Embrace and celebrate with the Lord. Discover where the Lord has passion and join Him. Learn what He likes and dislikes. Embracing God's wisdom and celebrating with obedient living gives Him glory and honor. You become a trophy of God's grace when you embrace and celebrate His character. It takes a lifetime of learning from the Lord, so don't be overwhelmed.

Embrace and celebrate His forgiveness, and you will find yourself forgiving; embrace and celebrate His peace, and you will discover that you are peaceful; embrace and celebrate His patience, and you will become patient. Moreover, make this a mantra in marriage and relationships as well.

Embrace and celebrate your spouse's interests. If shopping for special occasions is one of her passions, then embrace and celebrate. Let it sink in that she wants to look nice, especially for you. Be patient while she picks out an outfit and then help her buy some shoes that match. When you finish shopping, go for coffee and talk.

When you discover where someone else's passions lie, join them in celebration. Don't see someone's interests as competition. See their hobbies or activities of enjoyment as opportunities to join them, honor them, and get to know them better. Wisdom embraces and celebrates.

Lastly, embrace your current situation as God's will and do your very best to execute with excellence. You may not understand the next steps for your life, but the Lord does. Latch on to His train of trust and ride with Him to your next destination. But make sure to celebrate along the way.

Celebrate along the way so you can enjoy the fruit from your heavenly Father. God is working, so take the time to celebrate His goodness, mercy, and grace. Lives are being transformed as people are meeting Jesus face-to-face for the first time. The opportunity for the globalization of the gospel is unprecedented, so slow down to celebrate. Embrace your uncertain future and celebrate the current outstanding outcomes. Embrace and celebrate, and your relationships will flourish instead of frustrate.

Embrace God's eternal wisdom and celebrate the honor and grace He gives back.

CONFESSIONAL PRAYER

The people came to Moses and said, "We sinned when we spoke against the Lord and against you. Pray the Lord will take the snakes away from us." So Moses prayed for the people.
NUMBERS 21:7

Confessional prayer is coming clean with God. Our hearts know they are in need of repentance and forgiveness. Oddly enough, our sin may come on the heels of a great act from the Almighty. God may have previously worked mightily in our midst, but we forget to thank Him for His recent past provisions, and we rush to judge whether He or others will see us through our uncertain future.

We grow impatient when God does not give us immediate results, though we have seen Him work things out beautifully before. Unless we catch ourselves, we spiral down into fearful living. We know in our head that He is faithful, but our heart is drawn away by fear. So, confessional prayer comes full circle and comes clean with Christ. We get honest about our own grumbling and complaining. We take responsibility for our own bad attitudes. We can't change the other person with whom we have conflict, but by God's grace, we can change ourselves.

We can become better by remembering Almighty God is in control. We can throw ourselves on the need for His mercy and forgiveness. He listens to our contrite prayer of confession. He hears our cries. His Spirit brings about life transformation. There is no need to stay on the treadmill of temptation and tentative obedience. Step off with the Spirit's help and run by faith.

Our prayers of repentance are not reserved for God alone. Accountability grows when we ask for prayer over our awful attitudes. Yes, it is humbling and sometimes humiliating, but the prayers of godly people are levers for the Lord and a surge of the Spirit's support. Sin loses its grip when you invite people to pray over your process of repentance. We do much better when we ask a friend to pray that our lustful looks at an attractive person become glances of admiration and respect. We succeed at resisting sin when we know others are praying for us. We have a much higher probability for change when we confess our sin to God and to the saints who love us too much not to pray for us and hold us accountable.

Therefore, pulverize any preoccupation with sin by confessing your need for prayer and accountability. Sin slithers back into its dark corner when exposed by the light of confession and prayer. Reveal your secret sin to somebody you trust. Ask them to pray for you; it facilitates freedom and healing.

"Therefore confess your sins to each other and pray for each other so that you may be healed. The prayer of a righteous person is powerful and effective" (James 5:16).

MINISTRY MOTIVE

For the Lord your God has chosen them [priests]
and their descendants out of all your tribes to
stand and minister in the Lord's name always.
DEUTERONOMY 18:5

Unhealthy motives for ministry lead to burnout and regret. Our motive is not our need to be needed or to be recognized for our unselfish service. It is not our past guilt that we are trying to make up for with good deeds. Your service for the Lord becomes laborious when you strive in your own strength. You lose the joy that jolted you into ministry for Jesus in the first place. Our best ministry motive is our Master, Jesus.

Ministry is not meant to be about your service, but about His worship. Make sure you are not subtly shifting the attention toward your accomplishments instead of the Almighty's. Proper ministry motives point to the object of our ministry, the Lord Jesus. You are a conductor for Christ. He orchestrates His work through us. You pay the price of training and equipping, but He pulls off His concert of grace. As Christ's conductor, you point the baton away from yourself.

Minister in the Lord's name on behalf of others and help them discover their God-given talents and gifts. Lead them to bring their skills and abilities together in a beautifully harmonious piece of music on behalf of their Master. Seek to understand what others do best. Connect them with others, and then watch God do the rest. If you fulfill your ministry role properly, you may be forgotten, but He will be remembered.

So, stand and minister in the Lord's name. Do not stand and minister in your name or the name of an institution. Stand and minister in the name of your Savior, Jesus. The Bible says, "Paul greeted them and reported in detail what God had done among the Gentiles through his ministry" (Acts 21:19). God is our motive for ministry. He called us to carry out His will and implement His plan.

It all comes back to Christ. Live as one chosen and called by Christ. Called people cannot help but embrace and recognize their Caller. Christ called, you answered and obeyed. You do what you do because of Him. He called you to this career. He called you to your city to minister on His behalf.

Focus first on the One who called you, and second on your calling. Your calling is a means to an end: glorifying God. It is not the destination. He has chosen you for Himself. Almighty God owns you. You minister in the Lord's name, so make your ministry motive your Master, Jesus. Allow yourself to decrease as He increases. The early church leaders modeled that for us.

Stop and assess your ministry motives.
Are they promoting your Master, Jesus?

DECEMBER 12

SERVE THE SERVANT

Be careful not to neglect the Levites as long as you live in your land.
DEUTERONOMY 12:19

Vocational servants of the Lord need to be served because they constantly serve. Those who serve the Lord on our behalf are special servants. They are special because God called them out to a life totally abandoned to Him and to people. Everyone who follows Jesus is called to do the will of God, but His ministers, missionaries, and ministry leaders have a mandate from their Master. They are called to a specific area of service for Him. It may be teaching, preaching, leading, singing, worshiping, administrating, or equipping. This is their vocation and how they make a living.

Servants of the Lord can be overworked and unappreciated. It's hard to serve a congregation when you feel as if everyone is your boss. Serving the Lord as an employee of the church has the potential to create a seven-day workweek. A pastor or staff member may have a family activity planned, but if a funeral or relational crisis arises within the fellowship, they are called on to intervene.

Service is second nature to servants of the Lord, but we don't need to neglect their needs. If we do, their faith will become fragile, their emotions frazzled, their bodies fatigued. They will feel financial pressures and may tire of "being good." Servants of the Lord need to be served before they burn out or bail out. Their smile may mask their hurt, so come alongside them and pray for them.

Vocational ministry leaders are not immune to sin. In some ways their temptations are more intense. They represent God, and Satan cannot stand for the Lord's servants to remain faithful. He takes advantage of their vulnerabilities and tries to lead them into immoral acts. So, surround your vocational Christian workers with prayer and support. Serve your servants of the Lord with prayer. Pray for them daily to be filled and led by the Spirit. Pray for them to be secure in their Savior, Jesus, and to find their confidence in Christ. Pray for them to worship God with a fresh faith and a pure heart. Pray for them to share their burdens and be accountable. Pray for them to pray.

Prayer is an act of worship and love. Prayed-for people pull through by faith and they feel loved. Pray about how to best serve the precious servants of God in your life. Sincerely serve them, as this gives them staying power and praying power. This honors both the Lord's servant and Almighty God.

The elders who direct the affairs of the church well are worthy of double honor, especially those whose work is preaching and teaching. For Scripture says, ... "The worker deserves his wages" (1 Timothy 5:17-18).

TREASURED POSSESSION

For you are a people holy to the Lord your God.
The Lord your God has chosen you out of all the peoples on
the face of the earth to be his people, his treasured possession.
DEUTERONOMY 7:6

God followers are His chosen and treasured possessions. If God possesses you, He treasures you. Of all the people on the face of the earth, you were set apart by Almighty God when you believed in Jesus. He looks at you differently since you were saved by His grace. Your value proposition increased dramatically once you trusted Christ as the propitiation for your sin. Your salvation was not a casual exchange of old beliefs for new ones. It was your crucifixion and your resurrection. Your old way of living died, and the Holy Spirit brought you to life in Christ. It was a transformation of your character to His. You are eternally possessed and valued by God.

Do not underestimate God's valuation of your life. The world may scoff at your faith and even call it foolish to worship the unseen God. Unbelievers have no baseline for belief, so they devalue and ignore followers of Jesus as irrelevant and antiquated. Enemies of your Savior may seek to play down your commitment to discipleship as fanatical and call it a "phase you are going through." But don't rate your religion based on how others value your faith. Your self-worth flows from faith in your heavenly Father. Look to Jesus for affirmation and validation. He is your source of strength and security.

Let Almighty God appraise your life and work. His appraisal of you is off the chart in eternal valuations. Your increased value to the Lord is not based on a 3 percent annual inflation rate. Your increased value to the Lord is based on how much He has of you. So, surrender everything to Him. Surrender your worries; surrender your relationships; surrender your work; surrender your aspirations; surrender your fears. The more you give over to Him, the more valuable you become. You are His precious child and treasured possession. More than gold and silver is to this world, you are to God. He loves you. God is your owner.

Therefore, it is imperative you refer often to His owner's manual, the Bible, on what to learn and how to live. Following Jesus is a lifetime of obedience and growth. You never arrive but only graduate to new opportunities for faith. So, give it all up for God. You are His and His alone. Value yourself as He does: more precious than all the wealth of this world. You can hold your head up because you are His. You are a child of the King. In Christ, you experience true riches. See yourself as God does: a reflection of His Son, Jesus. You are His valued possession, holy and His.

"For he chose us in him before the creation of the world to be holy and blameless in his sight. In love he predestined us for adoption to sonship through Jesus Christ, in accordance with his pleasure and will" (Ephesians 1:4-5).

ARROGANT DEFIANCE

So I told you, but you would not listen.
You rebelled against the LORD's command and in
your arrogance you marched up into the hill country.
DEUTERONOMY 1:43

Arrogant defiance destroys our fellowship with God. It destroys our relationships with people. It destroys our security. It destroys our peace. Arrogant defiance doesn't listen to reason, because it already has everything figured out. It is a caricature of confidence and acts as if it has it all together but in reality, struggles in fear. Arrogant defiance laughs at warnings and ignores wise counsel. Relational and financial wreckage is in its wake. Arrogant defiance may seem sincere, but sincerity betrays its hurling forward into foolish activities. It may finally wake up to reality only to find itself defeated and crushed under the weight of unwise decisions.

This is the dark side of driven leaders. They can become intoxicated with power, and think they are invincible because of past success. In fact, pride can feed the lie that your past success guarantees your future success. Pride can blind the need for teachability. Pride breeds an arrogant attitude devoid of accountability. It is a deadly combination that leads to a devastating character flaw.

We all need the benefit of prayer and wise counsel. There is no need to plow ahead without prayer. A door may be open, but it does not mean you need to walk through. A door may be closed. Be patient. Do not force it open with manipulation or manpower. Take the time to pray and exercise due diligence. Let God lead you.

The Lord does not underestimate the enemy. He knows what it takes to defeat Satan, sin, and self. He knows whether you are ready or not to move forward in faith. He will provide the needed resources, relationships, and wisdom. He has a mentor in the wings for you to learn from; do not go at it alone. Humility positions you to receive God's grace.

Therefore, lean heavily on the Lord before you lead others. Your leadership and influence affects more people than you realize. Almighty God has entrusted their safety and security to you. Be courageous but temper your attitude with wisdom. Be a visionary but lead in patient humility. A humble spirit defeats arrogant defiance. Surrender to your Savior, and the enemy will see you're serious. Arrogant defiance will be conquered with the help of your heavenly Father. Stay if He says stay. Go if He says go.

An individual conquered by Christ is able to conquer the enemy's strongholds. Submission to your Savior defies arrogance.

NEWLY MARRIED

If a man has recently married, he must not be sent to war or have any other duty laid on him. For one year he is to be free to stay at home and bring happiness to the wife he has married.
DEUTERONOMY 24:5

Newly married couples need to focus intently on each other. Your first year of marriage sets the stage for the following years. If you get off to a rocky start, you will carry those wounds into subsequent years. Marriage is meant to be a marathon, not a sprint. So do not shortchange yourselves starting out. Be intentional in your intimacy and in your seeking to understand each other.

At the outset of marriage there are fewer distractions that divert you from getting to know each other. Now is the time to learn how to love and serve one another because marriage, in the beginning, begs for more time and attention. It is your opportunity to have an all-out interest in each other. Marriage isn't meant to get leftovers of energy, communication, and intimacy.

An unattended marriage is like a garden without a gardener. As time passes, neglect produces a crop of weeds that choke out the fruits and vegetables. A mismanaged garden lacks a meaningful harvest. So it is in marriage, without planting seeds of love, cultivating patience, and weeding out selfishness. Your first year of marriage is an opportunity to store up a barn full of good memories. Serve unselfishly and see God work, for your wedding was only the beginning of His good work.

Moreover, make the first year of marriage a time to focus on God. Use this time to study the Bible and its teachings about how to be a husband. As the husband, take the lead as spiritual leader of your home. Grow in your confidence to be Christ's servant to your wife. She needs you to lead on behalf of the Lord. Pray daily with her and for her. Go to church with her, take sermon notes, and engage with her in worship with praise and adoration of Almighty God.

Love each other unconditionally, forgive liberally, and serve unselfishly. Embrace and celebrate differences, think the best of the other's intentions and try to outserve each other. Apply these disciplines, and you are off to a good start in your marriage.

Mandate quality time for your marriage with daily conversation and weekly dates. Live in anticipation and excitement about what Almighty God has in store for you. Minister to each other in your marriage, and your marriage will become a ministry to others. So, grow old together joyfully, always learning how to love better.

Marriage is meant to be a picture of our relationship with Jesus. Ask God to move your marriage forward for Him.

ADJUST PLANS

David inquired of the Lord, and he answered,
"Do not go straight up, but circle around behind
them and attack them in front of the poplar trees."
2 SAMUEL 5:23

Many times, plans are made to be adjusted. The Lord is in the business of leading and guiding us through the planning process of discovery. It is imperative that we remain nimble, flexible, and open to His leadership. What worked yesterday may not work tomorrow. God's wisdom is the GPS we need to navigate His plans and locate His destination.

Do not be afraid to scrap the old plan and script a new one. God delights in leading you through the informal back door, and not necessarily the formal front door. What your friend experienced may be just the opposite of your experience. This is why it is wise to follow Christ's critical path.

The path of Jesus may seem perilous, but you can be guaranteed His presence is in the middle of your planning adjustments. If you remain bound by your plan, you may miss the freedom of His. Yes, it is somewhat embarrassing to change course for the umpteenth time. However, better to make a midcourse correction and suffer a little shame, than to wait too long and be humiliated by stubbornness.

The plan of God requires ongoing prayer that asks Him to purify your motives and clarify His plan. Ask Christ to confirm your coordinates with His direction. Whatever path you are blazing, He has been there before. It is typically harder to discern God's best when you are encountering someone or something for the very first time. There are many unknowns and so many opportunities to pursue. So over-apply due diligence by not rushing into first-time experiences with blind optimism. If you do, you might regret it. Trying to rush God's will is frustrating and will cause you to fret. God's will, reflected upon and clarified, is encouraging and will cause you to rest. Just make sure the Holy Spirit is guiding your steps.

If you make His minor adjustments daily, your course does not seem as radical. If you refuse to discern His plan daily, then one day you will wake up in need of a revolutionary reaction. So, let God lead you down what may be the unconventional road of His will. Humility is allowing the Lord to lead in a different direction. Wisdom is getting it done while leading others to do the same. Expect the plan to need adjustment and trust God with the outcome. Adjustable plans are the best laid plans. Hold your plan with an open hand, which rests in the hand of the Lord.

"Many are the plans in a person's heart, but it is the Lord's purpose that prevails" (Proverbs 19:21).

DECEMBER 17

BRIDGE BUILDER

Like water spilled on the ground, which cannot be recovered, so we must die. But that is not what God desires; rather, he devises ways so that a banished person does not remain banished from him.
2 SAMUEL 14:14

Sometimes, people do dumb and even shameful things. Their unwise choices may have inflicted great harm and even compounded into calamity and crisis. Sin caused them to suspend their good sense and biblical worldview for a season. They are confused, alone, and humiliated. They may not be at a point where they're ready to admit their mistakes, but deep down in their soul they wonder how much they have disappointed God and those who love them the most. They feel confused, for sin complicates matters. They are caught in a web of deceit that will not let them go. They have lost perspective and seem to be swirling down into a spiritual and a relational vortex. Not only are they estranged from their loved ones, but they are also estranged from their heavenly Father. Separation from God is a lonely place. It is the love of God and your love that will bring them back to their senses.

Relational bridge-building is not easy, and it takes time. But it can become necessary to woo the wandering one back home. Yes, they have made their bed, and now they are sleeping between its twin sheets of fear and insecurity. However, the bridge you are building leads to a bed of acceptance and peace.

No one wins in a vicious and venomous volley of blame. Instead, a bridge-builder prays—he prays to first be changed. He will accept blame and replace perceived rejection with action-oriented acceptance. A bridge-builder calls, writes, and sends gifts of encouragement and even takes the initiative to over-communicate. A bridge-builder seeks to understand and then love the estranged one at their point of need.

Maybe your child is living with a roommate who's pushing your son or daughter in the wrong direction. Reach out and get to know this person who is negatively influencing your child. By God's grace, become the influencer of the influencer. Invite them into your home and love them to God. Let your home become a magnet of grace that draws them into a reminder of what's good and right. The bridge you build may not be crossed immediately. But just its presence speaks volumes to your availability, care, and compassion.

One day, circumstances will unravel for your estranged loved one. When it does, you want your bridge of love and acceptance staring them right in the face. Stay faithful as a relational bridge-builder, just as the cross of Christ is God's bridge to you. The cross you bear is your bridge to broken people. So, continue to pray and pursue this Christ-honoring outcome.

"All this is from God, who reconciled us to himself through Christ and gave us the ministry of reconciliation" (2 Corinthians 5:18).

EXTEND KINDNESS

"Don't be afraid," David said to him, "for I will surely show you kindness for the sake of your father Jonathan. I will restore to you all the land that belonged to your grandfather Saul, and you will always eat at my table."
2 SAMUEL 9:7

Kindness is a killer application for the Christian. It is killer in the good sense of the word. Kindness kills fear and replaces it with hope. It kills insecurity and replaces it with security; it kills rejection and replaces it with acceptance; it kills pride and replaces it with humility. Kindness kills the bad, so the good can have room to grow.

Like the effect of weed killer on unwanted weeds, kindness gets to the root of sin and infects it with grace and love. As a follower of Jesus, what compels you the most is the gargantuan kindness He has bestowed upon you. Though you were undeserving, God's kindness captured you. He captured your mind and, in the process, flooded it with kind thoughts toward others, even your adversaries. He captured your mouth and filled it with kind words of affirmation and encouragement, extending them to those thirsting for verbal kindness. He captured your behavior, converted it to other-centeredness, so now you are guilty of random acts of kindness.

Gratitude to God for His kindness is a sterling reason to extend kindness to others. However, gratitude also results from our horizontal relationships. You feel compelled to be kind to a family member of a friend because of the kindness they extended to your child or spouse. You want to support those who support you and those you love. It may be a graduation gift, your presence at a wedding, or a hand-written thank-you note. It is the gift that keeps on giving. It seems you cannot pay forward enough with kindness. No one has ever complained of receiving too much kindness. You cannot overdose anyone on kindness. On the contrary, it is healing and wholesome.

Kindness is a picture of Christ. It is God-like. Therefore, defuse the explosives of harsh words and replace them with kind ones. Otherwise, you can say the right words in an unkind way and defeat your purpose of being open and honest. People cannot hear what you say if the manner in which you communicate is unkind. A kind delivery of hard words has a much higher probability of acceptance. Kindness comes from a grateful and prayerful heart that is focused on Christ. You cannot help but be kind when you are captured by divine kindness. Extend the quality of kindness that has been extended to you.

"Make sure that nobody pays back wrong for wrong, but always strive to do what is good for each other and for everyone else" (1 Thessalonians 5:15).

EGO'S SNARE

Absalom's hair got caught in the tree. He was left hanging in midair, while the mule he was riding kept on going. … During his lifetime Absalom had taken a pillar and erected it in the King's Valley as a monument to himself.
2 SAMUEL 18:9, 18

Ego has the propensity to "hang you out to dry." It snares your soul, as an enlarged ego tends to shrivel your heart. Ego entangles a man's motives around self-interest and self-credit. An ego has an insatiable desire for recognition and power. It is sad to watch. An unchecked ego is your enemy that will lead you down pitiful paths of regret. An out-of-control ego exaggerates self-importance and creates conceit.

Conceit and Christ-centered living are mutually exclusive. Either Jesus is calling the shots or Jesus is just a front for an ego-infested life. Unless your Christian vocabulary and behavior is void of ego, you are just using God to get your way for your benefit and your glory. E-G-O stands for Edging God Out. It is all about self. Everyone recognizes ego's effect, except the one mastered by its deception.

Defuse ego's illusion with truth before it implodes your life. The Holy Spirit takes a submitted ego and transforms it for effective eternal results, so ask God to daily bend your ego toward Him. Eventually, His influence will develop habits in your life that channel the energies of your ego into kingdom pursuits. Do not allow your ego to estrange you from eternity. Joy in living becomes service to others and intimacy with your heavenly Father. Money, power, recognition, and control all fade in importance. What becomes valuable is pointing people to Jesus. Your motivations become mercy, humility, and justice.

Humility, accompanied by confession of your need for God and people, will pin ego to the ground so that you can then walk unencumbered with Christ. Ego says yes to self, humility says no; ego says yes to power, humility says no; ego says yes to fame, humility says no; ego says yes to always being right, humility says no; ego says look at me, humility defers to Jesus; ego erects monuments to man, humility builds the kingdom of God. The Bible says this about Moses; "He regarded disgrace for the sake of Christ as of greater value than the treasures of Egypt, because he was looking ahead to his reward" (Hebrews 11:26).

Today, die to your ego and live for Christ. Seek out others to forgive and others from whom you can ask forgiveness. You can make the first move in forgiveness because you have nothing to lose and everything to gain. So, harness your ego to the hull of heaven's ship, as an eternal perspective edges out ego.

What's the state of your ego?

DECEMBER 20

EXHORT TO ENCOURAGE

"You love those who hate you and hate those who love you. You have made it clear today that the commanders and their men mean nothing to you. I see that you would be pleased if Absalom were alive today and all of us were dead. Now go out and encourage your men."

2 SAMUEL 19:6-7

It is easy to obsess over your agenda and forget to encourage those closest to you. Your attention and energy gets so wrapped up in your needs that the needs of others vanish from your interest. You can love more what you don't have and neglect what you do have. Those who know you best do not feel the love. In some cases, they may interpret your absence of attention as hate, so refocus and reengage with reality.

A good place to start is by encouraging those who have remained loyal and committed during your time of disengagement. They have been true and faithful to you and to the Lord. Let them know, in no uncertain terms, how grateful you are for them. You can tell them with a barrage of verbal encouragement or show them with acts of service. Take the time to make them coffee or take out the trash. Whatever you do, do not be hesitant to shower with them appreciation and affirmation. No one can be encouraged too much, so be ever mindful of not giving enough encouragement.

Spend your relational capital by encouraging your friends with an opportunity, gift, or words of wisdom. What you have is for the benefit of others. If you do not take the time to encourage them, they will go to someone who will.

Your teenage child needs your encouragement. They may act cool and self-sufficient, but they want you to pursue them with radical encouragement. Schedule a biweekly dinner just to listen to the heart of your child. Listening and understanding allows you to apply encouragement at their greatest point of need.

Encourage by asking questions. Proper questioning communicates care. People need to be encouraged to ask the right questions and then discover God's answers. This may be the most effective way to encourage someone. Always point them back to God and His game plan. God's vast reservoir of encouragement is virtually untapped. Human encouragement is finite; God's encouragement is infinite. Therefore, encourage others to engage with eternity. Your heavenly Father's encouragement is everlasting. Your encouragement is good, but His is great. So, be relentless in encouraging others to go from good to great. Be encouraged to encourage.

"But encourage one another daily, as long as it is called 'Today,' so that none of you may be hardened by sin's deceitfulness" (Hebrews 3:13).

POSITIONED FOR BLESSING

That person is like a tree planted by streams of water, which yields its fruit in season and whose leaf does not wither—whatever they do prospers.
PSALM 1:3

Blessing comes for those who are in a position of dependency on Almighty God. We are blessed when the roots of our faith draw from the waters of God's Word. This is wise positioning for a Jesus-follower. When we take the time to plant our faith by the banks of God's living water, we come alive. This is where the fruits of humility, honesty, and humor grow. It's the water of God that hydrates our souls, not man's generic substitutes.

We may attempt to plant our lives next to a stream of self-sufficiency, only to find ourselves thirsting. It is the water of God's Word that we are to drink day and night because it creates abundant life. The effects of God's Word are not always immediately evident. It takes time for it to make its way into the root system of our beliefs. Eventually an eternal perspective begins to take shape as we become saturated in the Word of God.

Plant your life close to an understanding and an application of Scripture. The Bible is your baseline for belief and behavior. When God sees someone who is immersed in the principles of His Word, He has found someone He can trust with His blessings. He extends His best to those who are planted next to the truth of His Word. He bears fruit through those who depend on Him.

The fruit of a faithful life flourishes over time. Your influence compounds as you follow Christ. It may seem like you are in an insignificant season. This is not true. All seasons with your Savior are significant. You may live in a confusing season, but your confusion is Christ's opportunity to bring clarity. Faithfulness brings clarity during uncertain times. Do not wish away this season; it is a time for you to go deep with Him.

You may be thriving in a season of prosperity, feeling tempted to walk away from God and continue on your own. But in doing so, you leave the spirit of humility and dependency on God. He brought you this far. So, stay faithful as your finances flourish, and be more aggressive in your generous giving. Live for the Lord, not for yourself.

Faith in Him is not always flashy. The wicked try to define a better way. They want to lead you astray. But Jesus is the way. Faith in Him bears the fruit that matters. It is the fruit of children who honor their parents; it is the fruit of fidelity between husbands and wives; it is the fruit of an unselfish friendship; it is the fruit of a caring culture at work, home, and church; it is the fruit of wise and generous giving; it is the fruit of fearing God and having a friend in Jesus. Therefore, by faith, stay in a position to be blessed.

"Blessed is the one who trusts in the Lord" (Psalm 40:4).

INTIMACY TRUSTS

Those who know your name trust in you, for you,
Lord, have never forsaken those who seek you.
PSALM 9:10

God's name is above every name. It is at the name of Jesus that every knee will bow and confess Him as Lord. It is much better and much more desirable to know His name this side of eternity. No name is close to carrying the weight, reverence, respect, devotion, and influence than that of the Lord Jesus Christ. By knowing His name, we begin to understand the attributes of the Almighty. Patience, peace, holiness, love, discipline, mercy, and grace all emanate from the name of Jehovah, our one and only God of creation. Because we know Him, we trust Him. Intimacy trusts.

Our heavenly Father wants us to have an informed faith. If we don't, we miss intimacy because our faith is based on a caricature of Christ. There can be knowledge without faith, but there can be no faith without knowledge. Knowledge carries the torch before faith and illuminates its path. Paul defined his faith experience when he proclaimed, "I know whom I have believed" (2 Timothy 1:12). A blind faith is as bad as a dead faith. Know Him, and you will trust Him. He is there for us to seek Him.

When we wrap our rope of faith around the mooring of our Master, we are secure. No storm of life will cause us to drift, because we are anchored in Him. We trust Him because He is utterly and thoroughly trustworthy.

Jesus' name is not only a good name; it is a great name. His name is wonderful. His name is beautiful. His name is to be honored and cherished because He is our God. Feel free to drop His name often to those who need encouragement or rebuke. No need to hold back the name of Jesus. He is Jehovah, Jireh, Elohim, El Shaddai, and Adonai. His is the name of the One we trust. We point people beyond ourselves to One who is much, much more capable. We name the name of Christ. As your trust in His name grows, so will your intimacy with Him.

Lastly, intimacy with individuals requires trust. This is the nature of intimacy with God or man. You cannot get to know someone authentically and not be positioned to trust them. If they overwhelm you with hypocrisy, you will lose respect and trust. But when you get close to genuine followers of Jesus, you see beyond their quirks. You appreciate their uniqueness and embrace their differences. You honor them for being who they are and you better understand each other's worlds.

"May the God of hope fill you with all joy and peace as you trust in him, so that you may overflow with hope by the power of the Holy Spirit" (Romans 15:13).

BENEFITS OF HUMILITY

You save the humble but bring low those whose eyes are haughty.
PSALM 18:27

Humility is the doorway to God's salvation. It is an entrance into an exciting life with the Lord. God saves the humble, but brings low the haughty.

The haughty find it hard to take responsibility for their ill will and anger. They blame others while becoming victims of their own pride. Haughty eyes have blurred vision of God and shy away from serving people. It is all about "what's in it for me?" It stiff-arms our Savior. The eyes of the haughty are cold, callous, and distant. The haughty are consumed with themselves and have but a faint remembrance of Christ. They don't remember what they wish to forget. Haughtiness forgets humility.

Humility, on the other hand, woos the blessings of God. It has bountiful benefits. God's presence permeates an environment of humility. The Lord looks out for the family members or work associates who value humility. He saves them from unwise decision-making and irresponsible living. He saves them from themselves.

Humility encourages honesty. It encourages honesty about our dreams and disappointments. Humility learns how to process disappointments. God saves the humble from bitterness and replaces it with brokenness. Humility is a prerequisite for relational success. A humble heart helps husbands and wives learn how to complement each other's strengths and weaknesses. It cultivates appreciation of each other's differences. It checks our conversations before we position ourselves for a win/lose dialogue. Humility first understands and then seeks to be understood. It deflates pride and inflates patience. Humility is quick to honor and slow to blame. It keeps us in the good graces of God and people.

Run from false humility formed out of fear, deception, and pride. Instead, cultivate authentic humility through prayer, honesty, and community. Surrender daily to your Savior with a sense of overwhelming dependence on Him. We are to submit on our knees, so that He doesn't have to bring us to our knees.

Humility is best harnessed in the context of a Christ-centered community. Invite people you respect into your life because "a companion of fools suffers harm" (Proverbs 13:20). Haughtiness is hurtful. Humility is beneficial, so sign up for its benefits.

"'You save the humble, but your eyes are on the haughty to bring them low'" (2 Samuel 22:28).

FIRST CHRISTMAS

*"Today in the town of David a Savior has been born to you;
he is Messiah, the Lord. This will be a sign to you:
You will find a baby wrapped in cloths and lying in a manager."*
LUKE 2:11-12

The focus of the first Christmas was Jesus. It was His day. There was no competition from commercialism seeking economic gain. The gifts were given to Him. God was the recipient of gratitude and generosity. There was an appreciation for the Almighty's descent into the decadence of humanity. There was a religious respect and humble worship from those who traveled great distances from diverse religions and cultures. On that day, Jesus unified sincere seekers of truth.

The first Christmas, however, was not without controversy. Politically, Jesus was a lightning rod (some things never change). Government leaders felt threatened. Involuntary spies were sent to verify His presence. Once His birth had been verified, the powers-that-be went to work. Insecurity and fear drove people to commit irrational acts. What started as a celestial coronation for the Prince of Peace ended with jealous leaders taking severe and deadly action. The Christ-child was driven from their pitiful, but powerful presence. They destroyed other God-fearing people in the process.

We can learn from the first Christmas, to keep Christ central in worship and society. He is the wonder of our worship. He is the reason for our giving gifts. It is because we celebrate His birthday that we pause to pray, reflect, and follow His will in a more robust and intentional manner. Our Master came to earth, born of a virgin, and made Himself a man. He took on the form of a servant, though He could have crowned Himself as King. He was God who dwelt among us, as one of us. He pointed us to the love and forgiveness of His heavenly Father. But, sometimes we forget Him, even on His birthday.

Let's start by inviting the Almighty back into our churches with fresh and revitalized reverence in worship, evangelism, and discipleship. Let all of us who name the name of Jesus revisit Him in the awe and worship of that first Christmas. Let's exclaim with enthusiasm to a hurting world that He has come to heal broken hearts and revive sick souls.

We unapologetically celebrate His birthday with passion, because God is with us. He is transforming us into the likeness of His Son. Let's make this Christmas like the first Christmas. The first Christmas fuels our faith and recalibrates us to Christ.

Let's invite the Holy Spirit to fill our hearts with forgiveness, joy, hope, peace, and love while we worship our Lord together.

MERRY CHRISTMAS

"Today in the town of David a Savior has been born to you; he is the Messiah, the Lord." … Suddenly a great company of the heavenly host appeared with the angel, praising God and saying, "Glory to God in the highest heaven, and on earth peace to those on whom his favor rests."

LUKE 2:11, 13-14

The birth of Jesus is meant to be a grand celebration. The angels in heaven, accompanied by a celestial choir, kicked off Christ's party. It was something to behold. It was not a passive holiday greeting. It was instead a bold and jubilant, *Merry Christmas!*

It was merry because there was a festive spirit in the air. Eternal God had come to meager man. Our Creator came face-to-face to correspond with us and care for us. The celebratory scene in heaven cascaded toward earth and crashed upon unsuspecting shepherds. God started His gleeful disclosure with those whose labor illustrated His heart. Shepherds knew shepherding. And now that the Great Shepherd Jesus had come, the flock of His fellow man could dance a merry jig.

Mary, the mother of Jesus, was overtaken by gratitude to God for being chosen by Him. In the beginning of God's revelation to her, she experienced surprise. She felt she did not deserve this type of recognition or honor. But it was not about her. It was about her baby, Jesus. He would save the world from their sin, and she would serve as his mother. Once she took all this in, she suddenly exploded in praise and adoration to God. Mary's prayer still shouts, *Merry Christmas!* 2,000 years later!

How many more opportunities today do you and I have to exclaim gratitude to God? He has chosen us. By faith, Christ indwells us. This intimacy with the Almighty drives us to our knees in appreciation and awe. Because of this heartfelt joy, our life and lips cannot help but announce to a wandering world, *Merry Christmas! Merry Christmas!* and *Merry Christmas!* Yes, you too, can experience a *Merry Christmas!*

So, be valiant with your gracious greeting, *Merry Christmas!* Indeed, trying to prevent a Christian (especially on the birthday of Jesus) from being merry, is like telling a child who just received a favorite toy to cease from joy and laughter. It is not possible. It is ludicrous to think one or many can stop Jesus-followers from celebrating His birthday with a *Merry Christmas!* We are merry Christians because it is a *Merry Christmas!*

You cannot take "merry" out of Merry Christmas any more than you can take "thanks" out of Thanksgiving. Therefore, be merry, so that your *Merry Christmas!* is authentic and inviting. It is good to not take Merry Christmas for granted, because it reminds us to not take God for granted. Be merry this Christmas. He is.

Merry Christmas to all, and to all a grace filled life!

HEART-DESIRES

May he give you the desire of your heart and make all your plans succeed.

PSALM 20:4

Desire determines focus. We desire food when hungry, and then we savor a nice meal; we desire water when thirsty, and then we guzzle cool liquid refreshment; we desire for people to like us, so we serve them at their point of need; we desire financial freedom, so we work hard and smart and save money; we desire love and respect, so we give love and respect.

Certain desires can be bad. We can desire fame for ego's sake. This is a dangerous desire. We can desire a physical relationship outside of marriage or with someone other than our spouse. We become consumed with selfish desires and then discover we are all alone.

Our heart desires need a Christ-centered context. Right heart-desires surrender to the authority of Almighty God. It is impossible for an untamed heart to totally trust God. An untamed heart still wants to call the shots and include God as needed. This is a recipe for unhealthy desires. If anyone had the potential to strike out on His own without God's input, it was Jesus. But even Jesus said, "Yet not as I will, but as you will" (Matthew 26:39). Aligning His heart-desires with God's, Jesus eagerly desired to eat the Passover meal with His friends before He suffered (Luke 22:15).

How do we align our heart-desires with His desires? Start by aligning the general purpose of your life. Commit your life to bringing glory to Him. Ask yourself: Do your speech, conduct, attitude and vocation bring glory to Jesus? Do you leverage your roles in life for the glory of God? Do you seek to be an employee who brings glory to God in your work so He will use that to evangelize your associates? Your character development will draw them to Christ. Your unconditional love for the lost will draw them to salvation.

Now, define your other desires. Christ's vocational purpose for you may be to become an excellent lawyer, student, minister, athlete, or technician. Wherever your labor, execute your employment for God's glory. After you have prayerfully planned out your desires, trust God for their success. He is the one who brings our plans to fruition. A farmer knows how to plow and plant, but God causes the crop to grow. So, create the best plan by faith, and then ask the Holy Spirit to ignite it into action.

Wake up every morning and invite your Savior's desires into your heart, and by God's grace, watch your plans succeed.

DECEMBER 27

TRUST OVERCOMES FEAR

Though I walk through the valley of the shadow of death, I will fear no evil;
For You are with me; Your rod and Your staff, they comfort me.

PSALM 23:4 (NKJV)

Fear engages in an ongoing assault on our heart and mind. If left unchecked, fear can whip up our imagination into an anxious frenzy. Though only an ounce of what we fear may come to pass, we tend to give it a ton of attention. It is madness when we are overcome by fear.

It may be the fear of death that dilutes our faith; it may be the fear of failure that drives us to control; it may be the fear of rejection that keeps us from speaking up; it may be the fear of financial ruin that refrains us from risk-taking; it may be the fear of divorce that shatters our dreams of a fulfilling family; it may be the fear of losing a job that becomes a self-fulfilling prophecy.

Though any number of fears may preoccupy our thinking, we are not alone. Jesus walks with us through our valleys. He may not deliver us out of the valley, but He most certainly does not abandon us in the valley. He walks with us through the valley of doubt; He walks with us through the valley of shame; He walks with us through the valley of transition; He walks with us through the valley of disease; He walks with us through the valley of the shadow of death. Our fear, many times, is but a shadow of Satan's. It seems like reality, but it is not. We have no need to fear because our heavenly Father casts His long light of love that clears all shadows.

The light of Christ guides us through the shadows of our soul. Death stands next to our life's path and attempts to cast a shadow, but the light of heaven guides our way. We trust Jesus and overcome fear. We trust the Lord with the known and the unknown. In our valleys, we can't forget our faith and be consumed by our fears. We must slow down and let the Lord love us through times of loss.

No amount of pain can separate you from the love of God. Pain may be smothering your soul, but do not give up on God. Immerse yourself in the Psalms where David practically drowns in doubt, but by faith, wisely lifts an arm to the Lord. No one suffers well alone. It is with the Almighty and the prayers of others that we make it through. So go to Christ for comfort. His tools of trust invite us: He repairs our broken spirit with His rod and His staff. He comforts our crushed heart with His caring touch. At the very least, the Lord will bring clarity to your confusion. Saturate your soul with truth, and you will flush out your fears. Trust Him as you face your fears, whether of death or life.

Trust in the Lord and let Him overcome your fear.

PEACE-FAKING

Do not drag me away with the wicked, with those who do evil,
who speak cordially with their neighbors but harbor malice in their hearts.
PSALM 28:3

Peace-faking is futile and it becomes frustrating for everyone. It is like shadow boxing with someone's intentions. You think you understand what they mean, but their actions betray their true beliefs. A peace-faker is a professional at concealing his real feelings. For whatever reason, peace-fakers hide behind plastic smiles while their anger simmers beneath the surface. Maybe they are afraid of rejection. Maybe they are intimidated by the opinions of others. Or maybe, on the base side, they withhold their true intentions for their future advantage. When you are around peace-fakers you never know where you stand. They have learned the manners of deceit that do not rock the boat until they are ready to reveal their true selves. Peace-faking eventually sucks the life from its relationships.

This happens in marriage. A passive man, by nature, does not reveal his true feelings to his overly aggressive wife. Marital bliss conceals his concerns for a season, and he falls into a pattern of pretending he doesn't mind neglecting his own needs. However, malice begins to bubble, and hatred haunts his thinking. Eventually he wants out. He can't stand the sight of the one to whom he vowed a lifetime of commitment and love.

Therefore, it is imperative that we are all real in our relationships. The worst type of dishonesty may be living a lie. The Lord does not linger with liars. Dishonesty dissolves trust with its deceit, and dissimulation is a deterrent to trusting relationships. Proverbs 10:18 states, "Whoever conceals hatred with lying lips and spreads slander is a fool."

However, peace-faking can be overcome by faith. Faith is a facilitator of honesty. There is no need for us to conceal our concerns or hide behind our fears. We can trust God to bless our honesty when we are hurt or misunderstood, so speak up and share your true self. Openness leads to authenticity. It is risky—but rewarding—to be authentic.

The true peace that comes from expressing yourself is liberating. Those who have intimidated you in the past will take notice of your resolve to be real. They will respect you as one who has a prayerful opinion and expresses it with humility. Those with whom you engage in healthy conflict may disagree with your ideas, but they will respect your well-thought-out response. Avoid peace-faking and call the bluff of those who exhibit behaviors that cultivate peace-faking. Peace-faking is for fools and the immature. It is a waste of time and has no place for followers of Jesus.

Faith flourishes in unfeigned living,
so overcome peace-faking by faith.

BE STILL

"Be still, and know that I am God; I will be exalted among the nations, I will be exalted in the earth."
PSALM 46:10

Be still with your Savior, for it positions you to see and hear God. Stillness sets you free from busyness that can betray your trust in God. It is hard to be still in a society that values busyness and suspects stillness. We are made to feel guilty if we are not constantly on the go. Why else would we stay habitually connected to computers and caffeine? However, busyness is not a badge of honor, but a sad and seductive addiction. Overdone busyness is a lack of focus on God and His provision, but to "be still" is the standard for serious followers of Jesus.

Practicing stillness regularly means you trust God with the big things such as relationships, the future, finances, family, a job, and your health. Stillness also means you come to understand the small things and don't sweat them because you know your Savior is in control. Stillness aligns our hearts with Almighty God. It is in our expressive stillness that we muse on His grace.

Yes, there are seasons of busyness that make stillness seem foreign. An infant requires intense attention. A move to another home involves significantly increased activity. Launching a business or a ministry is an all-consuming affair. Starting something new most likely means you are extremely busy. However, do not use your busyness as an excuse to ignore God. Push back from your fatigue that comes from forgetting to be still. In your busyness, you can still carve out time with Christ to be still. Busyness is not meant to be a habit; it's meant to be for a time. You are not designed to stay there.

Be still and rest; be still and reflect; be still and think; be still and pray; be still and write; be still and enjoy your family; be still with no agenda; be still and see things more clearly; be still and know He is God.

It is in your stillness that you see God for who He is, high and lifted up, deserving of your honor, praise, and adoration. God grows bigger when you slow down and rest in the shadow of His stature. It is in your stillness that you see the unseen activity of the Almighty. The Holy Spirit is melting hard hearts. He is orchestrating authorities in your life to bend them and you toward God. He is drawing men and women to Himself in the middle of Christless cultures. Stillness shows you what your Savior is up to and gives us a lively hope that can be yours. Stillness shows you the way. Stillness is God's way of working with you. Stillness saves time.

Be still, and you will see God exalted among the nations and throughout the earth.

GOD'S PURPOSE ACCOMPLISHED

"For God has put it into their hearts to accomplish his purpose by agreeing to hand over to the beast their royal authority, until God's words are fulfilled."
REVELATION 17:17

God will accomplish His purpose. It may be with or without us, but He will execute His will. God does not back down or hold back when it comes to the fulfillment of His wishes. He knows what is best and is bent toward carrying out His good will. Nothing can stop God from accomplishing His purpose.

War cannot stop His purpose because He will draw people to Himself during the atrocities of war. Illness cannot stop His purpose because He will reveal His care, compassion, and sometimes healing, during the eventual breakdown of the body. Death cannot stop His purpose. God will graduate believers in Christ to heaven and non-believers in Christ to hell. Sin cannot stop His purpose because Christ defeated sin by His death on the cross. Sinners cannot stop His purpose because there are consequences for wrong and, ultimately, judgment by God. Satan cannot stop God's purpose because what the devil means for evil, God can use for good.

God's purpose is a freight train that travels down the tracks of obedience and disobedience, saints and sinners. Its momentum on behalf of mankind cannot be stopped. He will not be denied. Even the delay of His ultimate purpose gives more lost souls the opportunity to get on board by placing their faith in Jesus. He will ultimately reign on earth as King of kings and Lord of lords!

In the meantime, there is still time for others to voluntarily bow to His kingship, instead of ultimately being forced to bend their knee to God. His purpose will happen, so it makes sense to work with God, and not against God, to accomplish His purpose.

So what is the purpose of God? One purpose of God is to adopt everyone into His family who believes Jesus is His Son. "For God so loved the world that he gave his one and only Son, that whoever believes in him shall not perish but have eternal life" (John 3:16). Anyone who calls on the name of the Lord will be saved, and this accomplishes one of God's greater purposes.

Another purpose of God is seeing you complete the work He has given you to do. Jesus said it best: "I have brought you glory on earth by finishing the work you gave me to do" (John 17:4). Your individual obedience to God accomplishes His purpose for you. This is a significant thing. Your obedience matters. You are contributing to the greater heavenly mosaic of God's glorification. Your fulfillment of God's purpose helps others do the same. So, stay laser-focused on executing God's purpose. Pray about it and seek the Scripture to better understand God's purpose for you.

God's purpose will be accomplished. Find out where He is working and join Him to fulfill His mission.

COMING SOON

"Look, I am coming soon! My reward is with me, and I will give to each person according to what they have done."
REVELATION 22:12

Jesus is coming soon to wipe away all sin and sorrow. He is coming to eradicate sin, suffering, and death. He is coming to cast the devil into the lake of fire for eternity. He is coming to reward everyone according to what he has done. He is coming to reign on earth as the King of kings and the Lord of lords. Jesus is coming back a second time. He came to earth the first time in a humble stable—as a precious baby—destined to be a simple servant of God. He is coming a second time boldly upon a cloud of glory, as a wise warrior of God.

Jesus will wield the Word of God, leading a train of angels in worship of God. He came the first time to teach and preach that the kingdom of God is at hand, and He will come the second time to establish the kingdom of God on earth. He gave His life during His first mission on earth, and He will take life on His second mission to earth. His first coming justified our sin. His second coming will judge our sin.

Jesus submitted to kings His first time to earth. Kings will submit to Him at His Second Coming. What the disciples wanted and expected the first time will be accomplished at the Second Coming. They wanted to serve Jesus in His Kingship, but they missed a step. The Messiah had to ransom the sin of humankind first.

As faithful followers of Jesus Christ, we invite Him to come. We long to see our Lord. We can go to Him or He can come to us. Either way is okay. Whichever is best in His big scheme of things is what we should most desire. The more time there is between His two comings, the more time we have to be about His kingdom business.

The promise of Jesus' Second Coming compels His followers to loving obedience. We do not want to be loafing when He returns. We want to be submissive to His lordship in our individual lives. We want to model, for a lost and dying world, that we have a hope that is eternal with Him, now and forever. We want to continue our fervent prayer of, "Thy kingdom come on earth as it is in heaven." We want to serve the bride of Christ, His church, with unselfish love and dedication.

When He comes, Jesus will quietly, lovingly, and most gently wipe away our tears. Our tears of sorrow will be removed, never to be seen again. We will keep our tears of joy as part of our heavenly reward. When He comes, we will be transformed and be like Him. We can't wait.

**Come, Lord; we are ready. Come quickly.
We can't wait. Come Lord Jesus, Come!**

HOW TO BECOME A DISCIPLE OF JESUS CHRIST

Then Jesus came to them and said, "All authority in heaven and on earth has been given to Me. Therefore go and make disciples of all nations, baptizing them in the name of the Father and of the Son and of the Holy Spirit, and teaching them to obey everything I have commanded you. And surely I am with you always, to the very end of the age."

MATTHEW 28:18-20

Holy Scripture gives us principles for becoming a disciple and making disciples:

1. BELIEVE: "If you declare with your mouth, 'Jesus is Lord,' and believe in your heart that God raised him from the dead, you will be saved" (Romans 10:9).

Belief in Jesus Christ as your Savior and Lord gives you eternal life in heaven.

2. REPENT AND BE BAPTIZED: "Repent and be baptized, every one of you, in the name of Jesus Christ for the forgiveness of your sins. And you will receive the gift of the Holy Spirit" (Acts 2:38).

Repentance means you turn from your sin and then publicly confess Christ in baptism.

3. OBEY: "Anyone who loves me will obey my teaching. My Father will love them, and we will come to them and make our home with them" (John 14:23).

Obedience is an indicator of our love for the Lord Jesus and His presence in our life.

4. WORSHIP IN COMMUNITY: "They broke bread in their homes and ate together with glad and sincere hearts, praising God and enjoying the favor of all the people" (Acts 2:46-47).

Worship and prayer are our expression of gratitude and honor to God and our dependence on His grace. Community and evangelism are our accountability to Christians and compassion for non-Christians. Study God's Word and apply His knowledge, understanding, and wisdom to your everyday life.

5. LOVE GOD: "'Love the Lord your God with all your heart and with all your soul and with all your mind.' This is the first and greatest commandment" (Matthew 22:37-38).

Intimacy with God is a growing and loving relationship. We are loved by Him, so we can love others and be empowered by the Holy Spirit to obey His commands.

6. LOVE OTHERS: "Love your neighbor as yourself" (Matthew 22:39).

We are able to love other people because our heavenly Father first loved us.

7. MAKE DISCIPLES: "And the things you have heard me say in the presence of many witnesses entrust to reliable people who will also be qualified to teach others" (2 Timothy 2:2).

The reason we disciple others is because we are grateful to God and want to obey His instruction to make Him known throughout the world.

HOW I BEGAN TO FOLLOW CHRIST

My process for finding God covered a span of nineteen years, before I truly understood my need for His love and forgiveness and the importance of a personal relationship with Jesus Christ. Many people in my life helped me learn more about who God is. My mother took me to church at age twelve so I could learn about faith through the confirmation process. My grandmother modeled her walk with Jesus by being kind and generous to everyone she encountered. In college, I began attending church with Rita (my future wife) and her family. Weekly relevant teaching from an ancient book—the Bible—began to answer many of life's questions. I was intrigued by questions like "What is God's plan for my life?" "Who is Jesus Christ?" "What is sin, salvation, heaven, and hell?" "How can I live an abundant life of forgiveness, joy, and love?" The Lord found me first with His incredible love, and then when I surrendered in repentance and faith in Jesus, I found Him. For two years, a businessman in our church showed me how to grow in grace through Bible study, prayer, sharing my faith, and service to others. Each day I discover more of God's great love and His new mercies.

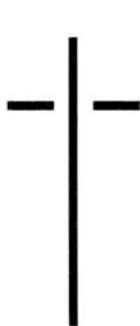

MEET THE AUTHOR
BOYD BAILEY

Boyd Bailey is the founder of Wisdom Hunters, Inc. By God's grace, Boyd has ministered in over 86 countries across the globe through Wisdom Hunters' daily devotionals and through several devotional books. For over 30 years, Boyd has passionately pursued and proclaimed wisdom through his career in full-time ministry, executive coaching, and mentoring. Since becoming a Christian at the age of 19, Boyd has begun each day as a wisdom hunter, diligently searching God's Word for Truth and, by God's grace, applying it to his life. In his writing, Boyd shares wisdom with thousands of others.